BUILDING SUSTAINABLE SOCIETIES

BUILDING SUSTAINABLE SOCIETIES

A Blueprint for a Post-Industrial World

DENNIS C. PIRAGES
editor

M.E. Sharpe
Armonk, New York
London, England

Library of Congress Cataloging-in-Publication Data

Building sustainable societies: a blueprint for a post-industrial world/
Dennis C. Pirages, editor.
p.   cm.
Includes bibliographical references.
ISBN 1-56324-738-0 (hardcover: alk. paper).
ISBN 1-56324-739-9 (pbk.: alk. paper)
1. Sustainable development. 2. Human ecology.
3. Economic development—Environmental aspects.
I. Pirages, Dennis.
HC79.E5B846   1996
338.9—dc20
95-40079
CIP

Printed in the United States of America
The paper used in this publication meets the minimum
requirements of American National Standard for
Information Sciences—Permanence of Paper for
Printed Library Materials, ANSI Z 39.48-1984.

EB (c)   10   9   8   7   6   5   4   3   2   1
EB (p)   10   9   8   7   6   5   4   3   2   1

Contents

Acknowledgments

This book is a product of the Harrison Program on the Future Global Agenda in the Department of Government and Politics at the University of Maryland. I would like to first thank Professor Emeritus Horace Harrison for the foresight and support that made possible the conference from which this book came. I would also like to thank the dedicated group of graduate students who played a major role in the conference and publication process. These include Michael Alberty, John Audley, Geoff Dableko, Nicole Kerber, Sean McCluskie, Clark Merrill, Jonathan Olsen, Serap Rada, Gigi Ramadan (Samman), Stacy VanDeveer, and Shayne Weyker. A special thanks is due to Don Beane, who did a tremendous job in seeing the manuscript through the production process. I would also like to acknowledge the cooperation of the journal *Futures*. Much earlier versions of the introduction and chapters 16 and 18 were published in *Futures*, Volume 26, Number 2.

BUILDING SUSTAINABLE SOCIETIES

Introduction

Dennis Pirages

The industrial revolution has reached an advanced stage and its effects are now clearly visible all over the planet. An industrializing and growing world population will soon reach six billion, and the resource demands of these growing numbers continue to escalate. But this ongoing "modernization" is now threatened by significant changes taking place in relationships between *Homo sapiens* and the physical environment in which the species has evolved. The perceived successes of the industrial way of life have created rising expectations and patterns of material consumption that are no longer sustainable on a global scale. Both the feasibility and desirability of continued industrial growth are being questioned, and doubts about the long-term viability of traditional forms of progress continue to increase.

An ongoing debate over the future of resource-intensive growth has advanced well beyond the early skirmishes over the potential "limits to growth" in a finite world.[1] More difficult questions about the potential for the continued diffusion of industrial prosperity to those on the other side of the industrial divide—the bulk of the human race—are now being asked. The focus is shifting from assessing the limits to growth to an analysis of what types of modernization and development might be sustainable globally in the next century, given increasing environmental uncertainties facing a rapidly growing and more affluent human population. A crisis of sustainability is emerging out of these deliberations, as it becomes more obvious that an industrial way of life cannot be sustained globally for the bulk of the human race well into the next century. There is growing concern that many existing states may no longer be economically or politically viable, and that historical patterns of economic and social progress are being disrupted in many parts of the world.[2]

Concern over the long-term sustainability of the industrial model of human progress goes back several decades, although such worries were first publicly and forcefully voiced in the Brundtland Commission report, published in 1987.[3] In that report the learned commissioners officially sanctioned an ongoing discus-

3

sion of the nature of sustainable development. The commission loosely defined such development as that which "meets the needs of the present without compromising the ability of future generations to meet their own needs."[4] Prior to the report, most concerns about the welfare of future generations were rebuffed by technological optimism, the belief that future technological innovations automatically would make each generation better off than previous ones. The commission officially recognized that the inevitability of increasing affluence for succeeding generations could now legitimately be called into question. Thus, prescriptions for making development work, which have shifted from policies designed to meet the needs of the world's poorest to those promoting massive redistribution of wealth and the creation of appropriate technologies for agriculture, are now focused on the need for a systematic redefinition of the ultimate goals of the development process.[5]

The crux of what could be called the contemporary sustainability problematique is that a materially comfortable and much emulated way of life has been shaped by the material abundance of the industrial revolution, but it cannot be diffused to the bulk of the human race at acceptable environmental costs. This way of life is emulated not only because it is intrinsically comfortable, but also because the leading country to develop and refine it, the United States, dominates a worldwide telecommunications system that purveys images of the good life in an increasingly interconnected global village. It is not sustainable because the environmental impact of more than six billion human beings living at U.S. consumption standards would easily overwhelm the capabilities of natural systems to support human life as we know it on the planet. Thus, the legacy of generations that have operated under the assumption that more consumption is better, indeed essential, without concern for ecological limits, is the evolution and diffusion of a dominant social paradigm, or set of collectively held rules for progress and survival, that no longer gives useful guidance in confronting the sustainability issues of the next century.[6]

Sociocultural Evolution and Unnatural Selection

The survival and success of *Homo sapiens* have been assured over the centuries by evolutionary mechanisms that have adapted the human body and human behavior to changing environmental constraints. Information gleaned from human experience has been passed from one generation to the next through two parallel evolutionary processes. The biological genome, created through natural selection, is a storehouse of information that is the product of hundreds of thousands of years of experience with nature. Shaped by an often painful process of trial and error, surviving human phenotypes (bodies) now represent information that has kept the human body adapted to the requisites of changing physical and social environments. Those phenotypes that survive to reproduce contribute to this ever changing genetic pool of information, while the genes of those who don't reproduce can contribute no information to future generations. This process of natural selection relies primarily upon genetic mutations that provide the raw material from which new phenotypes can be created.

Throughout human history a basic congruence between the human body and the changing natural environment has been thus maintained. Conventionally accepted biological principles of natural selection hold that such interactive processes between human beings and nature have, over time, shaped the genetic package called *Homo sapiens*. Survivors pass on physical traits that have allowed humans to adapt successfully to changing conditions.

Sociocultural evolution, operating through spoken, written, and visual communication, is a parallel process by which survival-relevant information is passed from one generation to the next. Cultures can be considered to be similar to the biological genome; they can be thought to consist of packages of general information as well as survival-relevant values, beliefs, norms, ideas, etc., that are passed on through social learning.[7]

Homo sapiens has a distinct advantage over other species in evolutionary competition because of the ability to reflect, learn, evaluate, and to communicate, orally and in writing, extensive amounts of nongenetic information across generations. While many species seem capable of transmitting at least a minimal nongenetic behavioral repertoire from one generation to the next, human beings have a highly developed capability to communicate large amounts of potentially survival-relevant information. While the outer limits of human survivability are still determined by the interaction of the environment with the human genome, the oral and written flow of accumulated wisdom now plays a very significant role in adapting human behavior to the constraints of nature.

Sociocultural evolution is driven by adaptation processes similar to those which drive natural selection. Those cultures that are better adapted to the environments in which they are embedded flourish, often diffusing successful values and ideas to other cultures. Those that for one reason or another become poorly adapted fall into chaos and cease to be major contributors to the transmitted pool of sociocultural information.[8] Novel ideas (innovations) are the sociocultural equivalent of genetic mutations and provide raw material for the massive trial and error processes that comprise sociocultural evolution. While genetic changes propagate themselves through differential reproduction, new ideas must percolate through structures of power, privilege, and prestige. Even the best adaptive idea may fail to have an impact if it originates in an obscure place in a power matrix and finds no influential champions.

The survival-relevant portion of this body of cultural information, or dominant social paradigm, has evolved and continues to evolve in response to demographic, environmental, and technological changes, much as does genetically carried information. But there are important differences. Whereas biological selection, for the most part, operates harshly through the failure of maladapted organisms to reproduce, human societies theoretically can be proactive and modify maladaptive traits in anticipation of negative future consequences. Thus, particularly at current stages of evolutionary development, human beings have the capability of using foresight, research, and education to modify the sociocultural information passed from one generation to the next, thereby enhancing the potential for human survival.[9]

Compared to biological theories of natural selection, the study of sociocultural evolution is still in its infancy, but scientists in several disciplines have begun to investigate aspects of it. Biologists and geneticists have focused on an evolutionary linkage between genes and patterns of human behavior in the field of sociobiology.[10] Demographers have studied differential reproduction patterns, disease, and competition with other organisms as factors that have shaped the nature of contemporary belief systems.[11] Anthropologists have closely studied linkages between changes in the physical environment and cultural responses.[12] Others have looked at human adaptations to technological change.[13] These approaches all contribute some understanding of how human cultures evolve in response to ecological, technological, and demographic pressures.

There are also connections between the two parallel evolutionary processes. Genetic natural selection clearly influences the evolution of new ideas by shaping the survival potential of their carriers. And sociocultural evolution can significantly influence natural selection through the norms, values, and habits that directly and indirectly influence patterns of reproduction.

There are also many other similarities. For example, just as not every human gene is essential, or even functional, for the persistence of the species, not every piece of information carried by a culture is necessary or functional for the persistence of a society. And just as certain defective genotypes disappear over time as a result of natural selection, maladapted cultures can also decline or disappear as a result of poor social learning. But it is also possible for a defective genotype to persist across several generations before being extinguished, just as it is possible for a declining civilization to grind down for decades before disintegrating in the face of growing anomalies.[14]

Over long periods of history, however, many human societies have been at least modestly successful in adapting to the changing challenges of the physical and social environments. The cognitive component of sociocultural evolution—thoughts, perceptions, empirical knowledge, beliefs, values, goals, etc.—has, for the most part, given relatively valid guidance in coping with nature's constraints. And the institutional or structural component of this evolution has produced reasonably successful templates for replicating ecologically acceptable behavior.

But the industrial revolution and the related evolution of an industrial paradigm have led to dramatic changes in human numbers and impact, which are rapidly culminating in a growing discontinuity between the sustaining capabilities of the global ecosystem and the nature of the survival information being passed from one generation to the next. The global spread of a resource-intensive industrial paradigm is peaking at a time when, due to increasingly apparent environmental limitations, that paradigm no longer gives valid guidance for the long-term sustainability of the human race. The types of behavior that are now being rewarded and emulated are increasing the pressure on the global ecosystem and could, in the long run, lead to the decline or even extinction of the species. A concise way of putting it is that "Our value system, knowledge system, social organization and technologies co-evolved to fit the opportunities which the exploitation of fossil fuel energy provided. Our social systems reflect these medium-term opportunities rather than the long-run opportunities of co-evolutionary development with the renewable resources of the global system."[15] And not only is the dominant social paradigm now carrying inappropriate information, it also appears that the socialization mechanisms or agents by which information is passed on—families, churches, schools, etc.—are disintegrating, thus adding an additional dimension to the long-term survival problem.

Undoing the harm of several generations of such "unnatural selection" associated with the short burst of industrial affluence requires the equivalent of a human genome project in the social and behavioral sciences. Such a sociocultural genome project would focus on analyzing the cognitive and structural aspects of the existing dominant social paradigm and evaluating the usefulness of its components for future sustainability. Sequencing the sociocultural genome is a significant undertaking, but understanding the nature and impact of the information being passed from one generation to the next, and the potential collapse of the mechanisms by which it is transferred, is an essential part of the process of constructing more sustainable sociocultural organizations, ones that can provide appropriate ecological guidance in the more constrained environment of the next century.

Sustainability as Process

Making a transition to a more sustainable world is a long-term process, and the tasks, difficulties, and opportunities will vary for societies in different circumstances. In the affluent countries, for example, it would be exceedingly difficult, and perhaps impossible, to become more sustainable by "de-developing" to levels of resource consumption typical in impoverished countries. It would be even more difficult to convince leaders in the so-called late-developer countries to forego the perceived pleasures of industrial consumption. Thus, the move toward greater sustainability creates different agendas for different societies. And not only must the future limits of nature be conformed to, but some central elements of existing value systems and lifestyles must be retained. It is important to protect the natural systems that provide environmental services as well as the many positive aspects of the existing paradigm, which has become synonymous with progress.

Becoming more sustainable is also best envisioned as a continuing process because the constraints that shape human opportunities change over space and time. What is sustainable under one set of circumstances may well not be under others. A sustainable future for oil-rich Saudi Arabia would be quite different than one for resource-poor Japan. And changing environmental constraints and technological opportunities suggest that alternatives must be explored with the greatest possible flexibility, and that sustainability can and should be approached in diverse ways.

The worldwide spread of industrialization has had an unfortunate homogenizing effect on the transformed societies. Such homogeneity stifles diversity and the development of creative alternatives. Just as it is important to maintain genetic diversity in plant and animal species, human cultural diversity must be nourished so that there will be a reservoir of ideas from which future cultural adaptations can be selected.

In summary, greater planetary sustainability could be achieved by means of a fluid, open-ended process involving the continued modification of the sociocultural genome. The creation of more sustainable societies is best seen as a continuing process of positive change, a moving away from environmentally destructive kinds of development and toward a postindustrial vision, using different prescriptions to deal with different situations. Building and living in more sustainable societies, however, need not require general ecological penance such as force-feeding humanity vegetarian diets and creating a fashion industry based upon sackcloth. Rather, the move toward a more sustainable world can give people a new purpose, one that will replace the shopworn acquisitive work ethic of the industrial paradigm. Real intellectual excitement can be generated over devising ways to do more with less and increasing human satisfaction without substantially increasing planetary levels of material consumption.

Guidelines for Transition

New definitions of progress and the good life imply the need to move well beyond environmental economics and the associated internalizing of production externalities. Since the existing structure of consumer preferences reflects the experience gained during the age of abundance, market forces cannot be relied upon to ignite a transition. Thus, governmental institutions will be required to play a much stronger leadership role in changing existing structures of privilege and creating alternative options for human satisfaction.[16] New measures of welfare and progress will have to replace gross national product (GNP), the long-outmoded simplistic indicator of material throughput.[17]

Economist Herman Daly has suggested four alternative approaches to efficiency as ecologically relevant replacements for the throughput and output-per-man-hour definitions of progress that still pervade contemporary economics.[18] Daly's definitions and prescriptions offer useful guidelines for thinking about the extensive transformation in record keeping that is a necessary part of measuring the process of moving toward greater sustainability.

Daly suggests first improving what he calls *artifact maintenance efficiency* (AME) by lengthening the period of time that artifacts (products) are used. The longer a product can be kept in service, the less additional raw materials will be needed to make replacements. Maximizing AME means designing more durable, longer-lasting products that need fewer repairs. If products remain in service longer and need less maintenance, the less the overall environmental impact. While it seems only logical to use this type of efficiency as an indicator of progress and a societal guideline for the process of sustainable and ecologically sound economic development, it runs contrary to the consumer thinking and accounting practices deeply woven into the socioeconomic fabric of industrial societies. People are reluctant to pay higher prices in order to get more durable artifacts and are poorly informed about them. Thus, there are few obvious reasons for manufacturers to produce more durable, better-quality automobiles, refrigerators, television sets, etc. Short-term perspectives on consumption are encouraged by price competition, which often leads to production of cheap and shoddy artifacts, and planned obsolescence is an all too common economic reality.

Artifact service efficiency (ASE) is the effectiveness with which a given production potential and resource stream meets social needs. Improving ASE requires addressing controversial issues of product mix and distribution. Thinking globally, it would seem that a much more egalitarian distribution of basic artifacts would be likely to create more widespread human satisfaction. For example, transferring capital to poor countries where it could be used to meet pressing needs for food, clothing, shelter, and schools would seem to maximize ASE. Thinking locally, investments in more widespread mass transportation in urban areas might do the same thing. But markets are driven by purchasing power (effective demand) and there is presently little of it in poor countries or poor cities.

Daly also addresses the question of optimal environmental exploitation in sustaining future minimal levels of material throughput. *Ecosystem maintenance efficiency* (EME) refers to the extent to which an ecosystem can be made to efficiently provide a flow of resources on a reliable basis with minimal long-term damage. This involves making wise technological choices and investments, carefully exploiting abundant rather then scarce resources, replanting consumed forest products, using more renewable resources, and developing recycling wherever possible. *Ecosystem service efficiency* (ESE) refers to how the unavoidable impacts of industrial activity are allocated throughout the environment. For example, a more service-efficient and thus more sustainable society would be one that minimizes environmental destruction by diffusing pollution burdens widely throughout the ecosystem rather than concentrating them in only a few vulnerable areas.

The process of building more sustainable societies could thus be indexed, both qualitatively and quantitatively, by progress along these four dimensions.

For the industrially affluent countries there are ample opportunities to design processes that reduce environmental impact while preserving adequate production. But there are also ample opportunities for shifting consumption patterns from resource-intensive goods to various kinds of services, including education and entertainment. For countries on the other side of the industrial gap, enhancing sustainability could mean avoiding many of the economic and ecological pitfalls of traditional industrialization. Thus, China might leap beyond industrialization and make a significant contribution to reducing future global warming by foregoing fossil-fuel intensive fleets of privately owned vehicles in favor of efficient mass transit and enhanced telecommunications capabilities. Unfortunately, automobile manufacturers from Detroit to Tokyo are already devising strategies to capture the potentially huge Chinese market.[19]

Two Faces of Sustainability

It is useful and instructive to engage in abstract discussions of the nature of sustainability. It is also fulfilling to conjure up visions of the desirable characteristics of sustainable societies.[20] It is much more difficult, however, to move from abstractions to a more concrete politics of transformation.

Creating a more sustainable world not only involves changing how natural resources are used and allocated, but also reshaping values and institutions that have been molded by generations of increasing material affluence. There are, thus, two faces of the sustainability problematique. The first, and most obvious, looks outward at the requisites for maintaining a viable natural environment; the second focuses inward to assess and preserve, wherever possible, many of the ideals of the existing sociopolitical system. Simply put, the task of restoring a pristine environment should not and cannot be accomplished through the wholesale destruction of deeply ingrained value systems.[21]

The sustainability problematique is thus a cluster of environmental-sociopolitical paradoxes and problems associated with the attempt to face political, social, and economic issues resulting from the steady decay of industrialization while simultaneously building more sustainable alternatives that both preserve nature and many existing liberal human values. The decline of industrialization ironically complicates the transition.[22] While periodic recessions and "de-development" certainly reduce global pollution and resource consumption, sagging personal incomes and increased poverty lend themselves as easily to conservative retrenchment as to paradigm shift. It is difficult to explain to the army of unemployed and to the downwardly mobile that their predicament is making a great contribution to ecological well-being.

The irony of creating "pseudosustainability" through economic collapse is illustrated by an exchange with an Indian colleague at a conference during the recession of the early 1990s. When informed that the United States GNP and related consumption figures had stagnated or even declined over recent months, the colleague gleefully commented that at last Americans would be consuming a smaller share of the world's resources. But when reminded that U.S. foreign assistance would likely be a direct casualty of economic austerity, he quickly changed his assessment.

Making a Transition

Identifying the anomalies and problems that are part of the sustainability problematique and devising a strategy for transformation are complex tasks requiring a sociocultural genome project, and only a sample of some of the aspects of the problematique can be can be covered in this book. One priority is to redefine progress. Old definitions relying upon undifferentiated growth in gross national product give a misleading picture of any kind of progress, since they measure human labor, material throughput, and very little else of interest. Thus, the most malignant societies, in which violence is widespread, could easily be judged as "progressing" by virtue of growth in arms production, prison construction, and the funeral industry. Gross national product can thus be as much a measure of social ills as of prosperity and is totally unrelated to any of Daly's efficiency guidelines.

Scholars have pointed out the defects of using simple GNP as an indicator of development and progress for decades, but as yet there has been very little policy response to the critiques.[23] One of the most obvious anomalies associated with GNP is that the environmental disruption and resource depletion associated with obtaining coal, oil, nonfuel minerals and forest products, an "ecological bad," is an "economic good" and increases GNP. And there are numerous other social ills that also contribute to progress as measured by GNP.[24] In the United States and other industrial societies a crime wave and drug epidemic have contributed to the growth of police forces, the expansion of court systems, and the construction of more prisons. But it would be difficult to argue that this kind of growth indicates an improvement in the quality of life. Similarly, growth in other services is often highlighted as a positive development, but many times such services create nothing that generally enhances the human condition. Witness the tens of millions of dollars of GNP generated by the O.J. Simpson saga. In the United States, GNP also includes the labors of nearly one million lawyers and paralegals who enhance the quality of life through litigation!

There is clearly an opportunity to begin the process of transformation by developing and employing much more sophisticated indicators of progress and human well-being to guide economic policy. Daly's guidelines suggest alternate measures of long-term ecological progress that could easily replace GNP. Walter H. Corson's chapter in this book reviews some fledgling efforts to develop indicators of sustainability. The academic community could play a leading role in carefully researching sustainability issues, but since the sustainability problematique doesn't fall clearly within the domains of existing disciplines, it receives scant attention on university campuses. And, paradoxically, university budgets are being cut as part of the "new austerity" at a time when revision and expansion of relevant academic programs should be an integral part of the sustainability process.[25]

Major changes are also required in the political institutions and processes that have evolved within the industrial growth paradigm. Pluralistic political systems, with their checks, balances, and time-consuming procedures, have evolved in ways that frustrate rather than facilitate needed changes. The United States Congress, with its outmoded sets of privileges, rules, and procedures, is a classic case of political paralysis. The process of reinventing government must be expanded; politics must be completely overhauled and must emphasize ecological balance for this generation in order to promote the welfare of future generations.

To sum up, creating a more sustainable world must be a dynamic, complex, and continuous process that will require decades of concerted effort. Given a wide variety of human societies embedded in many different ecological contexts, there can be no single plan for creating a permanent condition called sustainability. Rather, developing a process leading to a more sustainable world and developing indicators of progress toward it are essential for strengthening the evolutionary linkage between *Homo sapiens* and the physical environment.

The chapters that follow investigate many of the important questions and issues to be addressed in moving toward global sustainability. The first section focuses on relevant institutional and value issues. This is followed by a section on international aspects of moving toward a more sustainable world. The third section concentrates on an important set of North–South issues associated with sustainable development. The last section addresses the challenges of transition and examines strategies for social change that progress toward sustainability will require.

Notes

1. Donella Meadows, et al., *The Limits to Growth* (New York: Universe Books, 1972).

2. Robert Kaplan, "The Coming Anarchy," *The Atlantic Monthly* (February 1994); Gerald Helman and Steven Ratner, "Saving Failed States," *Foreign Policy* (Winter 1992–93).

3. See Dennis Pirages, ed., *The Sustainable Society* (New York: Praeger, 1976); World Commission on Environment and Development, *Our Common Future* (New York: Oxford University Press, 1987).

4. World Commission on Environment and Development, *Our Common Future* (New York: Oxford University Press, 1987), 43.

5. See Sharachchandra Lele, "Sustainable Development: A Critical Review," *World Development*, 1991, 19(6): 607–21.

6. For an explanation of the dominant social paradigm concept, see Thomas Kuhn, *The Structure of Scientific Revolutions* (Chicago: University of Chicago Press, 1962); Willis Harman, *An Incomplete Guide to the Future* (New York: W. W. Norton, 1979); Dennis Pirages and Paul Ehrlich, *Ark II: Social Response to Environmental Imperatives* (New York: Viking Press, 1974).

7. For more detailed discussions of sociocultural evolution, see Stephen Sanderson, "Evolutionary Materialism: A Theoretical Strategy for the Study of Social Evolution," *Sociological Perspectives* 37, no. 1 (1994); William Durham, *Coevolution: Genes, Culture and Human Diversity* (Stanford: Stanford University Press, 1991).

8. See Joseph Tainter, *The Collapse of Complex Societies* (New York: Cambridge University Press, 1988).

9. See Hazel Henderson, *Paradigms in Progress: Life Beyond Economics* (Indianapolis: Knowledge Systems, 1991); Walter Truett Anderson, *To Govern Evolution: Further Adventures of the Political Animal* (New York: Harcourt, Brace, Jovanovich, 1987); Robert Ornstein and Paul Ehrlich, *New World, New Mind* (New York: Simon and Schuster, 1989).

10. See Edward Wilson, *Sociobiology: A New Synthesis* (Cambridge: Harvard University Press, 1975).

11. Henry Hobhouse, *Forces of Change* (New York: Little, Brown, 1989).

12. See C. R. Hallpike, *The Principles of Social Evolution* (Oxford: Clarendon Press, 1986); Marvin Harris, *Cultural Materialism: The Struggle for a Science of Culture* (New York: Random House, 1979); Tim Ingold, *Evolution and Social Life* (Cambridge: Cambridge University Press, 1986).

13. See Jacques Ellul, *The Technological Society* (New York: Knopf, 1964); Langdon Winner, *Autonomous Technology* (Cambridge: MIT Press, 1977).

14. For examples see Lester Bilsky, ed., *Historical Ecology: Essays on Environment and Social Change* (Port Washington, NY: Kennekat Press, 1980); Clive Ponting, *A Green History of the World* (New York: Penguin Books, 1993).

15. Richard Norgaard, "Sustainable Development: A Coevolutionary Point of View," *Futures* (December 1988): 617.

16. See Martin O'Connor, ed., *Is Capitalism Sustainable?* (New York: Guilford Press, 1994).

17. See Walter Corson, "Changing Course: An Outline of Strategies for a Sustainable Future," *Futures* (March 1994); Hazel Henderson, "Paths to Sustainable Development: The Role of Social Indicators," *Futures* (March 1994).

18. Herman Daly, *Steady State Economics* (San Francisco: W. H. Freeman, 1977), chapter 4.

19. See, for example, Steven Mufson, "Dreams on Wheels," *Washington Post* (28 December 1994).

20. Among the best of these is Lester Milbrath, *Envisioning a Sustainable Society* (Albany: State University of New York Press, 1991).

21. John Robinson, et al., "Defining a Sustainable Society," *Alternatives* (August 1990): 39.

22. For an excellent analysis of the decay of the industrial way of life see Joel Kasiola, *The Death of Industrial Civilization* (Albany: State University of New York Press, 1993).

23. See E.J. Mishan, *The Costs of Economic Growth* (London: Staples Press, 1967); Tibor Scitovsky, *The Joyless Economy* (New York: Oxford University Press, 1976).

24. See Robert Repetto, et al., *Wasting Assets: Natural Resources in the National Income Accounts* (Washington, DC: World Resources Institute, 1989).

25. See David Orr, *Ecological Literacy* (Albany: State University of New York Press, 1992).

Part One

Designing Sustainable Societies: Values and Institutions

Introduction

Moving toward a more sustainable world is a process that requires two parallel types of design activities. It is obvious that to build a more sustainable world, more efficient and ecologically sound technologies must be designed, in order to develop industrial processes that are less resource intensive, and such products as automobiles that get better mileage and pollute less. This involves devising different ways of doing things by creating new institutions and value systems to facilitate the development of a new sustainability paradigm or postindustrial culture. This process requires "unlearning" much of what has been internalized during the period of rapid industrial growth and replacing it with information, values, and ways of doing things that will be better suited to the next century.

The chapters in this first section address some of the key institutional design questions inherent in the attempt to build more sustainable societies. In the first chapter, Ken Conca suggests that a central issue associated with sustainability is the need to design a new set of institutions, since these shape individual incentives, values, and understandings. It is impossible to alter the ways societies transform nature without affecting many of the ways in which they are organized. He suggests peace and justice as core values to guide the process of institutional design. Conca identifies two dominant approaches to building a more sustainable world; a paradigm of limits and restraint, and one of optimization to promote qualitatively different kinds of growth. Using peace and justice as criteria, he evaluates these two approaches and finds both of them lacking. He concludes by suggesting five general principles for incorporating peace and justice criteria into a design for a more sustainable world.

William Ophuls focuses on the tension between liberty and freedom in presenting both a critique of industrial politics and prescriptions for sustainable polities. Liberty is defined as the freedom for human beings to do essentially as they wish, while freedom suggests subordination to higher ideals. Tracing the evolution of political thought, Ophuls finds that simple liberty cannot be the basis for a philosophy of sustainable politics. Rather, freedom manifest in devotion to a higher ecological purpose must be a cornerstone of postindustrial political philosophy.

Stephen Viederman complains that the term *sustainability* has been captured by the very interests that have made the world a less sustainable place. He then lays out his definition of sustainability, basing it on the creation of five forms of social capital that will support his three pillars of sustainability: economic security, ecological integrity, and democracy. He concludes by arguing that a fundamental redesign of society is required, that it should be based upon his three pillars, and that to support this effort all available forms of capital must be marshaled to meet social and equity goals.

This section concludes with Gar Alperovitz's analysis of the failure of both capitalism and socialism to provide a model for more sustainable societies. Socialist societies have a legacy of environmental disregard and disrepair. While capitalist societies have taken small steps toward environmental preservation, certain "system problems" make them inherently unsustainable. Alperovitz suggests that a design for a sustainable system must include a renewed focus on community and a reduction of the scale of political activity; like Ophuls, he concludes that we need a new way of defining liberty.

1

Peace, Justice, and Sustainability

Ken Conca

The central political challenge of sustainability is the need to design institutions that facilitate sustainable ways of living. A useful definition of the term *institution* is provided by Oran Young: "Institutions are social practices consisting of easily recognized roles coupled with clusters of rules or conventions governing relations among the occupants of these roles." Based on this definition, Young cites electoral systems, markets, and structures of property rights as examples of institutions.[1]

The challenge of designing institutions for sustainability is complicated by the fact that institutions are not created in a vacuum; all societies embody existing sets of deeply entrenched rules and roles, which shape the ways they affect the environment. Thus it is more accurate to speak of both institutional design and *redesign*, the latter being the alteration of those existing institutions that drive unsustainable practices. Defining the task as one of defining new clusters of roles and rules *and* redefining existing clusters leads us to a dilemma. Building new institutions is a task that involves profound social change, and thus requires a concentration of political power. But it is such concentrated political power, standing behind existing institutions, that makes their redesign problematic. We therefore must ask a question familiar to constitutional scholars: How can societies concentrate and institutionalize political power so as to achieve collective social goals such as sustainability without seeing that power corrupted or co-opted in the process? How can purposeful power and authority exist without their being abused?[2] As discussed below, this question has not thus far been central to the sustainability debate.

Where sustainability is concerned, the task of institutional design is complicated by the obvious fact that the scale of the system is not limited to individual national polities. Many of the powerful institutions that drive currently unsustainable practices are inherently transnational in extent—the institution of development, for example, as manifest in the practices of the World Bank, or the liberal international trading order, as encoded in the General Agreement on Tariffs and Trade (GATT).[3] Also found at the international level are many of the most glaring institutional vacuums—for example, the lack of sets of roles and rules that would facilitate the peaceful resolution of transnational environmental disputes, and the absence of coordination mechanisms to insulate local communities from the buffeting effects of international capital mobility and industrial relocation.

Any serious efforts to institutionalize sustainability must address these transnational dimensions. But efforts to both establish and change specific practices at the international level will shape not only our global ecological future but also core aspects of global society. This is because, together, institutions weave a political fabric that is seamless: it is not possible to alter the institutions governing society's transformation of natural systems without also affecting the practices by which people choose leaders, spend public funds, or engage in the political life of their communities. In an interdependent society, the institutions that perform any of these tasks shape all of them. And on an interdependent planet, the result of institutionalizing sustainability will be not just a more ecologically sustainable world, but also one that is either more or less peaceful, fair, efficient, free, or productive than it was before. For this reason, we must ask whether and how we can reconcile sustainability with other broad values we may hold for the world system.

Peace and Justice

This chapter focuses in particular on two sets of values, those we call peace and justice. There are of course many competing definitions of peace and justice, just as there are of sustainability. Given the essentially contested nature of these concepts, my concern is less with narrow and precise definitions than in pursuing the concept of process embodied in this volume. It should be possible to identify pathways that are broadly consistent with rendering world politics more peaceful and just, even as we struggle with the eternal question of how to define such values more clearly.

Thus, rather than trying to construct fixed and precise definitions of peace and justice, we need criteria to identify, under conditions of great uncertainty, specific social trajectories that move us toward these values—recognizing that our definitions of peace and justice may shift as we approach. In this context, a trajectory toward a *more* peaceful world is characterized by more effective mechanisms of nonviolent conflict resolution. Similarly, a path to a *more* just world involves systematic attempts to diminish gross disparities in individual life opportunities, access to power, and socioeconomic fairness.

Can institutions designed to promote sustainability also help to produce such a world? *Must* they, in order to be truly sustainable? Peace and justice are among many values in regard to which such questions could be posed; to focus on these two is clearly justifiable for a shrinking planet entering a new and uncertain era of world politics. But a more important reason to focus on peace and justice is that *neither is automatically implied by sustainability.* That an unsustainable future will be violent and unjust goes without saying; we already live in such a world. Problems as diverse as the destruction of forest ecosystems and the handling of hazardous waste reveal the intimate links among injustice, violence, and ecologically unsustainable practices.[4] But this does not guarantee that a sustainable future world will automatically be peaceful and just, or that it *must* be so simply to meet a particular definition of sustainability.[5]

Consider efforts to create an effective international regime limiting greenhouse-gas emissions (perhaps as a follow-on to the vague and general commitments made by governments at the Earth Summit).[6] One scenario involves a North–South bargain in which Third World governments limit the growth of future emissions in return for some combination of technology, financing, and deep cuts in the current emissions of the industrialized countries. One can imagine two radically different pathways toward such limits in the South: one based on land reform, community-scale renewable energy technologies, labor-intensive employment policies, active involvement of grassroots organizations, the expansion of opportunities for women, and support for traditional agricultural techniques; the other based on forced reforestation, coercive population control programs, the expulsion of local people to create "nature preserves," and technology strategies that concentrate rather than redistribute power and wealth. Both paths would reduce greenhouse gas emissions, but it goes without saying that they differ radically in their social and political implications. To argue that the coercive path would not in itself be sustainable may be true in the long run but misses the point. The question remains: must we compromise or at least defer some worthy social and political goals in order to attain others?

The focus on peace and justice also illustrates some important conclusions about the politics of sustainability: that there are *many* sustainability agendas; that these various agendas have profoundly differing implications regarding the values we may hold; and that each one's formula for concentrating and controlling political power is a crucial determinant of the values that agenda carries. Finally, the focus also serves a practical purpose: as will be discussed below, peace and justice should be seen not as abstract values, but rather as crucial *strategies* for placing sustainability more effectively on the agenda of world politics.

The rest of the chapter is organized into three sections. The first is an exploration of the two predominant paradigms of sustainability, with particular attention to how they treat (or mistreat) the question of political power. The second is an examination of the ways these paradigms promote strategies of international institutional change that take an ambiguous, shifting, and largely instrumental approach to problems of peace and justice. The final section sketches an alternative approach, one that treats peace and justice not as conflicting values but rather as explicit strategies for promoting sustainability.

Sustainability Paradigms

For many, the central political question of sustainability is not the relatively abstract one of how to simultaneously concentrate and control political power. The central question is how to get on with the business of environmental protection, sustainable development, and global environmental governance. This action-oriented agenda, which makes environmentalism a social movement as well as a philosophy, has not produced a single paradigm on how to proceed. Rather, there are at least two widely held paradigms for institutionalizing sustainability on a global scale. The first is what might be called a paradigm of *restraint*. Its central premise is that we must build limits into the system so that human activity does not exceed the carrying capacity of planetary systems. The classic statement of this perspective is found in *The Limits to Growth,* with its apocalyptic warning about the dangers of exponential growth in human numbers, output, and consumption.[7]

For others, "getting on with it" means something quite different: a paradigm not of restraints on growth but rather of *optimization,* one that promotes qualitatively different forms of growth. This paradigm, which is sometimes euphemistically described as "planetary management," is far more optimistic about our capacity to fine-tune social change and manage natural systems. It stresses not macrolevel global restraints but a more complex, micromanaged, interventionist agenda—literally, an attempt to optimize key aspects of the relationship between humans and nature. An introductory passage from *Our Common Future,* the influential report of the World Commission on Environment and Development, is illustrative:

> We can move information and goods faster around the globe than ever before; we can produce more food and more goods with less investment of resources; our technology and science gives us at least the potential to look deeper into and better understand natural systems. From space, we can see and study the Earth as an organism whose health depends on the health of all its parts. We have the power to reconcile human affairs with natural laws and to thrive in the process.[8]

Clearly, these two paradigms are ideal types. At the level of practice, there are examples of the two coexisting in a single institutional manifestation. The emerging international mechanisms for creating national protected zones of biodiversity, for example, involve a complex mix of restraints and hands-on management. Despite such examples, sharp distinctions have been drawn between the two paradigms by some of their leading advocates. For example, Herman Daly argues that

> we have acquired a tendency to want to . . . take total control of the spaceship earth. The September 1989 special issue of *Scientific American* entitled "Managing Planet Earth" is representative of this thrust. But, as environmentalist David Orr points out, God, Gaia, or Evolution was doing a nice job of managing the earth until the scale of the human population, economy and technology got out of control. Planetary management implies that it is the planet that is at fault, not human numbers, greed, arrogance, ignorance, stupidity, and evil. We need to manage ourselves more than the planet and our self-management should be, in Orr's words, "more akin to child-proofing a day-care center than to piloting spaceship earth." The way to childproof a room is to build the optimal scale playpen within which the child is both free and protected from the excesses of its own freedom. It can enjoy the light and warmth provided by electrical circuits beyond its ken, without running the risk of shorting out those circuits, or itself, by experimenting with the "planetary management technique" of teething on a lamp cord.[9]

The optimizers' rebuttal is no less pointed. Writing in the *Scientific American* edition to which Daly refers, William Clark explores the limits of one of the restraint paradigm's recurring analogies, in which the growth of human population and the expansion of economic activity, resource consumption, and waste generation is compared to the multiplying of bacteria in a petri dish. Clark argues:

> The analogy breaks down in the fact that bacterial populations have no control over, and therefore no responsibility for, their ultimate collision with a finite environment. In contrast, the same wellsprings of human inventiveness and energy that are so transforming the earth have also given us an unprecedented understanding of how the planet works, how our present activities threaten its workings and how we can intervene to improve the prospects for its sustainable development. . . . With this knowledge comes a responsibility not borne by the bacteria: the responsibility to manage the human use of planet earth.[10]

Thus it is not surprising that tensions between the two paradigms cannot always be reconciled at the level of practice. Efforts to build an effective international forestry regime have failed in part because tensions between gross restraint and fine-tuned optimization were not resolved. Such would-be mechanisms of international governance as the Tropical Forest Action Plan and the International Tropical Timber Organization have polarized the sustainable forestry community by stressing optimization over restraint.[11] The collapse of the proposed forestry regime at the Earth Summit, though driven by several forces, revealed similar tensions.

Much of the debate among environmentalists over the concept of "sustainable development" has been driven by the conflicting notions of these two paradigms.[12] The Brundtland Commission, which popularized the term, came down heavily on the side of the optimizers, as indicated in the passage quoted above. Critics responded that there was less need to optimize behavior in the South than to restrain growth in the North, the predominant force pushing against global limits.[13] A similar tension between restrainers and optimizers was seen in the recent debate over the North American Free Trade Agreement (NAFTA), which polarized the U.S. environmental community. Those environmental organizations more inclined to qualitatively redefine growth embraced the agreement, seeing a chance to turn Mexico into a model of Third World environmental management, while those groups more concerned with the cumulative effects of trade-driven growth remained in opposition.

That environmentalism has not been torn apart by these two widely differing paradigms is testimony to its complexity and multifaceted character as a social movement. Instead, what we see emerging at the international level is the simultaneous expression of both paradigms, in patchwork fashion. Regimes prohibiting activities such as whaling, trafficking in endangered species, or the use of ozone-destroying chemicals reflect the paradigm of restraint.[14] Instruments aimed at funding qualitatively different forms of economic growth, such as the World Bank's Global Environmental Facility, reflect the paradigm of optimization.[15]

Despite their differences, there are important similarities between the two paradigms. Both are political, in the sense that they define how collective choices should be made and, at least implicitly, who should have the power to make those choices. Also, both paradigms tend to frame the problem as one of altering the sum total of individual human behavior. The problem is much less frequently framed as one of redesigning institutions, with political institutions receiving particularly little attention. This is puzzling: institutions are, after all, the principal mechanisms for shaping individual values, incentives, and understandings, and thus for shaping behavior. And the sustainability agenda clearly implies the need for drastic change in the way institutions shape our values, incentives, and understandings. Indeed, there are few historical precedents for the sort of *political* transformation that sustainability implies, and they include such large-scale transformations as the origins of the modern nation-state system, the implementation of a nearly global system of colonialism, and the emergence of the modern welfare state.

The sheer scale of the political task at hand should humble us. Even if we had the technical capacity to either restrain the species or manage the planet—and we currently do not—we probably lack the skill to design the institutions that would carry out these tasks. But regardless of one's view on this point, we should also ask why the sustainability challenge is so infrequently even framed in political-institutional terms. The answer, perhaps, is not that politics is seen as unimportant, but rather that each of the predominant paradigms implies a clear political strategy. More specifically, each of the paradigms sketched above focuses on only one side of the dilemma of simultaneously concentrating and controlling political power.

Not surprisingly, the paradigm of restraint tends to stress the need to erect new international institutions—notably norms, laws, treaties, and other binding commitments—to control the environmentally destructive exercise of traditional political power. In contrast, the optimization paradigm leads one quite naturally to the use of *existing* institutions—in particular those bundles of institutions that make up the state and the market—to manage behavior in a fashion much more complex than merely restricting it. The optimization paradigm seeks to mobilize existing patterns of political authority toward a new purpose, while the restraint paradigm seeks to check existing political authority's pursuit of its traditionally destructive ends.

But if each paradigm reflects one side of the institutional designer's dilemma, the limits of each approach indicate that there truly is a dilemma. One the one hand, it is safe to say that most of the restrictive international regimes and norms favored by the restraint paradigm have not sufficiently concentrated political power and authority so as to truly and effectively restrict; they are too weak. The optimization paradigm suffers from the opposite problem: the political institutions usually charged with carrying out the task of optimization—the state and the market—are *too* concentrated, powerful, and authoritative. This pattern can be seen clearly, for example, in the effects NAFTA is likely to have in rural Mexico. Far from balancing one another in the classic liberal sense, state and market are working in tandem to draw into their domain those social groups in Mexican society that have traditionally been linked only peripherally to either institution. The result is likely to be devastating for local modes of production, subsistence, land maintenance, and community sustainability, particularly in rural areas. In this example the centralized state and the transnationalized market are literally out of control, in the sense of being beyond broadly social control; as such, they are themselves a large part of the problem of unsustainability.[16] Institutional tinkering for the purposes of some abstract notion of optimization is unlikely to reconstruct such social control, and much of the tinkering does not seek to do so.

The Paradigms of Peace and Justice

Because each paradigm fails to stress the need to both concentrate and control political power, neither provides a consistent framework for thinking about the links among peace, justice, and sustainability. Seen through the lens of either paradigm, the importance of peace and justice varies situationally: depending upon the circumstances, these values may appear as useful means to an end— sustainability—or as conflicting goals that undermine sustainability, or as worthy but lesser goals to be attained in some future world in which sustainability has already been guaranteed.

Consider the problem of peace and sustainability. Clearly, the paradigms of restraint and optimization both stress the folly of war. Restrainers see war as one of the myriad actions that must be restrained, given its inherent ecological destructiveness.[17] Optimizers often stress the financial and human resources wasted in war—resources needed to get on with the business of optimizing and managing. The idea of "ecological security" thus provides some common ground for the two paradigms, in that it stresses both of the concerns just described: it *restrains,* in that it defines war itself as a threat to human security; and it *optimizes,* in that it would free up defense budgets for the more important task of environmental management.[18]

But peace is more than just the absence of war; it also requires the creation and effective use of nonviolent mechanisms for dispute resolution. With few exceptions, the problem of peace in the 1990s is not "war," in the sense of organized violence between governments. Rather, the world faces a murkier task of dealing with organized violence *by* governments against groups that do not accept governmental authority, or organized violence *between* groups that make competing claims to *be* governmental authority.[19]

This places both the restraint paradigm and the optimization paradigm on uncertain and often uncomfortable ground, because they rely so heavily on strong and authoritative states being in place and remaining there.[20] The optimizer's goal of micromanaging behavioral incentives creates strong temptations to accept and work with the status quo distribution of power in a particular state—even if that power is gained or held through violent, coercive means. The restrainer's goal of erecting broadly restrictive international regimes would seem to be a check on abuses of state power, but in a world where the parties to international regimes are states, the temptation again may be to legitimize violent and coercive states. Under these circumstances peace can quickly become a subordinate value.[21]

The predominant paradigms leave us in equally ambiguous territory with regard to justice. The restraint paradigm tends to see justice as a goal to be deferred; we must first ensure the ecological foundations for its future pursuit. In its crudest form, the restraint paradigm explicitly subordinates any questions of distribution to a larger planetary imperative. This larger imperative is usually presented in the form of global-average environmental impacts, calculated by multiplying factors such as population and per capita impact.[22] In this mechanistic view of the world, making the average come out right does not require attention to the distribution around the average. A more sophisticated version of the restraint paradigm argues that restraints *provide* justice, albeit for future generations.[23] Thus, while the cruder version treats justice as a lesser goal, the more sophisticated version sees conflicting claims for justice, not all of which can be met.

In contrast, the paradigm of optimization stresses the absence of socioeconomic justice in the here and now as a major obstacle to sustainability. Poverty is seen as a leading cause of environmental destruction, and also as an indicator of suboptimality in the way that natural resources are being used and natural environments transformed.[24] This theme is sometimes developed in terms of local actors depleting and degrading local systems, and sometimes in terms of the "shadow ecologies" of the Western industrial economies on a planetary scale.[25]

The problem, again, is reliance on unreformed institutions to carry out the task of optimization. If states and markets are not instruments of justice, then changing the market-based distribution *among* states may not resolve the question of justice *within* societies and may even exacerbate existing inequities. Injustice in this case is not being eliminated by such international cooperation but merely shifted to the subnational level, where it is rendered less visible to global society. (The point is directly analogous to the well-known slogan that foreign aid consists of taking money from the poor in rich countries and transferring it to the rich in poor countries.)

The point, it should be stressed, is not that either paradigm is overtly hostile to the ideas of peace and justice, nor that either approach is inherently violent or unjust. Rather, it is simply that the paradigms take an ambiguous and situational stance toward these values: sometimes instrumentally embracing them, sometimes pragmatically deferring them, and sometimes implicitly rejecting them. The effect of this ambiguous stance, however, is unambiguous: goals of peace and justice tend to be pushed aside in favor of the one value that is presented in unambiguous, nonsituational terms—sustainability. In a world where peace or justice is seen sometimes as a conflicting claim, sometimes as a subordinate goal, and sometimes as a limited means, there are no guarantees that all visions of sustainability automatically push in the direction of greater peace or justice.

Peace and Justice as Strategies for Sustainability

These failures of the leading paradigms of sustainability—their inability to grapple with the problem of simultaneously concentrating and controlling political power, and their inconsistent stances toward the issues of peace and justice—are related. By not focusing squarely on the question of political power, our attention is steered away from questions of violence and injustice. But the causal arrow also points in the opposite direction: by not focusing explicitly on questions of peace and justice, the restraint and optimization paradigms fail to see how these values can constitute effective political *strategies* for designing a sustainable world. The claim is not that these values are always compatible with sustainability, any more than they are always consistent with one another; as with any set of core values, internal contradictions and complex trade-offs are inevitable when one moves from the abstract to the specific.[26] Rather, the strategic value of peace and justice is that, contradictions notwithstanding, they are the firmest pillars on which to build exactly the sort of political institutions needed for sustainability: institutions that are authoritative yet legitimate. This suggests a provocative possibility: Rather than laying down ironclad requirements for sustainability and then maximizing subordinate values of peace and justice within those constraints, it may be more effective to pursue the creation of more peaceful, just international institutions as a foundation for the very difficult social changes that global sustainability will ultimately require. It is clearly beyond the scope of this chapter to present a framework for fully integrating peace and justice criteria into the design of institutions for sustainability. Nevertheless, some general propositions about the foundational importance of peace and justice for sustainability can be presented:

Violence and Injustice Undermine Sustainability

A large body of evidence indicates that there are thresholds of violence and injustice beyond which the impact on ecosystems becomes too great for sustainability to exist in any meaningful sense. In the case of violence this is obvious: war is simply too ecologically destructive, and natural resources and ecosystems simply too inviting as targets, for sustainability to endure in an extremely violent, conflict-prone world. The same is true, though perhaps less obvious, in a highly unjust world. We are often reminded that the poor and powerless may have little choice but to adopt unsustainable survival strategies. It is less frequently noted, but clearly the case, that the rich and powerful behave quite similarly. In a world of gross disparities, the wealthy and powerful generally can and do behave unsustainably—and then export the consequences of their behavior, to the south side of town or the south side of the planet. This is the political reality underlying what economists euphemistically describe as "externalities" or "high discount rates." We sometimes assume that the world system's interdependence automatically corrects for this, in that the horrible consequences we foresee in our unsustainable practices will eventually touch everyone. If so, the task would be merely to make all key actors see their own stake in sustainability. Perhaps at some point in the future the world system will be so truly interconnected and the impacts so immediate that everyone will receive exactly their global-average dose of ecology's revenge. But until then, the capacity to unjustly export the effects of behavior or the costs of adjustment onto someone else represents, like war, an important limit on the possibilities for collectively sustainable behavior.

Violence and Injustice Erode Community

If some minimal dose of peace and justice is needed to ensure the ecological basis for sustainability, a stronger dose is required to ensure its social basis. A growing body of evidence strongly suggests that a sense of *community* is essential if there is to be effective collective action on problems of resource scarcity or ecological distress. The work of Elinor Ostrom, among others, has shown that community plays a central role in shaping norms and incentives for sustainable resource management.[27] Certainly the corrosive effects of violence and injustice are one of the principal forces undermining what sense of community we still have and inhibiting the construction of a sense of community on a broader scale. Institutions that are seen as operating violently or unjustly in their pursuit of sustainability may succeed in coercing short-term gains, but at the far greater cost of the destruction of any lasting sense of community.

Violence and Injustice Expose the Illegitimacy of Authority

Injustice and violence reveal political institutions that lack the legitimate authority required to implement the sort of far-reaching policy changes needed to promote ecological sustainability. Sometimes the signs are obvious: the Mexican government cannot possibly retain the legitimate authority to implement effective policies for sustainability in Chiapas, which exploded into violent rebellion on the very day of NAFTA's implementation. Often, however, the signs are not so obvious; modern institutions have an extraordinary capacity to render violence and injustice invisible. This is exactly the reason for careful attention, since these more subtle forms of violence and injustice often reveal that political authority is growing increasingly brittle and illegitimate—and thus ineffective for implementing the ambitious agenda of sustainability.

Peace and Justice Strengthen Civil Society

Merging the global struggle for peace and justice with the global struggle for ecological sanity may be the only way to effectively rein in existing, badly flawed mechanisms for collective social choice. Inefficient markets will produce an uninhabitable world faster than efficient ones—but efficient markets, if unfettered by other social goals and institutions, will get us there in due course. The same is true of the state: incompetent, incapable states may speed the journey, but competent and capable states, unfettered, seem to know the route well enough. Nor can we be sure that some form of mutual balancing between state and market will in itself be adequate; in much of the world, it is exactly this dynamic duo of state and market that has produced the driving force of ecological destruction—particularly when arrayed against indigenous peoples, traditional lifestyles, and autonomous communities bound tightly to neither state nor market. Third World examples, such as those of forest peoples in Brazil, Indonesia, India, and elsewhere, are by now familiar.[28] But they are by no means unique; the same thing is happening to the Cree communities in Canada's James Bay, and in farm communities all across America.

Clearly, we require capable governments and efficient markets, on scales ranging from local to global; neither state nor market is withering away, and both will play essential roles in environmental management. But it should be just as clear that we need to institutionalize what Talbot Page has referred to as a "two-tiered value theory"—a prior level of governance that creates the conditions for state-based and market-based policies.[29] Given their historical mandate to promote *unsustainable* practices, neither state nor market alone can manage social choice on this prior, or constitutive, level of governance.

Thus, if social choice is to be managed effectively on this level, the impetus must come from civil society. In an ecological context, and on an international scale, this clearly means some highly transnationalized form of civil society. The institutions that foreshadow the emergence of such a global civil society are not international regimes or global markets, but rather increasingly transnational social movements and globally linked networks of nongovernmental organizations.[30] Identifying and building upon common ground among movements for environmental protection, human rights, disarmament, and a new agenda for development is therefore a critical institutional innovation.

Peace and Justice Are Systemic Values

Because peace and justice are values that apply on a local as well as a global scale, focusing on them helps us to see the total system. We are often told that actions that may be positive on a local scale—such as those that raise a community's standard of living—may be profoundly violent and unjust on a larger scale—if those local acts add up to the devastation of planetary systems. This is one of the main arguments used by those who claim that noble social goals must wait until sustainability is guaranteed. We need to see that the opposite is also true: greater cooperation among governments, and income transfers among countries based on national averages, may look peaceful and just when our focus is at the interstate level; but in the absence of institutional reform, these same acts may be instruments of violence and injustice in more localized terms. Much of the so-called "sustainable development" agenda assumes that, whereas people may be bad (or at least selfish), political institutions are good (or at least neutral).[31] Seeing the total system forces us to reexamine such assumptions, because it reveals the shifting of adjustment costs from one level of social aggregation to another.

Conclusion

Clearly, peace, justice, and sustainability are not always convergent goals. But there is good reason to believe that all three require broadly similar political institutions—authoritative enough to concentrate political power for an ambitious agenda of social change, yet legitimate enough to allow for effective social control of power thus concentrated. Thus, placing peace and justice at the center of our analysis of the political challenge facing sustainability yields both conceptual and tactical gains: by doing so we call attention to aspects of the relationship among power, authority, and sustainability that the leading paradigms of sustainability have blurred, and we are guided toward the design of legitimate, authoritative political institutions.

Arguing that there are practical as well as ethical reasons to pay careful, explicit attention to peace and justice is clearly only a first step. A second and far more difficult step is to articulate some design principles for political institutions that embody peaceful and just approaches to sustainability. While this step requires careful thought and investigation, some of the broader guidelines for this exercise are already clear. We should not create new institutions (e.g., international regimes) that exacerbate the violence and injustice of existing institutions (notably unfettered states and markets). We need to see the total system, so as not to confuse reducing the violence and injustice of our institutions with merely exporting violence and injustice to a less visible but no less real place within the system. And we need to facilitate the emergence of a healthy, pluralistic civic culture of environmental awareness and concern. This means neither a technocratic mentality of planetary management nor a draw-a-line-in-the-sand instinct of shielding pristine nature from human encroachment. What is needed instead is a broadly shared understanding: violence against nature and violence against people are intimately linked, and institutions contributing to one problem cannot be the foundation for solving the other.

Notes

1. Young also points out that institutions are distinct from organizations, which are "material entities possessing physical locations (or seats), offices, personnel, equipment, and budgets." See Oran Young, *International Cooperation: Building Regimes for Natural Resources and the Environment* (Ithaca: Cornell University Press, 1989), 32.

2. See for example Stephen L. Elkin and Karol Edward Soltan, eds. *A New Constitutionalism: Designing Political Institutions for a Good Society* (Chicago: University of Chicago Press, 1993).

3. On the need to see GATT as an environmental institution, see Ken Conca, "Environmental Change and the Deep Structure of World Politics," in *The State and Social Power in Global Environmental Politics,* ed. Ronnie D. Lipschutz and Ken Conca (New York: Columbia University Press, 1993). This negative view of the GATT is not universally shared among environmentalists. In the context of recent GATT negotiations, some environmentalists have argued that trade promotes globally efficient uses of natural resources and provides poor countries with badly needed funds for investment in pollution control. For an exploration of the trade debate, see Hilary F. French, *Costly Tradeoffs: Reconciling Trade and the Environment,* Worldwatch Paper 113 (Washington, DC: Worldwatch Institute, March 1993).

4. On forests, see the sources cited in note 28 below. On hazardous waste, see Robert Bullard, *Dumping in Dixie: Race, Class, and Environmental Quality* (Boulder: Westview Press, 1990); Center for Investigative Reporting, *Global Dumping Ground: The International Traffic in Hazardous Waste* (Washington, DC: Seven Locks Press, 1990).

5. On the ambivalence of some forms of environmentalism toward peace and justice criteria, see Ken Conca, "In the Name of Sustainability: Peace Studies and Environmental Discourse," *Peace and Change* 19, no. 2 (April 1994): 91–113.

6. This example is taken from Conca, "In the Name of Sustainability."

7. Donella H. Meadows, et al., *The Limits to Growth* (Washington, DC: Potomac Associates, 1972).

8. World Commission on Environment and Development, *Our Common Future* (New York: Oxford University Press, 1987), 1.

9. Herman E. Daly, "Elements of Environmental Macroeconomics," in *Ecological Economics: The Science and Management of Sustainability*, ed. Robert Costanza (New York: Columbia University Press, 1991), 39. No citation is provided for the quoted passage from Orr. The special edition of *Scientific American* alluded to here has been republished as *Managing Planet Earth: Readings From Scientific American* (New York: W. H. Freeman, 1990).

10. William C. Clark, "Managing Planet Earth," in *Managing Planet Earth: Readings From Scientific American* (New York: W. H. Freeman, 1990), 1.

11. See Larry Lohmann and Marcus Colchester, "Paved with Good Intentions: TFAP's Road to Oblivion," *The Ecologist* 20, no. 3 (May/June 1990): 91–98.

12. For an overview of the sustainable development debate, see Sharachchandra M. Lélé, "Sustainable Development: A Critical Review," *World Development* 19, no. 6 (June 1991): 607–21.

13. See for example Larry Lohmann, "Whose Common Future?" *The Ecologist* 20, no. 3 (May/June 1990): 82–84.

14. For an overview of the provisions of these international regimes, see Helge Ole Bergesen, Magnar Norderhaug, and Georg Parmann, eds., *Green Globe Yearbook* (New York: Oxford University Press, 1992).

15. The Global Environmental Facility is jointly administered by the World Bank, the United Nations Environment Programme (UNEP), and the United Nations Development Programme (UNDP).

16. My treatment of the market as a "political" institution is based on the complex intertwining of property rights and personal rights in modern society. As Bowles and Gintis describe this relationship:

> The tension between property rights and personal rights has been felt from the very birth of liberal republicanism. . . . Were it possible to identify one sphere of social life as "economic" and another as "political," this ambiguity might be attenuated. . . . But this convenient division of social space, favored by liberal social theory and academic convention, appears arbitrary given the evidently political nature of corporations, markets, and other institutions commonly termed "economic," and in light of the transparently economic activities of the state.

See Samuel Bowles and Herbert Gintis, *Democracy and Capitalism: Property, Community, and the Contradictions of Modern Social Thought* (New York: Basic Books, 1987), 28–29.

17. On the environmental consequences of war, see Arthur H. Westing, ed., *Environmental Hazards of War* (London: Sage Publications, 1990); Seth Shulman, *The Threat at Home: Confronting the Toxic Legacy of the U.S. Military* (Boston: Beacon Press, 1992).

18. On the concept of ecological security, see Lester Brown, *Redefining National Security*, Worldwatch Paper 14 (Washington, DC: Worldwatch Institute, 1977); Jessica Tuchman Mathews, "Redefining Security," *Foreign Affairs* 67 (1989): 162–77; Norman Myers, "Environment and Security," *Foreign Policy* 74 (Spring 1989): 23–41.

19. This theme is also discussed in Michael Klare's contribution to this volume.

20. It is for this reason that what is sometimes described as "building institutional capacity" in the Third World has moved to the forefront of discussions of global environmental governance.

21. For an example of the stark consequences that may result from such subordination, see Nancy Peluso, "Coercing Conservation," in Lipschutz and Conca, *The State and Social Power*.

22. See for example the use of the equation $I = P \times A \times T$ (where I = environmental impact, P = population, A = level of consumption or affluence, and T = technology) in Paul R. Ehrlich and Anne H. Ehrlich, *The Population Explosion* (New York: Touchstone/Simon & Schuster, 1990). For a discussion of the social and political assumptions embedded in such reasoning, see Conca, "In the Name of Sustainability."

23. On the problem of intergenerational equity, see Richard B. Norgaard and Richard B. Howarth, "Sustainability and Discounting the Future," in Costanza, *Ecological Economics*.

24. Perhaps the definitive example of this perspective is WCED, *Our Common Future*.

25. See Jim MacNeill, Pieter Winsemius, and Taizo Yakushiji, *Beyond Interdependence: The Meshing of the World's Economy and the Earth's Ecology* (New York: Oxford University Press, 1991).

26. For a discussion of the value trade-offs implied by differing conceptions of ecological justice, see Alan S. Miller, *Gaia Connections: An Introduction to Ecology, Ecoethics, and Economics* (Savage, MD: Rowman and Littlefield, 1991).

27. Elinor Ostrom, *Governing the Commons: The Evolution of Institutions for Collective Action* (Cambridge: Cambridge University Press, 1990). See also Luther Gerlach, "Negotiating Ecological Interdependence Through Societal Debate: The 1988 Minnesota Drought," in Lipschutz and Conca, *The State and Social Power*.

28. Ramachandra Guha, *The Unquiet Woods: Ecological Change and Peasant Resistance in the Himalayas* (Berkeley: University of California Press, 1989); Nancy Lee Peluso, *Rich Forests, Poor People: Resource Control and Resistance in Java* (Berkeley: University of California Press, 1992); Susanna Hecht and Alexander Cockburn, *The Fate of the Forest: Developers, Destroyers, and Defenders of the Amazon* (New York: Harper Collins, 1990).

29. Talbot Page, "Sustainability and the Problem of Valuation," in Costanza, *Ecological Economics*.

30. Ronnie D. Lipschutz, "Reconstructing World Politics: The Emergence of Global Civil Society," *Millennium: Journal of International Studies* 21, no. 3 (Winter 1992): 389–420; Kathryn Sikkink, "Human Rights, Principled Issue-Networks, and Sovereignty in Latin America," *International Organization* 47, no. 3 (Summer 1993): 411–41.

31. For a brief but effective rebuttal to this argument, see Robin Broad and John Cavanagh, "Beyond the Myths of Rio: A New American Agenda for the Environment," *World Policy Journal* 10, no. 1 (Spring 1993): 65–72.

2

Unsustainable Liberty, Sustainable Freedom

William Ophuls

Medieval theology, or the Roman corruption of morals, poisoned only their own people, a small part of mankind; today, electricity, railways and telegraphs spoil the whole world. Everyone makes these thing his own. He simply cannot help making them his own. Everyone suffers in the same way, is forced to the same extent to change his way of life. All are under the necessity of betraying what is most important for their lives, the understanding of life itself, religion. Machines—to produce what? The telegraph—to despatch what? Books, papers—to spread what kind of news? Railways—to go to whom and to what place? Millions of people herded together and subject to a supreme power—to accomplish what? Hospitals, physicians, dispensaries in order to prolong life—for what? How easily do individuals as well as whole nations take their own so-called civilization as the true civilization: finishing one's studies, keeping one's nails clean, using the tailor's and the barber's services, travelling abroad, and the most civilized man is complete. And with regard to nations: as many railways as possible, academies, industrial works, battleships, forts, newspapers, books, parties, parliaments. Thus the most civilized nation is complete. Enough individuals, therefore, as well as nations can be interested in civilization but not in true enlightenment. The former is easy and meets with approval; the latter requires rigorous efforts and therefore, from the great majority, always meets with nothing but contempt and hatred, for it exposes the lie of civilization.

—Leo Tolstoy[1]

Sustainable development is an oxymoron. Modern political economy in any form is unsustainable, precisely because it involves "development"—that is, more and more people consuming more and more goods with the aid of ever more powerful technologies. Such an economy *produces* nothing, it merely *exploits* nature. Such an economy reckons without the laws of thermodynamics and other basic physical laws: these ordain limitation as the price of life and guarantee that the invisible hand will generate the tragedy of the commons.[2] To put it another way, such an economy is based on stolen goods, deferred payments, and hidden costs; it continues to exist or even thrive today only because we do not account for what we steal from nature or for what posterity will have to pay for our pleasures or for what we sweep under the ecological carpet. In sum, development as commonly understood is intrinsically unsustainable.

In addition, to treat sustainability as if it were a merely technical problem—how can we make economics compatible with ecology?—is to miss the point almost entirely. The ecological crisis calls into question not our means, but our ends; not our ability to sustain so-called development, but its very meaning and purpose.[3] Therefore, achieving a form of development that is truly sustainable over the long term—that is, one that does not involve more and more people consuming more and more goods with the aid of ever more powerful technologies—will necessarily require a radical change in our basic values, perhaps even in our very notion of "civilization."

Above all, the standard discussion of sustainability begs an enormous political question. That is, even supposing that development as usual were technically possible and morally desirable, would it be politically feasible? I believe the answer is no: the basic premises of modern political economy are not only ecologically self-destructive but socially and psychologically damaging as well, and the aftermath of this damage is a large part of the reason that governance is in such trouble almost everywhere in the modern world today. In short, the most critical challenge confronting us is not economic but political sustainability—for moral and social collapse will hit us sooner and with more devastating effect than the ultimate ecological collapse.

To reduce the question of political sustainability to more manageable proportions, I propose to focus on the tension between liberty and freedom, for this core political issue illuminates the profound challenge to modern values that lurks within the ecological crisis. In effect, I shall respond to the question Ivan Illich raised about the developed world's near total dependence on so-called energy slaves: "The energy crisis focuses concern on the scarcity of fodder for these slaves. I prefer to ask whether freemen need them."[4]

I begin with Isaiah Berlin's famous distinction between negative and positive freedom.[5] The former means the freedom to do what we want, provided only that our acts do not directly injure others; in other words, what *liberty* usually denotes in the modern, or "liberal," tradition (so this is the term I shall use from now on). By contrast, positive freedom means subordinating desires to ideals in order to achieve some more virtuous or nobler state of being that better accords with our "higher nature." Freedom thus resides in self-fulfillment, not self-indulgence: to promote the former and check the latter, it follows that restraints on individual liberty may be necessary.

Berlin marshals a powerful case in favor of liberty and against freedom (in the positive sense): it is possible, he says, "to coerce men in the name of some [worthy] goal . . . which they would, if they were more enlightened, themselves pursue, but do not, because they are blind or ignorant or corrupt." Or, to put it more bluntly, tyranny can be (and has been) justified in the name of freedom, so let us for God's sake cleave to liberty at all costs, abandoning any hope of fulfilling our "higher nature" by political means. Moreover, since individuals differ fundamentally in their psychological makeup, they must be allowed to pursue their own self-defined ends, lest they be oppressed. Thus we must not only eschew the kind of ideologies that lead to tyranny, but we must learn to tolerate the astonishing diversity that results when individuals are liberated from traditional social restraints.[6]

Alas, although liberty is undeniably attractive as a political principle—who would not wish to be free of all constraints except the need to keep the peace?— the theoretical cogency of the libertarian position is belied by the practical outcome it has produced. Polities founded on the concept of negative freedom, or mere liberty, are now experiencing not only ecological degeneration from without, but also moral decay from within—precisely because they believe in nothing positive.[7] That some more positive ideal of freedom is indispensable will be clear once we understand how mere liberty engenders a process of moral entropy that leads ultimately to social collapse.

To be brief, centuries of ecclesiastical abuse and sectarian warfare in Europe had utterly discredited theocracy as a political principle and had even called into question the moral authority of the church. Thus when Thomas Hobbes made the satisfaction of individual wants, rather than the achievement of religious ends, the basis of politics, he became, as Marx said, "the father of us all." That is to say, he became the philosophical author of the modern way of life in general and of modern political economy in particular. With Rousseau being the major exception, those who followed Hobbes embraced his premises and built on his foundations. The result was the edifice known as classical liberalism: a philosophy of political economy that exalts the liberty of the self-interested individual to pursue sensual happiness. That government exists to gratify the hedonistic desires of selfish individuals thus became the defining principle of modern politics in all its forms (including Marxism, for as Marx's homage indicates, it too is founded on Hobbesian premises).

The moral implications of liberalism were grasped immediately by the Marquis de Sade, who carried Hobbes's emancipation of human passions from traditional moral restraint to its logical conclusion: all is now permitted. In *Juliette*, de Sade says that "self-interest . . . is the single rule for defining just and unjust." It follows that justice or morality is a fiction: "there is no God in this world, neither is there virtue, neither is there justice; there is nothing good, useful, or necessary but our passions, nothing merits to be respected but their effects."[8]

Thus de Sade was not merely a libertine and a pornographer: he was a genuine Enlightenment philosopher and authentic—if perverted—liberal whose folly and tragedy consisted in trying to advance the cause of sexual liberation too far in advance of its time.

That others did not at first follow de Sade's lead in demanding total personal liberation was due primarily to the powerful effect of inertia in human affairs and, more particularly, to the moral legacy of the Middle Ages, which despite growing secularism still permeated Locke's "civil society" (i.e., the social foundation upon which liberal political institutions rest). To make a long story short, however, by the end of the nineteenth century more and more people began to understand—either with horror, as in the case of Dostoyevsky, or with at least partial approbation, as in the case of Nietzsche—that the Sadean conclusion was inescapable: if God is dead, then all is indeed permitted.

Equally important, however, is that although Hobbes unleashed the human passions, he also gave them an important new outlet: economic development. The energy hitherto expended on religious and social conflict was now to be turned to promoting "commodious living" through the production and enjoyment of the "conveniences" of life. In essence, forms of Hobbesian political economy are an attempt to solve the problem of power politics with economic production: men who are sufficiently rich in goods will wish to enjoy their prosperity in peace, so governments need do little more than administratively divide the spoils.[9] To put it another way, Hobbes invented bourgeois civilization, which is based on converting passions into interests—that is, on sublimating political ambition and personal libido into a drive for goods instead of for power or dominance. The distinguishing features of that civilization followed both logically and historically: independent proprietorship as the ground of liberal polity; and the famous Protestant ethic as the moral basis of liberal society. (The latter was especially important in checking the passions of bourgeois man: although the Protestant ethic justified economic self-enrichment and social self-aggrandizement, it also spiritualized them by making wealth and status a function of rectitude.) Unfortunately, the very success of economic development in the latter half of the nineteenth century undercut these pillars of bourgeois civilization: the independent entrepreneur was largely replaced by the dependent wage earner, who lived not to produce, but to consume; not to become worthy in the eyes of the deity by acquiring worldly estate, but merely to possess and enjoy worldly goods.

At the same time, the animus against organized religion continued to undercut traditional morality. Thus the moral climate of Western civilization shifted dramatically in the first decade of the twentieth century: both the moral legacy of the Middle Ages and the Protestant ethic that had no longer restrained or channeled the passions effectively. The change in mores was epitomized by the famous Bloomsbury group. As the great economist John Maynard Keynes, one of its most prominent members, said, "We repudiated entirely customary morals, conventions, and traditional wisdom. We were, that is to say, in the strict sense of the term, immoralists." These "immoralists" pioneered the way for the rest of us: whereas Keynes was obliged to keep his own homosexuality relatively quiet, he and his friends made it possible for "the love that dares not speak its name" to be shouted from the rooftops today.[10]

To speak more generally about the nature of this new moral climate, bourgeois man (and I will get to bourgeois woman in a moment) was no longer content with mere political and economic liberty. He began to clamor for social and psychological liberty as well—that is, for "liberation" from the inner repression involved in submitting to the demands of "civilization." (Although Freud often receives the credit or blame for this development, he is really only a convenient symbol for a cultural upheaval affecting everything from high art to popular attitudes.) Twentieth-century history is therefore the record of how the "immoralism" of the avant-garde spread to the common man. That is to say, it is the chronicle of an orgy of "desublimation," an explosive release of hitherto repressed fantasies and desires, along with a resolute rejection of the social conventions that presumed to channel or forbid their expression.

In this fashion, the moral entropy that is intrinsic to the liberal order has slowly but steadily eroded both the moral legacy of the Middle Ages and the bourgeois rectitude of the Protestant ethic. A vicious circle of decay in both morals and mores has propelled us toward a social collapse whose details— crime, broken families, drug addiction, and the like—are so well known as to require neither documentation nor discussion. However, a closer look at two aspects of the vicious circle will further illuminate my general point.

With respect to crime, for example, the principal duty of the liberal state is to keep the peace by suppressing deviant behavior. For this reason it is often called "the night watchman state." As we all know, however, the watchman has fallen down on the job: despite prisons packed to the rafters with vicious criminals, there are even more out prowling the streets. Indeed, in a stark admission that the authorities have lost control of the nation's capital, already one of the most heavily policed cities in the country, the mayor of Washington in October 1993 asked the president to send in the National Guard to help stem the rising tide of murder and mayhem. How could it be that the liberal state of today—especially in the United States, but increasingly in all other modern polities as well—is failing to perform its one essential function (and a purely negative one at that)?

Leaving aside all sociological complexities, the answer is that crime is the logical and, indeed, inevitable consequence of living by Hobbesian premises. When all members of the society live purely to satisfy their own appetites, they are not only thrown into a fierce competition with each other for access to the sources of satisfaction, but also into a Sadean moral wasteland in which that satisfaction is the ultimate and only value. Eventually all that restrains them is fear of the watchman's club—and when that ceases to intimidate, crime is bound to flourish. Those who take to a life of crime in the urban wastelands of today are simply good Hobbesians: if the sovereign does not provide enough of the necessary and appropriate "conveniences" of life, then you owe the state and society neither loyalty nor obedience. As Hannah Arendt put it, "Hobbes foresees and justifies the social outcasts' organization into a gang of murderers as a logical outcome of the bourgeoisie's moral philosophy."[11] In sum, the practical effect of Hobbesian polity is paradoxically to encourage just the kind of lawless violence that it is supposed to prevent, because living by Hobbesian premises over the long term fosters a vicious circle of antisocial behavior that tends toward the state of nature and the war of all against all.

A second aspect of the impending social collapse that needs further elaboration is family breakdown. The disintegration of the little society of the family is a truly ominous development, foreshadowing the ultimate collapse of the larger society. Recent experience shows that social programs are of limited use in overcoming major family failures: what children do not learn at home they are very unlikely to learn elsewhere. Schools, for instance, cannot by themselves civilize each new cohort of barbarians. To put it more formally, the family is the primary arena in which ego learns to moderate its narcissistic demands and harmonize itself with some larger social entity: loyalty, integrity, responsibility, self-control, and the like are all learned primarily in the family setting. In short, the family is where we acquire civility, the ability to live constructively and well in civil society. If the family fails to model and inculcate civility or to bind the child to the community, then society no longer serves as a bulwark against selfishness, it becomes instead a mere arena for it—a place where fundamentally amoral and asocial beings struggle for personal advantage with little or no thought for the welfare of others, much less the general welfare. The decay of the family thus portends a bleakly Hobbesian future.

This provides the appropriate context for the promised discussion of bourgeois woman. To get right to the point, feminism heralds the final collapse of civil society and therefore of liberal polity. Women's liberation means precisely what it says: women now want to be just as "liberated" as men, just as "free" to pursue their own selfish ends. To obviate any possible misunderstanding, I am neither blaming women for deciding to play by men's rules—given the economic conditions and moral climate created by generations of male selfishness, they really had little choice—nor am I suggesting that some reactionary status quo ante be restored. I am simply reporting what I believe to be the social and political consequences of women becoming good liberals looking out for Number One in the great marketplace of life. For the fact is that, whereas men long ago abandoned the family for the marketplace, women until very recently upheld both family and civil society by not living according to Hobbesian premises: men lived for money, women for love. Woman's role in bourgeois society was thus utterly anomalous: putting aside all ambition for herself, she was to be the gentle custodian of traditional virtues, the warm champion of the heart against the head, and the loving incarnation of home and hearth. And in so doing, she provided the social and emotional glue that held together a society otherwise given over to self-interest. In short, women formerly devoted themselves to resisting moral entropy: they tended our inherited moral capital and thereby preserved the civil society that is absolutely indispensable to the success of the liberal polity. Now that they are no longer willing to make that sacrifice, both civil society and liberal polity are in jeopardy, and the future is, once again, bleakly Hobbesian.

To sum up this brief discussion of moral entropy, we must understand that narcissism and egotism are fundamental to liberalism. Its inner logic as a political and social doctrine is absolutely clear, even though few yet dare to follow it to a licentious Sadean terminus (because, thanks largely to the efforts of generations of mothers, our morals and mores have not yet been completely destroyed). Liberalism means exactly what it says: liberation of the self from all social or moral restraints except the necessity to keep the peace. Liberal society is thus, as Keynes openly acknowledged, frankly and intrinsically immoral. The liberal polities of today are therefore confronted with the prospect of moral and social collapse, followed swiftly by political breakdown or even chaos.

The fatal flaw in Hobbes's political philosophy was identified centuries ago by Aristotle:

> For as man is the best of the animals when perfected, so he is the worst of all when sundered from law and justice . . . [because he] is born possessing weapons for the use of wisdom and virtue, which it is possible to employ entirely for the opposite ends. Hence, when devoid of virtue man is the most unholy and savage of animals.[12]

By renouncing the aim of perfecting the political animal—that is, of teaching him to use his "weapons" for wise and virtuous ends, instead of for contrary ones—the liberal polities founded on Hobbesian premises effectively abandoned the vocation of politics. It was thus inevitable that "the best of animals when perfected" would be progressively "sundered from law and justice" and gradually turned into "the worst of all"—into an immoral creature of will and appetite who must be ruled by force, if he can be ruled at all. In the end, therefore, although the negative concept of freedom is attractive on many grounds, both theoretical and practical, *mere liberty is not and can never be the basis for a workable philosophy of politics over the long term.* Man's "weapons for . . . wisdom and virtue" *must* be directed to positive ends, or the resulting social order is bound to be both "unholy and savage."

So much for the diagnosis. What is the cure? It is implicit within the diagnosis. Despite the dangers that Berlin quite rightly points out, we cannot do without positive freedom, without some ideal that accords with our "higher nature," and to discover this ideal will be the great task of twenty-first century politics. I would like to sketch very briefly my own understanding of what this task will involve.

First, we need a politics of consciousness. The story of modern civilization has been one of increasing "command" or "mastery" of the material environment, as humans have appropriated more and more matter and energy for their own ends, in order to live higher on the ecological hog and to support greater numbers. We have called this "progress," but it now stands revealed as a self-destructive strategy for meeting basic human needs, both material and cultural. Indeed, not only is such a way of life intrinsically unsustainable, but it is not at all clear that it promotes genuine human happiness. As Tolstoy plaintively asks, what is the *point* of all this progress? In short, having nearly exhausted the possibilities of material development, we are left with little choice but to foster spiritual development instead. That is, we critically need some concept of a "higher nature" that we wish to fulfill and some ideal of an authentic freedom that would result from its fulfillment, for only thus will the human race be able to control its wants and moderate its demands. We need, in sum, a new social vision that makes growing in wisdom, rather than gratifying our appetites, the central purpose of human life.

Next, we need a recovery of morality. The story of modern civilization has been one of progressive demoralization in all three senses of the word: the corruption of morals, the undermining of morale, and the spreading of confusion. We can see clearly the problems such demoralization has already caused and the ominous terminus toward which it tends. It is now apparent that virtue, like wisdom, must be cultivated and indeed inculcated by the social and political order, or these "weapons" will be turned to perverse ends and destroy both the society and the polity.

Nor is morality the insoluble problem that hard-core rationalists pretend it is: we do know in a general way what personal and political virtue are. For example, Tzu, Socrates, and Gandhi, to pick three sages from very different eras and traditions, agree fundamentally on the nature and meaning of human life and also, in a more general way, on the political implications that follow from this understanding. In other words, with all due respect for the difficulty of the task, there would appear to be plenty of room for a reasoned middle ground between a fundamentalist dogmatism that wants to inflict a narrow-minded moral code and a laissez-faire relativism that denies both the necessity and the possibility of constructing one.

Moreover, to approach the problem in a way that may be more congenial to the modern scientific temperament, it seems that we have at least the beginnings of a new theory of natural law. That is, we now know enough anthropology, biology, ecology, psychology, and history to make some educated guesses about what would constitute a just, workable, healthy, and, last but not least, ecologically sustainable social order. For example, whatever their sectarian differences, all schools of depth psychology agree on one thing: both individuals and cultures must reckon with the forces of the unconscious, or they will be subject to the famous "return of the repressed"—that is, to the danger of individual madness and mass psychosis, a danger to which we are exposed today thanks to the radical sublimation that is the poisoned fruit of liberalism. One of the goals of a genuinely enlightened polity would therefore be to foster a constructive engagement with the unconscious through myth, rite, ritual, and self-exploration—a way of life conducive to psychological balance and health. Similarly, the clearest teaching of ecology is limitation: natural systems work on the basis of feedback mechanisms that constrain organisms in ways that foster orderly communities and, ultimately, a harmonious biosphere. Restated in moral terms, this comes close to being a scientific justification for the wisdom of things and for the control of appetite by the higher human faculties. Or for a kind of neo-Confucian concern with the character and quality of our relationships with the natural and social order. In short, politics founded on naturalistic principles discovered by human reason would seem to be possible. Indeed, I can see no other ground upon which to construct a viable political theory of the sustainable society—a theory that would permit us, despite all the shortcomings of human nature, to live harmoniously with our fellow creatures and virtuously with our fellow human beings.

This leads naturally to the third and final requisite of a future politics: the restoration of government. The story of modern civilization in its political aspect is one of emancipating the human passions and maximizing individual liberty. Although the effects were indeed liberating at first—not only with respect to civil liberty and human rights, but in many other ways as well—in latter days liberalism's destructive aspects have come to predominate. In short, as with material development and political economy, we have almost exhausted the possibilities of selfish individualism as a ground of government, so we shall have to find a new one.

Indeed, the fundamental problem with liberal polities is that they do not actually govern, except in the most minimal sense. According to my dictionary, to govern means to control, guide, direct, and restrain. This is precisely what liberal governments are not supposed to do in theory and what they try not to do in practice. (Now, of course, they are more and more obliged to do so by force of circumstance—but largely to remedy problems, rather than to achieve positive ends.) To govern in the true sense, however, is always to control, guide, direct, and restrain in accordance with some political and social ideal. Otherwise it is not government, but democracy at best and tyranny at worst. In sum, we now need to govern—to control, guide, direct, and restrain individuals who would otherwise behave selfishly and destructively, so that they respect the interests and needs of the larger human and natural community of which they are a part.

It seems that Rousseau was right. As he predicted, the unbridled individualism and unrestrained hedonism of liberal polity have proven to be morally and socially destructive. A politics based on mere liberty is unsustainable: to achieve real freedom, we must govern our appetites. Whether we like it or not, therefore, we must be politically encouraged to higher ends than self-gratification and self-aggrandizement. We must, in other words, be "forced to be free." But this does *not* mean to be tyrannized, only to be *governed by our own consent* in accordance with some notion of morality and some vision of the good life. And Rousseau was convinced, as I am, that to be so governed leads ultimately to a greater happiness than can be found in gratifying ego's desires—to the genuine felicity that only arises when we give ourselves to some higher purpose, some larger enterprise, than mere appetite.

This then is the political challenge of the twenty-first century: to invent a new form of politics that manifests this higher purpose and promotes this larger enterprise—but that also preserves, as far as possible, the basic civil and human rights which are the precious fruit of liberalism.[13] That to do this will be far from easy or free of risk goes without saying, but we seem to have little choice, for moral and social collapse and its likely political aftermath are the inevitable and appalling alternative.

I cannot conclude without noting that the challenge does not end there. Modern civilization, the peculiar way of life based on the ideas of the Enlightenment, represents not a break with all past civilization, as is sometimes thought, but rather an intensification and amplification of many of its worst tendencies, which are antithetical to real freedom. Modern civilization did not invent war, poverty, oppression, and exploitation, even though it has made these more devastating and widespread than ever before. The task before us is therefore even greater than implied above: we must not only reinvent politics as an arena of wisdom and virtue that sustains authentic human freedom, but we must also transform civilization along the lines envisioned by Rousseau—as well as by Thoreau, who maintained that the ultimate goal of civilization was to produce "a more experienced and wiser savage."

The human race has reached a critical point in its social evolution when it has no choice but to make peace with its biological origins and to learn how to live once again as a member and partner of the natural community rather than its dominator and destroyer. In other words, we must rediscover how to live as our savage ancestors once lived—in nature, rather than apart from it, much less above it. We must invent the civilized analogue of the hunter-gatherer way of life, the only truly sustainable mode of human existence the planet has ever known. This is not a call to return to the Stone Age: we have many possibilities open to us that were not available to our forebears, for we have been enormously enriched and enlightened by the long experience of civilization (or at least so one hopes). Nevertheless, how such a profound transformation of civilization toward a more experienced and wiser savagery can be achieved is obviously an immensely difficult problem, for it will clearly entail quite radical changes in the way we think and act.

Just how radical is suggested by one of the most poignant and pointed critiques of modern civilization ever uttered. Breaking into a filmed interview on the destruction of the Amazon rain forest, an anonymous Kayapo Indian woman shouted, "We don't want your dams. Your mothers did not hold you enough. You are all orphans."[14] It is perhaps too simple to say that the good society is one in which your mother—and by extension your father, your community, and indeed your entire way of life—holds you enough, so that you grow up feeling that the world is a good place and that life is intrinsically satisfying just as it is, and that there is thus no need to make it more satisfying by accumulating endless wealth and power at others' expense. But this at least points in the right direction: to become more experienced and wiser savages, we shall have to create cultures so rich and nurturing that we would have no need to pursue happiness, we could simply enjoy it.

Notes

1. Cited in Karl Loewith, *Meaning in History* (Chicago: Chicago University Press, 1949), 99.

2. William Ophuls, *Ecology and the Politics of Scarcity* (San Francisco: W. H. Freeman, 1977; William Ophuls and A. Stephen Boyan, Jr., *Ecology and the Politics of Scarcity Revisited,* rev. ed. (New York: W. H. Freeman, 1992).

3. It is necessary to insist upon this point because we live in a society that is means-driven: we allow our economy and technology to determine our values, instead of vice versa. Thus one of the most important actors in the American political system over the past fifty years has been the private automobile, which has completely reshaped both our landscape and our culture to suit its own requirements. What is worse, we suffer from the delusion that the solution to every problem is a better mousetrap. But if it is our ends that are in need of revision, better mousetraps are beside the point. They are, as Thoreau said, but "improved means to an unimproved end." In this light, the enormous effort expended in recent years on inventing devices to make the market less ecologically destructive has been mostly wasted, because we lack the political will to implement the measures that would be truly effective. In sum, ends are crucial, means ancillary: only a clear and compelling vision of the end we wish to achieve—a society that is truly sustainable over the long term—can give us the political will to discover and then to implement the means necessary to its achievement.

4. Ivan Illich, "Energy and Social Disruption," *The Ecologist,* no. 4 (1974): 49–52.

5. Isaiah Berlin, *Four Essays on Liberty* (New York: Oxford University Press, 1969).

6. In the work cited, Berlin tries to solve the core problem of contemporary liberalism: how can one justify individual liberty when a large part of its original rationale has evaporated? In high mass-consumption societies dominated by gigantic corporate enterprises, both public and private, it is no longer possible for most individuals to acquire Lockean "estate" (as opposed to mere possessions) through individual initiative. Thus independent proprietorship, the original ground of liberal politics, no longer exists to any significant degree. In response, Berlin tries to shift this ground from economics to psychology, from social independence to individual difference. Unfortunately, or so I argue below, this will not work: psychological liberation is not a viable basis for sustainable polity, much less liberal polity, over the long term, so the end of independent proprietorship probably means the end of genuine liberalism as well.

7. In fact, even the theory lacks cogency today, for the classical liberal position on

injury—my fist's freedom stops just short of your nose—is no longer tenable. We can scarcely breathe without harming, hindering, or constraining others—at least not in large, crowded, complex, interconnected societies such as our own.

8. Cited in James Davison Hunter, *Culture Wars* (New York: Basic Books, 1991), 313.

9. Or so the theory has it. In practice, of course, modern political economy soon developed its own characteristic form of power politics. In this connection, we should note the crucial role of Western imperialism in postponing the Sadean scenario: in the name of empire, the Hobbesian power drive was exported overseas; with the end of empire, it must be accommodated entirely at home.

10. Keynes citation from Gertrude Himmelfarb, "Manners into Morals: What the Victorians Knew," *American Scholar*, 57, no. 2 (Spring 1988): 226. No moral judgment is implied by my use of this example. I ask not whether any particular form of behavior, such as homosexuality, is good or bad and should therefore be permitted or not. My question is political: is it possible to have a viable society in which all is permitted?

11. Hannah Arendt, *The Origins of Totalitarianism* (Cleveland: Meridian, 1958), 142.

12. Aristotle, *The Politics,* trans. Rackham (New York: Putnam, 1932), 1253a, 30–33.

13. It should be obvious that my own notion of a sustainable society is fundamentally Rousseauean, or even Socratic, but I am not at this point arguing for this or that vision—only that there must be some higher purpose and some moral basis for sustainability. In any event, radical paradigm shifts cannot simply be dreamed up and then imposed on the society. Thus any new vision will emerge slowly and organically, only after prolonged and searching debate involving large numbers of people. Nevertheless, the shift must first be conceived or originated by particular human minds, and my purpose is to encourage others to become involved in the debate by articulating their own vision of a politically and ecologically sustainable civilization.

14. Documentary film, *Amazonia: Voices from the Rainforest,* cited in *San Francisco Chronicle,* 31 May 1991, E6.

3

Sustainability's Five Capitals and Three Pillars

Stephen Viederman

The words *sustainable* and *sustainability* have lost any semblance of meaning. In the last few years, for example, we have become accustomed to hearing the oxymoron "sustainable growth." The World Bank recently established a vice presidency for environmentally sustainable development, presumably to differentiate this from the rest of the development bank funds. Peter Passell, the *New York Times* economics columnist, has written that " 'Sustainability' is a budget concept (seeking the deficit level we can live with) that could soon come into vogue."[1] And President Clinton has established his own Council on Sustainable Development, which includes among its members eight corporations—including two that are on the Council on Economic Priorities "toxic ten" list—six national environmental organizations, six cabinet and agency heads, and a "diversity contingent." The message of the council seems rather clear: "sustainability" is about business and the environment. The Environmental Defense Fund is a member organization, but where, for example, is the Children's Defense Fund? *The New York Times* recently reported that Coca-Cola had decided to change its advertising agency because it was unhappy with its latest slogan. Perhaps the new slogan should be "Coke—the Sustainable Cola!" The fact that it doesn't mean anything should not deter them.

Why do we spend so much time trying to define sustainability? The German

Thanks to Matthias Finger, John Rensenbrink, Linda Stark, and Doug McKenzie-Mohr for comments on this chapter.

novelist, Günter Grass, suggests an answer: "Only what is entirely lost demands to be endlessly named; there is a mania to call the lost thing until it returns."[2] We were once sustainable, or so we believe; we know we are not now sustainable, and we yearn to be so once again.

The term has been misused and overused. Perhaps we should seek some other word to convey what we have lost and what we want to restore. I think not. I think we need to recapture the word, provide it with real meaning, and begin a process of dialogue. There is no running away from it. "All philosophy" said the Stoic philosopher Epictetus, "lies in two words, sustain and abstain." What better message for the twenty-first century! Abstain from the destruction of the natural world upon which all life and production depends, in order to sustain a just and humane relationship between nature and humanity.

Sustainability is usually presented as a technical problem, but it is much more than that. It is ultimately a question of what a society values, not in the technical economic sense of valuation, but in the sense of human concerns. It is, as Peter Gleick reminded us, "a social construct." It is a vision of the future. As such it is and must be as much the domain of the poets and painters, of "experts" and activists, as it is the domain of economists and ecologists. Women, people of color, the poor, and others must be included in the envisioning process in order to reflect the variety of our culture, and to reach a genuine consensus. This is not an issue of "political correctness" but of democratic necessity. While we should be concerned with the technical means of achieving sustainability, we cannot be preoccupied with them. Whether something we can define as "sustainable" is achievable is open to question. Still, the search for it is necessary if the present human condition is to be improved.

The Capitals of Sustainability

"Words, like eyeglasses," observed the eighteenth-century French moralist Joseph Joubert, "blur everything that they do not make clearer." Thus, yet another definition is offered in the hope of clarifying what we are about.:

> Sustainability is a community's control and prudent use of all forms of capital—nature's capital, human capital, human-created capital, social capital, and cultural capital—to ensure, to the degree possible, that present and future generations can attain a high degree of economic security and achieve democracy while maintaining the integrity of the ecological systems upon which all life and all production depends.

Before proceeding, some definitions are in order.

Capital is used broadly to define any form of wealth available for life and production. Its use here is not intended to diminish other aspects of the forms of capital identified, such as the aesthetic value of nature, or the spiritual purpose of humans. Neither is it assumed, as in conventional economics, that capital as a concept must be quantified.

Nature's capital is the stock that yields the flow of natural resources. It is both renewable and nonrenewable. It includes inputs into the economy, in terms of resources, and relates to the outputs of the economic system, in terms of the assimilation of wastes.

Human capital refers to the people and the bodies of knowledge that contribute to community and to production.

Human-created capital refers to products and technologies created by humans, including the built environment.

Social capital is what Harvard political scientist Robert Putnam calls the "civic-ness" of regional life, including such things as participation in the political life of the community, newspaper readership, and membership in associations from sports clubs to the Lions Club, from unions to choral societies. This is participation "that seems to depend less on *who* you are than on *where* you are," and that underlines the importance of the relationship to place. Social capital is the reservoir of mutual trust, civic involvement, and reciprocity, which grows as "virtuous circles." It is necessary, I would argue, for economic security and ecological integrity, particularly because of its connection to place, and it is at the heart of democracy.[3]

Cultural capital, as defined by Berkes and Folke, "refers to factors that provide human societies with the means and adaptations to deal with the natural environment and to actively modify it," for better or worse.[4] This includes the life stories and creation myths that are part of all cultures and that can help or hinder our search for sustainability. Witness, for example, Native American views of the world, as opposed to what Richard Norgaard has observed are "the forces of modernity's progressive, mechanical, hierarchical life story" that pauperized the coevolving natural and cultural worlds.[5] Cultural capital is, in part, the dream of a universe. It is also at the core of the life of the community, giving the community its distinctive character.

The Pillars of Sustainability

To continue with the definitions within the definition:[6]

Economic Security is the control that individuals and communities have over their own economic lives, and the degree to which they are capable of shielding themselves from external economic shocks. The right to sustainable livelihood, for example, is central to economic security. Kenneth Dahlberg's "buying locally and eating locally" (chapter 16) is an important aspect of economic security. Economic security involves recognition on the part of individuals and communities of the need to achieve a balance between the scale of the economic system and the limits of the ecosystem in which it operates. Economic security should contribute to a sense of interdependence among individuals and among communities based upon mutual interests and equality of power.

Ecological integrity is maintained when individuals and communities live in harmony with natural systems. Clean air, clean water, and land use appropriate to meet human needs and the needs of the ecosystem are essential elements of ecological integrity, as is the prevention and recycling/reuse of waste.

Democracy is characterized by citizen participation in community decision making through democratic processes supported by appropriate citizen education. Harmony is fostered through efforts to increase equity, justice, and political, religious, ethnic, racial, cultural, sexual, and gender tolerance. Diversity is accepted while a sense of wholeness is sought; equalization of power is a goal.

These "pillars" of sustainability are created and supported by the forms of "capital" described above. There can be no ecological security without prudent use of natural capital: the ways we use all the capitals will determine the degree to which we can attain economic security and democracy.

How Definitions Differ

This definition of sustainability reflects an extension of past public-policy efforts that emphasized efficiency, equity, and liberty. Here economic security and ecological integrity go beyond efficiency to include a concern for sufficiency. Economic security is also an extension of equity. Democracy extends the concept of liberty. The social contract is redefined to include ecology as an essential element.

In the past, the sustainability of ecological systems has received much of our attention. Concerns for equity and the economy, often as servants of the natural systems, have only more recently been addressed. However, to achieve sustainability, communities must control and prudently use all the capital available to them to balance the needs of economic security, ecological integrity, and democracy. They are inseparable.

This definition differs from many others that tend to focus on economics and the environment while neglecting participation and democratic processes. In addition, by focusing on community, it suggest an appropriate scale for our discussion of sustainability. Furthermore, economic security is very different from economic development, which, as the term is often used, is not sustainable.[7]

And the reference here to "control of capital" raises directly the issue of power, which is omitted from all other definitions of sustainability. These usually imply that a benevolent guiding hand will ensure degrees of equity, fairness, and distribution, but they do not address these central issues directly. Based on conventional economics, these definitions usually assume that "rising tides raise all ships." This, clearly, while it may occur in a single number, is not the case, in any larger sense.

As suggested by Costanza and Daly, we can do little more for future generations than provide them with the where-with-all and hope that they have the wisdom and intelligence to use it in an appropriate manner.[8] At the same time we must recognize that in important respects this generation and the next are on the cusp. Future generations will be structured into creative or destructive pathways by our choices.

Above all, the definition makes clear that the changes necessary to achieve sustainability are structural and systemic. Currently, the political system is driven by money, with voters as bystanders. The economic system fails to respect the environment, equity, or justice, assuming that the common good will be achieved through continued economic growth, and trickle-down theory has yet to demonstrate any degree of effectiveness. The social system reflects deep divisions based upon gender, sexual, racial, and ethnic intolerance. Overall the systems are broken, and a new system that honors the pillars of sustainability—economic security, ecological integrity, and democracy—is sorely needed.

Issues of Sustainability

Having put forward what is admittedly a rather grandiose prescription, it is well to reflect upon the first principle of sustainability: the humility principle. This reminds us of the limits of human knowledge, and by extension, the limits of our capacity to manage, especially on ever increasing scales—globally. It was perhaps reassuring recently to hear no less a manager than former World Bank president Robert McNamara say that he once believed that all problems had solutions but that he no longer does. And as Hayek reminded economists in his 1974 Nobel lecture, we too are now being called upon to solve the problems that we ourselves have created.

Again, a novelist provides the context. In the opening pages of his novel *Ragtime*, E. L. Doctorow describes the murder by his mistress of the well-known architect, Stanford White. THE CRIME OF THE CENTURY was the headline emblazoned across the front pages of New York's tabloids, but, Doctorow observed, "It was only 1906 and there were ninety-four years to go."

Closer to our subject, Marc Sagoff has recently retold the story of Petersham, a prosperous farming community in Massachusetts whose "habit of investing . . . and in improving their general living conditions argues that they looked forward to permanence." Today no one farms in Petersham, now the Harvard Forest. Despite the fact that "the practices the farmers used were impeccable from the perspective of sustainability" the farms of Petersham went out of production between 1850 and 1870. The cause: the opening of the Erie Canal in 1830 and the development of railroads. The farms of the Middle West accessed eastern markets and attracted eastern capital for expansion, producing foodstuffs in greater quantity and more cheaply than the farmlands of New England.[9]

Indeed, how were they in Petersham to know what was to come—and how are we today to know what upheavals await us? That we cannot manage the future, despite what would appear to be the efforts of the best and the brightest—witness *Scientific American*'s September 1989 issue, "Managing the Planet"—does not mean that we cannot envision what a sustainable society might look like. Technicians seek neutral solutions without a strong sense of the moral imperatives that fuel visionary thinking.

The envisioning process—and it must be a continuing process, not a one-shot affair—helps us to understand our values, individually and as a society. Discussions of sustainability are fundamentally efforts to decide who we are. A vision of a desirable future helps us to define alternative paths and in the process to avoid, to the degree possible, the shocks of Petersham. We can plan in a linear fashion from now to then. But we must also play the role of the historian or archaeologist of the future, working backward from then to now, in the attempt to identify barriers to success. This historical reflection helps us to identify and begin to address the issues of systems and structures.

Envisioning helps us to be *proactive* rather than being constantly *reactive* to assaults over which we feel we have little control. In the absence of envisioning, we make victims of ourselves. Envisioning also helps us to make the essential distinction between the management of events—which are the symptoms of the problems we face—and the sorts of system changes that must be our goal.

Envisioning also provides us with the possibility of establishing milestones to assist us in assessing our program along the way. Without a vision of the future we do not, in effect, know where we are going and, therefore, what we are measuring. However, we must be cautious, that is:

• Do our measures describe transient fluctuations or long-term trends?
• Is what we measure truly the result of our own actions, or the product of other forces? Are we comfortable with the units of measurement normally used—numbers?
• Are we disaggregating sufficiently to avoid traps such as that presented by a rising GNP that masks increasing disparities between rich and poor?

Since sustainability is an exercise in human values, "a social construct," what then are the appropriate measures?

Our goals must be clear and generally accepted. Is, for example, the goal zero toxins, as proposed in the Principles of Environmental Justice agreed upon at the First National People of Color Environmental Leadership Summit, or some higher level of toxic emission, as generally found acceptable by the larger, nationally based environmental organizations to be accepted?[10]

Because envisioning is a process that must be participatory, it helps us to recognize that priorities may vary given the level of development of a particular group or community. This has important political and substantive implications, especially for assessment. For example, at the risk of oversimplification, in the North, concerns about sustainability tend to be focused on global environmental issues. Green plans in Norway, the Netherlands, New Zealand, and Canada are reflections of these concerns, and goals do not include economic security and democracy. In the South, however, the issue is framed much more in terms of social equity regarding, among other issues, the use of natural capital and the availability of clean space to ensure future development. "The concerns of the South to address local community poverty and ecosystem issues," observes the Green Forum in the Philippines, "are not contradictions but form the necessary building blocks for the sustainability of the larger global whole."[11]

Envisioning also helps us to see the system as a whole. "Our task," E. F. Schumacher reminds us, "is to look at the world and see it whole." And by looking at the whole, Johan Galtung points out, we begin to recognize that there are no side effects or by-products or externalities; these are simply artifacts of too narrow a paradigm.[12] When we see that there are only effects and products, when we see the relationships among economic security, ecological integrity, and democracy, we have made significant progress toward the solution of our problems.

Global Considerations

Is there a fundamental contradiction between an effort to see the "whole" and addressing issues of "local community poverty?" I think not, but there is a tension that must be understood and dealt with, and this relates to the scale of our efforts toward sustainability.

Clearly our overall goal must be planetary. But, as David Orr has observed, "how can we manage the globe, if we can't manage the back 40?" I argue that for visions to be meaningful and permit meaningful participation, we must operate on scales (place) and in time frames (pace) that do not exceed the limits of our knowledge, and that give us confidence in the results of our efforts. In effect we must focus on places where people can see the horizon, can see and feel the consequences of their actions, both positive and negative. We must begin with the community, which as Wendell Berry has suggested is a "neighborhood of humans in place, plus the place itself: its soils, its water, its air, and all the families and tribes of the nonhuman creatures that belong to it."[13]

By seeing the place as a part of the whole, we are forced to recognize the importance of cooperation as a human value, juxtaposed against the supposed economic value of competition. For example, trade, in this admittedly ideal construction, becomes an exchange of surpluses from local production and use, one that serves mutual needs and desires. This is only one of the many important system changes that I have already identified as central to any degree of sustainability.

Perhaps the system most in need of overhaul is the global economic system— I never suggested sustainability would be easy. The question "Can a global economy work?" is often asked. However, a more important question is seldom raised: "Can there be economic security, ecological integrity, or democracy in a global economy?"

In a world economy characterized by virtually uncontrolled capital mobility, sustainability is likely to be unattainable. Why? Economic security is virtually impossible at the level of the family, the community, the state, and limited even at the national level. There is no locus of control that respects the three pillars of sustainability. Note, for example, a report on the 1993 gubernatorial election in New Jersey. The challenger blamed the incumbent for having lost 280,000 jobs as a result of the large tax increase he pursued three years ago. The *New York Times* reporter astutely observed: "Beyond the campaign oratory, there is a broader question: How much can a governor, or any state official, do about a state's economy, especially when market forces operate not only nationally but internationally?"[14]

The global economy underlines the lack of connection between production and place, as demonstrated by the historian William Cronon in his history of Chicago. This in turn limits the commitment of the corporation to place, except perhaps in the very short term, which is then reflected in the corporation's lack of commitment to the social and ecological infrastructure of the place. What is allegedly good on a global scale for Kodak or Xerox when those companies lay off ten thousand workers is not good for Rochester, New York, where they are based.

Capital's search for the cheapest place destroys community and ecology, because neither play any role in the definition of value in a global economic system. Intel is expanding its chip manufacturing plant in New Mexico because the state is providing them with a $2-billion bond issue, and millions of gallons of water—in the desert!—in return for at most a thousand jobs, many of which will come from out of state.[15] Mercedes-Benz's decision to locate in Alabama could hardly have been based upon the amenities available in the area: the school system was found to be unconstitutional by the state court system, and the governor had just been forced from office for improprieties.[16]

Citizenship is love and commitment to place, in addition to civic duty, which is impossible without love and commitment to place. There can be no real community nor citizenship in a capital mobile world. Therefore, there can be no sustainability.

Clearly, system change is essential if there is to be any move toward sustainability. We are experiencing not an economic recession but rather economic stagnation. The answer then is to not to continue applying worn out Band-Aids but to think in terms of a fundamental redesign based on the pillars of sustainability—economic security, ecological integrity, and democracy, using the available capital, in all its forms, toward our social and equity goals.

We have seen the faults of socialism. Capitalism has many cultures relating "to the meaning found in work, the attitude toward stakeholders, the styles of managing employees, the various negotiation tactics," among others things.[17]

But the necessary superiority of capitalism has not been demonstrated. As does any human institution, it has flaws, but capitalism itself can and must be changed. What lies between and beyond socialism and capitalism is perhaps the greatest challenge facing the search for sustainability.

Notes

1. Peter Passell, "Economic Scene: Sustainability, or Seeking the Deficit Level We Can Live With," *New York Times,* 12 August 1993, D2.

2. Quoted in *Utne Reader,* no. 60 (November/December 1993): 116.

3. Robert D. Putnam, *Making Democracy Work: Civic Traditions in Modern Italy* (Princeton: Princeton University Press, 1993); and Robert D. Putnam, "The Prosperous Community: Social Capital and Political Life," *American Prospect,* no. 13 (Spring): 35–42.

4. Fikret Berkes and Carl Folke, "Investing in Cultural Capital for Sustainable Use of Natural Capital," in *Investing in Natural Capital: The Ecological Economics Approach to Sustainability,* ed. AnnMari Jansson, et al. (Washington, DC: Island Press for the International Society for Ecological Economics, 1994), 128–46.

5. Richard Norgaard, *Development Betrayed* (New York: Routledge, Chapman and Hall, 1994).

6. This classification is adapted from Elizabeth Kline, *Defining a Sustainable Community* (Medford, MA: Center for Environmental Management, Tufts University, 1993).

7. See, for example, John Pezzey, *Sustainable Development Concepts: An Economic Analysis,* World Bank Environment Paper no. 2 (Washington, DC: World Bank, 1992).

8. Robert Costanza and Herman Daly, "Natural Capital and Sustainable Development," *Conservation Biology* 6, no. 1 (March 1992): 37–46.

9. Mark Sagoff, "Settling America or the Concept of Place in Environmental Ethics," *Journal of Energy, Natural Resources and Environmental Law* 12, no. 2 (1992): 349–418.

10. Charles Lee, ed., *Proceedings: The First National People of Color Environmental Leadership Summit, October 27, 1991* (New York: United Church of Christ, Commission on Racial Justice, 1992) xiii–xiv.

11. Maximo Kalaw, Jr. "The Justice-Ecology Debate," *Green Forum* 4, nos. 1, 2 (July 1993): 8–9.

12. Johan Galtung, "Environmental Politics Beyond Rio Waiting for UNCED: Waiting for Godot," in *Rebuilding Communities: Experiences and Experiments in Europe,* ed. Vithal Rajan (Devon, England: Green Books in association with World Wide Fund for Nature, 1993): 25–34.

13. Wendell Berry, "Decolonizing Rural America," *Audubon Magazine,* March/April 1993.

14. Iver Peterson, "In New Jersey, A Debate Over Lost Jobs," *New York Times,* 19 October 1993, A14.

15. Southwest Organizing Project, *Intel Inside New Mexico* (Albuquerque: Southwest Organizing Project, 1994).

16. E. S. Browning and Helene Cooper, "States' Bidding War over Mercedes Plant Made for Costly Chase," *Wall Street Journal,* 17 November 1993, 1.

17. Charles Hampden-Turner and Alfons Trompenars, *The Seven Cultures of Capitalism* (New York: Doubleday, 1993), 1.

4

Sustainability and "the System Problem"

Gar Alperovitz

Let me begin by suggesting that the conventional debate on "sustainability" is itself fast becoming unsustainable. I obviously mean to be provocative—but also quite specific.

At one level there is a growing consensus that to avoid compromising the needs of future generations any political-economic system must significantly reduce ecological stress, repair past environmental damage, and generate sufficient momentum so that net environmental deterioration is halted. Although precise definitions vary, many now recognize that "sustainability" also requires both an institutional structure and a culture with the capacity to achieve these bottom-line results *in an ongoing fashion.*

Yet I believe it has also become increasingly obvious that neither of the two major "systems" of the twentieth century—capitalism and socialism—are organized in a manner compatible with achieving these goals. If this is so, the conventional debate will obviously need to push much deeper in order to confront the underlying design characteristics of these and other systems to see if any are—or might be—sustainable. The debate in its present form is unsustainable. Put another way, whether we like it or not, the sustainability crisis is pushing us willy-nilly beyond itself to "the system problem."

The assistance of Thad Williamson in preparing this article is gratefully acknowledged.

Socialism

The easiest place to begin to consider this contention is with socialism, a system that, at least in currently known variants, has produced disastrous—and clearly unsustainable—ecological results in the twentieth century. Throughout Central Europe and the former Soviet Union, the push for cheap energy and maximum industrial production—together with a wanton disregard for public health—have created vast ecological wastelands in which filthy air, polluted water, and heavy toxic emissions have despoiled ecosystems and threatened human life.

In 1988 air pollution in more than a hundred cities in the former Soviet Union was over ten times higher than legal standards. Sixty-five percent of Poland's river water has been deemed too polluted even for industrial use, and large segments of the Polish population are not served by any waste treatment facilities.[1]

Energy efficiency in each of the former socialist countries of Europe has lagged 50 percent behind even modest U.S. levels. Much energy is produced by filth-generating brown coal plants, many without any pollution controls whatsoever. At the end of the 1980s it was estimated that one out of every seventeen deaths in Hungary was due to air pollution. "Wherever you point your finger on the map," one Russian scientist recently observed, "there is another horrible place."[2]

Behind such statistics—and many more could be cited—was a domineering, growth-at-all-costs centralized government bureaucracy, and an ideology that suggested that nature could and should be bent to human will whatever the consequences. The governing authorities of the socialist states lacked the will— and probably the capacity—to hold economic operations accountable to true social costs, and local communities had no means of contesting the antiecological values of central power. As ecological economist Ken Townsend has observed, "rationality" converted forests of rich diversity into monocrop fields and attempted to reverse the flow of entire river systems.[3]

Sadly, reports from postcommunist Russia are hardly more encouraging. In Moscow, a city where 80 percent of the smokestacks have no filters, trees and vacant land are being ravaged with few restrictions. Cancer rates are soaring; a factory was recently built on top of a radioactive dump. Says a pained city official, there is simply no awareness "that there are ecological consequences . . . everyone now is just thinking about when they get rich."[4]

That socialism has produced such results can be traced to certain basic properties or design features of the system. For instance, state-run agencies are compelled to expand by the pressure of internal grow-at-all-costs management dynamics and the general expansionist goals of the system. At the same time, such institutions are compelled to reduce and externalize costs, hence to pollute and degrade the environment if this "saves" money—as it commonly does.

Not only are socialist systems based on growth imperatives, they produce extreme hierarchies of power that reduce both liberty and the capacity of citizen groups to effect positive change. Status hierarchies also generate invidious comparisons, hence an unquenchable thirst for "more" as an expression of a peculiarly socialist form of consumerism: "my dacha is bigger than yours!" The outcome is a structurally determined pattern of growth that is destructive of the environment.

What needs to be stressed, however, is not simply criticism of the result, but rather that the *institutional architecture, power relationships, and dynamic properties of socialism make ecologically disastrous outcomes all but inevitable.*

The problem is *systemic.*

Capitalism

We have little difficulty recognizing such structural conceptions when we look "outward" toward another system. But what of our own system? Are the environmental problems of capitalism also systemic? Is the trend toward increased environmental degradation and the continuing escalation of resource consumption a minor side effect of the system? Or is it a necessary result of our own system's design?

The trends are not encouraging to those who would like an easy answer. Although there are occasional breakthroughs, such as the elimination of DDT, and many small reforms, what obviously counts are long-term results. Consider natural resource consumption; as the World Resources Institute has recently noted:

> The United States consumes nearly 3 times as much iron ore as India, 4.6 times as much steel, 3.6 times as much coal, 12 times as much petroleum, 3 times as many head of cattle and sheep, and 1.7 times as much roundwood. The United States has less than one-third the population of India, so per capita consumption differences are significantly larger. In particular, U.S. consumption of all sources of fossil energy is so large that per capita emissions of carbon dioxide, a principal greenhouse gas, are 19 times those of India.[5]

Alan Durning reports that since 1940 we Americans alone have used up as large a share of the earth's mineral resources as did *everyone* in history on the planet previously.[6] If this voracious level of consumption—and the deeper sources of growth and consumerism from which it springs—are ever to be confronted, we will clearly have to go well beyond proposals to increase taxes on consumption and advertising.

Again, to cite only one of numerous obvious long-term outcomes connected with pollution and toxic wastes, chemical production in the United States increased by 115 percent between 1970 and 1992 alone. Yet as of 1992, only 22 of the 70,000 chemicals in commerce had been fully tested for human health effects; only 1 percent had even been identified for testing by the Environmental Protection Agency (EPA). There are no health data at all on 80 percent of the approximately 50,000 industrial chemicals (a category excluding pesticides, food additives, cosmetics, and drugs) in use. EPA data from 1988 shows that 79 percent of all hazardous waste in the United States is generated by the chemical industry—and nearly a thousand new chemical substances are put on the market each year, some of which are likely to be harmful, even in small quantities. Yet if all the laboratory resources currently available worldwide were put to work, it would only be possible to test five hundred products per year![7]

We all know that capitalism as an economic system has certain basic properties: its profit-maximizing imperatives make it dependent upon continued expansion and continually higher levels of resource use. It too generates pressures to externalize costs and to pollute. It also produces extreme income and status hierarchies, cultural inequalities, and materialist aspirations.

Capitalism also creates certain kinds of power relationships—most obviously, the concentration of economic and political power in the large corporation. This is not because corporate leaders are "bad people," but rather because this is the logic of the system. Our business executives *must* take care of business—or they will be *out* of business!

Countless studies—and common observation—indicate that corporate institutions also commonly have the capacity and interest to wield disproportionate political influence, to manipulate regulatory agencies, thwart citizen action groups, and impact both electoral politics and legislation. Moreover, the income hierarchies generated by capitalism have an obvious effect on politics: those with more money tend to have more power, and their money gives them a disproportionate capacity to dominate the broader public interest. It is also no accident that toxic dumps end up in poor and minority communities.

It is important to recognize that growth in capitalist systems is not motivated simply by hunger for profit but also by fear. The logic and dynamics of the capitalist system are such that companies *must* cut costs if they are to withstand competition. They *must* externalize: if a company willingly spends money on a pollution reduction problem and then must raise its prices to cover the cost, it risks finding its market share reduced by a less conscientious rival firm.

A community given the choice between, say, continued logging of declining forests or loss of jobs is simply by reason of fear in a weak position to resist growth politics. On a larger scale, we see cities and states prostrating themselves in order to attract corporate investment—not simply out of greed, but because the consequences of not continuing to grow are so severe and so obvious: high unemployment, continued social breakdown, and, of course, negative political outcomes for incumbent government officials. For communities—as for capitalist firms—it is very often a matter of "grow or die."

The same proposition unfortunately commonly holds for most individuals as well. The materialist aspirations many so easily condemn are in large measure often the flip side of pervasive economic insecurity. Consider the life cycle of a typical middle-class American: one goes to college in order to get ahead and thus incurs debt. To pay off the debt requires accumulating as much money as possible, and then it's time for a family, children, and if you're lucky, a mortgage. More responsibilities, and more pressure to accumulate as much as possible—now. Parents come to realize that if they don't live in the right neighborhood, their child's education will suffer. And they had better start saving for college. And by the time that's over, the question "Who will take care of me?" in old age or sickness becomes central.

For the vast majority of Americans, whatever security one gets is fragile at best. At any time—and this is now as true for white-collar managers as for blue-collar workers—one might be laid off as a result of a downturn in the economy, a corporate buyout, a new technology, or even simply a change in the exchange rate.

The only way to get any real security is first and foremost to avoid failing. It is therefore *always* wise to strive for "more"—as much as possible—*now*—since tomorrow may well bring "less"—and thus to continue on the materialist merry-go-round. In this situation, it is hardly surprising that mass insecurity should generate adulation of the rich and the secure in the system, nor that the capacity to consume so often becomes a measure of self-esteem and status. Meanwhile, the corporate need to sell—and the type of products most widely promoted—also generates pressures for higher consumption and further impacts the buy-and-consume materialist culture.

I have been dwelling on such widely recognized features of our own system for a reason: that these are "system properties" is obvious—and this in turn implies that the unsustainable outcomes we regularly observe are just as inherent in the nature of capitalism.

But of course, we all know very well that our system is characterized by such institutional, structural, and power "design features." The problem is that we rarely call a spade a spade. *Most important, the implications are seldom incorporated into analyses of the challenge of long-term sustainability.*

Confronting the System Issue

If in truth the problems of capitalist countries, like those of the former socialist states, are systemic in origin, then indeed by definition they cannot be solved unless systemic change occurs. Again, this is readily accepted when we look "out" at another system; but it is much more daunting when we look "in" at our own.

Part of our difficulty in confronting the system issue on the environmental front is that we often have trouble distinguishing between reforms that help ameliorate the worst aspects of environmental degradation and those changes that actually result in altering *trends*. At the most general level, positive movement that diminishes harmful impact on the environment of course occurs within capitalist systems. Legislation is passed that helps control pollution; progress is made in eliminating lead and chlorofluorocarbons; there are improvements in the reduction of sulfur oxides, carbon monoxide, and particulates.

Let me urge, however, that it is absolutely essential that we discriminate much more clearly among the following three categories of change: "A," occasional breakthroughs; "B," token reforms and "gains"; and "C," *significant long-term trend reversals.*

Although most of our environmental debate is focused on fostering occasional breakthroughs, token reforms, and "gains"—and certainly efforts at policy reform reflect this—a great deal of evidence points to the conclusion that the basic *outcome trends* that matter most in terms of sustainability are commonly *not* significantly affected by the A and B type improvements.

I have sketched some of the obvious consumption/resource indicators above. With certain small exceptions, a composite study of long trends in twenty-one environmental factors recently compiled by the organization I head confirms general worsening of various other ecological outcomes in each of nine industrialized countries surveyed over the past twenty-five years.[8] This despite the fact that the quarter century began with the first Earth Day and extended through a flurry of legislation, reform, and green planning, the establishment of environmental ministries, and growing ecological consciousness and grassroots activism. Had economic growth been anywhere near the levels that business and government leaders in the nine surveyed nations wanted, the trend toward environmental degradation would have been far, far worse.

If the basic trend data we are beginning to see in numerous areas is even close to accurate, what we are in fact confronting *is* a system problem. Put another way: if most trends can be only marginally altered by traditional reforms, the dynamic system properties of capitalism are obviously incompatible with the goal of an ecologically sustainable future.

Furthermore, if it is truly the case that both capitalism and socialism are systems inherently designed in ways that are incompatible with sustainability—that neither system can produce desired ecological outcomes precisely because of their inherent architecture and dynamics—then either there is no way out of the box, or clearly we will ultimately need to come up with a different system design.

Logically and in all honesty, we must acknowledge that there may not be an alternative way forward; that there may not be an answer to this problem. Quite simply, one possible option is that it may be impossible to build the institutions and the culture required to achieve real sustainability.

However, if we do not buy this pessimistic conclusion—and I do not—then just as clearly we need to begin to engage in a serious discussion of system designs compatible with the principles of sustainability.

The question is, are we prepared to face up to the cold realities of such a challenge?

Yes, I know the old saw—"you can't change the system!" But no, I do not believe you can hide from what is self-evident forever. Hence, I propose that we at least try to think about the issue, and that we begin a serious dialogue. As Joan Rivers likes to say, "Can we *talk?*"

Community

What is needed, ultimately, is a system that not only stabilizes existing negative ecological trends but reverses those trends and produces positive outcomes. How might we begin to sketch at least some of the properties of a system that might undercut the pressures which generate nonsustainable outcomes?

When the question is put in this manner, I believe we can at least begin to think about some elements of a solution, if not as yet a total answer.

Given the space limitations—and simply by way of illustration—one primary system property, as Herman Daly and John Cobb emphasize in their book *For the Common Good,* almost certainly must be the constitution of a culture of community or "common good" as a necessary condition of sustainability.[9] I do not, however, believe this can simply be stated as a matter of abstract philosophical vision. "Community" has visionary (and moral and ethical) aspects, of course, but sustainability over time requires that the culture of community be *institutionally* based—which means it must be embodied in structures that generate, reinforce, sustain, and nurture it.

The logical issue is straightforward: in both capitalist and socialist systems any firm has an incentive to pollute its local community if this means lower costs. But if, say, the community were to own the firm, it would have little incentive to pollute itself. Again, simply by way of illustration, such an "institutional design" would at least structurally internalize most costs.

This is not to say that what is logical is easy to do institutionally. However, the growing interest in community land trusts—an increasingly common local institution—suggests one possibility of some quite practical social innovations which by their very nature bring the whole community into the same institutional structure.[10] Might there be experimentation to slowly push the frontier of institutional development of this kind well beyond its present modest levels?

In fact, just below the surface of most conventional inquiry a myriad of so-called "community development corporations" of all shapes and sizes have sprung up and are now involved in housing and business activities in almost every major locality. "Community-based," populist-style economic development has also spawned hundreds of democratically controlled worker-owned firms and thousands of co-ops. Some are operating plants of significant scale in such industries as steel. There has even been a surprising growth of community-owned municipal enterprises. Elsewhere small-scale public firms are engaged in everything from methane production and real estate development to cable television.[11]

Such institutional fragments—or "seedlings"—just possibly prefigure community forms more consistent with sustainable development than present capitalist or socialist models. If we agree that the experience of being part of a community is one necessary element of a sustainable system, then one obvious need is to assemble and assess such fragments and build upon the best of them.

A related issue is how community life might be better undergirded. Capitalist development in practice destroys the basis of community integration and wholeness as a matter of course: companies come and go, and jobs rise and fall. Often as not the social fabric is undermined, the local culture disintegrates, the community fragments, and young people leave. A system that engendered the core idea "we're all in it together" would also ultimately have to be better structured to stabilize the basis of local community experience.

Scale

Another fundamental issue is that of scale. One major problem in generating a culture and politics that can constrain forces that produce trends inimical to sustainability is the size of the polity in question: It is extremely difficult and expensive to build a social consensus in a large polity. It may be—I think it is—impossible in a continental system.

The question of scale used to be part and parcel of the study of political theory; today scale is making a comeback in regional studies and among ecological activists in the bioregional movement. It's also certainly coming back in the developing world, the former Soviet Union, and Canada—as "breakdowns" of big nations occur left and right.

In the United States, we have yet to confront the gigantism of the continental scale of our country. For instance, many discussions of social and political theory related to sustainability, and many proposals for change in the United States, utilize comparative European models: the Scandinavian countries did this, the Germans did that, the Dutch did this. The truth, however, is that all of the European geographic polities are of an order of magnitude so vastly different from our own as to make most comparisons questionable. For instance, West Germany, home of the postwar economic miracle, can be tucked into the state of Oregon. France fits inside Texas. The Netherlands is minuscule. Compared to the United States all are *very* small geographic polities.

If we agree that the size of a polity has implications for consensus building, then we need to look to entities that are smaller than the continental national government: states or groupings of states within a region, for example. Hence, smaller-scale and semi-autonomous regional polities with increased powers and responsibilities vis-à-vis the national government might ultimately be another necessary element of a new system—if, that is, democracy and sustainability are serious objectives.

Another possibility for future development might involve regionally scaled public enterprise. This, in fact, was the regional-ecological concept behind the original "grassroots democracy" inspiration of the Tennessee Valley Authority—*before* it was subverted by a variety of political-economic and military pressures (especially during World War II). Despite the current wave of privatization and much rhetoric condemning public enterprise, many studies show that under the right conditions public enterprise can also be efficient in strictly economic terms.[12]

Liberty

A third illustrative requirement of any serious design is obviously liberty for the individual citizen. As Robert Heilbroner has warned us, even the worthy goal of ecological sanity can all too easily lead in the direction of authoritarianism.[13] The danger lies in imposing a moral vision of the ecologically sound society without paying attention to the need for an underlying institutional structure that sustains liberty.

The classic conservative position, as expressed for example by Milton Friedman, Henry C. Simons, and even the traditionalist Russell Kirk, is that it is the small independent property-owning capitalist who provides the system basis of a free person and a free culture.[14] The entrepreneur stands on his own feet! The *idea* of liberty in this system reinforces the "material base," and the material base reinforces the idea system.

At one time the conservative theory in fact worked to a certain degree as one foundation for liberty. The United States was largely a system-culture based on *individual,* property-owning, independent small businessmen and businessmen farmers for much of its first two centuries. Leaving aside the fact that all capitalist firms tend to externalize costs and thereby threaten the environment, the problem today is that the basis for this system theory of liberty simply no longer exists. Only 15 percent of American society by any stretch of the imagination can legitimately be called entrepreneurs and small farmers.

In a new system design, what institutional structures might conceivably guarantee liberty? Apart from suasion, ethical vision, social reforms, and legislation, the task is to determine a structural basis that might allow citizens an independent place to stand so they can resist authoritarian tendencies in the polity and surrounding culture.

Some possible directions suggest themselves: Peter Drucker has proposed treating jobs as a form of "property right," which—like small landholdings in an earlier era—might now provide a more stable basis for preserving and extending individual liberty.[15] The academic community is certainly familiar with this concept: everyone at a university knows that if you want to be independent, you better have tenure! Otherwise you don't have the "liberty" to say what you want to say.

Another method, which appeals, interestingly, to both Democratic and Republican politicians, involves earned income credits—actually, "something for nothing" for those who work: money, added to wages as a means of strengthening a worker's capacity to support a family and remain independent.

Yet another intriguing approach is found in the state of Alaska. The principle that the community as a whole should share in the benefits of natural resource development is made operational via the Alaska Permanent Fund, but it is done in a way that also gives support to the individual. Royalties are divided annually, with each individual citizen receiving a fixed amount (over $900 in recent years) as a matter of right and the rest going to the state's general fund.[16] Of course, this example is deeply flawed because it depends so heavily on the exploitation of oil and often involves environmental degradation of many other kinds. However, the institutional mechanism for providing at least some additional support to individuals is suggestive of practical possibilities that might one day be developed in other areas.

What is essential is that a sound *basis* for liberty must be central to the design and institutional architecture of any system that has sustainability as its goal. Not only is liberty desirable in itself, but quite simply, without liberty, genuine accountability becomes impossible. In a system without true liberty, the state dominates society, while the resulting culture promotes passivity rather than the aggressive watchfulness that sustainability—and democracy—require.

The Inevitability of Change

Again, a system that was less driven to a culture of materialist consumption would likely provide structural support for an alternative culture—one in which greater personal security, the nurturance of community, and the cultivation of meaningful work were all possible. It might even affirm human spiritual concerns.

Put another way, the entire culture of grow and consume is reinforced by the *lack* in our current system of community life and support for true personal fulfillment sufficiently meaningful to sustain an attractive way of living other than consumerism.

Some of us still have glimpses of what an alternative feels like, of course—for instance, the broader values associated with the best of some religious traditions. But when communities are constantly undermined by economic pressures, when individuals and families must constantly move in search of the next decent job, and when the local factory must pollute the community because it has fundamentally different goals than the community, then the culture of growth and consumption expands simply by virtue of being the only game in town.

Nothing in everyday life teaches that there is a common, community interest.

Once we begin to move beyond sketching possible "elements" of a sustainable system to the question of how these diverse elements might one day be integrated into a larger whole, numerous other issues—and possibilities—arise. For instance, if there were more security and more time to truly participate, we might actually face the challenge of defining democracy in a way more compatible with true sustainability. If we so choose, increases in productivity and a more equitable income distribution could result in a shorter work week—not in more goods and more pressure on ecological systems but in more free time. One result might be that more people would be able to participate in the political process—which in turn is a precondition for holding planners and governments to higher standards of accountability for sustainability.

Even to entertain such questions is to suggest the need for a far-ranging inquiry that might begin with various elements but that would ultimately lead toward the integration we call a "system." This in turn poses the age-old problem of transitions.

System change is obviously an extraordinary occurrence. Yet it is also obvious that in fact systems change all the time—that, historically speaking, they come and go like the phases of the moon. What may seem impossible today becomes tomorrow's reality. Indeed, I would wager that the political and economic forms we take for granted today will almost certainly not be the dominant forms of the next century. The real question is not whether there will be change, but given the growing social strife, pain, and violence in our country, and indeed around the world, whether the inevitable change will be democratic and sustainable.

A useful paradigm to consider is the idea of "reconstruction"—the invention within an existing system of new forms and institutions that point in a different direction and that provide the foundation for a different system architecture. Reconstruction as a paradigm for change involves a nuanced combination of the ongoing way of doing business with a new way of thinking, through incremental institution-building steps.

Momentum, not ideas, usually governs in history. However, in a time of crisis—and especially one of lost belief—ideas matter profoundly. As the sustainability crisis deepens, I believe we will be forced to undertake a profound dialogue about issues at the very core of our nation and of the future—something akin, perhaps, to the debate the founders had at the outset of the Republic.

A new science—one pluralistic in its approach, problem-focused, holistic rather than reductionist, and tolerant of uncertainty—what philosophers of science Silvio Funtowicz and Jerome Ravetz have called a "postnormal" science—is also needed.[17]

Members of the academy, of course, have the time and resources to help start that kind of national discourse, and to begin the process of moving the systems debate from the margins to the very center of our national life. If we are to take the issue of sustainability seriously, it is, I think, the responsibility of people who enjoy the luxury of time and knowledge to do just that.

Notes

1. USSR State Committee for the Protection of Nature, *Report on the State of the Environment* (Moscow, 1989), cited in Hilary French, *Green Revolutions: Environmental*

Reconstruction in Eastern Europe and the Soviet Union, Worldwatch Paper 99 (Washington DC: Worldwatch Institute, 1990), 5, 11; see also Larry Tye, "Poland is Left Choking On Its Wastes," *Boston Globe,* 18 December 1989 (cited by French).

2. Facts on Eastern Europe from French, *Green Revolutions,* 11, 12, 23; quote from Margaret Shapiro, "Capitalism Compounds Moscow's Ecological Mess," *Washington Post,* 21 May 1993.

3. Kenneth N. Townsend, "Steady-State Economies and the Command Economy" in *Valuing the Earth: Economics, Ecology, Ethics,* ed. Herman E. Daly and Kenneth N. Townsend (Cambridge: MIT Press, 1993), 275–96. See especially 277–82; 279 in particular.

4. Shapiro, "Capitalism Compounds Moscow's Ecological Mess."

5. *World Resources 1994–95* (New York: Oxford University Press), 17.

6. Alan Durning, *How Much is Enough* (New York: W. W. Norton, 1992), 38, citing Ralph C. Kirby and Andrew S. Prokoprovitsh, "Technological Insurance Against Shortages in Minerals and Metals," *Science,* 20 February 1976.

7. Trend data from *OECD Environmental Data Compendium 1993* (Paris: Organization for Economic Co-operation and Development), 241; only 22 of 70,000 chemicals tested from General Accounting Office, "Environmental Protection Issues," GAO/OCG–93–16TR (Washington, DC: GAO, 1992), 13; and other facts on chemicals from *The World Environment 1972–1992,* 249, 253, 261, citing data from OECD, Environmental Protection Agency, and the landmark National Research Council study, *Toxicity Testing* (Washington, DC: National Research Council, 1984).

8. National Center for Economic Alternatives, *Index of Environmental Trends* (Washington, DC: Sage Communications, 1995).

9. Herman E. Daly, Jr., and John Cobb, *For the Common Good* (Boston: Beacon Press, 1989). See especially chapters 8 and 9, "From Individualism to Person-in-Community" and "From Cosmopolitanism to Communities of Communities," 159–89. The authors note on p. 360 that "the goal of the changes proposed in this book is a bottom-up society, a community of communities that are local and relatively small."

Commenting on Daly's earlier work on "steady-state economics" as well as *For the Common Good,* Douglas Booth perceptively notes that "the expansionist nature of capitalist institutions raises serious doubts about whether capitalism could even survive at the microeconomic level in the context of macroeconomic steady state limitations on resource flows." Booth concludes, "[A] steady state economy requires relatively radical changes in both macroeconomic and microeconomic institutions in order to be successful." Douglas E. Booth, "The Macroeconomics of a Steady State," *Review of Social Economy* (Summer 1994): 14, 18–19.

10. There are now roughly a thousand land trusts involving a million members and volunteers and encompassing over 2.7 million acres of land in the United States. Camas Hubenthal, "Land Trusts Save Forests," *Gaining Ground,* Spring/Summer 1994; *Gaining Ground* is the journal of the Global Action and Information Network, Santa Cruz, CA.

11. For a brief listing see Gar Alperovitz, "How Cities Make Money," *New York Times,* 10 February 1994. For a longer listing, see Jeffrey Shavelson, *A Third Way* (Washington, DC: National Center for Economic Alternatives, 1990).

12. See, for example, Brendan Martin, *In the Public Interest?* (London: Zed Books, 1993); William Ashworth, *The State in Business: 1945 to the Mid-1980s* (London: Macmillan Education, 1991); and Henry Parris, Pierre Pestieau, and Peter Saynor, *Public Enterprise in Western Europe* (London: Croom Helm, 1987), which notes that many apparent inefficiencies in public enterprise are due to less rigorous market conditions than those faced by private corporations, rather than the fact of public ownership itself.

For a partisan but useful account of the successes of public enterprise in Canada and an overview of the public-private issue, see Herschel Hardin, *The Privatization Putsch* (Halifax: The Institute for Research on Public Policy, 1989). For a recent, careful study of public enterprise success under adverse conditions in the Third World, see Barbara Grosh, *Public Enterprise in Kenya: What Works, What Doesn't, and Why* (London: Lynne Rienner, 1991).

13. Robert Heilbroner, *An Inquiry Into the Human Prospect* (New York: W. W. Norton, 1974). Heilbroner warned that neither capitalist nor socialist systems appeared able to deal adequately with the ecological challenge (89–94); he also suggested that "the passage through the gauntlet ahead may be possible only under governments capable of rallying obedience far more effectively than would be possible in a democratic setting" (110) and that a "drift toward the strong exercise of political power" was likely, "a movement given its initial momentum by the need to exercise a much wider and deeper administration of production and consumption" (130–31).

14. Milton Friedman, *Capitalism and Freedom* (Chicago: University of Chicago Press, 1962). See chapter 1, "The Relation Between Economic Freedom and Political Freedom"; for a succinct account of Kirk's thought and influence, see George H. Nash, *The Conservative Intellectual Movement in America* (New York: Basic Books, 1979), 69–76; Henry C. Simons, *Economic Policy for a Free Society* (Chicago: University of Chicago Press, 1948). See chapter 2, "A Positive Program for Laissez Faire."

Both Friedman and Simons strongly warned against the dangers of monopoly for their vision of "economic freedom"; Simons, who worried that "the corporation is simply running away with our economic (and political system)," strongly advocated the breaking up of corporations into smaller firms and even urged that local public ownership would be preferable to private monopoly if such monopoly was unavoidable (57–59).

15. Peter Drucker, "The Job as Property Right," *Wall Street Journal*, 4 March 1980.

16. See monthly and annual reports of the Alaska Permanent Fund, (Juneau, AK), 1991–93.

17. Silvio O. Funtowicz and Jerome R. Ravetz, "The Worth of A Songbird: Ecological Economics as a Postnormal Science," *Ecological Economics* 10, no. 3 (August 1994): 197–207.

Part Two

The Changing Global Context

Introduction

The existing international system is a product of the worldwide expansion of the industrial revolution. Although the colonial empires that once helped to sustain industrial growth in the wealthy countries were largely dismantled during the independence movement that followed World War II, the system that remains is characterized by uneven development and a significant gap between the wealthy countries of the "global North" and the poorer, nonindustrialized countries of the "global South." Many arguments in support of the move toward a more sustainable world have a hollow ring in countries that are just now taking steps toward industrialization. The existing international system is becoming increasingly interdependent while remaining largely anarchic, a heavy emphasis on national sovereignty and free trade being remnants of industrial ideology.

A search is now under way for more sustainable models of development and new approaches to ecologically sensitive international trade. A North–South dialogue on possibilities for more environmentally sustainable development has already begun (see Part III). But the supposed virtues of unrestricted trade among unequal partners still go largely unchallenged. Building a more sustainable international system requires both rethinking the meaning of development and the rules that currently govern international commerce.

The authors of the chapters in this section concentrate on the planetary bargains that must be struck in order to build a new global system. Thomas Wathen investigates the linkage between international trade agreements and environmental protection. He points out that current trade policies encourage individual consumption, resource-intensive growth, and specialization in production, and that trade officials are insulated from political pressures. The mandate of the

General Agreement on Tariffs and Trade (GATT) and its successor, the World Trade Organization (WTO), is to break down all barriers to trade among countries and to expand international commerce; preserving environmental integrity has never been part of the GATT mandate. Thus, any trade disputes among WTO members involving free trade versus environmental protection are usually resolved in favor of the former. Wathen argues that national economies are being increasingly globalized and that efforts to promote sustainability will suffer unless advocates for the environment can gain an effective voice in making trade policy.

Michael Alberty and Stacy VanDeveer focus on the potential for future international agreements to address major issues of sustainability. Expressing concern that global greenhouse warming presents a profound challenge to sustainable development and the welfare of future generations, they examine the Montreal Protocol on ozone depletion to see whether it might be useful in dealing with global warming and related issues of sustainable development. After making a careful comparison between ozone depletion and potential global warming, the authors conclude that the issues are so different that the Montreal Protocol is of little use as a model for agreements on global warming and sustainable development.

Peter Brown is concerned with creating a more "transparent " type of sovereignty that will facilitate compliance with international agreements. Grounding his arguments in the political philosophy of John Locke, he argues that governments should assume the role of trustees for current and future generations. In Locke's model a contract is conceived to exist between the governed and the trustees, requiring the latter to discharge certain duties both toward the governed and on behalf of the governed toward others.

When the Cold War drew to a close, the so-called peace dividend was supposed to usher in an era of relative prosperity. There would be vast sums of money diverted from defense spending, and new political configurations; issues of global environmental degradation could thus be addressed. Michael Klare points out in chapter 8 that things haven't worked out that way. For a number of reasons, the peace dividend is being eaten up by other military security problems, including environmental cleanup necessitated by war and preparation for it, the proliferation of schisms around the world, and the perpetuation of traditional national security concerns and spending.

5

Trade Policy: Clouds in the Vision of Sustainability

Thomas A. Wathen

Introduction

The recently completed negotiations to expand the General Agreement on Tariffs and Trade (GATT) and create the World Trade Organization (WTO), along with the debate over congressional approval of the North American Free Trade Agreement (NAFTA), have highlighted the role of trade policy in environmental protection. Trade agreements are the principal policy mechanisms for regulating international commerce, greatly influencing governments' management of natural resources and regulation of polluting industries. Unfortunately, since current trade policy seeks to increase individual consumption, encourage resource intensive economic growth, promote global specialization, and insulate international trade officials from local political pressure, trade institutions are moving rapidly away from emerging concepts of sustainability. Efforts to promote sustainability must include trade policy reform or sustainability will be eclipsed by the world's pursuit of a global economy. This chapter explains the complicated nexus between trade and environmental protection and shows how current trade policy is at odds with emerging principles of sustainability. It also suggests how environmental policy makers can begin reconciling trade policy with their sustainability goals.

Two Worldviews Collide

Fifty years ago a new economic vision for the world emerged from the Bretton Woods Conference. That historic conference in New Hampshire, which resulted

71

in the formation of the International Monetary Fund (IMF), the World Bank, and the International Labor Organization (ILO), also sought to create a global economy. Maintaining that trade conflict was one of the root causes of World War II, the U.S. and British governments proposed the formation of an International Trade Organization (ITO) to regulate and encourage greater world trade. While the ITO was eventually dropped because of opposition from the U.S. Congress, two dozen countries approved the ITO-less General Agreement on Tariffs and Trade (GATT) in 1947.[1]

Based on the "comparative advantage" theory of nineteenth-century economist David Ricardo, the philosophy behind the GATT has come to be popularized as "free trade." Free trade advocates argue that rather than discouraging imports through high tariffs, a country should specialize in producing the goods it makes most efficiently and trade with other countries for the goods they produce most efficiently. Such trading, the comparative advantage theory holds, increases overall economic activity in the world, making all countries better off than they would be with isolated economies.[2] Beyond these economic benefits, free trade was embraced through the GATT as a way to achieve international political stability by fostering cooperation and interdependence among nations. Five decades after Bretton Woods, free-trade visionaries have succeeded in advancing the vision of a global economy as the paramount social and economic global objective for the twenty-first century.

As additional countries embraced the GATT at a gathering of world diplomats in Annecy, France, in 1949, the Oxford University Press published Aldo Leopold's *A Sand County Almanac*. Like the GATT, Leopold's classic book signaled the emergence of a new vision for global social and economic development. Influenced by the young science of ecology, Leopold put forth the concept of a "land ethic" by arguing that conservation practices were too shortsighted to adequately protect natural resources:

> A system of conservation based solely on economic self-interest is hopelessly lopsided. It tends to ignore, and thus eventually eliminate, many elements in the land community that lack commercial value, but that are (as far as we know) essential to its healthy functioning. It assumes, falsely, I think, that the economic parts of the biotic clock will function without the uneconomic parts.[3]

Advanced in the postwar years by people inside and outside of the scientific community, the ecological perspective gained momentum with the reception of Rachel Carson's 1962 book *Silent Spring*. Warning of the harmful effects of widespread chemical pesticide use, Carson added pollution prevention to Leopold's resource stewardship as necessary for the protection of natural ecosystems. A third dimension was added by Paul Ehrlich, when he warned of the threat of exponential human population growth. By the time the Brundtland Commission issued its 1987 report *Our Common Future*, environmentalists had succeeded in putting forth their overall vision for the twenty-first century: the paramount global social and economic objective should be to make economic and human development environmentally "sustainable."

Despite the emerging consensus behind sustainable development, when trade representatives from ninety nations met in Punta del Este, Uruguay, in 1986 to renegotiate the GATT, only a few trade policy analysts or environmental policy analysts understood how important trade negotiations would become for environmental protection around the world. The connection became apparent to everyone by 1991, when a three-member dispute panel of GATT trade arbitrators ruled that the embargo provisions of the U.S. Marine Mammal Protection Act (MMPA) were an unfair trade barrier to Mexican fishermen seeking to sell tuna in the United States. The MMPA bans the sale in the United States of tuna from fishing vessels, like those in Mexico, whose fishing practices kill more dolphins than U.S. standards allow. In their decision, the GATT dispute panel determined that trade sanctions cannot be used by one country to protect the natural resources of another country or in the global commons.[4]

The GATT tuna-dolphin ruling illustrates how the movement to promote free trade is beginning to clash with the growing movement to achieve environmental sustainability. In their attempt to remove all possible barriers to free trade, trade policy makers want to "harmonize" environmental regulations to international standards.[5] They also seek to remove trade sanctions from environmental laws and treaties such as the Montreal Protocol on ozone depletion.[6] In time, trade policy will permeate all areas of domestic and international environmental protection. New changes in the GATT will affect government regulation of timber production, wildlife trading, marine fishing, agriculture, pesticide residues, energy use, hazardous waste shipments, toxic chemical production, recycling, packaging, product labeling, biotechnology, and food safety.

Trade Policy Making

International trade policy concerns the buying and selling of commercial goods and services across national borders. As with other border issues, like immigration, rules are set by each national government. Rules for international trade are set within the parameters of international trade agreements—a patchwork of multilateral, bilateral, and regional accords. Like all international treaties, a trade agreement has only the power that each country is willing to grant it. Traditionally, international trade agreements have derived their power from the mutual dependency of nations and the threat of retaliation. For example, if a country violates a trade agreement by blocking imports from a neighboring country it may find it cannot export its goods to that country or other countries.

The GATT has been the principal multilateral trade agreement for establishing international trade rules and has spawned the WTO to provide a forum for settling trade disputes. Over a hundred countries have signed the GATT, including former and current communist countries. Another thirty countries, mostly developing countries, abide by the rules, but are not formal "contracting parties" to the agreement. In the past, the GATT principally encouraged lower tariffs on raw materials and manufactured goods. From the time the agreement was first struck in 1948 until 1987, the average tariff tax surcharge for goods entering the United States fell from 40 to 5 percent.[7] Over the years, as tariffs fell, the GATT countries turned to reducing "nontariff" barriers such as quotas and government subsidies.

However, the GATT's overall success in increasing trade has been limited.[8] A great deal of worldwide trade is exempted from its provisions. Developing countries can easily sidestep GATT rules, and agricultural commodities are largely excluded. Services, like banking and shipping, have not been subject to the GATT in the past and a special Multifiber Arrangement (MFA) places quotas on textile imports into western countries. Expanding the GATT to cover more goods, include services, and eliminate more nontariff barriers was the focus of the Uruguay Round of GATT negotiations.

While the GATT provides universal trade rules on some goods, regional trade zones exist that allow free trade in many goods and services. The largest and most advanced of these regional trade zones is the European Community (EC). The EC is made up of twelve countries, with other European and Scandinavian countries scheduled to join and dozens of former European colonies enjoying special status. A comprehensive federation that includes a common parliament, the EC may eventually bind European economies together through a single currency, unified business regulation, unrestricted movement of labor, and free trade in commodities, products, and services.

To compete with the EC, the United States entered into a free trade agreement with Canada in 1989. A subsequent three-way negotiation between the United States, Canada, and Mexico resulted in approval of the more expansive North American Free Trade Agreement (NAFTA) in 1993. NAFTA does not aim for the level of political and economic integration found in the EC; neither a joint parliament, a single currency, nor free migration is envisioned. Rather, NAFTA's purpose is the promotion of a freer exchange of products, commodities, and investments. While the free-trade zone is initially limited to the United States, Canada, and Mexico, Central and Latin American countries could eventually become a party to similar agreements, creating a western hemispheric free trade zone from Alaska to Argentina.

Although the influence of multilateral and regional trade agreements has increased, the vast majority of trade is still governed by agreements between two countries. A myriad of quotas, tariffs, and other agreements control trade between the United States and every other country. Sometimes, as with Israel and Canada, a broad free trade agreement is negotiated; more often a separate agreement is struck for each imported product or raw commodity. Although adjustments are made for individual products and countries, U.S. tariffs fall into to these categories:

1. *Most Favored Nation (MFN) Tariffs*—MFN tariffs are those that the United States has agreed to under the GATT. Currently they average 5 percent of the cost of the product.
2. *Smoot-Hawley Tariffs*—Tariffs set under the Tariff Act of 1930 (Smoot-Hawley Act) average 40 percent and are imposed on non-GATT countries. However, the United States does grant MFN tariffs to non-GATT countries such as China.
3. *Developing Country Tariffs*—Generalized System of Preferences (GSP) is a waiver of tariffs given to developing countries for particular products.

Most trade policy is oriented toward regulating imports. However, many countries have laws that restrict the export of various products. The U.S. Export Administration Act denies export licenses on civilian goods when the government believes exporting the product will undermine foreign policy, endanger national security, or the good is in short supply. The U.S. Arms Export Control Act restricts trade in weapons and other military supplies, while the U.S. Department of Agriculture prohibits the export of some valuable commercial plant species, like tobacco plants.

The Growing Reach of Trade Policy

The Uruguay Round "Final Act,"[9] ratified by the GATT member countries, requires nations to yield more of their sovereignty over commerce to international institutions. The Final Act expands international trade rules to cover farm production, services, intellectual property, foreign investments, and domestic business regulation. The Final Act also tightens the GATT rules that govern each country's domestic standard-setting process. Here is a brief outline of the expanded powers agreed to in the Final Act.

Agriculture: The GATT traditionally excluded agriculture from its rules because the European Community, the United States, and Japan extensively support farmer and agribusiness income through price supports, subsidies, and import controls. To combat this support, agricultural exporting countries formed the Cairns Group to push for access to these three markets. Although France and Japan initially balked, trade negotiators eventually agreed to include more agricultural commodities under the GATT and to phase out many farm subsidy programs. The former measure was seen as necessary to gain concessions from Third World countries on issues like intellectual property rights and foreign investment.

Services: The Uruguay Round established a new side agreement called the General Agreement on Trade in Services (GATS). Initially, it was envisioned that GATS would seek to reduce restrictions on a wide variety of services, from construction to accounting. However, most U.S. professional organizations and companies sought exemptions for their particular service industry. As a result, GATS will begin by exempting three-quarters of all service industries. Trade policy makers hope that once GATS is established, future negotiations will expand the list of services included.

Intellectual Property Rights: In an effort to protect trademarks, copyrights, and patents, GATT negotiators fashioned another new side agreement called Trade-Related Intellectual Property Rights (TRIPs). This agreement is of enormous interest to companies marketing pharmaceutical products, motion pictures and videos, books, computer software, and brand-name products. TRIPs will require countries to treat foreigners seeking patents and copyrights the same as they treat their own nationals when granting them intellectual property rights. It also establishes minimum durations for some patents and copyrights and sanctions patents on natural substances. Developing countries will have a ten–year grace period before they are subject to the new rules. Intellectual property rights are viewed warily by developing countries, who fear they will be deprived of the basic technology needed to improve health care and develop their economies, and that they will ultimately be forced to pay patent royalties to Western multinational corporations on genetic resources first discovered in their developing countries.

World Trade Organization (WTO): Uruguay Round negotiators also approved the formation of a World Trade Organization (WTO), a reincarnation of the ITO President Harry Truman jettisoned in 1948. The WTO will have more resources than the GATT Secretariat has to monitor compliance with trade agreements and to enforce them. The WTO will become an international agency, like the United Nations or the International Monetary Fund, applying the trade rules established under the GATT (for goods), GATS (for services), and TRIPs (for intellectual property rights) and other multilateral trade agreements. Upon replacing the current GATT regime, the WTO will become the permanent forum for trade negotiation and dispute resolution, with an enhanced ability to amend trade rules. Rather than the consensus vote required to amend GATT in the past, the WTO will be able to change trade rules with a two-thirds vote of the member countries.

Stronger Enforcement: In the past, the GATT's enforcement powers were weak. Now, dispute panel rulings will be considered final decisions unless the WTO Council unanimously agrees to stay the ruling within sixty days, although a new appeal process from these decisions was established. Formerly, dispute panel rulings only had the force of recommendations, unless ratified by a unanimous vote of the GATT Council.

Foreign Investment: Particularly in developing countries, foreign investors are often required to enlist local partners, agree to make products for export only, use local material in the manufacturing process, or transfer technology to the host country. A working group was formed to develop trade-related investment measures" (TRIMs) that could lower these barriers to investment in the future.

Textiles: Textiles are covered by the GATT's tariff schedules but are also governed by a separate Multifiber Agreement (MFA) that allows import quotas. Uruguay Round negotiators took steps to bring textiles more fully under the GATT and begin reducing quotas.

Developing Countries: The GATT contains special exemptions for developing countries because the governments of such countries maintain that the GATT rules favor developed countries. The Uruguay Round took some steps to bring more trade with developing countries under the GATT, such as allowing the phasing in of new rules, but the GATT trade rules will continue to affect trade between developed countries more than North-South trade.

Impacts on Environmental Policy

Before the Uruguay Round, two principles established in the GATT had the potential to affect environmental regulation: multilateralism and nondiscrimination. The multilateralism principle requires that actions affecting trade between countries must be taken under widely accepted international rules; the nondiscrimination principle requires that all trading partners be treated equally and foreign companies have the same rights as domestic concerns. The Uruguay Round established a third principle, "harmonization," to bring domestic and international environmental regulation in line with these GATT trading principles. Harmonization requires that, with few exceptions, domestic business regulations not exceed international standards. As is outlined in the following discussion, adoption of the harmonization principle will enable the WTO to have an enormous impact on domestic and international environmental policy making.

Environmentally Damaging Imports: The 1991 GATT tuna-dolphin dispute panel ruled that "extraterritorial" enforcement of domestic environmental laws through trade sanctions violates the GATT multilateralism principle. The ruling stated that laws regulating the process by which a product is harvested or produced are harmful to free trade because they can be used to discriminate against the imports of foreign companies.[10] The Uruguay Round Final Act retains the GATT wording that the tuna-dolphin panel interpreted in its decision. The wording of the Final Act could compromise the Endangered Species Act, the U.S. African Elephant Conservation Act, the Migratory Bird Act, and a host of other U.S. environmental laws that regulate imports.[11]

Environmentally Damaging Exports: The GATT forbids export restrictions on goods destined for the territory of any other GATT member country. Exceptions can be made to preserve natural resources, but only if domestic companies are also denied access to these resources. To the degree that the Uruguay Round successfully increases the authority of the GATT, this provision could begin undermining efforts to stop exports of raw logs, hazardous waste, banned pesticides, or other goods and commodities.

Business Standards: The expanded GATT will classify environmental standards as "technical barriers to trade" (TBT).[12] TBTs include standards on the product itself or on the process by which a product is grown, harvested, manufactured, or shipped. Under the terms of the Final Act, all governmental and nongovernmental bodies that set business standards will be required to abide by the "Code of Good Practice for the Preparation, Adoption and Application of Standards," which states that national standards must be based on international norms. This is an application of the harmonization principle and it mandates the use of international standards for the regulation of industrial and agricultural products, where such international standards exist or are imminent. The Final Act also calls for the development of international standards where such standards don't exist. Exceptions are allowed only where the international standards will be "ineffective" or "inappropriate." However, these exceptions must be "no more trade restrictive than necessary," with the determination left in the hands of WTO dispute panels. U.S. environmentalists view these TBT provisions as threatening a wide range of existing domestic environmental laws and stifling future innovative domestic environmental standards.

Health Standards: The Final Act contains a series of provisions designed to limit the way countries regulate the harvesting, processing, production, and marketing of food. The food provisions are contained in the new agreement's agriculture section, under the heading "Sanitary and Phytosanitary Standards" (SPS).[13] A SPS is any standard that concerns the processing, inspection, packaging, labeling or contamination of food—this includes standards for pesticide residues. With adoption of the Final Act, only those domestic laws that comply with existing international standards will be presumed to meet GATT requirements. Any stronger laws can be challenged by exporters, requiring the regulating country to prove that the law is not an unfair barrier to trade. The Codex Alimentarius, a United Nations agency, is named as the agency that will set international standards for food. A 1992 congressional research service report shows that a fifth of Codex's standards are lower than comparable U.S. standards.[14] Environmentalists have criticized this international agency for being dominated by business interests.

Risk-Assessment Criteria: The Final Act establishes universal risk-assessment criteria to be used in setting pesticide residue levels and other health standards.[15] The criteria will require risks to human health to be balanced against the economic benefits of a harmful activity. Such a balancing is already found in the Federal Insecticide, Fungicide and Rodenticide Act (FIFRA), the U.S. pesticide law that environmentalists have long criticized as too weak. Although it is used in FIFRA, this balancing approach differs from the approach taken in other U.S. laws, which base their standards primarily on human health effects. For instance, the Delaney clause of the Food and Drug Act requires the Food and Drug Administration (FDA) to prohibit food additives and levels of pesticide residues that pose a risk of cancer.

Government Subsidies in Environmental Programs: If a government program funds environmental cleanup or the preservation of natural resources, the provision of those funds can currently be challenged under the GATT as an unfair trade subsidy, if the program benefits domestic companies that export goods or restricts the import of foreign products. The Uruguay Round negotiators refused to allow domestic subsidies for environmental programs, except for limited one-time payments to help a producer comply with new environmental regulations.[16]

State and Local Environmental Laws: The Final Act requires each country to bring the laws of their subnational governments into line with international standards. This can be read as a requirement that the U.S. government pass legislation overriding any state or local law that deviates from international standards—indeed, a GATT dispute panel was formed to hear Canada's challenge to U.S. state liquor laws. On 7 February 1992 the panel ruled that the laws in thirty-eight states discriminated against Canadian beer imports by subsidizing U.S. products. The panel further concluded

> that both parties [U.S. and Canada] agreed that under United States constitutional law, GATT law is part of the United States federal law and, being based on the Commerce Clause of the Constitution, overrides, as a general matter, inconsistent state law.[17]

However, because of constitutional and political concerns, it is more likely that this GATT language will compel Congress to insert specific preemption clauses into a vast array of environmental statutes that now allow state and local governments to exceed federal standards or to use federal funding as leverage to bring states into GATT compliance.

International Environmental Agreements: A February 1992 environment report put out by the GATT Secretariat shows that GATT officials clearly object to using trade rules to enforce international environmental treaties:

> [I]t is very unlikely that using a trade measure would be the most efficient way of dealing with domestic environmental problems. Is this conclusion altered by

the evident internationalization of such problems? When competitiveness concerns are at work, the answer is no. . . . First, it would block an opportunity for a mutually beneficial expansion of trade. Second, it would not necessarily cause the other countries to alter their environmental policies.[18]

Based on this general opposition, the GATT Secretariat maintains that international environmental agreements with trade sanctions should require a waiver from the GATT. In most cases, a waiver would require a two-thirds vote of the 103 voting members. This means that trade ministers from at least 69 countries must support an environmental accord with trade sanctions in order for it not to be in conflict with the GATT. However, international environmental agreements rarely contain language deferring to the GATT. In the event of a conflict between the GATT and an international environmental agreement, each national government will be forced to decide which agreement is more important.

There are at least twenty-four international environmental agreements that have trade provisions.[19] For instance, the Montreal Protocol on Substances that Deplete the Ozone Layer requires the signatories to ban the importation of CFCs from countries not signing the agreement. Likewise, the Basel Conventions on the Control of Transboundary Movements of Hazardous Wastes allows countries to limit the import or export of hazardous wastes. The Wellington Convention on Pacific Long Drift Net Fishing requires countries to prohibit the import of fish or fish products that are caught using a long drift fishnet.

Trade Policy versus Sustainability Policy

Current trade policy seeks to increase individual consumption, encourage resource-intensive economic growth, promote global specialization, and insulate international trade rule making from local political pressure. Principles of sustainability are evolving with nearly opposite goals in mind. A quick comparison of some of the underlying principles of the GATT with those often advanced for sustainability illustrates these differences (see Table 5.1).[20]

Impacting on Sustainability in Specific Areas

As the GATT and other trade rules become embedded in international and domestic law, their influence will be far-reaching. To demonstrate how trade policy can undermine efforts to promote sustainability, here is a closer look at potential impacts regarding agriculture, forestry, marine fisheries, pollution control, toxics, and solid waste.

Agriculture

The economic benefits of free trade are predicated on fostering competition and

Table 5.1

Trade and Sustainability: A Comparison

	Trade policy	Sustainability policy
Production and consumption	To develop the full use of resources and to expand the production and consumption of goods (GATT preamble).	To eliminate patterns of production and consumption that deplete natural resources.
Economic growth	Trade and economic policy should be conducted to ensure a large and steadily growing volume of real income and effective demand (GATT preamble).	Trade and economic policy should be conducted to ensure the long-term availability of natural resources.
Environmental standards	Environmental standards should be harmonized between nations on as wide a basis as possible (Final Act's TBT and SPS provisions).	Environmental standards should be established at whatever level is necessary (or desirable) to protect the environment and preserve natural resources for perpetual use.
Community orientation	The world is best served by a global economy based upon specialization and trade.	A sustainable world may require greater self-reliance and diversified local economies.
Democratic decision making	All GATT proceedings are held in secret and there is no public right to information.	Sustainability will require the active participation of all concerned citizens, internationally and locally.

specialization. For agriculture, this paradigm means that large-scale, capital-intensive farming will be favored. Such agriculture relies on fertilizers, pesticides, and monoculture production. These practices have led to the decline of family farms in both the developed and underdeveloped worlds, undermining rural communities that were rooted in smaller-scale, diversified farming and increasing migration to the cities. Some environmentalists feel organic farming practices and other alternative sustainable farming methods are more suited to these diversified farms.

On a global level, unrestricted trade will result in environmental improvement in some areas while accelerating degradation in others. For instance, trade agreements can be used to challenge both price and conservation subsidies. Agricultural price subsidies have led to surplus production in Europe and the United States. This overproduction comes at the expense of wildlife habitats, groundwater quality, and soil retention. An end to subsidized and protected agriculture may mean that farming decreases in the United States, Europe, and Japan. But this decrease will be offset by increases in the developing countries, which will mean environmental problems are shifted from North to South. Moreover, agricultural subsidies can also take the form of soil conservation programs, wetland and habitat protection programs, and other government programs aimed at encouraging environmentally sound farm practices. Some of these helpful programs may be discouraged with enforcement of trade agreements.

Trade policies will also harmonize the regulation of pesticides. The GATT Final Act instructs countries to harmonize their pesticide standards with international standards, like those established by the Codex Alimentarius. The Codex sets less stringent standards on the use of cancer-causing pesticides than the Delaney clause of the Food and Drug Act. Moreover, the Codex standards allow much higher levels of pesticide residue than U.S. law. For example, Codex allows DDT levels on bananas and peaches that are fifty times higher than U.S. allowable levels. Also, two pesticides that have been banned in the United States, heptachlor and aldrin, are allowed under Codex standards.[21] Higher pesticide residue levels will not only pose increased risk to U.S. consumers, they will also encourage greater use of DDT, heptachlor, and other dangerous pesticides in Third World countries.

Before the United States–Canada Free Trade Agreement (FTA), Canada regulated pesticides solely on the basis of safety. By contrast, the U.S. FIFRA requires that the economic benefits of a pesticide be considered before its use can be restricted. Consequently, Canada licensed 20 percent fewer pesticides than the United States before the FTA.[22] But in signing the FTA, Canada agreed to begin weakening their pesticide and food irradiation regulations in order to "harmonize" them with U.S. standards. Last year, the United States weakened several food safety rules in compliance with NAFTA. Now, through the GATT, the United States is similarly agreeing to weaken its laws to match prevailing international standards. The GATT could also undermine efforts by U.S. environmentalists to enact so-called "circle of poison" trade restrictions. These restrictions would prohibit the export of pesticides banned in the United States to farmers in other countries and prohibit the import of products with residues of the banned pesticides. Local and state pesticide laws, like California Proposition 65, are also vulnerable to challenges under both GATT and NAFTA harmonization provisions.

Forestry

In an effort to slow the destruction of tropical forests in developing countries, forty-four nations signed the International Tropical Timber Agreement (ITTA) in 1983. The ITTA encourages countries with tropical forests to process timber domestically, to reduce logging and garner greater income in wood processing. This goal is at odds with the GATT because the ITTA approach encourages local wood processing industries by restricting the export of raw logs.[23] Indonesia,

Malaysia, Brazil, the Philippines, and Thailand have all enacted restrictions on the export of unprocessed logs, in keeping with the goals of the ITTO. Japan and the European Community have used the GATT in the past to challenge these tropical timber export restrictions. Canada and the United States also have restrictions on the export of raw logs, to slow the cutting of temperate forests.

Free trade agreements can also impact on domestic forest conservation programs. One central principle of GATT is that a government subsidy can be viewed as a trade barrier if it favors domestic industry. Before the FTA was signed, U.S. timber companies challenged a tree planting program undertaken by the Canadian province of British Columbia, claiming that it constituted an unfair subsidy. Rather than face a trade challenge under GATT, the government of British Columbia discontinued the program.[24]

At the same time, governments such as those of the United States and Canada subsidize timber production in their forests. These production subsidies, which have been sharply criticized by environmentalists, can be challenged under the GATT. The United States, for example, has imposed special duties on softwood imports from British Columbia because of government subsidies given to the province's timber companies.

Marine Fisheries

Traditionally, marine fisheries have been treated as a common resource, open to all. This freewheeling approach, however, has given way to national laws and international agreements that limit catches and regulate fishing methods. A nation can limit catches in coastal waters through establishment of an "exclusive economic zone" reaching two hundred miles offshore. The United States proclaimed such a zone in 1976 with passage of the Magnuson Fisheries Conservation and Management Act. Most fishing within the zone is reserved for U.S. fishermen. At this time, there are no provisions in the GATT or NAFTA to equalize foreign access to coastal fishing. However, equal access is in keeping with the sort of economic integration being pursued by the European Community and is envisioned by those trade policy makers who favor unrestricted foreign investment. In fact, concerns about coastal fishing rights for foreign trawlers has held up Norway's entry into the EC.[25] One provision of the Magnuson Act, however, may violate existing GATT principles. The act requires the United States to regulate fishing beyond the two-hundred-mile limit when such fishing endangers salmon or other anadramous species. These species, including salmon, spawn in freshwater streams on the mainland. This provision constitutes an extraterritorial application of U.S. law, which the tuna-dolphin dispute panel held violates the GATT, although international marine law may sanction U.S. control of these anadramous fisheries.

Besides the MMPA, there are several U.S. laws that prohibit fishing techniques that harm marine species. The 1990 Dolphin Protection Consumer Information Act prohibits the importation of fish caught in large drift nets, in addition to regulating the use of "dolphin-safe" labeling. The Pelly Amendment to the Fishermen's Protective Act forbids the import of fish products from countries that violate U.S. fishery conservation programs. The GATT tuna-dolphin panel's rationale on the MMPA could be employed to challenge these laws.

Internationally, the 1989 Wellington Convention on Pacific Long Drift Net Fishing prohibits use of these nets over a large area of the Pacific Ocean because drift nets trap large numbers of nontarget fish, seabirds, and marine mammals along with the intended catch. The multilateral ban may not in itself violate the GATT, since the signatory countries have voluntarily suspended drift-net fishing; however, the agreement has a provision which prohibits importation of any fish or fish product which was caught using a drift net. This provision, aimed at countries who have not joined the ban, is a trade sanction discouraged by the GATT tuna-dolphin panel. The U.S. High Seas Drift Net Fisheries Enforcement Act was passed to uphold the drift-net treaty.

Air and Water Pollution

Free-trade advocates maintain that when economic growth is fostered through trade, air and water pollution is reduced, because producers and governments can spend increased wealth on pollution abatement.[26] But efforts to reduce pollution can also be undermined by free trade.

Because their emissions and effluent occur in their home countries, foreign companies are largely unaffected by domestic efforts to control point sources of air and water pollution. However, if a government provides incentives for pollution reduction through tax credits, loans, or grants, these programs can be challenged as unfair government subsidies. During the Bush administration, the U.S. Non-Ferrous Metals Producers Committee asked the U.S. trade representative to challenge a Canadian government program offering investment credits and loans to lead, zinc, and copper smelters to install sulfur dioxide scrubbers for acid rain reduction. The industry association claimed the program violated the FTA because it gave Canadian smelters an unfair competitive advantage over U.S. smelters.[27] Marketable permit schemes and other market incentive programs may be vulnerable to similar challenge under the GATT and NAFTA because innovative schemes would fail to meet the GATT's harmonization requirements and could place foreign companies at a disadvantage. For example, government grants of pollution credits may be viewed as an unfair trade subsidy to domestic companies.

The lowering of investment barriers envisioned by the GATT and NAFTA will result in a shift of production to countries where manufacturers' costs will be lower. When lower costs take the form of lax environmental regulations, free trade agreements can result in pollution havens. This regulatory flight phenomenon was the principal concern of environmental organizations opposed to

NAFTA. The maquiladoras factories along the U.S.–Mexico border provide a vivid example of regulatory flight. These factories now include dozens of U.S. furniture manufacturers who, according to a 1991 General Accounting Office study, relocated to escape Southern California's stringent clean air standards for paint coatings and solvents.

The GATT and NAFTA can also limit restrictions of nonpoint source pollution such as auto fuel efficiency standards, pesticide regulation, and soil conservation programs. The Corporate Average Fuel Economy (CAFE) standards and the "gas guzzler" tax have been challenged by the European Community as discriminatory against trade in European luxury cars.[28] California's innovative auto emission standards, which prompted the Ford Motor Company to engineer the cleanest-burning commercial automobile ever marketed, could also be jeopardized.

Toxic Chemicals and Hazardous Waste

The United States regulates most toxic chemicals through the Toxic Substance Control Act (TSCA). Like pesticide regulations, TSCA will be subject to challenge under the GATT and NAFTA on the grounds that it constitutes a trade barrier for foreign companies. Such a challenge already occurred under the U.S.–Canada FTA. Seven months after the FTA went into effect, the EPA announced a seven year phase-out of asbestos. The Canadian government challenged the ban in U.S. federal court, claiming it violated the FTA's prohibition against "unnecessary" obstacles to trade.[29] The same challenge could be made to environmentally related product standards set by the Consumer Product Safety Commission (CPSC). The CPSC banned asbestos in hair dryers and set regulations for formaldehyde in building insulation.

The GATT will similarly impact all laws and international agreements governing the generation and disposal of hazardous waste, especially efforts to reduce the shipment of hazardous waste overseas. Environmentalists advocate strict international regulation of hazardous waste disposal. Free-trade advocates, on the other hand, believe hazardous waste should be imported and exported as freely as any commodity or service. The Basel Convention seeks to control the international movement of hazardous waste through notice-and-consent procedures and by designating some hazardous waste trafficking as illegal. The GATT Secretariat raised concerns about the Basel Convention in the past, because the convention calls for restrictions on the import and export of hazardous waste from countries that are not parties to the agreement.[30]

In the United States, hazardous waste is regulated under the Resource Conservation and Recovery Act (RCRA) and the Comprehensive Environmental Response, Compensation, and Liability Act (CERCLA), which includes the Superfund. Both laws control the transportation and treatment of hazardous waste. Canada and the European Community already used the GATT to challenge a U.S. Superfund tax on foreign petroleum products; under the principle of harmonization, RCRA and CERCLA regulations could be made to meet international standards dictated by the GATT and NAFTA.

As a result of the GATT and NAFTA, industrial production may increasingly be shifted to countries with less stringent hazardous waste disposal laws. A 1990 Mexican government report found that only 35 percent of U.S. companies inside the Mexican border complied with laws on handling toxic wastes.[31] If free-trade advocates win further easements on investment restrictions in developing countries, more hazardous waste generators could relocate to Third World regulatory havens.

Solid Waste Reduction

An effective way to control hazardous and solid waste is to discourage its generation in the first place through bans, product content standards, and mandatory recycling. A few local communities have pioneered bans on products such as polystyrene containers to curb solid waste. These local bans could face challenges under the GATT's new harmonization requirement. Any efforts to control the content of consumer products, such as the New Jersey law limiting the use of harmful metals in batteries, can also be challenged as restrictions on free trade. Likewise, laws regulating the labels on "environmentally friendly" products may be challenged, as Mexico tried unsuccessfully to do with the "dolphin safe" label law.

Laws that require the recycling of a product or regulate the content of packaging are more prevalent and are equally vulnerable to challenge under the GATT and NAFTA. After passage of the FTA, the Conference Board of Canada, a Canadian business group, urged the Canadian government to challenge recycling laws in the United States that require recycled fiber in newsprint, claiming that these laws violate the FTA.[32] The European Court, which settles disputes between the Common Market countries, overruled a Danish recycling law on trade grounds. In 1988, companies wanting to sell nonreusable containers in Denmark objected to a 1981 Danish law requiring that all beer and soft drinks be sold in returnable containers. Although the Danish government had never refused to admit containers from other countries, the court said the law was an unfair trade barrier.[33]

Engaging Trade Policy

On 29 October 1993, President Bill Clinton gave a stirring call to action: This is the end of the Cold War. This the dawn of the 21st century. In these moments we have to reach deep into ourselves, to our deepest values, to our strongest spirit and reach out, not shrink back.[34]

This president, whose administration has embraced international efforts to preserve biological diversity, reduce global warming, and curb population growth, was unfortunately not talking about environmental sustainability. He was talking about NAFTA and his speech to a gathering of U.S. business representatives illustrates the powerful intellectual and political momentum that trade policy has achieved in recent years.

The WTO may not become the monolithic, all-powerful entity that many environmentalists fear, but trade negotiators are trying to greatly expand their power and influence. Tim Groser, a New Zealand trade representative, told free-trade backers in his country, "I think you've got to see this [GATT] as the first step toward more radical change in the long term."[35] With the Uruguay Round's Final Act, trade policy makers are striving to make environmental policy and other social policy subservient to trade policy, in the fervent belief that free trade will "float all boats."

But free-trade partisans are among many constituencies battling to influence social policy. To be sure, free-trade advocates have successfully monopolized trade policy up until now, but that is because, the limited scope of existing trade agreements, relegated the GATT to the backwaters of governmental affairs. As the new WTO strives for greater influence, its ambition will be checked by other international, national, state, and local political forces.

Still, rarely has an environmental issue emerged as quickly or carried such high stakes as trade policy. The trade policy arena is becoming the forum for worldwide economic policy making. As a result, no area of environmental protection will be untouched by trade policy considerations. This means that environmental scholars need to research and analyze the complex connections between trade and the environment, in order to craft proposals for environmentally sound trade policy. Unfortunately, since trade policy is subject to an intricate array of commerce rules, the issue is being portrayed in highly rhetorical and confusing ways. Creative and diverse thinking is needed to understand how trade policy can be fashioned to truly enhance environmental protection.

Given the demanding nature of this issue, scholars and others can make many contributions to the emerging policy debate. For instance, international economists should be challenged to understand the intricacies of environmental problems and their solutions instead of reacting defensively to scrutiny. Too often economists repeat the claim that free trade improves the environment by increasing growth, as though the claim were an intellectual talisman to ward off environmentalists. As impressive as their economic modeling may be, one cannot read through free-trade policy studies without being struck by the often superficial analysis of environmental problems. The environmental dilemma is not limited to pollution spewing out of a smokestack, the paradigm so favored by economists. It is an intricate and uncertain interplay between exhaustible resources, natural ecosystems, growing populations, and the pollution load that individual organisms can tolerate. To fashion trade policies that truly enhance environmental protection, environmental and trade policy makers must be able to answer the questions, how can trade contribute to sustainability and how can such a contribution be made to happen?

Trade organizations also need study. The GATT, NAFTA, EC and Organization for Economic Cooperation and Development (OECD) are becoming political forums with the potential to undermine efforts to achieve environmental sustainability. Laurence H. Tribe, a constitutional law scholar and a "strong supporter of the free trade principles of the Uruguay Round," wrote that the GATT implementing legislation in the United States will result in a legal regime that "entail[s] a significant shift of sovereignty from state and local governments to the proposed World Trade Organization (WTO), in which the interests of these entities would be represented exclusively by the U.S. Trade Representative."[36] If decisions made by trade negotiators in Geneva ultimately shape environmental policy at the national or local level, citizens need to understand and participate in the process. Without such participation, the commercial sector will have an easier time influencing trade negotiations and will use the resulting trade agreements to undermine national, state, and local environmental laws.

Moreover, trade is a major governmental tool for policy making. Just as they do with tax policies, governments use trade rules to favor one commercial sector over another or to pursue broader social policy. For example, the U.S.–Canada FTA gives special treatment to fossil fuels.[37] Likewise, it is routine for trade negotiators to abandon trade liberalization in order to protect national security or advance a goal like the eradication of illegal drugs. Environmental policy will not receive similar consideration without citizen involvement. Unfortunately, trade policymaking is a closed process. In March 1992, the OECD formally rejected participation of nongovernmental organizations. Similarly, the GATT and NAFTA negotiations were closed. Such secrecy undermines the tradition of citizen participation that has long spurred environmental policy making on the national and international level.

Conclusion

While understanding that the growing influence of trade policy is potentially harmful to environmental protection efforts, those working to achieve sustainability should also see trade policy as an important political opportunity. In attempting to supersede environmental policies, trade policy makers are being forced to confront the environmental consequences of commerce. In 1991, an OECD task force on trade and the environment wrote:

> In most cases, prices and markets do not fully account for environmental benefits and costs, and in some cases (e.g. genetic diversity), it is almost impossible to put a market price on environmental factors. Because trade flows reflect market forces as well as national environmental regulations, they can have negative effects on the environment where environmental regulations are inadequate.[38]

Similarly, a GATT Secretariat report illustrates how the debate on trade and the environment provides an opening to tackle the broader challenge of economic development and sustainability:

If the policies necessary for sustainable development are in place, trade promotes development that is sustainable. Alternatively, if such policies are lacking, the country's international trade may contribute to a skewing of the country's development in an environmentally damaging direction, but then so will most of the other economic activities of the country.[39]

Already, trade policy makers are recognizing that the WTO needs to reconcile trade and environmental policy. In Marrakech, Morocco, where the Uruguay Round Final Act was signed on 15 April 1994, trade ministers established a work program on trade and the environment and formed a Trade and Environment Committee to carry it forward. In the United States, the Clinton administration has announced that it also intends to address environmental concerns in future trade agreements.

These opportunities are eagerly being seized upon by both trade and environmental advocates, who are reaching out to each other through a variety of collaborative processes. Under the auspices of the Consensus Building Institute, which is based in Cambridge, Massachusetts, specialists including current GATT officials, trade ministers, and noted environmentalists have agreed to engage in an informal dialogue on environmental issues before the WTO Trade and Environment Committee meets. The dialogue also includes a research consortium, where trade and environmental scholars and experts will be asked to prepare policy proposals for the dialogue group. A similar collaborative initiative, aimed at influencing U.S. trade officials, is being organized by the Berkeley Roundtable on the International Economy (BRIE) at the University of California, the Council on Foreign Relations, the National Wildlife Federation, and the Nautilus Institute for Security and Sustainable Development. Meanwhile, the Sierra Club, Friends of the Earth, and other environmental organizations have been collaborating with the United States Council for International Business on a series of meetings designed to establish common ground among U.S. environmental organizations and large U.S. corporations engaged in global commerce.

Environmentalists and scholars interested in sustainability have much to gain by convincing trade policy makers to embrace the goal of sustainability. For instance, Robert Repetto of the World Resources Institute believes that trade and investment incentives can be used to induce cooperation in international environmental protection.[40] Hilary French of the Worldwatch Institute predicts that the demands of world trade will "spur movement toward internationally agreed measures to internalize costs—be they taxes, regulations, or labeling programs."[41]

The rise in importance of the GATT and other trade institutions reflects the increasing globalization of national economies. Consequently, efforts to promote sustainability will be eclipsed by the world's pursuit of a global economy unless environmental advocates and scholars can influence the processes that underlay global commerce. The opening up of trade policy making, as reflected by the growth in collaborative dialogues such as the three identified, provides a great opportunity to do just that.

Notes

1. Alan C. Swan and John F. Murphy, *Cases and Materials on the Regulation of International Business and Economic Relations* (Albany, NY: Matthew Bender, 1991), 219.

2. Ibid., 194.

3. Aldo Leopold, *The Sand County Almanac* (New York: Oxford University Press, 1949; reissued in paperback 1967), 251.

4. GATT Secretariat, *International Trade 1990–91,* vol. 1, 1992, 15.

5. Steve Charnovitz, "Environmental Harmonization and Trade Policy," in *Trade and the Environment: Law, Economics and Policy,* ed. Durwood Zaelke, Paul Orbuch, and Robert F. Housman (Washington, DC: Island Press, 1993), 267.

6. GATT Secretariat, *International Trade,* 30.

7. William B. Kelly, "Functioning of the GATT System," in *The Uruguay Round: A Handbook for the Multilateral Trade Negotiations,* ed. J. Michael Finger and Andrej Olechowski (Washington, DC: World Bank Publication, 1987), 81.

8. *The Economist,* Special Edition on World Trade, 22 September 1990.

9. Trade Negotiations Committee, *Final Act Embodying the Results of the Uruguay Round of Multilateral Trade Negotiations,* 15 December 1993, MTN/FA, UR–93–02461.

10. GATT Secretariat, *International Trade.* 15.

11. Robert Housman, *Testimony of the Center for International Environmental Law on Behalf of the Sierra Club and Defenders of Wildlife,* before the Subcommittee on Foreign Commerce and Tourism, Senate Committee on Commerce, Science and Transportation, 3 February 1994.

12. GATT Final Act, "Technical Barriers to Trade Rules," ch. III.5.

13. GATT Final Act, "Agreement on Sanitary and Phytosanitary Measures," ch. II.4.

14. Donna Vogt, *Sanitary and Phytosanitary Measures Pertaining to Food in International Trade Negotiations,* Congressional Research Service report to Congress, 11 September 1992, 22.

15. GATT Final Act, "Agreement on Sanitary and Phytosanitary Measures," ch. II.4, article 16, 15 December 1993.

16. Robert Housman, *Testimony of the Center for International Environmental Law,* 16.

17. GATT panel ruling, "United States—Measures Affecting Alcoholic and Malt Beverages," 7 February 1992, 5.

18. GATT Secretariat, *International Trade 1990–91, Trade and the Environment,* 25.

19. Thomas Wathen, *A Guide to Trade and the Environment* (New York: Environmental Grantmakers Association and the Consultative Group on Biological Diversity, 1992), 67.

20. GATT passages have been paraphrased to allow for easier comparison.

21. Mark Ritchie, "Trading Away Our Environment: GATT and Global Harmonization," *Journal of Pesticide Reform* 10, no. 3 (Fall 1990).

22. Steven Shrybman, "Selling the Environment Short: An Environmental Assessment of the First Two Years of Free Trade between Canada and the United States," in *Paying the Price: How Free Trade is Hurting the Environment, Regional Development, Canadian & Mexican Workers* (Canadian Centre for Policy Alternatives, 1991), 11.

23. C. Arden-Clarke, "Conservation and Sustainable Management of Tropical Forests: The Role of the ITTO and GATT," World Wildlife Fund discussion paper, November 1990, 5.

24. Steven Shrybman, *Selling Canada's Environment Short: The Environmental Case Against the Trade Deal* (Toronto: Canadian Environmental Law Association, 1988), 12.

25. "EU Shifts Focus to Norway As Three Nations Agree to Join," *The Journal of Commerce,* 3 March 1994.

26. G. Grossman and A. Krueger, "Environmental Impacts of a North American Free Trade Agreement," Woodrow Wilson School of Public and International Affairs, paper 158, Princeton University, 1992.

27. Shrybman, "Selling the Environment Short," 9.

28. Commission of the European Communities, *Report on United States Trade Barriers and Unfair Practices,* 1991, 34–37.

29. Corrosion Proof Fittings v. EPA, 947 F.2d 1201 (5th Cir. 1991).

30. GATT Secretariat, *International Trade 1990–91,* "Trade and the Environment," appendix I, iv.

31. Hilary F. French, "Costly Tradeoffs: Reconciling Trade and the Environment," Worldwatch Paper 113 (Washington, DC: Worldwatch Institute, March 1993), 31.

32. "Risk of Trade War Wrapped in Recycled Newsprint," *Toronto Globe and Mail,* 27 June 1990.

33. "Commission of the European Communities v. Kingdom of Denmark—Case 302/86," *Report on Cases Before the Court,* vol. 8, Luxembourg, 1988.

34. *New York Times,* 29 October 1993.

35. "GATT Success Will Be No Bonanza for New Zealand—Negotiator," Reuter 15 April 1992.

36. Laurence H. Tribe, letter to Hon. Robert Byrd, United States Senate, 19 July 1994.

37. *U.S.–Canada Free Trade Agreement,* article 906.

38. OECD, *Joint Report on Trade and Environment,* para. 15, 14 May 1991.

39. GATT Secretariat, *International Trade 1990–91,* vol. 1, Geneva, 1992, 3.

40. Robert Repetto, *Trade and Environment Policies: Achieving Complementaries and Avoiding Conflicts, WRI Issue and Ideas,* July 1993, 3.

41. Hilary French, "Costly Tradeoffs: Reconciling Trade and the Environment," Worldwatch Paper 113 (Washington, DC: Worldwatch Institute, March 1993), 59.

6

International Treaties for Sustainability: Is the Montreal Protocol a Useful Model?

Michael A. Alberty and Stacy D. VanDeveer

It is difficult to oppose the sentiment behind the Brundtland Commission's assertion that "sustainable development is development that meets the needs of the present without compromising the ability of future generations to meet their own needs."[1]

The trouble lies in trying to put this principle into practice with regard to specific problems, such as global warming. If in our pursuit of economic well-being we release large quantities of carbon dioxide into the atmosphere, how can we avoid a climatic disaster for future generations? It has become conventional wisdom that the regime established by the 1987 Montreal Protocol on Substances that Deplete the Ozone Layer is the appropriate model for solving other global environmental problems.[2] We will challenge this wisdom by arguing that it is unlikely the successes of the Montreal Protocol can or will be replicated in a global warming regime. The implications of this failure for ecological sustainability will also be explored.

The Montreal Protocol was the result of a unique collection of factors and conditions that simply do not exist for current international attempts to forge a climate-change regime. Therefore, in the case of global warming it is unlikely nations will move beyond the commitment-to-norms-and-principles stage to implement the type of significant abatement targets and schedules put forward in the Montreal Protocol. As a result, economic activities will in all likelihood continue to be carried out with little regard for their impact upon the environment. However, if human institutions fail to in some way reconcile the pursuit of economic development with the need for ecological sustainability, the danger that nature will do it for us will remain.

What Would an "Effective" Regime Look Like?

The effectiveness of a regime should be measured primarily in terms of how effectively it solves the problem it was created to address.[3] In the early stages of regime formation, success may depend on agreement among all parties involved on certain important goals or principles. According to Levy, Keohane, and Haas, "effective institutions begin with commitments 'merely' to norms and principles and either lack regulatory rules or possess only very weak ones. This is exactly as it should be."[4] This is certainly the path taken in the Montreal Protocol. What began as concern in the scientific community about the potential hazards of chlorofluorocarbons (CFCs) evolved into a series of ever tougher international agreements to regulate their use. By the use of these building blocks, the framework convention-protocol model takes advantage of changing scientific knowledge and gradually breaks down the reluctance of key actors to participate.

In much the same way that the concept of sustainable development needs to become operationalized in order to become more than an empty shell, the effective regime has to get past the initial commitment to "mere" principles and eventually implement the level of regulation necessary to remedy the problem at hand. The ozone regime made that critical move, but with regard to the global warming regime, this task will be much more difficult. The overall objective of the Climate Change Convention[5] is to stabilize concentrations of greenhouse gases (GHGs) in the atmosphere at a level that will allow the planet and its residents to avoid serious harm. The Climate Change Convention currently requires developed countries to reduce their GHG emissions to 1990 levels by the year 2000. But will this be enough of a reduction?

Unfortunately, the answer to this question appears to be a resounding no. Bert Bolin, the chairman of the Intergovernmental Panel on Climate Change (IPCC), recently stated:

> Stabilising developed country emissions of carbon dioxide, as is presently being aimed for, is only a very modest first step towards stabilising atmospheric concentrations of this gas. Because CO_2 emissions remain for such a long time in the atmosphere, even stabilising total global emissions would not stabilise atmospheric concentrations for several hundred years.[6]

The IPCC's latest findings indicate that even if CO_2 emissions were capped at their present levels, the amount of CO_2 concentrated in the atmosphere would continue to increase for at least two hundred years. This increase would push surface temperatures beyond the point at which the earth's climate would be disrupted. According to the IPCC, even to hold the atmospheric concentration of CO_2 at *double* today's amount will require cutting global emissions of the gas well below 1990 levels. The IPPC predicts that a doubling of the current CO_2 concentration in the atmosphere would increase surface temperatures on earth by from 3 to 8 degrees Fahrenheit.[7] More recent estimates from 1995, however, suggest that future temperature increases may be somewhat less than the IPPC projections. In fact, stabilizing emissions appears to be easier than stabilizing the CO_2 composition of the atmosphere. However, the latter is necessary to slow future temperature increases and will require significant *reductions* in global CO_2 emissions.

The decreases needed to achieve the overall goal of the Climate Change Convention are sobering. At a June 1988 conference in Toronto, representatives from forty-eight nations concluded that a reduction in CO_2 emissions by roughly 20 percent of 1988 levels by the year 2005 would be necessary to stabilize the atmosphere.[8] Two years later the IPCC decided even more significant reductions would be necessary. It proposed an immediate 60 percent reduction of CO_2 emissions, accompanied by a 15-to-20 percent decrease in emissions of methane.[9] After examining the most recent scientific data at the ninth session of the Intergovernmental Negotiating Committee (INC) in Geneva, some scientists argued that achieving a "slow warming" target of 1.0 degree Centigrade by the early part of the twenty-first century would require the developed countries to reduce their CO_2 emissions from fossil fuels by 75 percent of current levels.[10]

Any attempt to move the Climate Change Convention from its current weak commitments to the types of decreases needed to successfully address global warming will be met with significant resistance. Consider the type of sacrifice that would be required just to meet the recommendations of the Toronto conference. Cutting CO_2 emissions just from fossil fuel combustion by 20 percent would require a return to the type of fossil fuel use patterns last seen in the 1960s.[11] Most governments are unwilling to risk taking such drastic action. At the February 1994 INC meetings, many governments, including those of Australia, Brazil, China, Japan, Russia, and Saudi Arabia, argued against any further strengthening of the Climate Change Convention.[12] Because of the inability to get enough support, efforts in Geneva to officially propose greater GHG emission reductions failed. The September 1994 meetings also failed to move beyond the commitment to freeze CO_2 emissions at 1990 levels by the year 2000.[13]

An effective global warming regime would be one that promotes sustainability by reducing GHG emissions enough to protect future generations from significant temperature increases. Current efforts are clearly not sufficient to meet that challenge, and emissions levels are likely to grow. The United States Energy Association (USEA) projects an increase in world energy demand of from 130 to 200 percent by the year 2020.[14] Against this backdrop, even more significant reductions in GHG emissions will be necessary in the future.

Major Differences between Ozone and Climate Change

Why did the ozone regime apparently succeed where the climate change regime has so far failed? Rowlands suggests that if an international environmental agreement has modest economic costs, appears fair and equitable, has a high probability of attaining compliance by all parties and is supported by a consensus of the scientific community, then cooperation will occur.[15] Others have suggested that factors such as a relatively small number of key actors and keen public awareness should also be considered in determining whether or not cooperation will occur.[16] All of these factors were present to some degree in the case of ozone depletion. They are largely absent with regard to global warming.

The Costs of Change

CFCs were not so critical to the economic activity that supports day-to-day human life that parties to the Montreal Protocol were willing to tolerate the risks involved with depletion of the ozone layer just to continue their use. Phasing out CFCs does not involve any wrenching social or economic adjustments that would justify scrapping the treaty. In addition, policymakers and industrial users of CFCs were satisfied that while ready substitutes for CFCs were not available at the time the Montreal Protocol was signed, they would be in the near future.[17] Fueling this belief was a 1986 announcement by Du Pont that suitable alternatives to CFCs could be developed within five years, given the correct market incentives.[18]

Industrial opposition was not a significant barrier to CFC regulation. Leading producers of CFCs had diversified their activities to the point that these were not significant contributors to their yearly revenues. Du Pont, for example, received 2 percent of their annual profits from CFC production in 1987.[19] Du Pont also believed that they could earn $1.8 billion in windfall profits in the period prior to the development of a substitute; in essence, Du Pont's research and development efforts to find CFC alternatives would be subsidized by consumers.[20] Therefore it is significant that the Montreal Protocol gave industry the necessary time and incentives to develop CFC substitutes.

When the parties reconvened in Montreal in late 1986 they had a reasonably accurate picture of how the costs of CFC abatement stacked up against the risks of ozone depletion.[21] Overall compliance costs for the Montreal Protocol were estimated at several billion dollars a year for some years.[22] The United States government estimated that U.S. compliance would cost between $1 billion and $2.7 billion from 1989 to 2000 and between $20 billion and $40 billion from 1989 to 2075.[23] It was estimated that 80 percent of CFC use in the developing countries could be wiped out with relatively low cost, with the final 20 percent costing approximately $550 million to $700 million per year. The United States considered these costs a bargain given EPA calculations that adherence to the

Montreal Protocol would save three million lives and $6.4 trillion for the American economy over a twenty-five-year period.[24]

Fossil fuel combustion, however, drives global economic growth. The ability to "freely" dump CO_2 into the atmosphere is an integral part of the global economic order. GHG abatement costs will dwarf those of the Montreal Protocol. In fact, depending on the action being advocated, controlling GHGs could be the most expensive international program ever proposed. Economist Thomas Schelling suggests a serious effort at controlling CO_2 emissions could reduce worldwide GNP by 2 percent *in perpetuity*! For the United States alone this would mean the loss of $10 trillion in GNP over the next sixty years.[25]

For example, a 20 percent reduction in CO_2 by the year 2000, followed by a 50 percent decrease by the year 2100, would cost roughly $95 billion a year, effectively doubling gasoline prices.[26] The U.S. Council of Economic Advisers argued that a 20 percent cut in CO_2 would end up costing somewhere between $800 billion and $3.6 trillion.[27] Even just slowing CO_2 emissions by 40 percent of what they would be normally by the beginning of the next century could cost the equivalent of a $100-tax per ton of carbon emitted. This would result in a forty-cent increase in the price of a gallon of gasoline.[28] The political firestorm the U.S. Congress witnessed over a proposed twelve-cents-per-gallon gasoline tax increase illustrates how difficult selling of global warming costs might be.

Policy makers will also face much stiffer resistance from the numerous industries with a vested interest in the continued combustion of fossil fuels. The oil, coal, and automobile industries, to name just a few, are likely to exert considerable resources pressuring governments to oppose GHG emission reductions. At the September 1994 meeting of the Climate Change Convention in Maastricht in the Netherlands, lobbyists from the coal and oil industries, with support from Kuwait and Saudi Arabia, worked diligently to suppress and water down the IPCC's scientific findings.[29] In the United States, groups such as Global Climate Coalition and Citizens for a Sound Economy have successfully persuaded key government officials that significant GHG reductions will cost nearly $100 billion a year, resulting in the loss of hundreds of thousands of jobs.[30] The drawn-out struggle over the Clean Air Act of 1990, despite considerable public support and only $25 billion to $35 billion in costs at stake, provides another sobering point of reference.

In the face of serious domestic opposition and significant economic sacrifices, it remains highly unlikely that any state will be willing to accept significant GHG reductions in anything like the foreseeable future. To make such decisions, governments must be certain that "business as usual" will result in specific and very painful consequences. Governments have cooperated to combat ozone depletion because of the relatively low costs involved and the perceived availability of substitutes for CFCs. Those same conditions are absent with regard to global warming.[31]

Developing Countries and "Side Payments"

The original Montreal Protocol contained mandates that significantly decreased the production and consumption of various CFCs and halons. Representatives from developing countries argued it was unfair to require those countries to sacrifice future economic progress because of a problem largely created by the industrialized nations. Because population increases and economic growth would significantly boost CFC emissions in the developing countries, allowances were made for these countries in order to ensure their cooperation.[32]

Developing countries, as defined in article 5 of the Montreal Protocol, received a ten-year postponement of the enforcement of the protocol mandates.[33] CFC production was allowed to continue at a rate ten percent higher than the protocol's consumption limits in order to guarantee the Article Five countries' supply of CFCs was not disrupted in the interim. These provisions were thinly veiled side payments designed to create a winning coalition in favor of an agreement. Without these enticements, key actors in the developing world would have refused to participate in the ozone regime due to perceived inequities.

These de facto side payments were insufficient, however. At the second annual review conference in London, representatives of India and China made it clear they would not sign the Montreal Protocol unless a funding mechanism was created to help developing countries pay the incremental costs of CFC regulation, including the costs of acquiring more sophisticated technologies.[34] Negotiators at the London meetings knew that failure to bring China and India into the agreement would render the Montreal Protocol functionally worthless at some point in the future.[35] In China, for example, only one out of every ten households had refrigerators, but the government planned to ensure that every home had one by the turn of the century.[36] The resulting increase in CFC emissions would overwhelm even the best abatement efforts of the industrialized nations.

Thus, the London Amendments[37] created a multilateral fund to assist Article Five countries in securing cleaner technologies and meeting the incremental costs of compliance with the Montreal Protocol. Estimates at the time indicated that Article Five countries would need approximately $2 billion in assistance from 1990 to 2008 in order to comply with the Montreal Protocol. Chinese and Indian compliance alone would require roughly $600 million.[38] However, the signatories have had difficultly reaching their financial goals. Members originally pledged $160 million to the fund with the understanding that another $80 million would be added when both India and China signed the protocol. Actual contributions to the fund, however, have fallen far short of these pledges.[39]

The multilateral fund has been a powerful precedent for subsequent international environmental agreements. Since the adoption of the London Amendments, efforts to create climate change and biological diversity conventions have had to include proposals for a heavily centralized multilateral fund to assist developing countries in complying with treaty provisions.[40] Focusing on this "global bargain" approach to environmental treaties has empowered politically weak states to command side payments.[41] The Montreal Protocol established the political necessity to make side payments, and the implications for any climate-change regime are staggering.

The Climate Change Convention commits developed countries to return their GHG emissions to 1990 levels by the year 2000. The convention went into effect on 21 March 1994, and the developed countries had until 21 September 1994 to submit their proposals for achieving that goal. But the commitment to 1990 emissions levels is inadequate to meet the intended goals of the convention. Serious attempts to address global warming will again require the active participation of the developing countries, particularly India and China.

North America and Western Europe have been responsible for approximately 60 percent of the total cumulative anthropogenic increases in atmospheric CO_2 since 1800, largely due to industrial processes.[42] Carbon emissions in the developing countries, however, are positively driven by population. The United Nations Population Fund predicts that the lesser developed countries as a whole will be emitting roughly four times the amount of CO_2 they currently emit by 2025.[43] It is conceivable that by the middle of the next century the developing countries will be responsible for close to two-thirds of annual global CO_2 emissions.[44] Thus the members of the international community are faced with the following unpalatable choices: they can either stick with 1990-level targets and have future emissions from the developing countries overwhelm their efforts, or they can make side payments to these countries in an attempt to entice them not to pollute as much in the future.

The first option is illustrated by examining the cases of China and India. There is no question that China's population, currently 1.2 billion, will continue to grow.[45] The Chinese government projects 23 million newborns each year for the next decade, putting China well on the way to the 1.3-billion mark by the year 2000.[46] In addition, China has experienced a spectacular economic boom. According to World Bank estimates, China's domestic economy has been growing at 12 to 13 percent every year since 1988. Accordingly, many economists now believe China's economy will double by the year 2000.[47] To fuel this rapid expansion, China is expected to increase its coal consumption by two or three times, an increase that will contribute significantly to global GHG emissions.[48] To put the increase in perspective, in 1990 China burned the equivalent of one billion tons of coal, contributing 11 percent of global CO_2 emissions.[49] Some have predicted the projected massive increase in coal consumption could increase current worldwide carbon emissions by as much as 50 percent.[50]

India's situation is similar to China's. The Indian population is expected to surpass one billion by the year 2000 and to reach 1.4 billion by 2025.[51] If these projections hold up, India's GHG emissions could easily overtake China's. To accommodate the demands of this growing population, India could burn enough coal to trigger a six-fold increase in its CO_2 emissions.[52]

The Climate Change Convention accepts as a given that the first priority of the developing countries is their own economic development, even if it means GHG emissions will continue to rise as they industrialize. However, unless developing countries change the type of economic growth they pursue, any actions by the developed countries to significantly reduce GHG emissions will be more than canceled out. Lashof and Tirpak project that even if developed countries take effective action, without the participation of developing countries, global temperatures would nonetheless increase by 40 percent.[53] Therefore, the participation of less-developed countries (LDCs) is crucial to any effective climate change regime. Following the Montreal Protocol model, then, will require massive multilateral side payments to ensure global cooperation and participation.

How large would the side payments have to be? The North, in addition to paying its own abatements costs, would have to pay the South to reduce its dependence on fossil fuels, modify agricultural practices, reduce population growth, and reverse deforestation—all at the same time. The costs will be gargantuan. A study done for the OECD places the total cost of necessary side payments in the range of tens, maybe hundreds of billions of dollars.[54] Others estimate the United States' contribution to the Global Environmental Facility (GEF) will have to exceed $14 billion if side payments are made to assist the developing countries in controlling their GHG emissions.[55] Since the donor countries to the Montreal Protocol's multilateral fund are having difficulty raising $240 million, it is doubtful the political will exists to raise amounts tens or hundreds of times larger.

Scientific Consensus

In 1974 Mario Molina and Sherwood Rowland, atmospheric scientists at the University of California at Irvine, published an article hypothesizing a link between the emission of chlorine- and bromine-bearing compounds, such as chlorofluorocarbons and halons, and the depletion of stratospheric ozone.[56] According to Molina and Rowland, these chemicals were stable enough to survive as they passed through the troposphere and into the stratosphere. Once in the stratosphere, chlorine acts as a catalyst and reacts with stratospheric ozone (O_3) to produce a molecular oxygen (O_2), thereby decreasing ozone concentrations.[57] For several years after the publication of the Molina–Rowland article the scientific community remained divided on how to interpret their findings. Despite this uncertainty, public campaigns by nongovernmental organizations (NGOs) convinced nine countries, including the United States, to ban CFCs as aerosol propellants.

By the mid 1980s public concern over ozone depletion rose again. It was discovered that despite the ban on CFCs in aerosols, global production of CFCs for other products was increasing rapidly. To address these concerns, twenty states and the European Community sat down in Vienna in March of 1985 to strengthen efforts to protect the ozone layer.[58] Because of continuing uncertainty within the scientific community, the most that could be agreed to was a weak framework document affirming the need to fight ozone depletion and pledging to continue international research efforts on the subject.[59]

Soon after the Vienna Convention, members of the British Antarctic Survey announced the discovery of a large thinning area in the ozone layer over Antarctica that appeared during the Antarctic spring.[60] Within a year the existence of the "ozone hole" was confirmed by American and British satellite data. As this data was made public, researchers at the Du Pont Corporation, the world's largest producer of CFCs, announced that their research confirmed the Molina–Rowland hypothesis.[61] The fact that Du Pont was willing to pinpoint CFCs as the likely culprit in ozone depletion significantly weakened opposition to a stronger ozone regime. At the end of 1986, international negotiations on ozone resumed in Montreal. By September 1987, twenty-four nations and the European Community signed the Montreal Protocol. Going beyond the weak provisions of the Vienna Convention, the Montreal Protocol mandated the staggered reduction of both the production and consumption of five chemical compounds (CFCs 11, 12, 113, 114, 115) and froze the production and consumption of three halons (1211, 1301, 2402).

With regard to global warming, there is almost universal agreement within the scientific community that anthropogenic sources of GHG emissions are contributing to the natural greenhouse effect.[62] The National Academy of Sciences (NAS) and the IPCC agree that the doubling of the amount of carbon in the atmosphere that is expected midway though the next century will cause an approximate rise in average global temperatures of 3 degrees Celsius, within a range of 1.5 degrees in either direction.[63] This is where the scientific consensus ends, however. It is agreed that the earth will continue to warm and that GHGs are contributing to that trend. Exactly how great the warming effect will be is not known (1.5 to 4.5 degrees Celsius is a fairly large variation). Nor is there agreement regarding how fast warming will occur, or how it will affect different regions of the globe.[64]

In addition, among scientists who believe some climate change is unavoidable due to GHGs, there is a significant split between preventionists and adaptationists.[65] Much of this uncertainty is due to the many limitations of the general circulation models (GCMs) used to predict climate change. GCMs divide the global atmosphere into large "boxes" or grid cells and then use various equations involving motion, energy, and mass to predict changes in everything from wind to humidity. To estimate the influence of GHGs in altering our climate, GCMs are run as a simulation from which climate changes are approximated from changes in the smaller sections of the earth and atmosphere.

Weather processes such as cloud formation take place on scales too small for the grid cells in a GCM to capture. While the list of feedback mechanisms not handled well by GCMs is long, cloud formation is a particularly important variable because clouds might cool the earth's surface by reflecting solar radiation back into space or they might cause warming by trapping radiation from the earth's surface. Failure to accurately portray cloud formation could result in serious distortions of a GCM's predictions. Other important factors in the global warming equation not well handled by GCMs include oceans and their circulation patterns, solar activity, polar ice sheets, and land surfaces. All of these contribute to the wide variations in predictions of future global temperature increases.

Recent developments in the science of global warming have added to the uncertainty by suggesting that the rate of warming might not be as fast as some originally believed. It used to be thought that CFCs contributed to global warming by destroying the upper stratospheric ozone layer and allowing ultraviolet radiation to reach the earth. Now it has been discovered that CFCs also deplete ozone in the lower stratosphere and these reductions produce a cooling effect that cancels out the warming effect. The IPCC now claims that since CFCs do not have any net role in global warming, any anthropogenic warming effect will be more gradual.[66]

Regarding global warming, there is nothing like the level of agreement present in the scientific community prior to the signing of the Montreal Protocol. According to one recent review of the state of GCM-generated knowledge:

> Modelling shows that the observed warming is consistent with the effect of increasing greenhouse gases partly offset by some cooling due to aerosols, but it is also within the bounds of variability caused by natural factors. We cannot yet state definitely that the warming is caused by increasing greenhouse gases, and this uncertainty is unlikely to be resolved for another decade or so.[67]

It is likely that decades will pass before we have the same indisputable evidence on global warming that the scientific community had supporting its case for the Montreal Protocol and subsequent amendments to it.

Faced with scientific uncertainty, politics will ultimately decide what actions, if any, are taken. With significant uncertainties about the magnitude, rate, and regional impacts of global warming, policy makers opposed to significant reductions in GHG emissions are finding a number of scientists to support their position.[68] As long as this scientific uncertainty persists, policy makers in general are likely to view with suspicion, rather than deference, any incipient epistemic community forming around the issue of climate change.[69]

Emission Sources

The likelihood of cooperation on efforts to prevent ozone layer depletion were increased because there were two centrally important actors; the United States government and Du Pont. In 1985 the United States, Japan, and the European

Community (EC) accounted for 70 percent of global CFC production, with the United States alone responsible for over 40 percent of production.[70] Du Pont accounted for 25 percent of global CFC production and controlled 50 percent of the largest CFC market, North America.[71] The United States and Du Pont had immense power by controlling such a large percentage of an economically small market. Any unilateral decision by the United States or Du Pont would have a significant impact on CFC prices and the behavior of other producers around the world.

It was precisely this unilateral power that allowed the United States to break down European and Japanese opposition to CFC regulations. In February of 1987, Richard Benedick, the head of the U.S. delegation at Montreal, announced that unless agreement on overall cuts in CFC production was reached, the U.S. Congress would unilaterally pass legislation closing U.S. markets to products using CFCs.[72] CFC producers outside the U.S. feared being kept out of their most important market by these proposed regulations. According to Aman, "The idea of an equal playing field took hold. If U.S. producers were to be regulated, it was best to have all producers *internationally* regulated."[73] Even though European countries, Japan, and most CFC-producing firms favored little regulation, the outcome they feared most was unilateral U.S. regulations. As a result, Japan and the EC agreed on the regulations now found in the Montreal Protocol.[74]

In comparison, the causes of global warming are much more varied and widely distributed around the globe. GHGs include, in order of their contribution to the warming effect, carbon dioxide (CO_2), methane, CFCs—although recently scientists have cast doubt on conclusions about their net contribution—and nitrous oxide. These GHGs are mainly the product of fossil fuel combustion, deforestation, cement production, and agricultural processes found all over the world. Certainly no one corporation or country has the unilateral power to compel an agreement on GHGs that the United States had in the ozone case. Since GHGs like CO_2 are a direct result of combustion, and therefore of almost every basic process in an industrial society, any threat to block GHG-related products from a market would lack credibility.[75] The causes and sources of GHGs are so decentralized and diverse, effective action on global warming will require the active support and participation of a majority of the nations of the world.

Winners and Losers

While there may have been some uncertainty about the causal mechanisms involved, there was never any serious doubt that increases in ultraviolet radiation (UVR) would be uniformly disastrous. In some tropical regions there might be less skin cancer, but it was known there would be an increase in the incidences of cataracts and in agricultural damage. There has never been any perception that some regions might actually benefit from increases in ultraviolet radiation.[76] In addition, effects such as skin cancer are easily comprehended by the average person.

The magnitude of the potential impact was confirmed by computer models sponsored by the Environmental Protection Agency (EPA) in the mid 1980s. One of these models indicated that a 5 to 11 percent increase in the amount of CFC emissions would produce 40 million additional cases of skin cancer and 800,000 fatalities over the next eighty-eight years.[77] A year later the EPA reported that newer findings indicated there would be 150 million new cases of skin cancer in the U.S. by 2075, with approximately 3 million deaths.[78] During the Montreal Protocol negotiations, diplomats were not questioning these scientific findings.[79]

Predicting the regional impact of climate change is one of the most uncertain aspects of global warming science, because changes in such variables as temperature, precipitation, and evaporation are likely to differ significantly from region to region. Countries in the northern latitudes may feel they will benefit from a rise in temperature because of improved agricultural productivity.[80] Semiarid tropical zones such as parts of India may even benefit from increases in monsoonal activity. At the same time, low-lying island and coastal nations fear the rise of surrounding waters that will accompany significant warming.[81] Developed countries may not suffer substantially with regard to health or economic output, but less-developed countries that depend heavily on agriculture may experience disastrous consequences from even slight temperature increases.[82] Overall, it is the nations least prepared to adapt to climate change that will suffer most from any significant warming.

Countries in which policy makers believe they may benefit from global warming will be reluctant to cooperate in any international effort that involves significant economic costs. Industrialized nations in particular believe they will lose little due to global warming and are unlikely to see any national interest in making costly economic sacrifices to reduce GHG emissions. The perception of "winners and losers" in the distribution of both impact and cost will seriously hinder any effort to abate GHG emissions. However, where public finances are tight, social programs and other investments needed to make wealthy societies more sustainable may lose out in the larger competition for funds created by the costs of climate-change mitigation.

If Not the Montreal Protocol, Then What?

Overall, there has been an unwillingness among the nations of the world to take the dramatic actions needed to address problems on the scale of global warming. We predict that actors in the climate regime will continue to pursue politically digestible but inexpensive and climatologically insufficient mandates such as those put forward in the Climate Change Convention. If, however, the current fixation with the framework protocol model embodied in the ozone protection regime can be overcome, it is possible that other means to sustainability can be found, by which we could begin to limit GHG emissions and increase sink reductions in the absence of a giant, globally negotiated climate-change regime. Such possibilities include increased scientific and technological research on issues related to climate-change mitigation and abatement; the protection of habitats and forests in both the developed and developing countries, including tree planting, reforestation, and debt-for-nature swap programs[83]; the reforming of multilateral development banks in order to promote ecologically sustainable lending[84]; and joint implementation projects that would help reduce CO_2 emissions, such as increasing energy efficiency, on which the developed countries would work with individual developing countries.[85]

Virtually everyone interested in issues related to climate change acknowledges a need for more research on both the environmental and social impacts of global warming and its control. Only the developed countries possess the financial resources needed for such large-scale research efforts. However, the research must be conducted in both developed and developing states, because GHG sources and the effects of climate change are very different across countries and levels of development. This policy has the additional advantage of enhancing domestic research and other scientific capacities in individual developing countries, a development goal in its own right, which has proven quite valuable in the pursuit of other ecological and public health related goals.[86] Areas of necessary research include the development of cleaner, more efficient energy and transportation systems and technologies; advances in agriculture and in ecological protection and restoration; and improvements in contraception and women's health. Research programs in these areas already exist in developed countries; they need only be expanded to include developing countries and to address the needs of a warming world. More research will not, however, guarantee greater scientific consensus. There will likely be a great deal of uncertainty surrounding climate change in general and the climate models in particular for the foreseeable future.[87]

As has often been the case with environmental and social policy initiatives, individual policies are often working at cross-purposes. Environmental analysis and impact statements should take GHG emissions into account. The results are often quite surprising. For example, the 1990 U.S. Clean Air Act, generally considered a climate-friendly piece of legislation because of its mandated reductions in both ozone-depleting and acid-rain-causing substances, may result in an increase in CO_2 emissions, because so-called clean coal technologies often require that more coal be burned to produce equivalent amounts of energy.[88] Sulfur emissions are reduced, but CO_2 emissions increase. In order to be effective, domestic policy coordination would have to be quite expansive, encompassing construction codes, energy and transportation efficiency, tax law, and numerous other government and private sector operations.

Many existing international organizations are also working against climate-change mitigation and abatement. For example, the World Bank continues to violate its own environmental regulations by approving loans for massive fossil-fuel-burning projects.[89] One recent World Bank–funded environmental fiasco is a $400-million project to build a series of large coal-fired power plants in India. It is estimated this project alone will double the amount of coal India burns and create the single largest source of GHG emissions in the world.[90] Institutions such as the United Nations and the World Bank have important environmental initiatives, but as is often the case with domestic policies, the left hand does not know—or does not care to know—what the right hand is doing. A public and academic dialogue has also begun about the connections between ecological protection and trade regimes.[91] This suggests that although the realms of development and trade are generally hostile to environmental concerns, institutions designed to promote trade and development are too important to ignore: they control too much capital and exert too much influence in setting development goals and policies around the world.

Joint implementation programs and regimes can be tailored to individual goals in areas of research, agricultural reform, forestry, habitat protection, and clean and efficient technology and energy production and use. These programs are also defensible on other economic and social grounds. For example, energy efficiency gains in the developing countries would reduce GHG emissions per energy unit and could free up capital for other development and environmental needs.[92] Joint implementation programs also offer diversity in initiative types and participants. The multifaceted approach of such programs may mean they won't be faced with challenges from various blocking coalitions, as a globally negotiated regime would be.[93] Finally, joint implementation programs, because they can be designed and implemented with specific issues and geographic areas in mind, can simultaneously incorporate other objectives and programs for sustainability.

These alternative paths require funding that will not be available if governments pursue the planetary bargaining model. If weaning ourselves of carbon dioxide production means making massive side payments to the developing countries, these payments will be drawn directly from funds for other projects that promote sustainability. For example, further reducing and eventually eliminating human population growth rates is an essential component of any set of climate-change mitigation initiatives. Family planning programs, educational opportunities for young girls, aid that targets the enhancement of economic opportunity and choice for women, and the provision of basic health services are cost-effective ways to help control future population increases and raise the quality of life for millions while simultaneously fighting global warming.[94]

Providing increased access to these services is potentially a much quicker, more politically expedient way to combat global warming, but it would require substantial funding in the future. Although the cost is small in comparison to that of the Montreal Protocol side payments model, such funding will likely be unavailable if that model is pursued. The 1994 United Nations Conference on Population and Development in Cairo stated that funding for these types of services will need to have to be increased from current levels of $5 billion to nearly $17 billion by the year 2000 if there is to be any hope of containing the earth's population to a "sustainable" 7.27 billion people.[95] So while the concept of sustainable development has contributed to our understanding of the trade-offs between economic development and environmental quality, it has cast little light on the trade-offs between the financing of its various objectives.

Conclusion

If the scientific community is correctly interpreting its evidence and computer models, then we are providing an unsustainable legacy for future generations. Without some unforeseen and radical transformation in the way we view costs, benefits, and the future, the planetary bargaining approach holds little hope for staving off serious disruptions of our climate. The argument is best summarized by Oran Young and Gail Osherenko:

> What worked in the ozone case . . . is not necessarily the best route to success in efforts to negotiate a climate change regime. It follows that those responsible for working out the terms of any given regime should make a conscious effort to evaluate the pros and cons of alternative paths to regime formation rather than fixating on the alleged virtues of a single route.[96]

The scientific, economic, and political circumstances that characterized the evolution of the ozone protection regime and the Montreal Protocol model were unique. While numerous lessons regarding international environmental cooperation can be drawn from the Montreal Protocol experience, this does not mean that its institutional model should or can be transferred to the problem of global warming. Such a myopic approach excludes the many lessons from other, quite different experiences and institutional models that could encourage progress toward an ecologically sustainable future. Policies to address climate change must be flexible, highly complex, and able to adapt over many decades to new scientific findings and empirical reality. If the Montreal Protocol model is emphasized, despite its having been proved not to be universally useful, there is a high risk that these possibilities will be ignored.

Notes

1. World Commission on Environment and Development, *Our Common Future* (New York: Oxford University Press, 1987), 43.

2. Alfred C. Aman, Jr., *Administrative Law in a Global Era* (Ithaca, NY: Cornell University Press, 1992); Richard Benedick, *Ozone Diplomacy: New Directions in Safeguarding the Planet* (Cambridge, MA: Harvard University Press, 1991); Harold W. Bernard, Jr., *Global Warming Unchecked: Signs to Watch For* (Bloomington, IN: Indiana University Press, 1993); Gary Bryner, "Implementing Global Environmental Agreements," *Policy Studies Journal* 19 (2): 103–14 (1991); David D. Doniger and Alan S. Miller, "Saving the World May Not Be As Hard As You Think," Center for Global

Change, 1990, photocopy; David Hurlbut, "Beyond the Montreal Protocol: Impact on Nonparty States and Lessons for Future Environmental Protection Regimes," *Colorado Journal of International Environmental Law and Policy* 4 (2): 344–68 (1993); Winfried Lang, "Is the Ozone Depletion Regime a Model for an Emerging Regime on Global Warming?" *Journal of Environmental Law* 9 (2): 161–74 (1991); Daniel A. Lashof, "Climate Plan Evaluation: USA," *Independent NGO Evaluations of National Plans for Climate Change Mitigation: First Review, February 1994* (Washington, DC: Climate Action Network, 1994); Irving M. Mintzer, "Cooling Down a Warming World: Chlorofluorocarbons, the Greenhouse Effect, and the Montreal Protocol," *International Environmental Affairs* 1 (1): 12–25 (1989); Stephen R. Seidel and Daniel P. Blank, "The Montreal Protocol: Pollution Prevention on a Global Scale," *Ambio* 19 (6–7): 301–04 (1990); Richard B. Stewart, and Jonathan B. Wiener, "The Comprehensive Approach to Global Climate Policy: Issues of Design and Practicality," *Arizona Journal of International and Comparative Law* 9 (1): 83–112 (1992); Pamela Wexler, "Protecting the Global Atmosphere: Beyond the Montreal Protocol," *Maryland Journal of International Law and Trade* 14 (1): 1–19 (1990).

3. Oran R. Young, "Global Environmental Change and International Governance," *Millennium* 19 (3): 342 (1990); Marc A. Levy, Oran R. Young, and Gail Osherenko, "The Effectiveness of International Regimes: A Design for Large-Scale Collaborative Research," photocopy, 1991.

4. Marc A. Levy, Robert Keohane, and Peter M. Haas, "Institutions for the Earth: Promoting International Environmental Protection," *Environment* 34 (4): 33 (1992).

5. United Nations Conference on Environment and Development, *Framework Convention of Climate Change,* final text, 9 May (New York: United Nations, 1992 [hereinafter Climate Change Convention]).

6. Lelani Arris, "Climate Change Treaty Goes Into Effect," INC *Press Release,* 19 March 1994, 1.

7. William K. Stevens, "Emissions Must Be Cut to Avert Shift in Climate, Panel Says," *New York Times,* 20 September 1994, B9.

8. Government of Canada. "The Changing Atmosphere: Implications for Global Security," in *The Challenge of Global Warming,* ed. Dean Abrahamson (Washington, DC: Island Press, 1988).

9. Intergovernmental Panel on Climate Change, *Scientific Assessment of Climate Change: The Policymakers' Summary,* World Meteorological Organization and United Nations Environmental Programme, 1990, 13, 17.

10. Susan Subak, "Six Torontos, Two Montreals . . ." *ECO Geneva* (INC9) no. 6, 18 February 1994: 1.

11. Dean Abrahamson, "The Challenge of Global Warming," in *Global Climate Change and Life on Earth,* ed. Richard L. Wyman (New York: Routledge, Chapman and Hall, 1991), 245.

12. It should be noted that this diverse group of countries has agreed on little else at INC meetings, other than an opposition to strengthening the Convention.

13. Stevens, "Omissions Must Be Cut."

14. Chris Carrel,"Clinton's Climate Inaction Plan," *No Sweat News* 2 (2): 26 (1993–94).

15. Ian H. Rowlands, "Ozone Layer Depletion and Global Warming: New Sources for Environmental Disputes," *Peace & Change* 16 (3): 260–84 (1991).

16. See for example Levy, Keohane, and Haas, "Institutions for the Earth"; and James K. Sebenius, "Designing Negotiations toward a New Regime: The Case of Global Warming," *International Security* 15 (4): 110–48 (1991).

17. Peter M. Haas, "Policy Responses to Stratospheric Ozone Depletion," *Global Environmental Change* (June 1991): 233.

18. Peter M. Morrisette, "The Montreal Protocol: Lessons for Formulating Policies for Global Warming," *Policy Studies Journal* 19 (2): 155 (1991).

19. Cynthia Pollock Shea, "Why Du Pont Gave Up $600 Million," *New York Times,* 11 April 1988, sec. 3.

20. Bernard, "Global Warming Unchecked," 74.

21. Peter M. Haas, "Stratospheric Ozone: Regime Formation in Stages," in *Polar Politics: Creating International Environmental Regimes,* ed. Oran R. Young and Gail Osherenko (Ithaca, NY: Cornell University Press, 1993), 170.

22. Thomas C. Schelling, "Some Economics of Global Warming," *The American Economic Review* 82 (1): 3 (1992).

23. U.S. Environmental Protection Agency, *Regulatory Impact Analysis: Protection of Stratospheric Ozone,* vols. 1–3 (Washington, DC: EPA, 1987).

24. Ibid.

25. Schelling, "Some Economics," 7–8.

26. U.S. Department of Energy, *Limiting Net Greenhouse Gas Emissions in the United States* (Washington, DC: GPO, 1991).

27. U.S. Council of Economic Advisors, *Economic Report of the President* (Washington, DC: GPO, 1990), 234.

28. Joel Darmstadter, *The Economic Cost of CO₂ Mitigation: A Review of Estimates for Selected World Regions* (Washington, DC: Resources for the Future, 1991), 51.

29. Stephen Willis, Greenpeace press release, "Scientists Confirm Need for Deeper Cuts in Greenhouse Gas Emissions," 16 September 1994.

30. Michael T. Hatch, "Domestic Politics and International Negotiations: The Politics of Global Warming in the United States." *The Journal of Environment and Development* 2 (2): 37, fn. 55 (1993).

31. Peter M. Haas, "Obtaining International Environmental Protection through Epistemic Consensus," *Millennium* 19 (3): 347–63 (1990); Levy, Keohane, and Haas, "Institutions for the Earth"; Morrisette, "Montreal Protocol"; Rowlands, "Ozone Layer Depletion"; and Sebenius, "Designing Negotiations."

32. Special considerations were also given to the former Soviet Union and Japan to insure their cooperation; the Soviets were allowed to continue the construction of a new CFC plant, and the Japanese were allowed to shift between various CFCs in their computer industries.

33. Article 5 exemptions apply to any developing country whose consumption of the substances controlled in the Montreal Protocol is less than 0.3 kilograms per capita on the date of the entry into force of the protocol, or anytime thereafter prior to 1 January 1999.

34. Jason M. Patlis, "The Multilateral Fund of the Montreal Protocol: A Prototype for Financial Mechanisms in Protecting the Global Environment," *Cornell International Law Journal* 25: 181–230 (1992).

35. Scott Barrett, *Convention on Climate Change: Economic Aspects of Negotiations* (Paris: Organization for Economic Co-Operation and Development, 1992), 50; and Haas, "Domestic Politics," 164.

36. Daniel F. Kohler, John Haaga, and Frank Camm, *Projections of Consumption of Products Using Chlorofluorocarbons in Developing Countries,* Rand Corporation Report N2458-EPA, 1987.

37. United Nations Environment Program, *Fourth Meeting of the Open-ended Working Group of the Parties to the Montreal Protocol,* United Nations Environment Program/Ozone Layer Program: WG.IV/L. 1/Rev. 1 (London: UN Publications, 1990).

38. Barrett, *Convention on Climate Change,* 50; Sue Montgomery, "Fund to Combat Ozone Depletion," *Development Forum,* September/October 1990, 9; UNEP, *Fourth Meeting,* 1.

39. Arjun Makhijani and Kevin Gurney, *Mending the Ozone Hole* (Takoma Park, MD: Institute for Energy and Environmental Research, 1992), 179–80; and Patlis, "Multilateral Fund," 223.

40. The Global Environment Facility (GEF) will act as an interim mechanism for channeling money to developing countries participating in the United Nations Convention on Climate Change and the Framework Convention on Biological Diversity. As of January 1994 the members of the Organization for Economic Cooperation and Development have pledged two billion dollars for 1994–98.

41. Alan S. Miller, "Global Environmentalism and North-South Relations: Bargain or Opportunity?" Center for Global Change, photocopy, 1994; Lawrence Susskind and Connie Ozawa, "Negotiating More Effective International Environmental Agreements," in *The International Politics of the Environment,* ed. Andrew Hurrell and Benedict Kingsbury (New York: Oxford University Press, 1992), 142–65.

42. Yasumasa Fujii, *An Assessment of the Responsibility for the Increase in the CO_2 Concentration and Intergenerational Carbon Accounts* (Laxenburg, Austria: IIASA, 1990), 20.

43. S. Okie, "Developing World's Role in Global Warming Grows," *Washington Post,* 15 May 1990.

44. Alan S. Manne, *Global 2100: Alternative Scenarios for Reducing Carbon Emissions* (Paris: Organization for Economic Co-operation and Development, 1992), 7; and Schelling, "Some Economics," 10.

45. World Resources Institute, *World Resources 1994–95: People and the Environment* (New York. Oxford University Press, 1994), 61.

46. Rajiv Chandra, "Continuing Population Explosion in China," *Inter Press Service,* 27 January 1993; Vaclav Smil, *China's Environmental Crisis: An Inquiry into the Limits of National Development* (Armonk, NY: M.E. Sharpe, 1993), 13; and WRI, *World Resources 1994–95,* 61.

47. Steven Mufson and Steve Coil, "China Offers Its Oil Riches on the Open Market," *Washington Post,* 20 March 1994, A34.

48. Bernard, *Global Warming,* 161; Vaclav Smil, "Barriers to a Sustainable China" Paper presented at the Harrison Program for the Future Global Agenda's Footsteps to Sustainability Conference, College Park, MD, 1993); WRI, *World Resources 1994–95,* 66.

49. WRI, *World Resources 1994–95,* 65.

50. Sebenius, "Designing Negotiations," 129.

51. WRI, *World Resources 1994–95,* 83.

52. Ibid.

53. Daniel A. Lashof and D. A. Tirpak, *Policy Options for Stabilizing Global Climate* (Washington, DC: Environmental Protection Agency, 1989), 40–43.

54. Barrett, *Convention on Climate Change,* 50.

55. Patlis, "Multilateral Fund," 223.

56. Mario J. Molina and Sherwood Rowland, "Stratospheric Sink for Chlorofluoromethanes: Chlorine-Atom Catalyzed Destruction of the Ozone," *Nature* 249: 810 (1974).

57. For a complete discussion of the evolution of the science of ozone depletion, see Makhijani and Gurney, *Mending the Ozone Hole.*

58. *Vienna Convention for the Protection of the Ozone Layer, Final Act* (Nairobi: United Nations Environment Program, 1985) [hereinafter Vienna Convention].

59. Benedick, *Ozone Diplomacy,* 20–22; and Haas, "Stratospheric Ozone."

60. J. G. Farman, B. G. Gardiner, and J. D. Shanklin, "Large Losses of Total Ozone in Antarctica Reveal Seasonal ClO_x/NO_x Interaction," *Nature* 315: 207–10 (1985).

61. William Glaberson, "Science at Center Stage in Du Pont Ozone Shift," *New York Times*, 26 March 1988, 41.

62. Daniel Bodansky, "The United Nations Framework Convention on Climate Change: A Commentary," *Yale Journal of International Law* 18 (2): 460 (1993); and Kathy Maskell, Irving M. Mintzer, and Bruce A. Callender, "Basic Science of Climate Change," *The Lancet* 342: 1031 (1993).

63. National Academy of Sciences, *Carbon Dioxide and Climate: A Scientific Assessment* (Washington, DC: National Academy of Sciences, 1979), 2; and IPCC, *Scientific Assessment*, xxv.

64. John Broome, *Counting the Cost of Global Warming* (Cambridge: White Horse Press, 1992), 8; IPCC, *Scientific Assessment*, xii; and Morrisette, "Montreal Protocol," 156.

65. Haas, "Obtaining Environmental Protection," 359.

66. Intergovernmental Panel on Climate Change, *Climate Change 1992: The Supplementary Report to the IPCC Scientific Assessment* (Cambridge: Cambridge University Press, 1992), 20, 29.

67. Maskell, Mintzer, and Callender, "Basic Science," 1031.

68. Robert C. Bailing, Jr., *The Heated Debate: Greenhouse Predictions Versus Climate Reality* (San Francisco: Pacific Research Institute, 1992); Richard Kerr, "Greenhouse Skeptics Out in the Cold," *Science* 246: 1118–19 (1989); Marshall Institute, *Scientific Perspectives on the Greenhouse Problem* (Washington, DC: George C. Marshall Institute, 1989); S. Fred Singer, ed., *Global Climate Change: Natural and Human Influences* (New York: Paragon House, 1989); S. Fred Singer, "Warming Theories Need Warning Label," *Bulletin of the Atomic Scientists*, June 1992.

69. Haas, "Obtaining Environmental Protection," 359–60.

70. David A. Wirth and Daniel A. Lashof, "Beyond Vienna and Montreal: A Global Framework Convention on Greenhouse Gases," in *A Global Warming Forum: Scientific, Economic, and Legal Overview*, ed. Richard A. Geyer (London: CRC Press, 1993), 511.

71. Haas, "Stratospheric Ozone," 165.

72. The distinct possibility that the federal courts and Congress might impose tough domestic CFC regulations is thought by many to have been a key motivating factor in President Ronald Reagan's support for an international agreement. See for example Alfred C. Aman, Jr., "Above the Boundaries: Ozone Depletion, Equity, and Climate Change," *Law and Policy* 15 (1): 1–13 (1993).

73. 1992, op. cit., 144.

74. Haas, "Stratospheric Ozone," 166.

75. Rowlands, "Ozone Layer Depletion," 272–73.

76. Peter M. Morrisette, et al., *Lessons Learned from Other International Agreements for a Global CO_2 Accord* (Washington, DC: Resources for the Future, 1990), 17.

77. Daniel J. Dudek and Michael Oppenheimer, "The Implications of Health and Environmental Effects for Policy," in *Effects of Changes in Stratospheric Ozone and Global Climate*, U.S. Environmental Protection Agency and United Nations Environment Program (Washington, DC: EPA, 1986).

78. Environmental Protection Agency, "Protection of the Stratospheric Ozone Layer," *Federal Register* 52: 47492–47496 (1987).

79. Benedick, "Ozone Diplomacy," 22.

80. Morrisette and Plantinga op. cit., 30.

81. Morrisette, "Montreal Protocol," 153.

82. Schelling, "Some Economics," 6.

83. William R. Cline, *The Economics of Global Warming* (Washington, DC: Institute for International Economics, 1992); Schelling, "Some Economics"; Mark Sagoff, "Set-

tling America, or the Concept of Place in Environmental Ethics," *Journal of Energy, Natural Resources and Environmental Law* 12 (2): 349–418 (1992).

84. Karen Capoor, Bruce Rich, and Rob Watson, *Power Failure* (Washington, DC: Environmental Defense Fund, 1994); Bruce Rich, *Mortgaging the Earth* (Boston: Beacon Press, 1994).

85. Sebenius, "Designing Negotiations," 121; Alan S. Miller, in this volume.

86. Peter Haas, Robert O. Keohane, and Marc Levy, eds. *Institutions for the Earth* (Cambridge, MA: MIT Press, 1993).

87. Bryner, "Implementing Agreements"; International Unit on Climate Change, "Are Climate Models Reliable?" Fact Sheet 15 (Geneva: United Nations Environment Program, 1992); Charles T. Rubin and Marc K. Landy, "Global Warming," *Garbage Magazine* (February/March 1993): 24–29.

88. Bryner, "Implementing Agreements."

89. Capoor, Rich, and Watson, *Power Failure.*

90. Pratop Chatterjee, "World Bank to Pay for Global Warming Disaster," Environmental Defense Fund press release, 13 September 1993.

91. See, for example, Earth Island Press, *The Case Against Free Trade: GATT, NAFTA, and the Globalization of Corporate Power* (Washington, DC: Earth Island Press, 1993); and Durwood Zaelke, Paul Orbach, and Robert Housman, *Trade and the Environment: Law, Economics, and Policy* (Washington, DC: Island Press, 1993).

92. Alan S. Miller, in this volume.

93. Gareth Porter and Janet Welsh Brown, *Global Environmental Politics* (San Francisco: Westview Press, 1991), 94–97; James K. Sebenius, "Challenging Conventional Explanations of International Cooperation: Negotiation Analysis and the Case of Epistemic Communities," *International Organization* 46 (1): 323–65 (1992).

94. Cline, *Economics of Global Warming;* Anne H. Ehrlich, in this volume; Schelling, "Some Economics"; Sebenius, "Designing Negotiations," 143; and Amartya Sen, "The Population Delusion," *New York Review of Books,* 22 September 1994.

95. Alan Cowell, "Conference on Population Has Hidden Issue: Money," *New York Times,* 12 September 1994, A8.

96. Oran R. Young and Gail Osherenko, "International Regime Formation: Findings, Research Priorities, and Applications," in *Polar Politics: Creating International Environmental Regimes,* ed. Oran R. Young and Gail Osherenko (Ithaca, NY: Cornell University Press, 1993), 260.

7

Transparent Sovereignty

Peter G. Brown

Since the end of the Cold War it is a commonplace that we need both a new vision and a new framework for foreign policy. President Bush talked of a new world order but was unable to articulate what it was, and the Clinton administration has been no better at setting forth its global purposes. A parallel difficulty afflicts the now nearly global concern with sustainable development. Sustainability—albeit still very much in the process of definition—has not been connected with a theory of state relations that grounds the concept in a vision of world order. This is a reason that it remains a peripheral public policy concern.[1]

Foreign Policy as Conceptual Failure

These tragic failures stem in large part from a common root: the ad hoc reliance on two unproductive vocabularies for thinking about foreign policy. One of these is realism—which holds that states not only may but should pursue whatever is in their national interest. The other is what Charles Beitz has called "the autonomy of states"—which holds that like individuals, states have the right to manage their own domestic affairs.[2] Neither vocabulary is promising. Realism falls into self-contradiction at the outset. It claims to be nonmoral but asserts a normative standard: that states *ought* to pursue their interests. This is a reason that few really believe in realism or the attendant national-interest standard. Even the most ardent proponents usually qualify their arguments by pointing out that states should pursue their "legitimate" interests. This leaves what needs analysis buried in the word legitimate and the real work about what we should do all undone. The best face that can be put on realism is that it is a device to oppose naive moralism in foreign policy, but absent a moral foundation for thinking about the

113

relations between states, it does not offer a means of discussing what to do. The autonomy-of-states vocabulary fails because the analogy with persons is inappropriate. States do not have bodies or memories, as persons do. States are made up of persons who have privacy rights, but the state itself has no such rights.

A promising reconceptualization of sovereignty is going on under the rubric of "transparent sovereignty," mostly in the context of the GATT, NAFTA, and other agreements in international trade. The root idea is that nations have to reveal actions they may be taking that could violate the requirements of free trade, such as providing subsidies. Similar requirements—but springing from a largely different source—arise in the context of nuclear proliferation.

It is obvious that states can be transparent along a variety of dimensions. So the question that needs analysis is *which transparency?* The normative dimension of the problem calls for some standard of conduct that generates a list of relevant considerations to be revealed.

The standard set out in the trade context derives from the ideal of perfectly functioning markets as the standard against which to judge deviance. This is in turn compatible with certain elements of neoclassical economic theory, which see the role of the state as correcting for market failures. The goal is increased efficiency, and thus happiness or utility, through facilitating mutually beneficial transactions between consumers and suppliers.

The trade negotiators ask the right question—what should states have to reveal?—but have gotten an unpromising response—only those things that interfere with perfectly functioning markets. This conception of transparency cannot be adequate *by itself* for two reasons. First, it rests on a moral theory, utilitarianism, which is incompatible with the preservation of persons both materially and morally. Second, the fascination with free trade takes no account of the relative scale of the world economy and the biosphere on which it depends. Let us explore each of these in turn.

The market/utilitarian doctrine fails to materially preserve persons because it has nothing to say about persons who cannot compete in markets. It cannot preserve people morally because it requires either too little or too much. If it says that all our obligations are discharged by mutually advantageous trades in the market, it recognizes no duties toward others. Insofar as it relies on the classical utilitarian standard of the greatest happiness of the greatest number, as Bernard Williams has pointed out, it requires too much.[3] This is because it makes each person's moral commitments to their own moral or religious life abridgable in order to satisfy the requirements of the principle of utility. We need to find a way of conceptualizing international relations that offers a coherent account of our obligations to other persons around the globe.

The market interference conception of transparency also fails to take into account our obligations to future generations, or to the biosphere itself. This vision is of an ever larger world economy providing more goods and services to more and more persons, with economic activity increasing severalfold. The fact that the *present* scale of world economic activity is already destabilizing the earth's climate and is a major factor in the loss of biodiversity is not a concern internal to this conception of transparent sovereignty. Accordingly, it places the well being of future persons and the biosphere in jeopardy.

Government as Trustee

A more promising account of transparency can be derived from seventeenth-century English philosopher John Locke's *The Second Treatise*. Ironically, though Locke never visited North America, this work is surely one of the most important books in American politics, since it was relied on heavily by Jefferson and other writers of our founding documents. Locke proposes that we think of governments as trustees for the preservation of persons. In Locke's conception, two large classes of duties derive from this conception: a set that pertains directly to persons by which the natural law obligation to preserve all mankind is discharged; and a set that is concerned with the preservation of the common resources of the earth for the benefit of all mankind. This standard offers a philosophical ground, but only a general one, for the concept of sustainability. When we speak of transparent sovereignty, it is the standard of trusteeship that should inform our inquiry as to whether a government is discharging its obligations.

Certain duties flow directly from the notion of trusteeship, but by itself it is a fairly formal concept: we can set up a trust to preserve anything for anyone. To know in detail how governments as trustees should behave, we have to appeal to some underlying moral principles. I have used Locke's theory, for the most part as set out in *The Second Treatise,* to specify these principles and their practical consequences.

Locke writes over and over again of the trust that the people repose in their government, and he speaks of those who govern as having a "fiduciary trust."[4] For Locke, people seek out government for the

> mutual preservation of their lives, liberties and estates, which I call by the general name, property. The great and chief end, therefore, of men's uniting into commonwealths, and putting themselves under government, is the preservation of their property[5]

In understanding Locke's theory of government, it is essential to keep in mind, as we will see, that "property" includes *life* and *liberty,* as well as estate. Much of the *Second Treatise* is devoted to the circumstances under which the citizens may legitimately rebel because the executive or legislator has violated the terms of the trust. The government conforms to the terms of the trust when it discharges its duties "to be directed to no other end but the peace, safety, and public good of the people."[6]

The root idea of the trust conception of government is of a fiduciary trust, in which the trustee has a duty to preserve and enhance the assets of the trust with a view to protecting the persons and property of the citizens. It draws on the general notion that certain persons can be given powers over certain assets, powers to act on behalf of and for the benefit of others. Trusts are set up because there is an asset to be managed for the benefit of someone, and typically a document sets forth the duties and privileges of the trustee. The general duties of the trustees are: (1) to act out of loyalty for the benefit of the beneficiary, not in the trustee's own interests; (2) not to delegate the entire administration of the trust; (3) to provide the beneficiaries with information concerning the trust; (4) to enforce claims on behalf of the trust; and (5) to make the trust property productive.[7]

In a trust conception of government, a constitution and laws are the trust documents or instruments. The assets of the trust are the natural resource base, the coercive powers of the state to tax and to provide for national defense, its legitimate ability to plan, to educate, and in other ways to foster the well-being of both its citizens and the community. Corresponding to the trustee's general duties, those who govern must act in the interests of the citizens, not their own interests; perform the duties of office—not delegate them; disclose information to the public; defend the assets of the trust and citizens from unjust interference, destruction and/or waste; and preserve and enhance the assets of the trust.

The trust conception's understanding of government duties is, then, as follows. First, *the trust conception recognizes the direct duty of the government to preserve and enhance the well being of all persons.* As beneficiaries of a trust, we expect our trustees to work for our well-being. For Locke the state is established in order that "the law of nature be observed, which willeth the peace and preservation of all mankind."[8]

The idea that government has an obligation to preserve its citizens can be supported—and has been—in modern democratic society without explicit reference to natural law by pointing out that no one setting up a government would agree to any other rule for fear of being in an unprotected group. No one is left out, and government is charged with equal protection. The trust model thus satisfies in a direct and straightforward manner the intuitive requirement that everyone counts.[9] For Locke, what it means to be a person is to be self-governing in two senses: persons regulate their own conduct and choose their own government.

As is clear from Locke's *Letter Concerning Toleration,*[10] Locke thinks that to be a person is to be capable of setting goals, holding moral or religious beliefs, and acting on those beliefs. When Locke speaks of the trustee's obligation to preserve all persons, he refers not only to food and housing but to the human capacity for worship and citizenship. Indeed, one of the things that worried Locke most, and a major source of his motivation in writing the *Second Treatise,* was the rise of religious intolerance and the destruction of persons both figuratively and literally because of their religious beliefs. The obligation of the trustee is thus not simply to keep people alive, but to preserve their capacity as persons capable of exercising choice.

Second, *the trust model holds that the legislative (and the executive) must discharge these obligations to the public good on the basis of impartial deliberation.*

> Whensoever . . . the legislative shall transgress this fundamental rule of society, and either by ambition, fear, folly, or corruption, endeavor to grasp themselves or put into the hands of any other absolute power over the lives, liberties, and estates of the people, by this breach of trust they forfeit the power the people had put into their hands . . . [11]
>
> The legislators must be freely chosen . . . and, so chosen, freely act and advise as the necessity of the commonwealth and the public good should upon examination and mature debate be judged to require. This those who give their votes before they hear the debates, and have weighed the reason on all sides, are not capable of doing.[12]

It is the obligation of legislators to debate public issues and decide on the public good in light of that debate. Those whose votes have been committed in exchange for campaign contributions cannot, for example, discharge this obligation.

Third, *the trust conception imposes an obligation to respect human rights and provides an account of those rights.* In civil society, according to Locke, persons have three clusters of rights.[13] First, there are those associated with democratic processes, exercised by electing representatives. "The liberty of man in society is to be under no other legislative power but that established by consent in the commonwealth."[14] Second, rights pertaining to the integrity of the body are absolute: "Every man has property in his own person; this nobody has any right to but himself."[15] Third, there is a set of rights to some minimal level of well-being. Though Locke's theory is sometimes taken to be a justification of absolute property rights, which would preclude government from redistributing wealth, this reading does not accord with the text.

The "law of nature" for Locke imposes a duty on each of us to preserve humanity, including a duty to assist the poor, or at least those incapable of working who would otherwise perish.[16] People leaving the state of nature and entering into civil government discharge their general duties for the preservation of humanity by delegating these duties to government:

> The first power, viz., of doing whatsoever he thought fit for preservation of himself and the rest of mankind, he gives up to be regulated by the laws made by the society, so far forth as the preservation of himself and the rest of that society shall require; which laws of the society in many things confine the liberty he had by the law of nature.[17]

Locke's "law of nature" thus captures the idea of obligations to which we have not consented; the social contract is the mechanism by which we confer on government the responsibility to carry out those obligations on our behalf.

A more contemporary derivation of government's duty to respect rights can avoid talking about natural law, as well as other theological aspects of Locke's argument. We can see ourselves as consenting to government on the condition that it look out for our well-being as persons—keeping in mind the full-bodied sense of person as self-legislating. Thus, individually we reserve rights against those people we ask to serve as trustees, just as beneficiaries of a financial trust have certain legal rights by virtue of their position. The golden rule—a nonvoluntary but uncontroversial source of obligation—also demands that we universalize: what we ask the government to do for us we ask it to do for all. Hence we delegate to government the duty to treat others as we wish to be treated ourselves. The idea that we *entrust* government to act as trustee on our behalf, along with acknowledgment of the golden rule, grounds our rights along with the rights of others, as it grounds government's obligations.

Fourth, *the trust conception explicitly prohibits waste.* A trustee's job is the conservation and enhancement of assets, and this has direct consequences for action. The fiduciary model recognizes that we have an obligation to leave material resources we find available for our use in a condition at least as good as the one we found them in. In *Second Treatise,* for example, Locke states that a man is entitled to appropriate from the commons whatever he has expended his labor on, "at least where there is enough, and as good left in common for others."[18] There is a duty to protect and conserve the commons for others, including future generations.

Edith Brown Weiss has developed the terms of the trust conception along similar lines in her article "The Planetary Trust: Conservation and Intergenerational Equity,"[19] an application of the trust idea to the emerging issues of planetary management. As presented by Weiss, the fiduciary trust framework imposes two duties on each living generation. One is the duty of *conserving options* so that future generations can survive and pursue their own visions of the good life. We are obligated to preserve biological diversity so that the benefits of a diverse gene pool will be available to our descendants. And we should conserve natural resources or invest in substitutes so as to leave our descendants as many choices with respect to resources as we have. Lastly, under this duty we should preserve our cultural heritage so that future persons can have enriched lives and learn from our mistakes and successes. The second duty concerns the *conservation of quality,* an obligation we discharge in two ways. One is by conserving natural resources and investing in substitutes so that the real prices of vital resources do not rise in the future. We are also obligated to conserve the unique natural resources of the world, such as places of unusual beauty, so that they can be enjoyed by our successors.

What bothered Locke most, in some ways, was that some people who owned potentially productive resources did not manage them for the common good. In *Some Thoughts Concerning Education* he wrote, "People should be accustomed from their cradles to spoil or waste nothing at all."[20]

On the fiduciary conception, waste in the management of resources can be understood in four different ways.[21] First, as the *over*harvesting of an otherwise sustainable resource so as to destroy the capacity of the resource to sustain itself. This would include overharvesting a forest or overfishing a bay. A second sense is the converse: the *under*harvesting of a replenishable resource, for example, letting a forest overmature to the point where trees that could otherwise be utilized die and become commercially unusable. (Of course, there are certain resources, those in the sacred sphere, that shouldn't be harvested at all. This concept of waste applies only to those goods that society has decided to assign to the sphere of the market.) In a third sense, waste refers to the *inefficient extraction* or use of a resource, for example by pumping oil wells at a rate that reduces the total amount that can be extracted, or using water for irrigation in a manner that needlessly loses much of it to evaporation. Fourth, waste can mean the *inefficient use* of a resource—using a furnace that sends unnecessarily large amounts of heat up a chimney, using a refrigerator that is poorly insulated, or a car that gets poor gas mileage. Government's role as trustee or steward of assets calls for policies to limit all these species of waste.

The fifth main element of the trustee's duties is that *the trustee must respect the virtues of commerce.* Securing a robust economy that provides for the needs of persons through trade and agriculture was one of Locke's primary concerns. Indeed much of the *Second Treatise,* written, of course, in a preindustrial period, is devoted to developing a theory that will ensure that productive resources, particularly agricultural land, will get into the hands of those who will use them productively, a goal that follows directly from Locke's abhorrence of waste. In an age—similar to ours—of uncertain harvests, malnutrition, and occasional famines, one would hardly expect otherwise.

> God gave the world to men in common; but since He gave it them for their benefit, and the greatest conveniences of life they were able to draw from it, it cannot be supposed He meant it should always remain common and uncultivated. He gave it to the use of the industrious and rational (and labor was to be his title to it), not to the fancy or covetousness of the quarrelsome and contentious.[22]

But the ultimate rationale for private appropriation of the commons is that it serve the common good.

> The provisions serving to the support of human life, produced by one acre of enclosed and cultivated land, are . . . ten times more, than those which are yielded by an acre of land, of equal richness, lying waste in common. And therefore he that enclosed land and has a greater plenty of the conveniences of

life from ten acres, than he could have from a hundred left to nature, may truly be said to give ninety acres to mankind.[23]

As Richard Ashcraft notes in his brilliant *Revolutionary Politics and Locke's Two Treatises of Government:*

> It is quite true that . . . under this view, particular individuals may be able to acquire considerable wealth as the outcome of their productive and beneficial actions, but to suggest that Locke ever sets men free from their natural law obligations such that wealth may be accumulated solely because individuals desire to do so and without social constraints on its employment is to reverse completely the thrust of his argument in *The Second Treatise.*[24]

In America the ordinary person believes, despite decades of court decisions to the contrary, that it is self-evident that private property holders can do whatever they want with the land they own. The trust conception puts these ideas in a different and unfavorable light and suggests constraints on titleholders' use of land so that the corpus of the trust is not lost or wasted. In the fiduciary conception, land is not something that can be used simply for the benefit of the present owner, but an asset that must be used for the common good as understood in a multigenerational context. It is a community resource. This view is compatible with the private ownership of real property, but the rights of the owner come with the responsibilities of a steward. Indeed, for Locke, even land that has been enclosed by someone "can still be looked on as waste"[25] and can legitimately be taken for the common benefit if it is not effectively cultivated. Private ownership and the market have their place, but in a larger moral framework.

Sixth, *the trust conception provides a framework for setting the obligations of foreign policy that is an alternative to the realism* that has dominated American foreign policy at least since the end of World War II.[26] Nowhere does Locke limit the scope of obligations to compatriots. He talks of our obligation to preserve all mankind, and this obligation creates a transboundary frame of reference for evaluating the conduct of other nations. It simply applies the golden rule across space: other governments have responsibilities of trusteeship, and we have obligations to help see that they are carried out.

The foundations of the alternative to realism are twofold. The first is the stipulation that "nature willeth the preservation of all mankind." The second is the principle that legitimate government can be derived only from the consent of the governed. In "Of Conquest," chapter 16 of *The Second Treatise,* Locke wrote: "Conquest is as far from setting up any government as demolishing a house is from building a new one in its place."[27] Legitimate governments have obligations to their citizens, and the legitimate national governments of the world are a community of democratically elected trustees. The trustees of one nation are obligated to respect the actions of other nations' governments with regard to the citizens of those nations. When living up to their duties as trustees, legitimate governments are to be free from interference in accord with the familiar idea of national sovereignty.

But the trust conception also provides the foundation for a powerful critique of the behavior of nations. Here is where it fills in the concept of transparent sovereignty in a much more satisfactory and full-bodied way than that associated with trade. Trustees that abuse or neglect fiduciary obligations may legitimately be held accountable by the community of nations for not discharging the obligations of the trust. The international community's treatment of the oppressive regime in South Africa for violating its fiduciary obligations toward its citizens shows that this is already done. Governments established without the consent of the governed, e.g., dictatorships, are obviously illegitimate. Nations that fail to respect the human rights of their own citizens are failing to discharge their responsibilities.

The trustee conception also provides a framework for addressing the *means* by which the duties of the trustee can be enforced. War is not, seen in this perspective, simply the continuation of politics by other means, as the realist Clausewitz would have it.[28] In foreign policy the trustee's fundamental duty to preserve humanity legitimates a form of modified pacifism. Since war involves the intentional killing of other persons, it violates the fundamental spirit of trusteeship. This creates a powerful presumption against it. But that presumption can be rebutted, and the tradition of just-war theory, which is compatible with and illuminated by the trustee model, provides the terms for setting out the rebuttals.[29] For example, a government that is otherwise discharging its duties may engage in war to repel an invasion—in fact, failure to do so would be a fundamental violation of fiduciary obligations to secure and foster the well-being of citizens.

When a government violates its duties to its citizens, the offending government may legitimately be sanctioned by other governments, or by international bodies such as the Organization of American States or the United Nations. When rights are systematically threatened or are not protected, or the health of the biosphere is significantly undercut, the most profound duties of the trustee are transgressed, and here other governments have the strongest obligations to intervene. But again, the underlying obligation of all trustees to preserve all humanity creates a strong presumption against force. Intervention, when time permits, should begin peacefully, diplomatically. Force is truly a last resort, to be relied upon only when all other means—from trade and other economic sanctions, to embargoes of nonhumanitarian goods and blockades—have failed.

For all of Locke's relevance to contemporary politics, his own understanding of trusteeship is lacking in one important respect. The scope of Locke's seventeenth-century moral concern is limited to human beings only. For Locke, "the earth and all that is therein is given to men for the support and comfort of their being."[30] Locke almost certainly has in mind here the passages from near the end of the first book of Genesis where God gives the earth and all the plants and animals to man for his use: ". . . have dominion over the fish in the sea, the birds in the air, the cattle, all wild animals on land, everything that creeps on the earth."[31] One of the obvious weaknesses of this point of view is that not everything in the world is, in any direct or immediate sense, useful to human beings. But more important, the findings of modern evolutionary biology obviously suggest a quite different perspective. The burden of much of Darwin's *The Descent of Man* is to argue that there is no basic difference in kind between humans and the other animals. For Darwin, humankind belongs to a community of indefinite age.

> Man with all his noble qualities, with sympathy he feels for the most debased, with benevolence which extends not only to other men but to the humblest living creature, with his god-like intellect which has penetrated into the movements and constitution of the solar system—with all these exalted powers—man still bears in his bodily frame the indelible stamp of his lowly origin.[32]

Indeed, a revision in the conception of the moral community we belong to seems to have been under way well before Darwin, though it does not reach as far back as Locke.[33] Expanding the scope of "community" in a way that takes into account the post-Darwinian conceptions of who "we" are broadens the scope but not the essential terms of the trust. The implications of acknowledging obligations of trusteeship to other species and even ecosystems has been articulately set out by ecologist Aldo Leopold in *A Sand County Almanac*. Leopold advocates a "land ethic" which

> changes the role of *Homo sapiens* from conquerer of the land-community to plain member and citizen of it. It implies respect for his fellow members, and also respect for the community as such.[34]

Of course, some of these obligations to the broader community of the biosphere will also be discharged in fulfilling the requirement to "leave enough and as good" for our descendants. Thus there is an obvious overlap between our obligations to our own descendants and to the communities that make up the biosphere itself.

Choosing the Trust Conception

Accepting the trustee model and actively applying it domestically and around the globe could transform the world. The reasons that favor the trust conception over the market model are numerous and overwhelming. The first and perhaps most obvious is that *the fiduciary conception captures the idea that governments and governors have a responsibility to care for citizens.* The notion that public servants hold a trust of service that they can betray or fail to live up to is common currency in our discussions about government, but the market model can make no sense of it. In fact the umpire model of government invoked by right-wing writers such as Milton Friedman[35] cannot even make sense of the duty of the trustee to behave carefully with the taxpayer's money! Umpires do not take care of money, trustees do. Of course, those who govern have responsibilities that go far beyond being careful with money, but the failure of the right to capture even that financial responsibility shows the poverty of its ideas.

Second, *the trust conception can help us decide what to do.* "Public goods" and "externalities" are key concepts of the market model, but these are formal terms that offer little guidance for political action. The idea of trusteeship, on the other hand, points to specific spheres of activity: conserving and enhancing natural resources as assets of the trust, and preserving the lives and capacities of persons. It can set the terms for deciding on things as diverse as the financing of public office, the preservation of our national parks, vaccinating our children, controlling population, and protecting the earth's ozone layer. It helps to set priorities and suggests a public agenda that reflects our deepest values.

Third, *the fiduciary conception has the capacity to address the special crises of natural resources and biostability we find ourselves faced with in the late twentieth century.* Market theorists, arguing that the market will ensure the efficient use of resources and generate alternatives and concentrating on aggregate supply, have held that scarcity is no longer a problem. Cornucopians like Julian Simon have made much of the fact that, for instance, the proven reserves of many resources such as fossil fuels continue to increase or at least remain constant in the face of *rising* use, while real prices are steady or falling. They point to the market as a fantastic creator of wealth, which since the end of the Middle Ages has generated unprecedented levels of income for large numbers of people. It has helped to replace, especially for Europe, a world in which there were chronic shortages of necessities like food, with a world of surpluses.

Indeed, the problem plaguing agriculture in many nations is not shortages but surpluses. Many of the world's agriculturally rich nations, such as the United States and many European countries, have explicit programs to *reduce* the amount of land that is farmed. If food shortages in the aggregate should redevelop, some of this excess capacity can be tapped again. Moreover, a portion of the large percentage of world grain production that is fed to livestock could be diverted to direct human consumption in the event it is needed. Indeed, in years of small harvests the market tends to make this allocation itself, by increasing the price of grain and thus causing livestock owners to reduce the amount of grain fed per animal, or the number of animals, or both. Further still, as the techniques of modern competitive agriculture take hold in parts of the former Soviet Union, it is probable that these regions will change from grain-deficit to grain-surplus arenas—though the timing of this turnaround is difficult to estimate.

But despite the successes of the market, waste is still a fundamental issue that political theory must address. First, food, water, and clean air are scarce for many people right now. The number of people in the world who are malnourished now is between 350 million and one billion.[36] Water for drinking, bathing, and irrigation is chronically short in many places.[37] Air pollution is so severe in many Third World cities as to be a major factor in ill health.[38] Because people like Friedman and Simon have nothing to say about distributive justice, their fascination with the *aggregate* success of the market blinds them to this ongoing violation of the terms of the trust. The trustee model, on the other hand, makes it a central concern by insisting on the preservation of all mankind.

The most honest answer to the question of whether the world is about to enter a *global* crisis in the supply of food or other natural resources would seem to be no. Not in the next decade. And perhaps not in the decade following that. But this doesn't mean that Malthus may not ultimately be right: the human population may outrun the food supply, though there is no evidence that we are near that threshold yet in the aggregate. Will there be severe shortages of the natural resources necessary to run a modern economy in the middle of the next century? Here, an honest answer can only be that we just don't know. Projections of future human populations could be off by several billion in either direction. We don't know what the rate of technological innovation will be and hence do not know what substitutes will be found for resources that would otherwise be in short supply.

But whatever the future holds there is now a *new kind of scarcity*. The very success of industrialized market economies is leading to a scarcity of ecological diversity and stability, and of coherent human communities. *Indeed, the problem in some dimensions is not that, in the intermediate term, we will run out of some of the basic inputs of industrialized economies, but that we won't.* Ecological diversity and stability are threatened around the globe by habitat destruction for housing and commercial development, the harvest of forest products, nonsustainable agriculture, the introduction of exotic species, pesticides, and a variety of other forces. But still more fundamental threats exist: the growth in the human population; the release of heat-trapping and other gases such as nitrogen, which are the byproducts of economic activity; and the thinning of the earth's protective ozone layer. These three factors are causing unprecedented biospheric disequilibria.

Perhaps the ultimate failure of the market model is its inability to take into account the fact that the economy is dependent on the biosphere. Suppose we did everything in accordance with the market model as presented by Friedman, or the more promising model that is the tradition of the center: markets would be competitive, the proper mix of public goods supplied, and all externalities would be internalized. *This leaves unaddressed the question of whether the resulting mix of human economic activity can be sustained by the biosphere on which it depends.* Indeed, the issue of biospheric health and integrity is off the scope of modern economics as a whole, while on the trustee conception it is a central concern.

A fourth reason for preferring the trust model is that *in recognizing our unavoidable interdependence, the trust conception rests on a more plausible account of our moral obligations than the market-failure model.* Trusteeship puts concern for the well-being of people, especially the vulnerable, at the center of government responsibility. Caring for each other is something that is unavoidable, not an anomaly to be explained in an otherwise self-interested model. What is at stake can best be captured by what Robert Goodin has called "the vulnerability model of obligations."[39] In this conception our fundamental responsibility is to *forestall threatened harms to one another.* The vulnerability model not only does a better job than the voluntaristic model in explaining how our obligations arise, it also does a better job of explaining what those obligations are. On the voluntaristic model I am obligated to do what I have agreed to do; but it provides no guidance as to what I should agree to do. The vulnerability model not only gives us a more plausible account of why we are obligated, but it fills in the details about what we should do. If my spouse is sick I should see that she gets appropriate medical care, sympathy, and my assistance in recovery. My help reduces her vulnerability. Even if I did not promise explicitly to do this, I would still have the obligation. The vulnerability model also explains our obligations to strangers, people to whom we are not linked by contract or promise. We may not justly pass by those outside our immediate community when they are in need. Their vulnerability and our ability to help yield obligation. At the same time our obligations do not extend to exhausting all our resources to assist others, or to forgoing our own journey, an insight captured by the New Testament story of the Good Samaritan.

Lastly, *the trust conception is comprehensive, since it contains an account of our obligations both through time and across space.* Most contemporary theories of the state provide no account of what we owe to noncompatriots, persons who live outside of our borders. But this cannot be satisfactory for two reasons. First, while theories of the nation-state assume that duties of justice stop at national borders, most accounts of morality refer to duties to all persons. Second, as the world gets more and more interconnected through the environment and trade, there is less reason than there ever was to believe that the effects of our actions stop at the border.

Once we see that traditional accounts of state legitimacy are unsatisfactory if they assume that duties stop at borders, it is an easy step to see that they are also inadequate if they see us as obligated only to our contemporaries. The results of our actions are no longer confined to the present, if indeed they ever were. One of the great strengths of the trustee model is that it gives an explicit account of our duties to future persons. Most theories of state obligation simply ignore the issue.

Defending the Trust Conception

An objection to the trust conception might hold that *in a variety of ways the trust model requires too much:* that it is too disruptive of our individual lives and plans by requiring excessive concern with the preservation of others. It is startling to note that the other-regarding aspects of the trustee conception are extremely modest when compared to the underlying moral assumptions of market-based models. The centrist market model finds its roots in classical utilitarianism, whose defects we have already considered. Recall that utilitarianism requires that we seek the greatest happiness of the greatest number. The market school accepts this obligation and then falsely claims that it can be discharged indirectly through voluntary exchanges. Note how strong the requirement is that *happiness* be maximized. It requires that our own projects and purposes always be subject to revision or cancellation if we could thereby achieve more happiness overall. If we are seeking something with a more modest account of our obligations to others, the trustee concern with only the *preservation* of all is far preferable. Ironically, the market account, which often seems so selfish, is at bottom altruistic in the extreme.

Nevertheless, the obligation to preserve all persons might seem especially demanding and disruptive once we recognize its global implications. But the underlying global duty of preservation is first of all an obligation of national governments. Our individual obligations are properly discharged indirectly through the governments of the world—the community of trustees.[40] The citizens of one nation have duties to those of another only when the other government does not or cannot discharge its duties. Trustees do have the conventional duties of aid in times when local resources are overwhelmed by natural disaster, civil strife, and the like, but their primary international duty is to work for a just world order where the rights of persons around the globe are satisfied by their own governments. Except for responding to natural disasters, in a just and well-ordered world we could legitimately attend only to compatriots.

This may be dismissed by realists as utopian. In the far from ideal world of the present, which is in part a result of an absence of coherent normative principles for governing international relations, the problem of how to deal with noncomplying states—international rogues—routinely arises. But as the twentieth century draws to a close with more than 100 millions persons dead as a result of war, it is the realists' position that must be seen as infeasible.

In the context of the trustee conception, response to governments that do not discharge their duties can be thought of, at least in the first stages, as *nations* adopting the principles outlined by Thoreau for individuals in *Civil Disobedience*.[41] A noncomplying state is in violation of a fundamental moral law, and the response of other nations should basically be noncooperation. Because of the interpenetrating nature of the world economy and the growing movement concerning basic human rights that is sweeping the globe, nonviolent material and moral persuasion should have more force than in the past. It is an important element of this nonviolent path not to let nations arm vast armies, so arms control is vital and must be enforced. Force should be used to deal with noncompliance only if it will save lives overall, though Thoreau might not have been comfortable with even this exception. In many cases the show of force may be sufficient.[42]

Trusteeship and the Preservation of Persons

Central to the idea of trusteeship is the obligation of the trustee to act in the interest of and discharge the obligations of the beneficiary of the trust. Though Locke's theory is often taken as a justification of private property rights, this overlooks the natural-law dimensions of his theory, which calls for "the preservation of all mankind." Conservative theorists interpret Locke's concept of property far too narrowly and ignore the fact that it makes perfect sense for Locke to talk of persons as having property in their religion.

Locke recognizes a cluster of three rights that are necessary for the preservation of persons: the right to bodily integrity and a moral and religious life of one's choosing, to participate in processes to elect those who govern, and the right to at least a minimal level of subsistence. Transparency of sovereignty along this dimension is to evaluate the behavior of governments as trustees with respect to their treatment and protection of their citizens concerning these rights.[43] Anyone who accepts the golden rule must also accept the idea of transparent sovereignty with respect to the protection of these three rights.

Trusteeship and the Preservation of the Biosphere

Central to the idea of state trusteeship is that the trustee is to conserve and enhance the assets of the trust for the citizens. The state is thus the steward of the natural world for this and future generations. The fact that many ecosystems on the earth's surface cross national boundaries gives further support to the interest of citizens of one state being able to "see into" the actions of others, and where treaties exist we must be able to check on compliance. The preservation and restoration of world commons like oceans, climates, and flyways further supports transparency, as does the proliferation of nation-states themselves. Free riders and deceivers can be detected only with transparency.

The idea that the life-support systems of the planet can be thought about in terms of discounted present values is anathema from the fiduciary point of view. On the contrary, the fiduciary state points in the familiar direction of sustainable yields as principles of forest and fisheries management and away from doctrines of complete substitutability. It favors what might be called "robust stewardship," on the grounds the many resources are not substitutable. For example, forests are not simply sources of wood but means to the preservation of the ecological health of streams and hatcheries.

It draws attention to the fact that some actions are irreversible, thus providing a philosophical ground for legislation like the endangered species act as a means for preserving not only resources but the aesthetic, moral, and religious choices of future generations with regard to nature. These arguments are especially easy to make in the context of the many religions which regard the natural world as God's creation.

Hence governments that do not protect the human rights of their citizens, or do not carry out their duties with regard to the global commons such as climate, oceans, and flyways, or fail to protect the biological diversity, forests, and farm- and marshlands within their borders are not discharging their fiduciary obligations. Land use and infrastructure planning, population control and reduction, and the management or avoidance of toxic substances are among the means to discharging these obligations.

A variety of compacts should be drawn up to outline these responsibilities. These would vary from human rights declarations and the Montreal Protocol already in place, the expansion of the Ramsar Convention for the protection of wetlands, and an international inventory of biodiversity and the strengthening of compacts to protect it. The climate convention signed at the 1992 conference in Rio de Janeiro should be considerably strengthened, and enforceable targets for greenhouse-gas reduction added.

Steps toward Transparency

The world sketched above is a long way from the one we have. The transition will not be easy, because the conduct to be regulated is that of those who do the regulation. But some steps can be taken now, and to some degree they are being taken already by nongovernmental organizations.

National Self-Reporting. Nations should be asked to report on their treatment of their own citizens with respect to human rights, and on their treatment of the common heritage of humankind.

Relying on the Independents. There are already groups such as Amnesty International, the Nature Conservancy, the Red Cross and Red Crescent, and many others who provide independent information with respect to the performance of the world's governments as trustees. The reports of these institutions should be compiled into an annual *Report on the World's Trustees,* which would reveal any conflicts between the self-reporting of nations and the findings of others.

Carrots. The OECD nations should increase their official development assistance (ODA) to the developing world to the percentage of gross national product (GNP) recommended by the OECD.[44] However, ODA should be conditioned on recipient nations' meeting the requirements of transparency.

Sticks. Additional sanctions, ranging from refusal to allow participation in the Olympics and trade sanctions and embargoes to the use of multinational peacekeeping and invasion forces, should be used to bring about compliance with the trustee standard of transparent sovereignty. Obviously, one should begin with the least violent sanctions. Because the United States has failed to preserve much of the common heritage of mankind that is within its borders, such sanctions should be applied against us.

How Trusteeship Makes the National Interest and State Autonomy Standards Useful

The national-interest standard, which is the core of realism, failed to provide an adequate framework for discussing the relationships between nations, in part because it left the concept of what was "legitimate" unanalyzed. By specifying the functions of governments, the trustee concept makes clear what it is that governments owe their own citizens, and those abroad. Once these duties have been discharged, governments are free to pursue the national interests as they see them. Similarly, these residuals are properly referred to as domestic concerns and can be legitimately screened from those who are not citizens or residents.

The system of sovereign states that evolved only a few centuries ago is under widespread attack from all directions. Transparent sovereignty will strengthen this system by restoring the public's trust in the institutions of government.

Notes

1. This chapter extends the arguments in my *Restoring the Public Trust* (Boston: Beacon Press, 1994) from domestic policy to international relations.

2. Charles R. Beitz, *Political Theory and International Relations* (Princeton: Princeton University Press, 1979).

3. Bernard Williams, "A Critique of Utilitarianism," in J. J. C. Smart and Bernard Williams, *Utilitarianism For and Against* (Cambridge: Cambridge University Press, 1973).

4. John Locke, *The Second Treatise of Government*, par. 156. All quotations of Locke's *Second Treatise* are taken from *The English Philosophers from Bacon to Mill*, ed. Edwin A. Burtt (New York: Modern Library, 1939), 403–503.

5. Locke, *The Second Treatise*, par. 124.

6. Ibid., par. 131.

7. This account of the duties of the trustee is taken, with modifications, from David C. Slade, Esq., *Putting the Public Trust Doctrine to Work*. Obtained from the Coastal States Association. Published November 1990.

8. Locke, *The Second Treatise*, par. 7.

9. Locke advances both theological and naturalistic arguments in favor of the idea that everyone counts. Theologically each person is a creation of God and valuable for that reason. But Locke also claims that persons in the state of nature "should be equal one amongst another without subordination or subjection" (*The Second Treatise*, par. 4).

10. John Locke, "*A Letter Concerning Toleration*," in *Locke on Politics, Religion, and Education* (New York: Collier Books, 1965), 104–46.

11. Locke, *The Second Treatise*, par. 222.

12. Ibid.

13. Locke's conception of rights roughly tracks with Henry Shue's tripartite cluster of rights set out in *Basic Rights* (Princeton: Princeton University Press, 1980).

14. Locke, *The Second Treatise,* par. 22.

15. Ibid., par. 27.

16. Locke is ambivalent on how much is owed the poor, though he says over and over again that persons with substantial property may not deny food and other necessities to those in need. See, for example, *The Second Treatise,* par. 183, where Locke writes: "He that hath and to spare must remit something of his full satisfaction, and give way to the pressing and preferable title of those who are in danger to perish without it."

17. Ibid., par. 129.

18. Ibid., par. 27.

19. Edith Brown Weiss, "The Planetary Trust: Conservation and Intergenerational Equity," *Ecology Law Quarterly* 2, no. 4 (1984): 495–581.

20. Quoted from Richard Ashcraft, *Revolutionary Politics and Locke's "Two Treatises of Government"* (Princeton: Princeton University Press, 1986), 266.

21. Here I follow Weiss, "Planetary Trust," 512–16.

22. Locke, *The Second Treatise,* par. 34.

23. Ibid., par. 37—later editions.

24. Ashcraft, *Revolutionary Politics,* 266.

25. Locke, *The Second Treatise,* par. 38.

26. I am indebted to Robert Sprinkle's discussion of realism in his unpublished manuscript "States, Corporations and the Ethics of Political Realism."

27. Locke, *The Second Treatise,* 175.

28. See, for instance, Roger Ashley Leonard, ed., *A Short Guide to Clausewitz on War* (New York: Capricorn Books, 1968), 57.

29. See, for example, Michael Walzer, *Just and Unjust Wars* (New York: Basic Books, 1977), for a discussion of the principles of just warfare.

30. Locke, *The Second Treatise,* par. 26.

31. Gen. 2:26, *Revised English Bible.* Lynn White, Jr., has suggested that the concept of "dominion" has done much to legitimate the destruction of the natural world—see "The Historical Roots of Our Ecological Crisis," *Science* 155, no. 3767 (10 March 1967): 1203–7—but this overlooks the responsibilities that go with a proper understanding of power, or dominion.

32. *Descent of Man,* 920.

33. As Keith Thomas notes in *Man and the Natural World* (New York: Pantheon Books, 1983): 242–43,

At the start of the early modern period, man's ascendency over the natural world was the unquestioned object of human endeavor. By 1800 it was still the aim of most people and one, moreover, which at least seemed firmly within reach. But by this time the objective was no longer unquestioned. Doubts and hesitations had arisen about man's place in nature in his relationship to other species. The detached study of natural history had discredited many of the early man-centred perceptions. A closer sense of affinity with the animal creation had weakened old assumptions about human uniqueness. A new concern for the sufferings of animals had arisen; and, instead of continuing to destroy the forests and uproot all plants lacking practical value, an increasing number of people had begun to plant trees and to cultivate flowers for emotional satisfaction.

These developments were but aspects of a much wider reversal in the relationship of the English to the natural world. They were part of a whole complex of changes which, in the later eighteenth century, had helped to overthrow many established assumptions and create new sensibilities of a kind that have gained in intensity ever since.

34. Aldo Leopold, *A Sand County Almanac* (New York: Oxford University Press, 1949), 240.

35. See for instance Milton Friedman, *Capitalism and Freedom* (Chicago: University of Chicago Press, 1982).

36. *World Resources* (New York: Oxford University Press, 1990), 8. In the "Food and Agriculture" chapter the following "mixed picture" is presented (84): (1) many of the gains from the green revolution have already occurred; (2) many regions have little potential for adding cropland, and what is in use is stressed to maintain current production practices; and (3) "the number of undernourished people has increased in absolute terms but has probably declined in percentage terms in most regions."

37. See *World Resources,* 6, 161–78.

38. Ibid., 8, 201–216.

39. This relies on Robert Goodin, *Protecting the Vulnerable* (Chicago: University of Chicago Press, 1985), 110.

40. This is far preferable to the onerous duties in classical utilitarianism, which makes us responsible for the *happiness* of all persons—far too strong a set of obligations to make it possible to preserve our own purposes and project. It is thus incompatible with a moral and religious life. This is brilliantly argued by Bernard Williams in his "Critique of Utilitarianism." It is also preferable to the account of Friedman, which says that we have *no* obligations to others, thus having an ethic that flies in the face of the fundamentals of the Judeo-Christian tradition. Welfare economics is still stuck with the principle of utility in principle, along with its requirement of too great an altruism, but dodges it in practice with the idea of the invisible hand and by not having any principle of distribution. The trustee doctrine steers a nice middle course between these two implausible accounts of our duties to noncompatriots.

41. Henry David Thoreau, *Walden and Civil Disobedience* (Cambridge, MA: Riverside Press, 1957).

42. The requirement to preserve all persons could seem to lead to distortions in another direction. How much should we spend to preserve someone? In an age of increasing sophistication of medical technologies, it could seem that trusteeship requires us to spend limitless amounts merely to keep people alive, a problem particularly acute with respect to the elderly. But the conception of the person as chooser and goal setter helps set the limit on expenditures: we are only obligated to keep those persons alive who have the potential for choice. By defining death as brain death we thus draw the line in the right place and keep the principle from being an open-ended authorization for expenditure.

43. *Subsidiarity.* National governments should also be transparent "from below." Local and regional groups should be strengthened which allow for more autonomy and control over resources within broad guidelines concerning respect for Locke's parsimonious list of human rights and global and national policies to protect the common heritage of mankind.

44. See for instance *1991 Report: Development Co-operation* (Paris: Organization for Economic Co-operation and Development, 1991).

8

War, Weapons, and Sustainability in the Post–Cold War Era

Michael T. Klare

When the Cold War finally drew to a close, many people in many countries hoped that the world community would at last be able to devote its full attention to other pressing international problems, in particular the problem of environmental degradation. For four decades, the attention of world leaders had been focused largely on military issues, especially the dangers arising from the ongoing arms competition between the United States and the Soviet Union. This competition consumed vast sums of money and so divided the international community that it was impossible to reach agreement on such vital world issues as the environment. It was widely assumed, therefore, that the end of the Cold War would not only free up enormous resources for common international sustainability endeavors but also permit increased global collaboration in the implementation of such efforts.

Unfortunately, things have not quite worked out that way. While the world does face a diminished risk of thermonuclear annihilation, and the rate of military spending has declined in some countries, a fresh outbreak of regional and internal conflict has diverted world leaders from other concerns and produced new schisms in the international community. The cost of U.N. peacekeeping operations has skyrocketed, and environmental concerns have again been pushed aside by issues of war and peace. And given the current state of affairs, we can have no confidence that this situation will improve anytime soon.

Unless this epidemic of armed conflict subsides, it is likely that international efforts to address the environment and other global problems will be subject to repeated setbacks and disappointments. This is true for several reasons:

1. *The Diversion of Global Resources.* Despite widespread hopes that the end of the Cold War would produce a significant reduction in global military spending, there has been only a modest decline in world military expenditures, and many nations continue to devote enormous sums to military purposes. Because of uncertainties regarding the level of military spending in Russia and the other former Soviet republics, it is difficult to put a precise figure on total world military expenditures, but current estimates place the figure at around a trillion dollars per year. Of this, approximately $240 billion is accounted for by military spending in the developing world—an amount that far exceeds total spending on health and education in less developed countries (LDCs).[1] So long as governments continue to devote sums on this scale to military preparedness and war, it will be difficult indeed to address critical environmental problems and to promote sustainable development in the Third World.

2. *The Environmental Effects of War.* Military preparation and warfare not only divert resources needed for sustainable development but also contribute to the further degradation of the environment. Research shows that military forces and arms industries, including the nuclear arms industry, are among the most prolific generators of toxic wastes and other threats to the environment.[2] The production of nuclear weapons, for instance, has produced vast quantities of radioactive materials for which no satisfactory method of long-term storage has yet been found.[3] Even more worrisome, the many ethnic and regional conflicts in Africa, the Middle East, Southeast Asia, and the Balkans have damaged fragile ecosystems and contributed to long-term environmental decline.[4] This damage has produced widespread hunger and starvation, created millions of new refugees, and spurred massive human migrations that in turn have been met with fresh bouts of anti-immigrant violence in many countries.[5]

3. *The Deepening of Local, National, and Global Schisms.* Perhaps even more damaging than the direct environmental impact of war and the preparation for war are such effects as intensified hostility between groups, clans, tribes, and states—hostility that prevents increased international cooperation in overcoming major environmental challenges. Although leaders of many nations pledged to work together in promoting sustainable development at the 1992 Earth Summit in Rio de Janeiro, the painful reality is that growing ethnic and regional conflict has deepened the divide between many countries and prevented government leaders from fulfilling promises made in Rio. So long as the world community remains so stressed and divided, it will prove very difficult to undertake major collaborative efforts in support of sustainable development.

4. *The Perpetuation of Traditional Concepts of Security.* Immediately after the Cold War's end, it was widely thought that states would abandon or downplay traditional concepts of "national security" based largely on territorial defense against external enemies, in favor of new concepts of "common security"

or "world security," based on cooperative international responses to global perils, including threats to the environment.[6] These concepts, as expressed in such documents as the Brundtland Commission's report *Our Common Future,* hold that the promotion of sustainable development is essential to the long-term safety and well-being of all human communities and thus should be accorded high priority by the world's governments. However, with the proliferation of ethnic and regional conflict, many governments, including that of the United States, are backing away from their commitment to such an approach and returning instead to more traditional concepts of security, with emphasis on military preparedness. Clearly, this trend is likely to result in a renewed emphasis on state-centered military endeavors at the expense of global environmental efforts.

Given these realities, it is evident that there is a close relationship between patterns of global conflict and the prospects for sustainable development. Unless the world community can overcome the divisive forces that are provoking regional and ethnic conflicts and release some of the resources that are now committed to military preparedness, our ability to promote sustainable development will remain limited. It is essential, therefore, that we better understand the causes and characteristics of modern wars, in order to enhance the world's capacity to prevent, ameliorate, and terminate armed conflict.

Analyzing Global Conflict

In attempting to characterize the momentous upheavals of the past few years, many analysts have used the metaphor of tectonic shifts, the movement of the giant plates that makes up the earth's rocky crust. Because these movements have the power to reshape continents and alter climates—sometimes cataclysmically—they represent an apt analogy for the dramatic changes now occurring in the human world. "Like the tectonic forces that move continents around on the surface of the earth," historian John Lewis Gaddis observed in 1992, the end of the Cold War and other recent developments suggest a massive shift in the "historic tectonics" of human civilization.[7]

The image of tectonic motion helps us to understand the scale of the changes now under way around the globe, and how surface events are the product of deeper sociohistorical forces. However, to adequately describe the security environment of the post–Cold War era, we need to supplement the tectonic metaphor with an additional image—one that effectively captures the profusion of ethnic, tribal, religious, and national conflicts that we see today.

To generate such an image, imagine that a large piece of glass is laid over a map of the world and then struck in several places by a large, heavy instrument: the result would be an intricate web of cracks spread across the world, with heavier concentrations in some areas but nowhere left unscathed. These cracks represent the many fissures in our multiethnic, multiclass, and multilingual societies—the divisions between rich and poor, black and white, Hindu and Muslim,

Muslim and Jew, Serb and Croat, Azeri and Armenian, Czech and Slovak, and so on. These fissures are being stressed by the tectonic shifts occurring beneath the surface, but it is along their jagged edges that the wars of the post–Cold War era are being fought.[8] However, to best describe this environment of conflict it is useful to combine the images: tectonic movements causing massive shifts *beneath* the surface that in turn accentuate and extend the cracks appearing *on* the surface.[9]

Tectonic Shifts

It is risky, of course, to attempt an analysis of these "tectonic shifts" when the world is still undergoing a process of profound transformation. But enough has already occurred on the surface for us to be able to begin to understand what is happening below. Four such shifts in particular are worthy of discussion:

1. *The Growing Pull of Economic Forces.* Not so long ago the "fate of nations" was determined largely by political and military factors—most significantly, the ability of the state to marshal a country's resources for war, conquest, or defense. Today, the state remains a major international actor, but its capacity to marshal resources for its purposes has been circumscribed by what has been called "supranational capitalism." As suggested by economist Robert L. Heilbroner, the global nexus of multinational corporations and international financial institutions has accumulated vast power and influence at the expense of national capitalism and state agencies. This, Heilbroner notes, endows supranational capitalism with the capacity "to rearrange the global division and distribution of political and economic power"—a capacity that when exercised is often "seismic" in its impact.[10]

It is, of course, impossible to establish a one-to-one correlation between broad economic phenomena and particular world events. But there is no doubt that the inability of the Soviet Union and its client states in Eastern Europe to keep pace with economic growth in the West contributed to the debilitation of communist regimes. Unable to generate funds for investment in economic and social revitalization, these regimes fell into stagnation and lost what remained of their political legitimacy. The result was a rapid slide from power, with little resistance from what had become a corrupt and demoralized ruling class.

The same economic forces are now exacerbating conflicts around the world. Because some groups and societies have adapted more successfully than others to the competitive pressures of global capitalism, socioeconomic divisions in multinational states are becoming more visible and pronounced, provoking increased conflict between those on opposite sides of these rifts. Thus, the breakup of Yugoslavia can be attributed partially to the desire of its stronger economic units, Croatia and Slovenia, to break away from their more disadvantaged fellow republics and to integrate more closely with the Western European economies. Similarly, the breakup of Czechoslovakia can be attributed in part to growing resentment in Slovakia over the faster pace of economic activity in the Czech Republic.

Even more destabilizing, perhaps, is the growing economic rift between the industrialized "North" and underdeveloped "South." Although some Third World countries have in recent years managed to join the ranks of the more affluent nations, most of the less-developed countries of Asia, Africa, and Latin America have seen the gap between their standard of living and that of the wealthier countries widen over the past decade. At the same time, the global spread of Western culture and consumption patterns via the mass media has given Third World populations an appetite for goods and services not attainable by the masses of the poor and unemployed. The result is increased North–South tensions of various sorts, ranging from the growing militancy of political and religious movements with anti-Western themes (for example, the Sendero Luminoso in Peru and the Muslim Jihad in Egypt) to increased South-to-North drug smuggling. Depressed economic conditions in the South are also causing increased migration to the nations of the North, itself a growing cause of violence in the latter.[11]

2. *The Global Diffusion of Power.* Accompanying the growth of supranational capitalism has been a continuing diffusion of political, military, and economic power from the United States and the Soviet Union—the two "poles" of the Cold War era—to other actors in the international system. As yet, no clearly defined system of power relationships has developed in place of the bipolar system and the tight alliances of the Cold War era. Rather, we see the emergence of a number of regional power centers—Japan in Asia, Germany in Europe, Russia in central Eurasia, the United States in North America—each of which is surrounded by a cluster of associated states. These centers cooperate with each other in some matters and compete in others; other states, not aligned with any of the main clusters, are forced to manage as best they can.[12]

The diffusion of political and military power and the realignment of global power relationships has multiple implications for world security. With the erosion of superpower influence and the proliferation of modern weapons, some newly strengthened regional powers have perceived a greater opportunity to pursue their own hegemonic ambitions, often provoking fierce conflict in the process, as in the case of Iraq's 1980 invasion of Iran and its 1990 invasion of Kuwait. Furthermore, the collapse of central state control over the outlying areas of the former Soviet Union has resulted in a series of ethnic and territorial clashes within and between former republics of the USSR. And the worldwide diffusion of modern weapons has contributed to the duration and intensity of regional, ethnic, and insurgent conflicts.

3. *Increased Popular Assertiveness at the Grassroots Level.* Paralleling the growth of globalized economic institutions and the diffusion of political power

among international players is the increased assertion of "people's power" at the local and national level. Wherever we look in the world today, we find grassroots citizens movements for fundamental change in key social, economic, and political structures. In some areas, including China, Haiti, the Philippines, Eastern Europe, and the former Soviet Union, this assertiveness has entailed a powerful drive for democratic rights; it has also, however, appeared as antiforeigner sentiment in Germany and increased anti-Semitism in Russia.

By far the most potent expression of this grassroots assertiveness is the militant expression of ethnic, national, linguistic, and religious affiliations by peoples who have previously lived relatively peacefully in multinational, multicultural societies. This expression takes many forms: the calls for secession by the constituent nationalities of the former Soviet Union and Yugoslavia; the militant assertion of Hindu fundamentalism in India; the Kurdish rebellion in Iraq; and the Palestinian Intifada. As suggested by Myron Weiner of MIT, " 'Peoples'— however they identify themselves by race, religion, language, tribe, or shared history—want new political institutions or new relationships within existing institutions"; when accommodation is not forthcoming, they are likely to escalate their demands in one way or another.[13]

The growing assertion of populist claims, whether of a political or ethnic nature, has significant implications for world security. At the very least, it is jeopardizing the ability of current leaders—in the North and South, the East and West—to retain their grip on power. In many areas, it has led to violent clashes between opposing groups. And in Yugoslavia, it has ignited a maelstrom of ethnic fury that threatens to engulf much of southeastern Europe.

4. *Population Growth and Environmental Decline.* The erosion of the state's authority and the intensification of ethnic disputes has been accelerated, in many cases, by a fourth tectonic force: rapid population growth and the discovery of harsh environmental limits. Population growth has not been by itself a cause of instability—historically, it has often contributed to the health and vigor of societies, as in the case of the United States. But when it exceeds the rate of economic growth, as in many Third World countries today, and when it contributes to the depletion of scarce resources, such as tropical forests and tillable soil, the ability of states to engage in long-term economic and social development is impaired— thus ensuring worse hardship and unrest in the future. The world's population now stands at about 5.6 billion people, and this figure is expected to double by the middle of the twenty-first century. Such an increase could theoretically be sustained if the world's resources were evenly distributed, and if new synthetics were developed to replace those natural substances that are being depleted. But the world's resources are *not* evenly distributed, and it is unclear that such new products as may be developed will be available at an affordable price to all those in need of them. As things stand now, many states in Asia, Africa, and Latin America (three regions where population growth rates are near an all-time high)

are not able to provide for growing numbers of young people, and will be less able to do so in the future. The consequences include a rising incidence of hunger and malnutrition, increased migration from the impoverished countryside to urban shantytowns, soaring unemployment (especially among the young), and the growing popularity of such extremist movements as the Sendero Luminoso in Peru, the Muslim Jihad in Egypt, the Bharatiya Janata Party in India, and the communist New Peoples' Army in the Philippines.[14]

Even if population growth is stabilized, moreover, the world would still be faced with intergroup conflicts arising from environmental decline. Although research on the conflictual consequences of environmental degradation is still sparse, enough is now known to indicate that ecological damage, especially when occurring in environmentally stressed areas of the Third World such as deserts, rain forests, hillsides, and coastal lowlands, can exacerbate intergroup competition and drive still more people into crowded urban shantytowns in foreign countries, where the prospects of meaningful employment are poor and the risk of unrest is high.[15]

Battle Lines

These "tectonic forces" act upon the peoples, states, and societies of the world in such a way as to exacerbate existing intergroup tensions and, in many cases, to provoke and intensify conflict. The resulting struggles take several forms, all of which have become all too common features of the current global environment. Of these, the four most significant are:

1. *Regional Rivalries.* The breakdown of the bipolar system and the accompanying diffusion of political power has given added impetus to interstate rivalries at the regional level, especially in East Asia, southern Asia, and the Middle East. Of particular concern are the continuing rivalries between China and Taiwan, North Korea and South Korea, India and Pakistan, Iran and Iraq, Iran and Saudi Arabia, Syria and Iraq, and Israel and Syria. These rivalries have all flared up periodically in the past, but they seem to have gained renewed intensity in recent years, as the inhibiting influence of the superpowers has declined and regional power equations have become more unsettled and uncertain. There could, in fact, be fresh outbreaks of fighting in several of these conflicts in the latter 1990s.

Several key factors will bear upon the relative propensity for renewed fighting among these pairs of adversaries. These include the degree of progress (or lack of it) in regional peace negotiations; the degree to which these states are hobbled by internal power struggles; the relative ability of the United States—now the world's sole superpower—to discourage adventurism on the part of regional powers; and the impact of global economic conditions on the ability and inclination of these states to engage in external conflict. No one can predict how these factors will play out in the years ahead, but it is reasonable to assume that a breakdown in the Mideast peace talks (or in other regional negotiations), coupled with a decline in U.S. influence and/or the emergence of aggressive leaders in one or more of these states, would increase the risk of new conflagrations.

Another key factor in all of this is the impact of weapons proliferation on the dynamics of conflict between regional rivals. All of the states named above are currently engaged in major military buildups of one sort or another—in many cases involving weapons of mass destruction—and thus every one of them has a reason to fear the arms acquisition programs of their adversaries; should any one of these powers achieve a sudden and unexpected increase in its net military capabilities—through, say, the acquisition of nuclear weapons or ballistic missiles—it could invite a preemptive strike on the part of its rival.[16]

2. Nationalism and Irredentism. Accompanying the breakup of large multinational states like Yugoslavia and the former Soviet Union has been a global surge in ethno-nationalist and irredentist pressures as groups that have been denied a state in the past—or have had their state submerged in a larger multinational entity—seek to establish—or reestablish—one, and as groups that are already in possession of a state seek to enlarge it so as to incorporate adjacent territories occupied by large numbers of their kinsmen. Such impulses have long been a major source of conflict, but seem to have gained renewed vigor in recent years, as the bipolar system has broken down and the balance of power between state authorities and populist forces has shifted in favor of the latter.[17]

Nationalist aspirations are at the heart of many of the conflicts now under way in the world, including those in Abkhazia, East Timor, Kashmir, Tibet, the West Bank and Gaza, and the Kurdish-occupied lands of Iran, Iraq, and Turkey. Major irredentist struggles include the Serbian's campaign to create a "Greater Serbia" out of the remnants of the former Yugoslavia, Armenia's push to gain control over Nagorno-Karabakh (now controlled by Azerbaijan), Russia's drive to repossess the Crimean Peninsula (ceded to Ukraine in 1954 by Nikita Khrushchev), and China's continuing efforts to repossess Taiwan. In addition, many security analysts fear that irredentist forces in Hungary will press for the incorporation of Hungarian-speaking regions of Slovakia, Rumania, and the former Yugoslavia into a "Greater Hungary."[18]

3. Revolutionary and Fundamentalist Crusades. Although the appeal of Soviet-style communism has largely disappeared, other revolutionary and millennarian movements continue to attract downtrodden and dispossessed peoples in many areas of the world. Such movements promise not just a change in government leadership, but also a sweeping transformation of society itself, typically involving the elimination of existing societal institutions and their replacement by more "righteous" or egalitarian structures. Movements of this sort appear to be gaining strength in areas where economic conditions have worsened for the majority, or for particular groups within society, and where the capacity or inclination of state authorities to overcome widespread impoverishment and inequity has diminished. In such areas, revolutionary and millennarian groups appear increasingly willing to employ violence in their efforts to transform society.

At present two major types of revolutionary crusade can be discerned: ideological or political movements, usually entailing a drive to end the exploitation of the poor by the middle classes and the rich; and religious fundamentalism, entailing a drive to subject all societal interactions to religious law and practice. Examples of the first type include the Sendero Luminoso in Peru, the Khmer Rouge in Cambodia, and the New Peoples' Army in the Philippines; examples of the second type include the Hindu fundamentalist Bharatiya Janata Party in India, the Islamic Salvation Front in Algeria, the Muslim Jihad in Egypt, and the various Islamic fundamentalist forces in Afghanistan.

4. *Democratic and Anticolonial Movements.* Lastly, the world is confronted with an assortment of prodemocracy and anticolonial movements in a number of areas—movements that tend to erupt periodically in strikes or civil disorders and/or to provoke repressive violence by the prevailing authorities. All of these movements reflect the tectonic increase in grassroots activism described earlier, and while they may experience setbacks in the short term, they are not likely to disappear or recede any time soon.

These movements take many forms, including popular drives for Western-style electoral democracy and human rights, as in Burma, China, Haiti, the Philippines, South Korea, Thailand, and Zaire; struggles by disenfranchised minorities (or majorities) to abolish unrepresentative or discriminatory governments, as in Northern Ireland; and efforts by subject peoples to cast off what are viewed as colonial systems of rule—even though the "colonizers" involved may be other Third World countries—as in East Timor, Kashmir, the Western Sahara, and the territories occupied by Israel.

Peacemaking, Peacekeeping, and Peace Enforcement

The tectonic forces described above and the intensification of internal, local, and regional conflict has placed enormous strain on the international community, forcing world leaders to expand U.N. peacekeeping operations and to consider new and enhanced methods of conflict control. The development of such methods, and their application to actual conflicts, is likely to remain a critical issue in world security affairs for the foreseeable future.

With the Cold War over and the superpowers no longer assuming responsibility for the maintenance of peace and stability within their respective spheres of influence, a greater burden has naturally fallen on the United Nations, which has responded by greatly expanding its peacemaking and peacekeeping operations around the world. Between 1988 and 1992, the United Nations established thirteen new peacekeeping operations—exactly the number initiated by the world body in the forty-two years of its existence up until that point.[19] At the end of 1994, UN peacekeeping forces were serving in Angola, Cyprus, El Salvador, Georgia, the Golan Heights, Haiti, Kashmir, the Kuwait–Iraq border, Lebanon, Liberia, Mozambique, Rwanda, the Sinai, Somalia, the former Yugoslavia, and the Western Sahara; all told, some 71,500 military and police personnel were involved in these operations.[20]

These operations have contributed to stability in many areas of the world and given the United Nations enhanced international visibility and respectability. And, while some have encountered setbacks and difficulties of various sorts, most analysts agree that conditions in these areas would probably be much worse without the presence of the United Nations' "blue helmets." Nevertheless, world leaders generally agree that current UN capabilities and methods will not be adequate to meet the wide range of conflicts and security challenges expected in the years to come. (Between 1948 and 1994, the United Nations spent $10.4 billion on peacekeeping operations, or an average of $226 million per year; in 1994, the cost of such operations was estimated at $3.8 billion and it was assumed that this figure would continue to rise in the years ahead.[21]) Accordingly, the UN Security Council has called upon Secretary-General Boutros Boutros-Ghali and his staff to suggest ways in which the United Nations' peacemaking activities can be improved. The development and implementation of these suggestions is likely to be the organization's top priority in the mid 1990s.

To inform the discussion of peacemaking initiatives, Boutros-Ghali published *An Agenda for Peace* in June of 1992. In this document, the Secretary-General identifies five key areas in need of improvement: *preventive diplomacy,* diplomatic efforts to avert conflict by persuading hostile parties to seek negotiated settlements; *peacemaking,* efforts to persuade nations already at war to cease their fighting and to settle their differences at the bargaining table; *peacekeeping,* the use of UN forces to monitor cease-fires and to prevent the reignition of hostilities; *peace enforcement,* the use of force to prevent or resist aggression by a belligerent in violation of UN resolutions; and postconflict *peace building,* efforts designed to alleviate human suffering and thus eliminate conditions that might contribute to the renewal of fighting. Boutros-Ghali proposed a number of initiatives in each of these areas and broke new ground by calling for the formation of a permanent peacekeeping force under United Nations control (currently such units comprise contingents drawn from the forces of member states on an ad hoc basis).[22]

The development of new approaches to the control of local and regional conflict has also been a matter of great concern in the United States, which has been under great pressure to step in and resolve certain ongoing crises, notably those in Bosnia and Somalia. While some U.S. leaders would prefer to delegate all such activities to the United Nations, others, including Presidents Bush and

Clinton, contend that the United States has an obligation to act in certain cases where no other option appears viable. Thus in December 1992, Mr. Bush ordered U.S. forces deployed in Somalia in order to restore order and protect the delivery of relief supplies. This action, and others of a like nature proposed by President Clinton, such as the venture into Haiti, have sparked a heated debate in this country over where and under what circumstances U.S. forces should be employed in such operations.[23]

Whatever the outcome of future debates in the United States and the United Nations on the use of force in humanitarian and peacekeeping operations, it is apparent that the problem of preventing and controlling local, ethnic, and regional conflict has become the most urgent world security concern of the post–Cold War era. Because such conflicts are likely to proliferate in the years ahead, and because no single power or group of powers is willing and able to assume full responsibility for the maintenance of global peace and stability, U.S. and world leaders will be forced to enhance existing peacemaking instruments and to develop new techniques along the lines suggested by Boutros-Ghali and others.[24]

Proliferation and Nonproliferation

Adding to the dangers posed by all of the patterns of conflict described above is the global proliferation of modern weapons and the technologies for producing them. Such proliferation entails not only the spread of nuclear, chemical, and biological (NCB) weapons—the so-called "weapons of mass destruction"—but also a wide range of "conventional" arms—the tanks, planes, guns, and missiles used by regular military forces. These weapons, both NCB and conventional, are finding their way into the arsenals of more and more nations, thereby stimulating local arms races and ensuring that future wars will be ever more lethal and destructive.[25]

The cumulative effects of proliferation can be measured by the growing military capabilities of recipient countries. Thus, in the nuclear realm, we find that the five declared nuclear powers—the United States, Russia, Great Britain, France, and China—have been joined by three undeclared nuclear powers—Israel, India, and Pakistan; Iran, Iraq, North Korea, and other would-be nuclear powers continue their efforts to develop such weapons, and several others retain a capacity to do so in the future, including Argentina, Brazil, South Africa, South Korea, and Taiwan.[26] U.S. intelligence officials have identified fourteen Third World countries that are believed to possess offensive chemical-warfare capability: Burma, China, Egypt, India, Iran, Iraq, Israel, Libya, North Korea, Pakistan, South Korea, Syria, Taiwan, and Vietnam.[27] Many of these countries have also engaged in research on biological weapons and have acquired ballistic missiles that can be used to deliver NCB warheads.[28]

Complementing the spread of NCB weapons and ballistic missiles is the proliferation of advanced conventional weapons. According to the Congressional Research Service, Third World countries spent an estimated $339.5 billion (in constant 1990

U.S. dollars) on imported weapons from 1983 to 1990—an amount that translated into some 13,010 tanks and self-propelled guns, 27,430 heavy artillery pieces, 2,920 supersonic combat planes, 38,430 surface-to-air missiles, and 53,790 surface-to-surface missiles, among other weapons.[29] These were used to sustain the Iran–Iraq war of 1980–88 and other regional conflicts, and to enlarge the arsenals of emerging powers in Africa, Asia, and Latin America.[30]

Arms proliferation is certain to remain a major security concern in the 1990s and beyond because it increases the danger that future wars will entail the use of chemical and/or nuclear weapons. We have already witnessed the extensive use of chemical weapons in the Iran–Iraq war, and in Iraq's subsequent campaign to liquidate Kurdish villages in strategic border areas. Chemical attacks were also threatened by Iraq against Israel in 1990 and 1991, leading Israeli officials to threaten possible retaliation with nuclear arms.[31] And officials of the Central Intelligence Agency have reported that India and Pakistan were prepared to use nuclear weapons in 1990, when it was feared that the fighting in Kashmir would spark a full-scale conflict.[32] Clearly, as the number of states with such capabilities increases, so does the risk that a major regional conflict will trigger the unintended or accidental use of NCB munitions.

In response to these perils, the world community has attempted to shore up existing nonproliferation regimes and to establish new ones in areas where none now exist. The existing regimes covering NCB weapons and ballistic missiles consist of the Nuclear Non-Proliferation Treaty (NPT), signed in 1968; the London Nuclear Suppliers Group (an association of producers of nuclear equipment who agree to restrict their exports of sensitive technology and materials); the 1925 Geneva Protocol for the Prohibition of the Use in War of Asphyxiating, Poisonous or Other Gases, and of Bacteriological Methods of Warfare; the Chemical Weapons Convention (CWC), signed in 1993 and not yet ratified; the Australia Group (an association of chemical producers who agree to restrict their exports of chemical weapons precursors); the Biological Weapons Convention (BWC), signed in 1972; and the Missile Technology Control Regime (MTCR), established in 1987.[33]

All of these treaties and agreements have proved effective in controlling some forms of NCB proliferation, and all have proved deficient in other areas.[34] As a result, determined proliferators such as India, Iran, Iraq, Israel, Libya, Pakistan, North Korea, and Syria have succeeded in acquiring the technology to produce nuclear and/or chemical weapons as well as ballistic missiles.[35] The United States and other major powers have attempted to strengthen the various nonproliferation regimes by expanding their membership, tightening restrictions, increasing the number and intrusiveness of allowable inspections, and bolstering the sanctions that can be applied in cases of unambiguous noncompliance.[36] These efforts are not likely to prevent all forms of NCB proliferation, but they will make it more difficult for prospective proliferators to obtain sensitive materials and technology.

Unfortunately, no such progress has been made in the field of conventional weapons. After the Persian Gulf War, representatives of the five permanent members of the UN Security Council (the United States, Russia, Britain, France, and China) met in Europe to develop some common guidelines for the control of conventional arms exports, but these talks foundered in 1992 when the Bush administration agreed to sell 150 F–16 fighters to Taiwan, and China, in protest, announced that it was pulling out of the talks. The United Nations has since established a voluntary "register" of member states' arms exports and imports but has not imposed any restrictions on what can be transferred from country to country. Thus at this point there are no international restraints on the trafficking of conventional arms, and likely belligerents in the Middle East and elsewhere have been able to stockpile large quantities of munitions.[37]

Conclusion

It is essential to develop improved methods of conflict control and avoidance for many reasons: to reduce the level of death and destruction in the world, to prevent the spread and escalation of conflict, to discourage the outbreak and extension of costly arms races, and to foster the development of democratic societies. These are, of course, more than sufficient grounds for seeking a reduction of global violence, but to these long-standing concerns, a new reason must be added: without such a reduction it will not be possible to mobilize global resources for sustainable development.

Without sustainable development, the deterioration of the global environment will accelerate and the economic divide between North and South, haves and have-nots, will widen, thus ensuring the further proliferation of ethnic and regional conflict. But unless we can reduce global levels of conflict and violence, we will not be able to undertake the measures needed to promote sustainable development. Clearly, we will have to make progress on both fronts simultaneously if we hope to make progress on either. How to do this is something that will require further study and experimentation, but it is painfully evident that the two sets of concerns cannot be separated.

Notes

1. Data extrapolated from U.S. Arms Control and Disarmament Agency, *World Military Expenditures and Arms Transfers 1991–1992* (Washington, DC: ACDA, 1994); and Ruth Leger Sivard, *World Military and Social Expenditures 1991* (Washington, DC: World Priorities, 1991).

2. See Bruce Van Voorst, "A Thousand Points of Blight," *Time,* 9 November 1992, 68–69.

3. See Matthew L. Wald, "U.S. is Unprepared to Disarm A-Bombs," *New York Times,* 24 September 1993.

4. For discussion of the environmental effects of warfare, see Stockholm International

Peace Research Institute, *Warfare in a Fragile World: Military Impact on the Human Environment* (London: Taylor and Francis, 1980).

5. For discussion of the relationship between environmental decline on one hand and ethnic combat, refugee flows, and migratory pressures on the other, see Thomas Homer-Dixon, "Environmental Scarcity and Intergroup Conflict," in *World Security: Challenges for a New Century*, 2d ed., ed. Michael T. Klare and Daniel C. Thomas (New York: St. Martin's Press, 1994), 290–313.

6. For discussion of these concepts see Seyom Brown, "World Interests and the Changing Dimensions of Security," in Klare and Thomas, *World Security*, 10–26. On the environmental dimension of the new security thinking, see Jessica Tuchman Mathews, "The Environment and International Security," in Klare and Thomas, *World Security*, 274–89.

7. John Lewis Gaddis, "Tectonics, History, and the End of the Cold War," occasional paper from the Mershon Center of the Ohio State University, Columbus, 1992, 4.

8. Most contemporary conflicts are described in Stockholm International Peace Research Institute, *SIPRI Yearbook 1993: World Armaments and Disarmament* (Oxford: Oxford University Press, 1993), 81–170.

9. The author first provided an analysis of this sort in "The New Challenges to Global Security," *Current History* (April 1993): 155–61.

10. Robert L. Heilbroner, "The Future of Capitalism," in *Sea Changes: American Foreign Policy in a World Transformed*, ed. Nicholas X. Rizopoulus (New York: Council on Foreign Relations, 1990), 114–15.

11. For discussion see Dennis Pirages, "Demographic Change and Ecological Insecurity," in Klare and Thomas, *World Security*, 314–31; Ivan L. Head, "South–North Dangers," *Foreign Affairs* 68, no. 3 (Summer 1989): 71–86.

12. For discussion see Lawrence Freedman, "Order and Disorder in the New World," *Foreign Affairs* 71, no. 1 (Winter 1991/92): 25–30.

13. Myron Weiner, "Peoples and States in a New Ethnic Order?" *Third World Quarterly* 13, no. 2 (1992): 318.

14. For discussion see Pirages, "Demographic Change."

15. These findings emerge from the Project on Environmental Change and Acute Conflict, a joint study of the American Academy of Arts and Sciences and the Program on Peace and Conflict Studies of the University of Toronto. See Thomas Homer-Dixon, Jeffrey Boutwell, and George Rathjens, "Environmental Change and Violent Conflict," *Scientific American* (February 1993): 38–45; Homer-Dixon, "Environmental Scarcity."

16. For discussion of arms race dynamics in the Middle East, see Geoffrey Kemp, *The Control of the Middle East Arms Race* (Washington, DC: Carnegie Endowment for International Peace, 1992), 15–115.

17. For discussion see David L. Horowitz, "Ethnic and Nationalist Conflict," in Klare and Thomas, *World Security*, 175–87; Weiner, "Peoples and States," 218–22.

18. See Stephen Engelberg, "Now Hungary Adds Its Voice to the Ethnic Tumult," *New York Times*, 25 January 1993.

19. Boutros Boutros-Ghali, *An Agenda for Peace* (New York: United Nations, 1992), 28.

20. See Roger Hill, "Preventive Diplomacy, Peace-making, and Peace-keeping," in SIPRI, *SIPRI Yearbook 1993*, 45–65; Paul Lewis, "UN, Busier than Ever Globally, Struggles with Peacekeeping Role," *New York Times*, 25 January 1993; United Nations, "United Nations Peace-Keeping Operations," background note, July 1994.

21. U.N., "United Nations Peace-Keeping Operations."

22. Boutros-Ghali, *Agenda for Peace*, 11–34. For further discussion of these various types of peacemaking, see Hill, "Preventive Diplomacy."

23. See for instance William H. Lewis, ed., *Military Implications of United Nations Peacekeeping Forces* (Washington, DC: National Defense University, 1993); Elaine Sciolino, "The UN's Glow is Gone," *New York Times,* 9 October 1993; Donald M. Snow, *Peacekeeping, Peacemaking and Peace Enforcement: The U.S. Role in the New International Order* (Carlisle, PA.: U.S. Army War College, 1993).

24. For a discussion of such proposals, see Robert C. Johansen, "Building World Security: The Need for Strengthened International Institutions," in Klare and Thomas, *World Security,* 372–97.

25. For an overview of proliferation issues, see W. Thomas Wander and Eric H. Arnett, eds., *The Proliferation of Advanced Weaponry* (Washington, DC: American Association for the Advancement of Science, 1992); Jonathan Dean and David Koplow, eds., "Symposium: World Security and Weapons Proliferation," *Transnational Law and Contemporary Problems* 2, no. 2 (Fall 1992).

26. See Zachary Davis, "Nuclear Proliferation and Nonproliferation Policy in the 1990s," in Klare and Thomas, *World Security,* 106–33; Leonard Spector, *Nuclear Ambitions* (Boulder: Westview Press, 1990).

27. Prepared statement of Rear Admiral Thomas A. Brooks, Director of Naval Intelligence, before the Seapower Subcommittee of the House Armed Services Committee, Washington, DC, 7 March 1991, mimeographed, 58.

28. See Aspen Strategy Group, *New Threats: Responding to the Proliferation of Nuclear, Chemical, and Delivery Capabilities in the Third World* (Lanham, MD.: Aspen Strategy Group; University Press of America, 1990).

29. Richard F. Grimmett, *Conventional Arms Transfers to the Third World, 1983–1990* (Washington, DC: Congressional Research Service, U.S. Library of Congress, 1991), 46, 74.

30. For discussion of the dynamics of the international arms trade see Klare, "Adding Fuel to the Fires: The Conventional Arms Trade in the 1990s," in Klare and Thomas, *World Security,* 134–54; Edward J. Laurance, *The International Arms Trade* (New York: Lexington Books, 1992); U.S. Congress, Office of Technology Assessment, *Global Arms Trade* (Washington, DC: OTA, 1991).

31. See Kemp, *Control of the Middle East Arms Race,* 101–112.

32. According to CIA proliferation expert Gordon Oehler, "When [India and Pakistan] were running up to the possibility of war, there was a real possibility that if it did go to war, it would be nuclear." Quoted in *Washington Times,* 31 October 1992.

33. For texts of the NPT, Geneva Protocol, and BWC, see U.S. Arms Control and Disarmament Agency, *Arms Control and Disarmament Agreements,* 1990 ed. (Washington, DC: ACDA, 1990). For current signatories of these agreements, see SIPRI, *SIPRI Yearbook 1993,* 765–81. For text of CWC, see SIPRI, *SIPRI Yearbook 1993,* 735–56. For discussion and comparison of these regimes, see Zachary S. Favis, *Nonproliferation Regimes: Policies to Control the Spread of Nuclear, Chemical, and Biological Weapons and Missiles* (Washington, DC: Congressional Research Service, 18 February 1993).

34. For discussion of the relative strengths and weaknesses of these regimes, see Davis, *Nonproliferation Regimes.*

35. For an assessment of proliferation activities, see Aspen Study Group, *New Threats.* More recent developments are covered in SIPRI, *SIPRI Yearbook 1993,* 240–53, 259–92, and earlier editions.

36. For discussion of these efforts, see Zachary Davis and Robert Shuey, *Current Issues in Non-Proliferation Regimes Policy* (Washington, DC: Congressional Research Service, 12 March 1993).

37. For discussion see Klare, "Adding Fuel."

Part Three

Sustainable Development and North–South Issues

Introduction

One of the most critical issues in moving toward a more sustainable world is the very important question of sustainable development. Although some claim this to be a contradiction in terms, it is obvious that development, as opposed to industrialization, can have many different meanings. Traditional forms of resource-intensive growth need not be confused with development of human potential. The mistakes of the industrial revolution, as it has unfolded in the global North, need not be repeated in the global South. It is, however, difficult to convince people that the images of the good life purveyed by the global media are not worthy of emulation. The investigation of the potential for and the nature of sustainable development has just begun, as has a global dialogue on how to nurture it.

One of the biggest impediments to future sustainable development is the rapid rate of population growth in much of the less industrialized world. Anne Ehrlich addresses the question of a sustainable global population in the first chapter of this section. Although the Earth's population has already passed through its period of most rapid growth, at its current rate of growth it will double in only forty-two years. Many less industrial areas of the world have already overshot the carrying capacity of the land, but populations continue to grow rapidly. While it is true that each person in the industrial world now walks much more heavily on the Earth in terms of resource consumption, the growing numbers of global poor aspire to consume as the rich now do. Ehrlich concludes that the human enterprise cannot be made sustainable until all countries recognize that the human race is collectively living beyond its means.

Herman Daly, one of the earliest advocates for "steady-state" societies, picks up on some of these themes, making the distinction between growth and development. The economy, a subsystem of the Earth, must develop without growing: To Daly, this is the essence of sustainable development. Human requirements can increase only at the expense of the Earth's other inhabitants. Thus, qualitative sustainable development means striving for *sufficient* per capita wealth for the maximum number that can be sustained over time under these conditions.

China is the laboratory in which many of these population and sustainable development ideas will be tested. With nearly one-quarter of the world's population, China has avoided an ecological disaster only by enforcing a one-child-per-family population policy. Vaclav Smil's chapter indicates that even with this rather draconic policy, the Chinese population is pressing against the carrying capacity of the land. He concludes by suggesting that the best managerial approaches and technical improvements would make at least some difference in the rate of overall environmental deterioration. Unfortunately, recent information from China would seem to indicate that its ecological future is in peril, given a sobering combination of rapid industrialization and liberalization of population policies.

Denis Goulet and Rekha Mehra both directly address the nature of sustainable development in their chapters. Goulet suggests that the focus must be on production of genuine wealth through authentic development, neither of which results from traditional industrialization. He concludes by posing three key ethical questions that must be addressed in the debate over sustainable development. Mehra argues that women can play an important role in sustainable development. Based upon her observations in the Philippines, she concludes that educating women and integrating them into economic activities is crucial to future sustainable development.

This section concludes with Janet Welsh Brown's chapter on North–South cooperation. Sustainable development of the global South requires close cooperation between the rich and poor countries. Countries in the global South have been encouraged to imitate the development patterns and lifestyles of the rich countries for at least two generations. A continuing dialogue on North–South cooperation on redefining progress is essential if the goals of the 1992 United Nations Conference on the Environment and Development are ever to be implemented.

9

Toward a Sustainable Global Population

Anne H. Ehrlich

Many definitions of *sustainable population* have been put forward. For a biologist, the simplest and most obvious one is a population of an organism that is within the carrying capacity of that organism's environment, that is, the maximum number of individuals of the organism in question that can be supported indefinitely without degrading the environment's capacity to support future populations. Carrying capacity thus is a function both of the characteristics of the environment—the resources it contains and its productivity—and of the organism—whether it is large or small and how much energy it expends to meet its needs.[1] Many more mice or grasshoppers ordinarily can be supported in a given area than elephants. And even animals of similar sizes may have very different energy needs because of different rates of metabolism; thus, more lizards than birds can be supported in the same area, other things being equal.

Similar definitions of sustainability have been offered for human populations. The often cited Brundtland Report defined *sustainable development* as "[development that] meets the needs of the present without compromising the ability of future generations to meet their own needs."[2]

Although the concept itself is easily defined, calculating the carrying capacity of an environment, even with regard to nonhuman organisms, is a very complex matter. Human beings, however, are not typical organisms. Their cultures, especially technologies, can dramatically change an area's carrying capacity for human populations, particularly in the short-to-medium term. Technology allows the manipulation of biotic resources to enhance production of desired organisms such as crops and livestock, and gives people access to resources that are not

151

available to other animals, such as metals and fossil fuels. An area's carrying capacity for traditional farmers or herders thus is much greater than for hunter-gatherers, and that for industrial societies is greater still. Nevertheless, despite humanity's great plasticity of behavior and capacity for environmental modification, expansion of the human enterprise will ultimately be limited by inescapable biophysical constraints.[3]

Furthermore, inefficiencies in resource use created by social systems, cultural practices, and lifestyle preferences generate a "social carrying capacity" that is smaller than the biophysical one. Less than optimal land-use patterns governed by tradition or inheritance customs would be an example whereby the social carrying capacity constrained a population to a size well within potential biophysical carrying capacity. Perhaps more important, increasing social carrying capacity to match the potential biophysical carrying capacity would imply a lifestyle for all individuals that maximized the number of people supported while ignoring the quality of their lives: the human equivalent of chicken factory farming.[4] Even though human ingenuity has enormously increased both kinds of carrying capacity, especially in the last century, social limits and inefficiencies will always be with us,[5] just as physical limits (exemplified at the extreme by the laws of thermodynamics) will.[6]

Estimating the world's carrying capacity for human beings therefore is much more difficult than for other animals, given our unique ability to mobilize resources, trade materials between groups, and manipulate environments to produce food and other resources for ourselves. Accordingly, to determine what a sustainable human population would be, a series of other questions must first be answered: For how long must the population be sustained? What kinds of lifestyles and technologies will be entailed? What levels of resource consumption will be required, and what options exist for resource substitution? How equitably will resources be distributed? How much and what kinds of environmental change are acceptable in the long term?

Today, most observers realize that the human population is not sustainable, in part because it is still expanding rapidly. A growing population in a finite environment is by definition unsustainable, at least in the long term. In 1995, the world's population passed 5.6 billion, and it continues to increase by more than 90 million people per year.[7] The 1995 rate of growth (births minus deaths) was over 1.6 percent per year; the Earth's population would double in forty-two years if this continued unchanged. Indeed, the world's population, which reached 2 billion in 1930, will pass 6 billion before the turn of the century and thus will have tripled in less than one lifetime.

Recent United Nations demographic projections indicate that the population is likely to pass 8.5 billion by 2025, reach 10 billion near midcentury, and ultimately stop growing a century later at 11.5 billion.[8] Of course, changes in reproductive rates or mortality rates could cause growth to be either considerably higher or lower than in this "medium" projection. The UN's high projection shows no end to growth, with the population soaring past 28 billion around 2150. Demographic projections customarily include no significant rise in death rates (although the AIDS pandemic in regions such as Africa has led to revision of some projections by biologists). The unsustainability of such growth hardly deserves comment.

More interesting is the low projection, which indicates global population will peak at 8.5 billion around 2050 and then slowly decline, reaching 5 billion again within a century. The key assumption leading to such a projection is that the average family size worldwide (currently 3.3 children per couple) will fall below "replacement reproduction" (where parents on average just replace themselves in the next generation: slightly more than two children per couple) early in the twenty-first century.

Until very recently, demographers never entertained the possibility of a sustained population decline; still less would they have considered it desirable. Even when they were overtaken by reality in several European nations, where very slow declines have been under way for up to two decades, demographers continued to assume that these populations would sooner or later return to a stationary situation (zero population growth). By generating a projection that allows a sustained decline, they may be tacitly acknowledging that such a path might have its advantages (although, of course, value judgments are never overtly attached to projections).

Symptoms of Overshoot

Whether the future demographic path will actually coincide with any of the United Nations' projections depends to a great extent on humanity's ability to support, even temporarily, a much larger population than today's. To biologists, the symptoms of population overshoot are already evident and increasing.We are doing what no responsible family or corporation would do—living on our capital. The capital in question here is our endowment of resources, both renewable and nonrenewable. That civilization is depleting reserves of nonrenewable resources such as metals and fossil fuels, especially petroleum, is not news to anyone, although many economists are convinced that in due course acceptable substitutes will be found.[9] Less appreciated but more worrisome are the depletion and degradation of putatively renewable resources, such as agricultural soils, fossil groundwater,[10] and biodiversity.[11]

Some 24 billion tons of topsoil have been estimated to be lost each year from the world's farmland, a loss of roughly 7 percent per decade.[12] A rate only a tenth as high would still clearly be unsustainable. A recent study of productive land by the United Nations Environment Programme has concluded that just since 1945, significant land degradation has occurred on every continent but Antarctica.[13] The affected lands include cropland, forestland, and grasslands; the causes are agriculture, deforestation, and overgrazing by livestock. Worldwide, an average of 11 percent of productive land has been moderately to extremely damaged, and another 6 percent has been lightly degraded. Moderate to severe damage implies some loss of productivity. Restoration would require a substantial investment of time and effort even in moderate cases; extremely degraded lands are beyond reclamation.

Many regions are already seriously short of fresh water, not only for producing food but in some areas even for domestic use.[14] Water is becoming a major limiting factor in areas such as the Middle East, northern India, much of China, and parts of Africa. In most of these regions, populations are still growing rapidly. In recent decades, a substantial increase in global food production has been accomplished in large part through irrigation, and much of that water has been obtained by tapping groundwater that collected over thousands of years during the ice age.[15] In many areas—including the Great Plains of the United States, one of the world's leading breadbaskets—aquifers are being drained at rates far above natural recharge. Agricultural land is increasingly being taken out of production as groundwater becomes so depleted that further pumping is uneconomic. In many places, competition for water has led to reduction or curtailment of supplies to farmers, who require large quantities but typically cannot pay as much for it. And in many industrialized areas, groundwater and surface sources have been seriously polluted with toxic substances and thus made unusable for agriculture or domestic consumption.

The accelerating loss of the planet's biodiversity is probably largely unappreciated by the general public, but it is of gravest concern to biologists. As land areas have been increasingly degraded by overgrazing or deforestation, or assaulted by human-created toxins from acid precipitation to pesticides, other organisms have lost their habitats, and more and more have been pushed to extinction.[16] As ecosystems are degraded or destroyed outright, the essential services that they provide for society are impaired or lost: maintenance of the gaseous composition of the atmosphere; moderation of climate and regulation of the hydrological cycle; cycling of nutrients (vital for agriculture), replenishment of soils and disposal of wastes; detoxification of poisonous substances; pollination of numerous crops; control of the vast majority of pests and disease vectors; provision of forest products, fisheries, and other foods and materials; and the provision of nature's vast genetic library, the source and inspiration for countless potential new products, from foods, medicines, and spices to industrial chemicals.

Most ecosystem services are taken for granted and valued only after they are lost.[17] Even if people knew how to replace these services—in most cases they do not—technological replacement would not be possible on the scale required. The attempts we have made to perform these services ourselves, such as management of the hydrological cycle by means of dams and water projects, produce results that are far from perfect and often unsustainable.

The profound changes being imposed on the Earth's ecosystems can be seen in the impact on the planet's biological production—the most fundamental resource of all, the basis of all food for ourselves and other animals. Net primary production (NPP) is the energy taken from sunlight and made available through the process of photosynthesis by green plants, algae, and some kinds of bacteria, less the energy used by the photosynthesizing organisms for their own life processes. Of the total amount of energy made available daily worldwide on land, humanity uses directly—for food, feed, fiber, and forest products—or indirectly—by diverting it into human-directed ecosystems composed of different organisms than would otherwise be present—or prevents the fixation—through degradation of natural ecosystems or conversion of them into less productive ones—some 40 percent.[18]

Human diversion of NPP from the oceans, which are much less productive than land despite their far greater extent, is a comparatively modest 2 percent. The NPP in ocean systems, however, is produced by highly dispersed, microscopic organisms, which are not likely soon to become an important part of the human diet. Rather, we will continue being dependent on fish, most of which are at the top of the food chain, as our marine food source, thereby harvesting only a tiny fraction of the oceans' NPP. This is not to say that human impact is minimal: the increasing depletion and in some cases commercial extinction of many fish stocks is a serious concern.[19] Humanity is also severely polluting harbors and estuaries and eradicating coastal wetland systems, all of which serve as nurseries for numerous important seafood species.

Feeding the Billions

As the world population continues to expand, producing enough food to keep pace becomes increasingly problematic.[20] The green revolution enabled food production to increase faster than the population from 1950 until the mid 1980s. Since then, global grain production, the human feeding base, has lagged on a per capita basis. Most of the land suitable for agriculture is already being cultivated, while increasing amounts are being taken out of production because of land degradation, depletion of groundwater irrigation sources, or urbanization. Green revolution technology—cultivation of high-yielding varieties of major crops, together with increased use of fertilizers and pesticides, and abundant water—has now been applied in most of the world and will soon have run its course. In most areas, diminishing returns from the increased use of fertilizer are evident. But no encore is in sight. While biotechnology is often promoted as the next revolution, its potential for expanding food supplies is quite limited; its value will lie more in giving crops better protection against disease and pests and perhaps the more efficient use of some nutrients.

No technology, moreover, can compensate fully for depleted or damaged soil or for the loss of arable land. Yet the green revolution itself, even as it dramatically boosts food harvests, often accelerates the deterioration of agricultural lands. Soil erosion is promoted by continuous cultivation, which is facilitated by synthetic fertilizers; and large-scale monocultures invite pests and crop disease, as mosaics of small-scale mixed crop cultures do not. Heavy applications of fertilizers and pesticides cause serious pollution problems, especially in surface and groundwater sources. And most of these problems are intensified when attempts are made to transfer the green revolution to moist tropical areas.[21]

Given the trends in the condition of our natural capital and the outlook for further increasing crop yields, Lester Brown of Worldwatch Institute several years ago warned that the global grain harvest was unlikely in the 1990s to increase faster than the population.[22] So far, history has not contradicted that prognosis.

Measuring the Impact

Human beings today are mobilizing resources on a scale comparable to or in some cases exceeding natural cycles. We are also threatening to destabilize major elements of the natural life-support system through such changes as defor-estation and desertification,[23] depletion of the stratospheric ozone shield, and the buildup of greenhouse gases in the atmosphere.[24] A population that allows the deterioration of its essential resource base and the destabilization of climate and other planetary processes is very far from sustainable. Compounding this unstable situation is the fact that the population may double again before its growth can be humanely stopped.

More than twenty years ago, Paul Ehrlich and John Holdren devised a simple equation to describe in very simplified terms the multiplicative effects of numbers of people and their use of resources in generating environmental impacts.[25] The equation—more accurately, an identity—is

$$I = P \times A \times T$$

where I represents the total impact (of a society or all societies); P is the population in question; A is the affluence (or consumption) of each individual on average; and T is the technology used to supply each unit of consumption.

Although reasonably accurate statistics are available for population sizes, no useful measure exists for total consumption per person or for technology. Indeed, the latter two are very difficult to untangle, and all three factors are by no means independent of each other. But a rough appreciation of the relationship can be gained by using per capita energy use as a measure of $A \times T$ (or AT). Considering the central role that energy use plays in generating virtually all environmental impacts, this is a useful approximation that, although greatly oversimplified, nonetheless offers some insight into human impacts.

By this measure, each person in an industrialized nation can be seen on average to have seven times the impact of a person in a developing nation.

Looking at the more extreme ends of the scale, the average American—whose per capita energy use is 50 to 100 percent higher than that of the average European or Japanese—has about thirty times the impact of a person in a very poor nation like Bangladesh or Chad. Thus, even though the populations of industrialized nations are growing relatively slowly—and in some cases, not at all—those populations consume a disproportionate share of the world's resources. The developed nations have only about a fifth of the world's population—1.2 billion—but they control and consume about four-fifths of most resources.[26] Consequently, they are causing far more than their share of damage to the Earth's life-support systems. And moreover, they are still striving to *increase* their consumption per person.

While the populations of most developing nations are growing much more rapidly—at an average rate of about 2.3 percent per year, excluding China—their collective contributions to deleterious global change are much smaller. But the potential for far greater contributions in the near future is considerable, given substantial growth in both their populations and their economies.[27]

Claims are often made by people in the industrialized world that the "population problem" is a problem only for developing countries, because populations in rich nations are growing much more slowly or not at all. Conversely, people in the Third World often assert that the problem isn't overpopulation, it is overconsumption by the rich.[28] As the $I = PAT$ identity shows, both are partly right. But overpopulation still drives much of the overconsumption in rich societies; clearly, if half as many people were consuming at the same rate per capita, they would be doing far less damage.

Meanwhile, the poor aspire and plan to consume as the rich do; in societies that are rapidly industrializing (such as Mexico or Taiwan), population growth drives rising consumption rates and increases pressure on resources. In poorer societies, which still tend to have the highest birthrates, population growth often has the effect of intensifying pressures on the land, accelerating land degradation, and deepening the people's poverty.[29] The consequences include large-scale displacement of people, as they migrate to cities, often overwhelming the cities' ability to accommodate them, or to other countries, where they hope to find a way to make a living. The United Nations Population Fund estimates that more than 100 million people were moving across borders each year in the early 1990s, and an unknown (but several times larger) number were moving within countries to areas where they hoped prospects would be better, usually the capital city.[30] Such migrants have often been called "economic refugees," but more and more of them are really environmental refugees fleeing from damaged and exhausted lands.

Biologists know well that when animal populations approach or exceed their local carrying capacities, more individuals are forced to live in less than optimal or marginal situations, while the more resource-abundant areas will become more crowded.[31] A male bird with a good territory in a well-populated area, for instance, may establish a second nest with another mate. That may be more advantageous to the second female and her offspring than finding a monogamous mate with a suboptimal territory.[32] For human beings, an analogous situation can be seen in heavily populated nations such as Bangladesh or Indonesia, where many of the poor are forced to live in either less productive or high-risk areas. Indonesia's crowding led to forced migration from Java to less productive is-lands—a largely failed policy; in Bangladesh, poor farmers on the chars of the Ganges Delta are vulnerable to severe floods and cyclones that have several times killed tens of thousands of people.

Population: The Good News

Not all the news about the population is bad, however. Demographers have reported a recent decline in the overall growth rate. On a global basis, the change is small—a drop from a rate of 1.68 in the late 1980s to about 1.60 percent in 1995. But it is significant nonetheless, since there had been almost no change for the previous twelve years.[33] The principal reason for the change was a sharp drop in the birthrate in China: in a country with 22 percent of the world's population, even a small change in demographics has visible global effects.

The drop occurred as the one-child family program was enforced again after some relaxation during the 1980s. The relaxation was necessitated by the rebel-lion of many couples who had girls after pledging for the one-child program. In a society with a long tradition of preference for sons, parents of daughters widely reneged on their pledges. Many had second children, but one unfortunate result was a sharp rise in female infanticide. Recently, there have been reports of Chinese women using ultrasound to determine the sex of their fetuses early in pregnancy and aborting females. A highly skewed sex ratio among children born in the last decade, with boys outnumbering girls by as much as 130 to 100 in some districts, lends credence to the reports. Parents appear to be unconcerned about the implications for social problems in the next generation or about whether their sons will find wives.

China's harsh population policies, including violations of human rights, have been much criticized in the West. They are, of course, consistent with Chinese policies in other areas, especially the suppression of political rights. In one sense, the population policies can be seen as a success, because without them, the population would by now be larger by several hundred million people. China's leaders seem acutely aware of the country's resource limitations; their nation is roughly the size of the United States, but has only half the amount of good agricultural land and 4.5 times as many people.[34] This awareness explains much of the severity of the Chinese population program.

The sudden change in the world growth rate was not caused only by changes in China, however. A significant decline in fertility was recorded in the late 1980s in several countries in sub-Saharan Africa, where birthrates had previously remained stubbornly high, even rising with improved health conditions in many cases.[35] The continent includes some of the world's poorest nations, and its rapid population growth, some 3 percent per year or more, has clearly hindered efforts to improve well-being. Bangladesh too, racked by poverty and underdevelopment for decades, has recorded a significant decline in fertility in recent years, apparently largely because of efforts to improve women's status and strong programs for maternal–child health and family planning.[36] Finally, already low fertility has fallen further in Central and Eastern Europe, where the political and economic turmoil accompanying the breakup of the Soviet Union has understandably led to fewer births.[37]

Population Policies

Despite increasing worldwide awareness of the danger of unregulated population growth and the establishment of population policies in many developing nations in the last three decades, only China has at least an implied goal of population reduction. While no nation has yet made an objective and comprehensive assessment of its resources and established population goals on that basis, many do have population programs with vaguer goals, such as improving the health of women and children or even slowing or stopping population growth. These population programs, mainly family planning programs, have met with mixed success.

Strangely enough, no industrialized nation has an explicit population policy— although most do have immigration policies—except for a few that are still pronatalist (notably France, which has been urging higher birthrates since a generation of young French men was decimated in World War I). In many nations, even the United States, implicitly pronatalist goals are still embodied in policies that provide family allowances and tax deductions for dependent children.

Although most industrialized nations have quite low birthrates and population growth rates, the United States and Canada still have comparatively high rates of natural increase (births minus deaths), not much below 1 percent per year. In the United States, a high immigration rate pushes the actual growth rate above 1 percent. Europe, Russia, and Japan have annual growth rates averaging around 0.2 percent. Some European nations are now experiencing negative population growth. Despite the well-known opposition of the Roman Catholic Church to the provision of contraceptives and especially abortion services, two predominantly Catholic countries, Italy and Spain, have the smallest average family sizes of any nation: 1.3 children per couple.

In contrast, annual growth rates in developing regions range upward from less than 1 percent in some East Asian nations to 3 percent or more in other parts of Asia and most African countries. Nations whose development has been most successful—by conventional standards—also are among the most successful in bringing their population growth under control: South Korea, Hong Kong, Singapore, and Taiwan. Substantial declines in birthrate and some success in development have also been achieved by Thailand, Sri Lanka, and Indonesia. But fertility in

India has fallen to only a modest extent, from an average of more than six children per family to just under four, although it was the first developing nation to establish a family planning program.[38] No significant decline has occurred in Pakistan and many Middle Eastern nations, where poverty and underdevelopment persist for the majority of people, despite wealth from oil in some cases.

Latin American nations have rates of population growth ranging from 1 to 3 percent. As in Asia, considerable variation exists among these nations in levels of both fertility and development. Several Latin American countries are "two-tiered societies," with very large disparities between the richest and poorest fractions of the population. Often in such situations, the rich behave reproductively and consume resources like citizens in industrialized nations, while the poor live in circumstances resembling those of people in the poorest nations: chronically undernourished, with high birthrates and infant mortality, and little access to clean water, basic sanitation, health care, family planning services, or education. Nonetheless, in several Latin American nations family planning programs have been significant successes, notably Mexico, Colombia, Costa Rica, and Brazil.

The situation in sub-Saharan Africa is disheartening in many respects. Nearly all African nations have annual rates of population growth between 2 and 4 percent, reflecting average families of from 5 to 8 people.[39] Development has all but stalled in most sub-Saharan nations; food production per person has fallen some 15–20 percent since 1969, as population growth has outstripped production. Much of the region has suffered repeated droughts, desertification, and other forms of environmental degradation.[40] Most African nations have simply lost ground in the development process as their economies, as measured by gross national product (GNP), have failed to keep pace with expanding populations. In some countries, especially in West Africa, severely deteriorating conditions have led to social and political breakdown.[41]

In much of the developing world, lower fertility seems related to economic growth, although the question remains: did the GNP "take off," as economists are fond of putting it, before or after fertility began to fall? Throughout the 1970s, correlations of fertility with development, as measured by GNP per capita, were weak at best.[42] Indeed, in countries such as China and Sri Lanka and in Kerala State in India, there was remarkable progress in reducing fertility but very little growth in per capita GNP, whereas Mexico and Brazil proceeded some distance along an industrial path with very little change in fertility. By 1990, however, a different relationship had emerged: many nations that had successfully reduced fertility earlier were enjoying economic booms.[43]

A recent World Bank study suggests a relationship between successful development and economic equity; countries with less disparity between the incomes of the richest 20 percent of the population and the poorest 20 percent tend to have higher rates of economic growth.[44] Nations where there is both economic equity and successful development have also substantially reduced their birthrates—notably the Asian "dragons," Hong Kong, Singapore, Taiwan, and South

Korea. Newer applicants to the club are Malaysia, Thailand, and Indonesia, whose economic success may be more mixed, and China, whose economic "takeoff" is so hot it may end in a crash.[45]

Despite the lack of progress in reducing birthrates in many developing nations, family planning programs in almost all of them are at least given government approval if not official support. These programs have existed in some countries since the early 1960s. Many programs were founded as a means to improve family health and well-being, and some have not moved beyond those goals.[46] But increasingly, developing nations are recognizing that rapid population growth can consume all the gains of economic development, and they have taken on the more ambitious goal of reducing the rate of population growth.

The mixed success of family planning programs, however, soon led to an understanding that simply offering contraceptives does not automatically cause birthrates to fall. Much more is needed to persuade people to plan for and have fewer children. At first, it was assumed that "successful development" would bring the desired demographic transition. But by the mid 1970s, social scientists had learned that certain aspects of development were crucial, but that most of the trappings of industrialization—airports, highways, factories, etc.—were irrelevant. What counted were reductions in infant and child mortality, longer life spans, the education and empowerment of women, and some form of social security for old age.[47] Possibly most fundamentally important is the education of women, because that education is then applied to improving the health, nutrition, and well-being of families, which in turn results in lower infant and child mortality. And the increased survival of children reduces the pressure to overreproduce as insurance for support in old age.

Empowerment of women—the securing of such basic rights as the right to vote, to own and inherit property, and to earn wages, as well as to control one's own reproductivity—is also critical, not only to achieve demographic goals but also for development. It surely is no coincidence that the most underdeveloped and persistently poor societies are also, by and large, those in which women have the fewest rights and are least educated. In much of sub-Saharan Africa, for instance, women do most of the farmwork, with help from their children, yet they cannot own the land and have no access to such things as fertilizer or improved seeds or expert advice. Improving the status of women and providing basic health care and education to all people, of course, results in many benefits besides smaller families and thus could rightfully be considered "no-regrets" strategies for successful development.

Addressing the Human Predicament

The growing precariousness of the human situation has been clear to environmentalists for some time. Now it is at last receiving the attention of political decision makers, as demonstrated by the 1992 United Nations Conference on

Environment and Development (UNCED) in Rio, the first such United Nations conference that included heads of state. It was followed in 1994 by the United Nations Conference on Population and Development (UNCPD) and another on women (both were at the "ministerial" level).

It also is increasingly apparent that no simple or superficial solutions will be sufficient to reverse the dilemma. Nor will addressing only one or two of the *I=PAT* factors be adequate in the long run—even though some measures, such as greatly increasing energy efficiency, switching to more benign energy sources, developing less damaging agricultural systems, and strengthening family planning programs are surely essential.

But the human enterprise cannot be put on a truly sustainable basis until it is recognized that we are now living beyond our means, and that a path toward a viable future must be carved out and agreed on. The next century or two will not be easy ones, when the principal task will be to manage the transitional overshoot phase, during which populations and resource use will inevitably further exceed the global carrying capacity and stresses on life-support systems will continue to mount. Humanely reversing the population explosion itself will require many decades to accomplish; so will reducing the material throughput of overindustrialized societies, kicking the fossil fuel habit, detoxifying and restoring damaged and decimated ecosystems, developing sustainable agricultural systems, and somehow avoiding serious international warfare in the process.

Without some clear vision of an attractive, attainable, shared future, these difficult decisions are not likely to be made. Each society should evaluate its own territory's carrying capacity, which includes resources available through trade with other societies, and determine what standard of living and what population is appropriate. Then policies to achieve these goals must be developed and adopted. Of course, these decisions cannot be made in isolation but will require an unprecedented level of cooperation and coordination with other societies.

In a short chapter, I cannot offer a total prescription to cure what ails the world, but I can suggest a few obvious directions in which to seek answers. It will be necessary for industrialized nations to curb their consumption and share with developing nations their technologies for efficient energy use and the development and deployment of alternative sources. Cooperation in curbing greenhouse gas emissions is critical. Providing the necessities of life for the poor in every nation should be a global priority. And all nations should be involved in the task of reversing the population explosion.

Some progress has begun to be made in international cooperation at the political level, as signified most prominently by international conferences and the agreements and processes that emerge from them. International agencies coordinate numerous activities having to do with the global environment; to an even greater degree, global economies are increasingly tied together through multinational industries and financial markets. But much more is needed. We can take heart that the Cold War has ended without a catastrophe; in fact, we are presented with the opportunity to create a new cooperative world structure. This is an opportunity we cannot afford to lose.

Notes

1. Gretchen C. Daily and Paul R. Ehrlich, "Population, Sustainability, and Earth's Carrying Capacity," *BioScience* 42, no. 10 (November 1992): 761–71.

2. World Commission on Environment and Development, *Our Common Future* (New York: Oxford University Press, 1987), 8.

3. See, e.g., P. R. Ehrlich, A. H. Ehrlich, and J. P. Holdren, *Ecoscience: Population, Resources, Environment* (San Francisco: W. H. Freeman, 1977), esp. chaps. 3, 4, 8, and 9.

4. Daily and Ehrlich, "Earth's Carrying Capacity."

5. Nathan Keyfitz, "Population and Development within the Ecosphere: One View of the Literature." *Population Index* 57, no. 1 (1991): 5–22.

6. P. R. Ehrlich, A. H. Ehrlich, and J. P. Holdren, *Ecoscience*, 33–35.

7. Carl Haub, *1993 World Population Data Sheet* (Washington, DC: Population Reference Bureau, 1993). This is the source for all population figures unless otherwise noted.

8. United Nations Population Fund, *State of the World Population, 1992* (New York: United Nations, 1992). UNFPA based its summary on United Nations Population Division, *Long-Range World Population Projections,* ST/SEA/SER.A/125 (New York: United Nations, 1991).

9. H. E. Daly and J. B. Cobb, Jr., *For the Common Good* (Boston: Beacon Press, 1989).

10. Sandra Postel, *Water for Agriculture: Facing the Limits,* Worldwatch Paper 93 (Washington, DC: Worldwatch Institute, 1990).

11. Paul R. Ehrlich and Anne H. Ehrlich, *Healing the Planet* (Reading, MA: Addison-Wesley, 1991), chap. 1; E. O. Wilson, "Threats to Biodiversity," *Scientific American* (September 1989): 108–16.

12. Lester R. Brown and Edward C. Wolf, *Soil Erosion: Quiet Crisis in the World Economy,* Worldwatch Paper 60 (Washington, DC: Worldwatch Institute, 1984).

13. L. Oldeman, V. Van Engelen, and J. Pulles, "The Extent of Human-Induced Soil Degradation." Annex 5 of L. Oldeman, et al., *World Map of the Status of Human-Induced Soil Degradation: An Explanatory Note,* rev. 2d. ed. (Waginengen, Netherlands: International Soil Reference and Information Centre, 1990). A summary of the findings can be seen in World Resources Institute, *World Resources 1992–93* (New York: Oxford University Press, 1992).

14. Peter Gleick, *Water in Crisis* (New York: Oxford University Press, 1993).

15. Postel, *Water for Agriculture.*

16. Paul R. Ehrlich and Anne H. Ehrlich, *Extinction: The Causes and Consequences of the Disappearance of Species* (New York: Random House, 1981); E. O. Wilson and F. Peter, *Biodiversity* (Washington, DC: National Academy Press, 1988).

17. Paul R. Ehrlich and Anne H. Ehrlich, "The Value of Biodiversity," *Ambio* 21, no. 3 (May 1992): 219–26.

18. P. M. Vitousek, et al., "Human Appropriation of the Products of Photosynthesis," *BioScience* 36 (June 1987): 368–73.

19. Peter Weber, *Reversing the Decline of the Oceans,* Worldwatch Paper 116 (Washington, DC: Worldwatch Institute, November 1993), chap. 12.

20. Lester R. Brown, et al., *State of the World 1994* (New York: Norton, 1994), chap. 10.

21. Anne H. Ehrlich, "Development and Agriculture," in *The Cassandra Conference,*

ed. Paul R. Ehrlich and John Holdren (College Station, TX: Texas A&M Press, 1988; Paul R. Ehrlich, Anne H. Ehrlich, and Gretchen C. Daily, "Food Security, Population, and Environment," *Population and Development Review* 19, no. 1 (March 1993): 1–32.

22. Lester R. Brown, *The Changing World Food Prospect: The Nineties and Beyond,* Worldwatch Paper 85 (Washington, DC: Worldwatch Institute, 1988).

23. Norman Myers, *Deforestation Rates in Tropical Forests and their Climatic Implications* (London: Friends of the Earth, 1989); WRI, *World Resources 1992–93,* chap. 8.

24. J. Houghton, G. Jenkins, and J. Ephraums, eds., *Climate Change: The IPCC Scientific Assessment, Intergovernmental Panel on Climate Change* (New York: Cambridge University Press, 1990); P. R. Ehrlich and A. H. Ehrlich, *Healing the Planet.*

25. Paul R. Ehrlich and John S. Holdren, "The Impact of Population Growth," *Science* 171 (1971): 1212–17. See also Ehrlich and Ehrlich, *Healing the Planet.*

26. P.R. Ehrlich and A.H. Ehrlich, *Healing the Planet.*

27. Paul R. Ehrlich and Anne H. Ehrlich, "How the Rich Can Save the Poor and Themselves: Lessons from the Global Warming," in *Proceedings of the International Conference on Global Warming and Climate Change: Perspectives from Developing Countries,* ed. S. Gupta and R. Pachauri (New Delhi: Tata Energy Research Institute, February 1989), 287–94.

28. A brief book that makes the latter point well (but says little about the role of population growth) is Arjun Makhijani, *From Global Capitalism to Economic Justice* (New York: Apex Press, 1992).

29. UNFPA, *World Population 1992;* World Bank, *World Development Report 1990* (Washington, DC: 1990).

30. UNFPA, *State of the World Population, 1993* (New York: United Nations, 1993).

31. Daily and Ehrlich, "Earth's Carrying Capacity."

32. Paul R. Ehrlich, *The Machinery of Nature* (New York: Simon & Schuster, 1986).

33. Carl Haub and Machiko Yanagashita, *1994 World Population Data Sheet* (Washington, DC: Population Reference Bureau); Carl Haub, "China's Fertility Drop Lowers World Growth Rate," *Population Today* 21:6 (June 1992). Shiro Horiuchi, "Stagnation in the Decline of the World Population Growth Rate During the 1980s," *Science* 257 (7 August 1992): 761–65.

34. Patrick E. Tyler, "China Lacks Water to Meet Its Mighty Thirst," *New York Times,* 7 November 1993; Patrick E. Tyler, "The Dynamic New China Still Races Against Time," *New York Times,* 2 January 1994.

35. John C. Caldwell, I. O. Orubulove, and Pat Caldwell, "Fertility Decline in Africa: A New Type of Fertility Transition?" *Population and Development Review* 18, no. 3 (June 1992): 211–42.

36. William K. Stevens, "3rd-World Gains in Birth Control: Development Isn't Only Answer," *New York Times,* 2 January 1994.

37. Haub, *1993 World Population.*

38. G. Narayana and John F. Kantner, *Doing the Needful: The Dilemma of India's Population Policy* (Boulder: Westview Press, 1992).

39. Haub and Yanagishita, *1994 World Population;* UNFPA, *World Population 1993.*

40. *World Bank, 1992;* WRI, *World Resources 1992–93;* Lester R. Brown and Edward C. Wolf, *Reversing Africa's Decline,* Worldwatch Paper 65 (Washington, DC: Worldwatch Institute, June 1985); Alan B. Durning, *Poverty and the Environment: Reversing the Downward Spiral,* Worldwatch Paper 92 (Washington, DC: Worldwatch Institute, November 1989).

41. Robert D. Kaplan, "The Coming Anarchy," *Atlantic Monthly* 273, no. 2 (February 1994): 44–76.

42. World Bank, *World Development Report 1980* (New York: Oxford University Press, 1980); Nancy Birdsall, "Population Growth and Poverty in the Developing World," *Population Bulletin* 35, no. 5 (Washington, DC: Population Reference Bureau, December 1980).

43. UNFPA, *World Population 1992.*

44. Sylvia Nasar, "Economics of Equality: A New View," *New York Times,* 8 January 1994, Business Day; Makhijani, *Economic Justice.*

45. Nicholas D. Kristof, "China Sees 'Market-Leninism' as Way to Future," *New York Times,* 6 September 1993; Nicholas D. Kristof, "Riddle of China: Repression as Standard of Living Soars," *New York Times*, 7 September 1993.

46. John A. Ross and Elizabeth Frankenberg, *Findings from Two Decades of Family Planning Research* (New York: Population Council, 1993).

47. Bernard Berelson, et al. "The Great Debate on Population Policy Revisited," *International Family Planning Perspectives* 16, no. 4 (December 1990); J. Bongaarts, W. P. Mauldin, and J. F. Phillips, "The Demographic Impact of Family Planning Programs," *Studies in Family Planning* 21 (1990): 299.

10

Physical Growth versus Technological Development: Odds in the Sustainability Race

Herman E. Daly

To appreciate the importance of the distinction between growth and development, we must first understand how the economy is related to its environment. The economy, in its physical dimensions, is a subsystem of the earth ecosystem. The ecosystem is finite, nongrowing and closed. A "closed" system is one that matter neither enters nor exits, but one that energy does enter and exit. In the earth ecosystem solar energy enters and exits and it is this throughput of energy that powers the material biogeochemical cycles on which life depends. Within this earth ecosystem the economy exists as an open subsystem. That means that both matter and energy enter from the larger system, and that both matter and energy exit back to the larger system. All physical economic processes of life and production are maintained by this metabolic flow-through of matter-energy from and back to the environment. The economy lives off the environment in the same way that an animal does—by taking in useful raw material and energy and giving back waste material and degraded energy. The rest of the ecosystem, the part that is not within the economic subsystem, absorbs the emitted wastes, and by biogeochemical cycles powered by the sun, reconstitutes most of the waste into reusable raw materials.

As the economic subsystem grows, it assimilates into itself a larger and larger proportion of the total matter-energy of the earth ecosystem. More and more of total life space is converted into economic space—that is, living space for expanding populations and space taken over to provide our raw materials and sinks for our waste materials. Consequently less and less life space remains outside the economy to provide the vital function of carrying out the biogeochemical cycles at the rates and through the pathways to which we are adapted. The earth *develops* without *growing*—that is, it evolves qualitatively without expanding quantitatively. The economy, as a subsystem of the earth, must at some point adapt itself to this same pattern of development without growth—which is what should be understood by the popular term *sustainable development.*

There is such a thing as a maximum scale of the economic subsystem—a point beyond which further growth of the subsystem induces collapse in the total system. Before that point there is an optimal scale—a point beyond which further physical growth, while possible, costs more than it is worth. An optimal scale, beyond which growth is antieconomic, exists even if we think of the nonhuman part of creation as having only instrumental value to humans and no intrinsic value in its own right. If we recognize the intrinsic value of other creatures, in addition to their instrumental value to us, then the optimal scale of the human niche would be smaller than if we recognized only instrumental value. A man is worth many sparrows, but a corollary is that a sparrow's worth cannot be zero. Since growth beyond the optimal scale increases costs faster than benefits, it makes us poorer, not richer, thereby reducing our ability to end poverty, and even creating more poverty. The belief that growth is the cure for poverty is an evasion of the real but politically unpopular answer, namely, development, with an emphasis on sharing and population control, as well as on increased productivity.

What conclusions should we draw from this description about how to act rightly in the world? Should we convert as much as possible of the matter-energy of the world into ourselves and our artifacts? Should that be the "central organizing principle" of society, to use Albert Gore's term? Indeed, growth has been and still is our central organizing principle—that is precisely our problem. We need a new central organizing principle, a fundamental ethic that will guide our actions in a way more in harmony with the way the world works. This ethic is suggested *by* the terms *sustainability, sufficiency, equity, efficiency.* Growth has become unsustainable. It has never been equitable, in that some live far above sufficiency, while others live far below. And no system that uses resources at a rate that destroys natural life-support systems yet does not meet the basic needs of all can possibly be considered efficient.

To capture the cluster of values expressed by sustainability/sufficiency/equity/efficiency in a sentence, I suggest the following: *We should strive for sufficient per capita wealth, efficiently maintained and allocated, and equitably distributed, for the maximum number of people that can be sustained over time.*

Some clarifications are needed. Note that the goal is sufficient, not maximum, per capita wealth. Sufficient for what? Sufficient for a good life. I will not try to define a "good life" but will note that not only man-made wealth but also preserved natural capital—biodiversity—is essential to it. What is maximized is the cumulative number of lives over time lived in sufficiency. This is very different from maximizing the population simultaneously alive. Too many people alive at one time overloads and destroys carrying capacity, resulting in fewer lives, or more lives lived below sufficiency, in subsequent time periods, and consequently a smaller cumulative total of lives lived in a condition of sufficiency. Too much consumption per capita at any one time leads to the same result. The value of efficiency, both technical and allocative, is affirmed because it allows more people to exist over time in conditions of sufficiency. Wealth "efficiently maintained" means that wealth as it depreciates is replaced by new production that gives greater (maximum) use or satisfaction per unit of resource used. Equitable distribution means that sufficiency is attained by all, and that the range of inequality above sufficiency is limited. It does not mean equal wealth for all. Some degree of inequality of wealth is necessary for justice, efficiency, and community. But the present range of inequality is vastly greater that what is consistent with community or necessary for incentives. The idea of sustainability, of course, is captured by the insistence on maximizing cumulative lives *over time*.

Since utilitarianism is the basic ethic underlying contemporary economics, it is useful to compare the above statement with Jeremy Bentham's utilitarian guideline, "the greatest good for the greatest number." Bentham's rule has the virtue of brevity but unfortunately contains an impossible double maximization. You cannot have two "greatests," because it is possible to have more people at a lower per capita good, or greater per capita good for fewer people. Logically it would have to be either "greatest good for a sufficient number" or "sufficient good for the greatest number." The principle here advocated is the latter, with *number* defined as the cumulative number over time.

The reason for that choice is that we have no notion of what a sufficient number over time would be—that implies deciding when the world should end. Standard economics, by its practice of discounting the future, is implicitly willing to say that beyond some point the future is worth nil and might as well end. Rejection of this view is part of the thrust of sustainability. Although both Christianity and thermodynamics teach that the world is not perpetual, we nevertheless affirm that life and longevity are good gifts of God and should not be wasted—at least not by us. Also, we do have some notion of how much is sufficient for a good life, even though there will be disagreement, and we will have to think in terms of a limited range rather than a single number. Much thought and clarification is needed here, but clearly at one extreme, life can be stunted by poverty, and just as clearly at the other extreme, life is not improved and is even harmed by surfeit and excess. It is not too much to expect that we could come up with a reasonable range of sufficiency limits, notwithstanding the chorus of econosophists who will ask, Who are you to impose your personal tastes on everyone else? and similar questions ad nauseam. If the cluster of values affirmed above were logically reducible to "personal tastes," and if continual growth were biophysically possible, then this common objection would have force. The fact that both presuppositions of this objection are clearly wrong is indicative of the low level of argument that is customary in what currently passes for serious economic discourse.

The product of population and per capita resource use at any point in time represents the *scale* of the human presence in the biosphere—the rate of total resource throughput. It is this total scale that is limited by the regenerative and absorptive capacities of the ecosystem, this scale that is sustainable or unsustainable. For a given sustainable scale of throughput we could choose to have many people consuming small amounts of resources per capita, or fewer people consuming correspondingly more resources per capita. This is the choice of "sufficient good," subject to which cumulative lives would be maximized.[1]

To put the above ethical principle into effect requires that we know something about carrying capacity—indeed this principle is operationally almost equivalent to the dictum "Thou shalt not exceed carrying capacity." For humans, carrying capacity includes much more than just population—it also depends on technology and per capita resource demands.

The impact of the economic subsystem on the total environmental system can be viewed as the product of four factors:

$$I = P \times Y/P \times T/Y \times I/T$$

where I = environmental impact; P = population; T = throughput; and Y = national income. In other words, environmental impact (I), equals *population* (P) times *affluence* (Y/P, or per capita income) times *technology*.[2] Technology (I/Y, or impact intensity of income) is separated into two factors ($I/Y = T/Y \times I/T$). The first of these, T/Y, is the throughput intensity of income; the second, I/T, is the impact intensity of throughput. Increases in P and Y/P measure "growth," while decreases in T/Y and I/T measure "development." Change in environmental impact is thus a race between growth—increases in the first two factors—and development—decreases in the last two. Growth in scale results from growth in population and affluence. Development occurs as a result of technologies that permit declines in both throughput per unit of income, and in impact per unit of throughput.

For the world as a whole, some orders of magnitude are instructive in figuring the odds on how this race is likely to turn out. P is projected to double in roughly the next forty years. Per capita gross national product (Y/P) in the high-income countries is on the order of 21 times higher than in low- and middle-income countries (i.e., 21: $21,000/$1,000, from Table I, *World Development Report, 1993*).[3] If the goal is for the poor and middle-income to catch up with the rich, and there is no further increase in the average per capita income of the rich countries over the next forty years, then to avoid greater impact on the environment than today, technology would have to improve by a factor of about $2 \times 21 = 42$. However, since the poor and middle-income constitute roughly 85 percent of the world's population today (the percentage will be higher in forty years), and the increase only applies to them, it should be $0.85 \times 42 = 36$ times.[4]

Is it feasible to increase the efficiency of our total use of the environment by a factor of 36 during the next forty years? This is what would be required to avoid any downward adjustment in population growth or aspirations of universal affluence, while keeping environmental impact constant at present, already damaging levels. Keep in mind that the large increases in "productivity" experienced historically have been in capital, land, or labor productivity—not in throughput productivity. In fact, one reason for the historical increase in labor, capital, and land productivity has been the large increase in resource throughput. In agriculture, for example, the productivity of capital, labor, and an acre of land have all increased thanks to a tremendous increase in resource throughput (fertilizer, pesticides, water, energy to run machinery). Productivity per unit of throughput in agriculture has actually fallen—that is, throughput intensity of income, T/Y, has risen—as throughput volume increased in order to raise the productivity of the complementary factors, capital and labor. The only basis for any optimism at all on this score is that precisely because we have been so negligent of resource productivity, there is now considerable room for improvement. Indeed, energy productivity has recently increased significantly, but nothing like a factor of 36 is visible on the horizon.

Reduction of the impact intensity of throughput, I/T, likewise offers little historical reason for rejoicing. Substitution of novel synthetics for natural materials has clearly increased environmental impact per unit of throughput—witness DDT, CFCs, PCBs, plastics, plutonium, detergents, biocides used in agriculture, and so on. Having had no evolutionary experience with these novel substances, the biosphere is entirely unadapted to them, and consequently their large-scale introduction is almost always harmful. The 36-fold improvement required in technology demands a reversal, not a continuation of past trends in technological development.

Why did we adopt such impact-intensive forms of throughput? Because the quest to produce more and more things for more and more people required ever more powerful technologies and novel substances. Why did we adopt such throughput-intensive techniques? To increase the productivity and income (affluence) of the major social classes, labor and capital. The sacrifice of resource productivity has been seen as a small price to pay for peace between labor and capital. Politically it has been easy to sacrifice the interests of the landlords and resource owners, since the ethical claim to rent is weak, and in any case the government is often the major resource owner. Not present at the table when this political bargain was made were any representatives of future generations or nonhuman species. Furthermore, the growth bargain could only make sense in an "empty world," which of course was—and still is—the regnant preanalytic vision. Thus, growth in affluence and population drove development down the path of least technological and political resistance, raising—worsening—the last two ratios.

This whole calculation assumes that the rich countries do not increase their per capita income beyond the 1993 figure of $21,000 during the forty years that it takes for population to double. So far the rich have shown no willingness to stand still while the poor and middle-income countries catch up. And the standard doctrine is that the rich should grow *more* to provide markets for the poor, that a rising tide lifts all boats. If we still lived in an empty world of superabundant natural capital, that would make some sense. But in a full world, growth is not the solution. If we look at the full world as a total system, even the metaphor is wrong, since a rising tide in one part of the world implies an ebbing tide somewhere else.

Since an X-percent change in any of the three factors—population, affluence, technology—will result in an X-percent change in the product, it follows that in an arithmetic sense all three factors are of equal importance in determining environmental impact. Nevertheless, it makes sense to ask in any concrete situation which factor is most likely to permit an X-percent change. As a very broad generalization one could say that the South has the most room for an improvement in P (a reduction in rates of population growth rates); the North has the most room for improvement in Y/P (a reduction in per capita consumption); and the formerly communist East has the most room for an improvement in I/Y (a reduction in the impact intensity of income). But again, all countries need to pay attention to all three factors. To bet on technological development alone, without policies to limit growth in population and affluence, is to ignore the odds and indulge in wishful thinking. It is a sucker's bet.

The old technological optimism about unlimited material growth is, I believe, discredited. But there is a new technological optimism regarding the possibility of tremendously increasing resource productivity, by even as much as a hundred-fold. Although it is clear from the foregoing that I do not share this optimism, I could be wrong. But even if I were very optimistic about technology in this sense, I would still advocate the policy that derives from the less optimistic view—namely, that the scale of throughput be limited to well within carrying capacity. If the efficiency optimists are right, the increase in resource prices resulting from such limitation will provide the incentive for exactly those technologies in which they have so much confidence. The cost of sustainability in terms of forgone services would be very small, perhaps even negative. While I would rejoice in such an event ex post, I would not want to borrow against it ex ante. Both optimist and pessimist should agree on limiting throughput within carrying capacity. Such a policy encourages the efficiency optimists to pursue their fondest dreams, while giving the pessimists some insurance against their worst fears.

Notes

1. The term *maximize* should not be taken to imply any precise mathematical solution of an ethical problem. It is a convenient way to bring efficiency into a problem of serving

more than one value. There are three values in play: sufficiency, sustainability, and equity. Efficiency, treated in the text as a fourth value, is really a derivative value in that its goodness derives from its ability to permit a greater degree of attainment of any one of the three basic goals, given some set level of attainment of the other two.

2. P. R. Ehrlich and J. P. Holdren, "Impact of Population Growth," *Science* 171 (26 March 1971): 1212–17.

3. World Bank income figures for different nations are converted into dollars using market exchange rates. Using purchasing power parity conversion rates, as done by the International Monetary Fund, would give a lower range of difference. The figures used should not be considered precise but only indicative of general magnitudes, which is all the argument requires. These figures are from World Bank, *World Development Report 1993* (Washington, DC: World Bank, 1993), Table I.

4. Information-handling technologies have shown productivity increases this large and larger, but that is an exception. And these improvements are not so relevant to poor countries whose needs are food, clothing, and shelter—not high-powered computers and Nintendo. Even in rich countries the amazing increase in information processing has done little to increase the relevance or insight contained in the information being so much more efficiently processed.

11

Barriers to a Sustainable China

Vaclav Smil

No decisive progress toward a globally sustainable civilization can be achieved without a gradual transformation of the Chinese environment and society. This is not impossible—but it will be exceedingly challenging. Emulating the Chinese, who have a fondness for numerical labels—Three Bad Years, Gang of Four, Five Black Elements—I will concentrate on the Five Great Barriers to China's sustainable development: limited ecosystemic resources and services; large—and in absolute terms, still rapidly growing—population; high rates of economic expansion; a historic lack of concern about environmental degradation; and the demise of the best, most sustainable traditions.

Limited Resources

Given China's huge population, even the country's most abundant natural resources—its hydroenergy potential is largest in the world, its coal deposits are second only to those of the United States—prorate to relatively modest endowments.[1] And the combination of China's location, terrain, climate, and long history of environmental abuse means that many critical ecosystemic resources are in low supply even in terms of nationwide averages: in some regions of the country shortages are already retarding the rate of economic development. I will concentrate on shortages of the three most important of these resources: water, farmland and forests.

Water

Of the 6 trillion tonnes (metric tons) of precipitation received by China during an average year (the mean of 630 millimeters), about 45 percent flows away as stream runoff.[2] About 40 percent of this flow, or 1.1 trillion tonnes, is potentially usable, and the actual recent annual withdrawals have totaled just over 500 billion metric tons. This prorates to per capita use of less than 500 tonnes a year, not even a quarter of the U.S. value and about 20 percent below the level in India.[3] But these abstract means are made up of relative southern abundance and northern shortages. The densely inhabited northern region comprises about one-third of China's territory, has about two-fifth of all the population, grows the same share of staple grains, and accounts for nearly 45 percent of all industrial output—but it receives only about one-quarter of the country's total precipitation, and its high evapotranspiration means that it has access to less than one-tenth of stream runoff.

The Huang He (the Yellow River) is the principal stream in North China and it is not replenished to any major extent as it flows through the very arid Loess Plateau, the world's most heavily eroded, and through the deserts of Gansu, Ningxia, and Nei Monggol Provinces. In the Huang He's basin less than 20 cubic meters of water runoff are available for each hectare of cultivated land, and no more than about 600 cubic meters per person. Comparable rates in the Chang Jiang (the Yangtze River) basin are, respectively, about 170 cubic meters per hectare and 2,800 cubic meters per person. And the Huang He's flow has repeatedly diminished in prolonged droughts, recently to just two-fifths of the long-term mean, when the river's normally very low early summer flow ceased for up to 200 kilometers from its mouth for more than a month. This brings high reliance on underground water reserves, but here the northern provinces, with less than 30 percent of all reserves, are also disadvantaged.

Water shortages have been affecting every major northern city. In 1985, 188 Chinese cities were short of more than 10 million tonnes of water a day, and in 40 of them, including the capital, these shortages have been serious enough to impede economic development. By 1990 China's urban water deficit reached 15 million tonnes, and some Chinese estimates for the year 2000 are as high as 88 million tonnes. Surface subsidence caused by excessive underground water pumping now affects virtually every major northern city.

Urban water shortages tend to attract disproportionate attention, but as in any populous Asian country, China's water is heavily used for irrigation, which creates a number of extensive environmental impacts. Among the populous countries, only Egypt, Pakistan, and Japan (each at about 75 percent) surpass China in their relative dependence on irrigation.[4] The most obvious irrigation problems can be seen on the North China Plain.[5]

The region's minimal slope (1:10,000), the unreliable summer flow of its rivers, and the enormous sediment load carried by the Huang He make extensive surface gravity irrigation impractical and cause excessive exploitation of aquifers during prolonged droughts. Scarcity of irrigation water on the plain is best illustrated by the average annual distribution of water per hectare: while the national mean is now close to 10,000 cubic meters, and the most intensively cropped southern areas receive over 30,000 cubic meters, the plain's fields average only about 4,000 cubic meters per hectare.

This combination of strained supply of irrigation, urban, and industrial water now affects an area extending over some 585,000 square kilometers from eastern Shandong through northern Henan and Hebei to southern and central Liaoning and including Beijing and Tianjin. This area, larger than France, now has a chronic annual shortage of nearly 4 billion tonnes of water, a deficit too large to be eliminated by harnessing more of the region's scarce capacities.

Compared to the huge volumes of water used in irrigation, household use of water by the rural population is almost negligible, but the extension of an adequate and safe water supply to most of China's population remains a distant goal. Running water is now available to just over 80 percent of all urban residents in 300 large cities, and in less than one-third of small cities and towns, and by the end of 1989 about 23 percent of the rural population had access to tap water, although only a fraction of this population had the water actually piped into their homes. Even during years of normal precipitation, between 50 and 80 million people in rural areas have to live with extreme shortages even of drinking water, and the prolonged droughts of the 1980s worsened this situation.

Farmland

There is a widespread consensus that official figures understate the extent of China's cultivated area. While the official total is now less than 95 million hectares, values between 130 and 150 million hectares have been offered on the basis of remote sensing, and the extrapolation of partially completed detailed surveys of China's land use put the total between 133 and 140 million hectares. The accuracy of these unofficial figures is unknown, but there is no doubt about major, continuous losses of high-quality, flat alluvial land throughout the densely settled eastern third of China. The magnitude and rapidity of this decline makes it a much more important concern than disputes about the area actually farmed.

Cultivated area has been declining as the gains from considerable reclamation efforts have been overwhelmed by losses caused by a combination of population growth, economic modernization, and natural degradative processes—heavy erosion, desertification, salinization, alkalization—which were either accelerated or initiated by improper land management. During the twenty years between 1957 and 1977, mass deployment of rural labor reclaimed about 17 million hectares of cropland—but losses amounted to 29 million hectares, for a net decline of 12 million hectares. Since 1978 the spurt of rural and urban modernization led to even higher rates of land loss due to housing and plant construction, and some recent declines also reflect the fact that wetlands, grasslands, and treed slopes that were converted into farmland during the 1960s and 1970s were returned to their natural state during the 1980s.

Official figures indicate a net loss of about 17 million hectares between 1957 and 1990, or an average of about 500,000 hectares a year. In relative terms this means a drop of more than 50 percent, from 0.17 hectare in 1957 to only about 800 square meters (0.08 hectare) per capita. Land absorbed by city housing, transportation links, and industrial and mining enterprises, and by rural houses, paths, and irrigation added up to about 40 million hectares between the mid 1950s and 1990. Environmental degradation, above all erosion and desertification, has been responsible for most of the remainder. A nationwide survey done during the 1980s found various degrees of excessive soil erosion on 31 percent of the land, desertification on 5 percent, salinization and alkalization on 6 percent, and waterlogging on 9 percent.

Cumulatively, these losses have seriously weakened China's long-term food production capacity. Given the 1990 crop productivity, the loss of about 40 million hectares is equivalent to forfeiting a base of food production capable of supporting some 370 million people! Even the recent moderated average annual loss of just over 500,000 hectares means a loss of food production capacity for 6 million people every year. The only way China's food output can keep up with both high population increases *and* substantial losses of arable land is by intensification of inputs. Inevitably, this trend, which requires higher inputs of synthetic fertilizers and more energy for irrigation, is taking Chinese farming further away from long-term sustainability.

Forests

When the publication of official statistics resumed in 1979, China's forested area was put at 122 million hectares, or 12.7 percent of territory. This total referred to fully stocked, productive forests, that is to growth whose canopy covers at least 30 percent of the ground. These forests contained about 9.5 billion cubic meters of wood, and their annual wood increment was estimated at 220 million cubic meters.

These figures appeared to confirm the success of reforestation campaigns that were claimed to have restored tree cover on 28 million hectares of land between 1949 and 1979. Soon new admissions modified the totals.[6] First the Ministry of Forestry stated that no more than one-third of all China's plantings since 1949 had managed to survive. Then came many reports on deforestation, including many of staggering provincial losses in just one or two decades, and the studies and descriptions of a deepening rural energy crisis detailed the pressure put on China's trees by the basic demand for fuel for cooking. The post-1979 surge of economic growth led to a 25-percent increase in timber logging between 1978 and 1986.

The well-established practice of falsifying afforestation claims continued during the 1980s: a survey by the Northwest Institute of Forestry in Xi'an indicated that half of reported national afforestation claims were false, and that the survival rate of planted trees was no higher than 40 percent. Consequently, the real rate of reforestation is only about one-fifth of the claimed total.

In addition, pest problems in China's forests are so severe that the area of annual infestation exceeds the area of total afforestation, and the annual economic loss caused by insect pests equals the state's total investment in forestry. Total annual wood losses caused by pests were put at about 11.5 million cubic meters. Another serious threat to China's wood resources is the inadequate prevention of forest fires and poor fire-fighting capabilities. Northeastern forests, the country's largest area of commercial timber stands, experienced 4,900 fires between 1949 and 1989, which burned or damaged about 10 million hectares, or roughly eight times the region's newly afforested area during the same period.

In spite of a slight decrease in China's total timber output after 1986, excessive felling in the few remaining areas of the country that contain mature natural growth has continued. By 1990, 25 of the state's 131 forestry bureaus had virtually exhausted their timber resources, 40 have enough wood for just five to ten years, and 24 for ten to fifteen years: this means that by the year 2000 nearly 70 percent of China's forestry bases will have no trees to fell.

Reports of continuous deforestation have been indicating rapid deterioration not only in the arid north but also in the rainy southern mountains, whose soils are much more prone to heavy water erosion. Officials of the Ministry of Water Resources admitted that the damage caused by deforestation in the Chang Jiang basin has already far outstripped what efforts to control soil erosion can restore. Forest cover in Szechuan, China's most populous province and one of the country's principal timber bases, is now down to about 12 percent from 19 percent in the early 1950s.

Consequently, it came as no surprise that the third survey of forestry resources undertaken by the Ministry of Forestry in 1989 found a combination of sharply declining forested area, diminishing growing stocks, and poorer-quality timber. During the 1980s the forest area decreased by 12.847 million hectares— nearly a 10-percent loss in a decade—with mature growth accounting for 60 percent of this large decline, roughly a 10-percent drop in a decade. As a result, 82 percent of China's timberland in 1990 comprised young or middle-aged stands. Harvestable timber reserves declined by 2.308 billion cubic meters, with mature stands contracting by 170 million cubic meters annually. Moreover, the growing stock ready for harvesting in mature forests now amounts to less than 1.5 billion cubic meters, and it could all be cut in just seven to eight years.

Total wood harvests averaged 344 million cubic meters during the 1980s, exceeding the sustainable rate by 97 million cubic meters, or nearly 40 percent. But merchantable commercial timber accounts for less than one-fifth of this volume, as about 150 million cubic meters of wood are cut to supply around 60 million cubic meters of logs for finished lumber and pulpwood. The rest of the phytomass, approximately 60 percent of the total felled volume, is wasted; the remaining volume of around 200 million cubic meters is fuel for China's energy-deficient countryside.[7] Phytomass is still the critical source of fuel for cooking and heating in most of China's rural areas, but even excessive harvests cannot satisfy minimum household energy needs.

The prospects are made even more worrisome by the extremely low productivity of new plantings and by what are almost certainly overestimates of China's currently forested land. The published figure for the average growing stock in forest plantings—28.27 cubic meters per hectare—makes it quite clear that there is little hope of replacing the felled mature forests, whose growing stock would be at least 80 and commonly up to 100 cubic meters per hectare. And unlike the figures for cultivated land, official figures for total forested area are almost certainly *over*estimates; there may actually be up to 30 percent less forestland. But as in the case of China's farmland, disagreements about the actual extent of forested area are much less important than the acute shortages of timber and the indisputably rapid rate at which forest is being lost.

The current Chinese annual per capita consumption of commercial timber is a mere 0.05 cubic meters per capita, only about a fortieth of the enormous U.S. consumption.[8] And the annual harvest of fuelwood prorates to less than three kilograms of fuel a day per rural household—while the surveys show that 11 kilograms of woody matter a day is the existential minimum. Inevitably, shortages of wood and other resources will be worsened by population increases of more than 200 million during the coming generation.

Growing Population

In the spring of 1994 China's population surpassed 1.2 billion, and although its recent growth rate has been a relatively low 1.1–1.2 percent a year, the huge base results in the addition of 13–14 million people. Such large annual increases will continue for the remainder of this decade, as several fundamental factors put strong upward pressure on China's birthrates. The most obvious one is the age structure of Chinese population, namely the presence of large cohorts of women of fertile age.[9] The number of women of peak childbearing age (twenty-one to thirty years) has culminated at about 125 million, after rising steadily from just 80 million ten years ago; by the year 2000 they will still total nearly 110 million. The effect of this unalterable reality would be modified only by a combination of delayed marriages, lowered fertility, and increased spacing of births.

Minimum marriage age could be changed by a legislative fiat—but in view of the widespread custom of early marriage it is highly doubtful if a major postponement—that is, to the late 20s—would be socially and politically acceptable. Perhaps the only chance for a successful adoption of this approach would be to combine it with a universal guarantee of two births. This birth control strategy is perhaps a better long-term alternative to the one-child policy, with its now numerous exceptions and local peculiarities.

Another important advantage of this approach is that it would result in a more acceptable fertility rate. While China's total fertility rate declined from 6 to less than 3 children with a surprising ease, the stall of further declines during the

1980s demonstrates the resistance of Chinese peasants to any policy forcing them to restrict average total fertility below 2.5 children. Fertility surveys show that virtually no Chinese women (less than 0.1 percent) want to be childless, and fewer than 5 percent of rural families would stop voluntarily at one child. Ideal family sizes translate to total fertility rates of 2.6 in rural areas and 2.0 in large urban areas—and they provide a perfect explanation for the prevailing stall in fertility declines.

Another tightening of state policies aside, the most important variable generating downward pressure on future Chinese fertility rates will be the continuation of a relatively rapid urbanization. For China this is still a novel phenomenon. The nationwide share of urban residents in 1980 (19.4 percent) was virtually identical to the 1961 rate, but the official Chinese statistics show an incredibly rapid increase of urban population to over 30 percent by 1984 and to 49.6 percent in 1988. In reality, most of this astonishing shift can be explained by administrative reorganizations: less than 200 million Chinese are actually residents of large cities.

On the other hand, Chinese urbanization is proceeding even faster at lower levels, as peasants are leaving villages for smaller cities and local towns. Farming privatization, accomplished between 1979 and 1984, resulted in a one-time displacement of some 75 million laborers. By 1990 China's surplus rural labor was more than 100 million, roughly equal to all of Africa's agricultural labor force, or more than three times the European total.

Given the substantial difference between urban and rural fertility rates, continued rapid urbanization should translate into gradually declining total fertility. But forecasts of these changes are highly uncertain at best. Migration to large cities may have only a marginal effect on fertility during the 1990s, and the growth of urban population in smaller cities and country towns may have a relatively modest impact on childbearing, as many migrants will still remain very much within the traditional family setting.

A large number of plausible scenarios combining a range of values for marriageable age, birthrate, total fertility, and urbanization rates can be used to forecast China's population growth. As already noted, perhaps the most realistic, because it is culturally the most acceptable, birth control strategy that could have kept China's population below 1.2 billion by the year 2000 would have been a two-child policy, with or without later marriage and with a strictly enforced policy that there must be at least four years between the births.

Barring a sudden shift toward truly drastic birth control, China's population at the end of the century will surely reach at least 1.25 billion and it may surpass the 1.3 billion mark, although perhaps only by a few million; a total between 1.26 and 1.28 billion appears to be most likely. The United Nations' 1990 medium variant projected 1.299 billion for the year 2000 and put the total for the year 2025 at 1.513 billion.[10] Even the most conservative forecasts add up to awesome cumulative totals: during the 1990s the country's population will grow by at least 125 million people, a total equal to today's Japan or roughly half of the current United States population. A generation later, in 2025, there will be most likely another 200 million Chinese, a gain larger than Indonesia's total population in 1990.

Economic Aspirations

On the whole, China remains fundamentally a poor country, a fact unrealistically overshadowed by recent reports on the rapid growth of the country's gross domestic product (GDP) and on the emergence of an affluent consumer class in a few of the richest coastal provinces and cities. Looking at nationwide means, the combination of privatized farming and high rates of economic growth, the effect of the aggressive, Western-oriented modernization initiated by Deng Xiaoping in 1978 resulted in a generally better supply of food and brought a modicum of material affluence to increasing numbers of urban residents and to many peasants—but the country's per capita GDP is still an order of magnitude lower than in rich countries.

The actual mean—most likely U.S.$1,000–1,500 per capita—is somewhere between the two extremes established by using official exchange rates—the method preferred by the World Bank—and by applying appropriate purchasing power parities—now the choice of the International Monetary Fund.[11] The first approach, yielding only about U.S.$400 per capita, greatly underestimates the real value; the second results in a figure of more than U.S.$2,000 per capita, clearly an exaggeration.

Whatever the actual level, bold developmental plans foresee near-term growth rates matching those of Japanese expansion during the 1960s and 1970s; that is, the aggregate GDP will advance 6–8 percent a year. Recent rates have been much higher, with the 1992 figure reaching 12.8 percent. Even when efficiently executed, such expansion would call for huge increases of energy and material input. International comparisons of basic quality-of-life indicators show the still very low to moderate levels of Chinese achievements and indicate the huge need for resource inputs during the coming decades.

These claims will come not only from a higher demand for better housing and more consumer goods, but also from the necessity to upgrade China's inadequate transportation, communication, and education infrastructures. Even if the comparison is limited to the populated eastern third of the country, the extent of China's railway system is comparable to that of the United States more than a century ago; good, multilane roads are even scarcer, efficient communication is largely restricted to cities, and China offers postsecondary education to a smaller share of its young people than does India. Eliminating these structural deficiencies will require rising consumption of energy and raw materials even if the country's average energy/GDP intensity continued to decline, as it has since modernization of the economy began in the early 1980s.

And the overwhelming majority of this energy and material must come from domestic sources: China cannot follow the Japanese model of economic development predicated on securing imported resources with exports of high-quality manufactures. This pattern has been successfully copied by Taiwan, Hong Kong, Singapore, and South Korea—for a country of China's size, such exchange can yield only a small share of total domestic needs.[12] Comparisons for the two most important resources, energy and food, make this clear. Japan imports about 90 percent of its primary energy consumption, and it produces virtually all of its meat with imported feed. If China imported 90 percent of its primary energy needs it would have claimed half the world's crude oil exports in the early 1990s, and even if China could afford to buy all the grain recently entering the world market it could meet no more than a third of its annual need.

Environmental Concerns

Attitudes are enormously important in confronting and managing environmental degradation; the existence of traditional and relatively widespread concerns about the state of ecosystems and the consequences of pollution is of inestimable help in conducting the requisite research, mobilizing public opinion, adopting effective management approaches, and ensuring appropriate state intervention. There is no doubt that the breadth and intensity of current environmental concerns in rich European countries, Canada, and the United States owe a great deal to a multitude of cultural, social, and scientific traditions embraced and promoted by the intellectual elite.

Some of these attitudes have ancient cultural roots, and their rejuvenation in modern societies has had a major influence on environmental affairs. Certainly the best examples are the admiration of unspoiled landscapes and the particularly deep emotional relationship of many European cultures with forests. Practical demonstrations of these concerns range from the adoption of sustainable forestry practices in eighteenth-century Europe and the establishment of large national parks in the nineteenth-century United States to the recent wave of extensive afforestation—most European countries now have more forest than two or three generations ago—and to fervent nonviolent protests against clear-cutting in Canada.

Perhaps the other two most notable strands of this complex amalgam are long-standing interest in the sustained productivity of land, institutionalized by British experimental stations and by American agricultural universities of the nineteenth century, and various natural conservancy movements, a phenomenon inspired by Rousseau and Thoreau and manifested in such disparate ways as the Boy Scouts' and E. T. Seton's wood lore and the activism of the Sierra Club and Greenpeace.

Unfortunately, China's recent past includes neither the elite concerns nor any more popular preoccupations with the state of the environment. Reasons for this range from ancient historical traditions—Chinese philosophy has always been preoccupied with questions of morality and the proper conduct and ordering of human relations, rather than with mankind's place in nature—to more recent political and economic realities. The poverty and violence of twentieth-century Chinese history have left little room for concerns beyond those of basic survival, and the most recent spell of economic prosperity has been marked by a frantic quest for enrichment and by higher material consumption. This frenzied rush is the understandable reaction to decades of Maoist deprivation—but it creates a climate inimical to any widespread appreciation of the environmental foundations of economic success. Consequently, popular Chinese environmental concerns are overwhelmingly just defensive reactions to the immediate effects of pollution, most commonly to excessive urban noise and air pollution. The ruling elites, preoccupied with the preservation of the old political orthodoxy and the corrupt dash for riches, focus on these matters only when it cannot be avoided—in crises such as urban water shortages—or when there is international pressure to confront regional and global environmental problems.

In terms of a historical analogy, China's development today is perhaps best compared to that of the United States in the last decade of the nineteenth century: the country is overwhelmingly preoccupied with growth, expansion, and rapid embourgeoisement. This would weaken environmental concerns even in a society with a much stronger tradition of elite involvement in such matters. No less important is the effect of these changes on the survival of some of the most environmentally commendable traditional practices.

Demise of Sustainable Traditions

No Chinese tradition could be of greater value in establishing a sustainable society than intensive agriculture based on heavy recycling of organic matter and on complex crop rotation. Many Western observers have seen these practices as a paragon of sustainable farming, forgetting or perhaps never even realizing that the best traditional European cultivation was very similar until the last decades of the nineteenth century.[13] Now, repeating the Western trend, Chinese practices are being displaced by modern commercial methods.

Heavy recycling of organic matter—crop residues, animal and human waste, grasses, and canal and pond mud—has declined precipitously since the early 1980s. Key reasons for this change have been the privatization of farming, the decreasing availability of organic waste, and increasing access to synthetic nitrogen. Privatization has favored less labor, and the collection, fermentation, and distribution of organic waste are among the most labor-intensive activities in traditional agriculture. The construction of sewers and water treatment plants in cities has deprived suburban farms of their main source of organic waste, and because of widespread rural energy shortages, large amounts of crop residue are diverted for cooking fuel. And by the late 1980s China became the world's largest producer of synthetic nitrogen in the form of urea from nearly a score of large new plants.

As a result, the use of synthetic nitrogen on an average hectare of Chinese farmland has soared past the high Japanese mean (in 1990 the means were about 200 and 140 kilograms N/ha), and organic recycling fell to a fraction of its traditional rates. Inevitably, this change has accelerated the qualitative decline of China's agricultural soils. Complaints about the demise of organic recycling have been coupled with reports of declining soil fertility, excessive use of synthetic fertilizers, and increasing water pollution from the dumping of sewered but untreated urban wastes. The organic-matter content of intensively cultivated soils on the North East China Plain fell from the natural level of 9 percent to 5 percent by the 1970s and to only 2 percent by the mid 1980s.

The decline of organic farming has been accompanied by undesirable simplification of cropping as cultivation has been getting steadily less diversified. In 1949 wheat and rice were planted on 43 percent of the total grain-growing area; in 1990 on 55 percent. Coarse grains were planted on more than a fifth of all sown land in the early 1950s, but by 1985 that figure had shrunk to less than one-tenth of the total. Cultivation of such traditional Chinese species as millet, mung beans, and red beans has become very rare.

The planting of soybeans—China's leading leguminous crop fixing a large part of its nitrogen need with symbiotic rhizobia—has increased since 1980, but it is still nearly 30 percent below the plantings of the early 1950s. Higher yields have not compensated for the combination of reduced planting and growing population: per capita availability of soybeans is now 35 percent below the mid-1950s rate. The decline of legumes planted as green manures has been great even in absolute terms. Such planting peaked at nearly 10 million hectares in 1975, but by 1990 it fell to just about 4 million hectares. Moreover, cultivation of soybeans has become extremely uneven, with a single province, Hunan, accounting recently for nearly one-quarter of the national total, while the newly rich, intensively farmed Guangdong has merely one percent.

The principal reason for abandoning green-manure cultivation is clearly the higher pressure to produce more food on limited land. To return to the peak plantings would mean to forego green harvests equivalent to about 20 million tonnes, enough to feed some 75 million people. American farmers can take huge amounts of marginal land out of production—especially when encouraged by laws that reward them for reducing soil erosion—and European farmers can reduce high-intensity fertilization—as a result of huge state farming subsidies—without compromising food supply in their respective societies. Chinese farmers have virtually no reserves of new land, and no land tied up in production for exports; consequently they have to meet rising demands for food by further intensifying cropping—that is, by turning to progressively less sustainable agriculture.

Looking Ahead

While it would be naive to underestimate the combined effect of these barriers to China's quest for a more sustainable society, it would be equally irresponsible to underrate the potential for effective remedies. Synergy among the five described obstacles will make it impossible to reverse the existing degradative trends during the next generation, but an aggressive adoption of the best available managerial approaches and technical improvements would make a major difference in the rate of the overall deterioration.[14]

I will mention just the most obvious and most desirable remedies, those that can make the greatest difference. Better pricing is a precondition of many effective changes. I am not even thinking about accounting for notable externalities, merely about pricing that covers the actual known costs of production. Given the ubiquity of irrational pricing in China, such changes would go a long way toward promoting more efficient use of water, energy, and wood.

Numerous measures can have major cumulative effects. In water management, these range from better matching of crops with natural moisture supply (sorghum needs less than corn) to simple, inexpensive microcomputer-controlled soil moisture assessments for optimal irrigation. In forest management they should include higher rates of woody biomass utilization as well as the extensive use of milling waste for heat generation or particle board production. In energy management there must be persistent diffusion of more efficient convertors, be they compact fluorescent lights, more modern household stoves, or better industrial boilers.

All of these options are within China's existing capabilities, and their effect can be significantly augmented by the extensive adoption of foreign techniques and by well-targeted aid for industries and processes primarily responsible for worrisome environmental degradation. Here the opportunities range from a variety of techniques for cleaner coal combustion to flue gas desulfurization and reduced production of chlorofluorocarbons.

But even a vigorous commitment by the Chinese and the best foreign assistance will not be enough to put China on a sustainable path during the next generation. A critical appraisal of Chinese realities offers no comforting outlook for the remainder of this century—or for the first decade or two of the next. The best that can be hoped for during the next twenty or thirty years is that a gradual moderation of degradative trends will result from reduced population growth, better management, and more efficient techniques. These changes would provide the necessary foundation for a more sustainable society by the middle of the next century.

Notes

1. Vaclav Smil, *Energy in China's Modernization* (Armonk, NY: M.E. Sharpe, 1988).

2. All factual information on the current state of China's environment comes from appropriate sections of the following three books which offer comprehensive assessments: Fu Lixue, et al., *Gaishan shengtai huanjing (Improving the Environment)* (Beijing: Xueshu shukan chubanshe [Science Book Publishing House], 1989); Vaclav Smil, *China's Environment: An Inquiry into the Limits of National Development* (Armonk, NY:

M.E. Sharpe, 1993); Qu Geping and Li Jinchang, *Population and the Environment in China* (Boulder, CO: Lynne Rienner Publishers, 1994).

3. World Resources Institute, *World Resources 1994–95* (New York: Oxford University Press, 1994), 346–47.

4. Food and Agriculture Organization, *Production Yearbook* (Rome: FAO, 1994), 15.

5. For details on the plain's irrigation see Huang Ronghan, "Development of Groundwater for Agriculture in the Lower Yellow River Alluvial Basin" and James E. Nickum, "All Is Not Wells in North China: Irrigation in Yucheng County," in *Efficiency in Irrigation,* ed. Gerald T. O'Mara (Washington, DC: World Bank, 1988), 80–84, 87–95.

6. Vaclav Smil, "Afforestation in China," in *Afforestation Policies, Planning and Progress,* ed. A. Mather (London: Belhaven Press), 105–17.

7. Shangwu Gao and Deying Xu, "Rural Energy and Fuel Forests in China," *Biomass and Bioenergy* (May 1992): 297–99.

8. Food and Agriculture Organization, *Forestry Yearbook* (Rome: FAO, 1994).

9. Griffith Feeney, et al., "Recent Fertility Dynamics in China: Results from the 1987 One-Percent Population Survey," *Population and Development Review* 15 (1989): 297–322.

10. United Nations, *Long-Range World Population Projections: Two Centuries of Population Growth* (New York: United Nations, 1992).

11. Vaclav Smil, "How Rich Is China?" *Current History* 92 (1993): 265–69.

12. Vaclav Smil, "Asia's Stumbling Giant," *Independent Monthly* (May 1994): 66–69.

13. F. H. King, *Farmers of the Forty Centuries* (New York: Harcourt & Brace, 1927).

14. For details on practical roads towards greater sustainability, see Vaclav Smil, *Global Ecology Environmental Change and Social Flexibility* (London: Routledge, 1993).

12

Authentic Development: Is it Sustainable?

Denis Goulet

Introduction

For the World Bank, the "achievement of sustained and equitable development remains the greatest challenge facing the human race."[1] Equitable development has not been achieved, however: glaring disparities continue to exist both within and among countries.[2] It will not do, therefore, merely to sustain the kind of development we already have.

The World Commission on Environment and Development defines as sustainable "development that meets the needs of the present without compromising the ability of future generations to meet their own needs."[3] This brief and apparently clear definition is nevertheless fraught with ambiguities. As the economist Paul Streeten notes, it is unclear whether one should

> be concerned with sustaining the constituents of well-being or its determinants, whether with the means or the ends. Clearly, what ought to matter are the constituents: the health, welfare and prosperity of the people, and not so many tons of minerals, so many trees, or so many animal species.[4]

Matters are complicated further, Streeten adds, because the term *sustainable development* can have at least six different meanings: (1) "maintenance, replacement and growth of capital assets, both physical and human"; (2) "maintaining the physical environmental conditions for the constituents of well-being"; (3) the "resilience" of a system, enabling it to adjust to shocks and crises; (4) "avoiding burdening future generations with internal and external debts"; (5) "fiscal, administrative and political sustainability. A policy must be credible and acceptable to the citizens, so that there is sufficient consent to carry it out"; and (6) "the ability to hand over projects to the management by citizens of the developing country in which they are carried out, so that foreign experts can withdraw without jeopardizing their success."[5] These diverse meanings are not analyzed or illustrated in this chapter; its more limited role is to clarify the question of whether development is environmentally sustainable. "Sustainable development" has now become the fashionable mantra in international policy circles. Although it is usually assumed that these two terms are compatible, this is not self-evident. As the economist Paul Ekins observes:

> There is literally no experience of an environmentally sustainable industrial economy, anywhere in the world, where such sustainability refers to a non-depleting stock of environmental capital. It is therefore not immediately apparent that, on the basis of past experience only, the term "sustainable development" is any more than an oxymoron.[6]

Sustainability requires simple living in which consumption and resource use are limited.[7] But development, as conventionally understood, demands continued economic growth, which may render sustainability impossible by further depleting nonrenewable resources and polluting the biosphere.

One cannot decide whether development is sustainable until two prior questions are satisfactorily answered:

- What is genuine wealth?
- What is authentic development?

Defining Wealth

In development circles, wealth means the accumulation of material, or economic, goods. It is identified with mass consumption, or at least with a society's access to an ever increasing supply of ever more diverse material goods. Yet genuine human riches may lie elsewhere: it is perhaps more accurate to assign only instrumental value to economic riches and to posit other, qualitative kinds of goods as constitutive of true human wealth. This quite different view of wealth appears in various sources.

a) *Carolina Maria de Jesus* was an impoverished single mother of three dwelling in São Paulo's Canindé *favela* (slum). Her diary, written on scraps of paper as an exercise in fantasizing to escape the squalor of her life, was accidentally discovered by a journalist in 1958 and became an instant best-seller in Brazil.

> I read that a woman with three children had committed suicide because she found it too difficult to live. The woman who killed herself didn't have the

soul of a *favelado*, who when in hunger goes through garbage, picks up vegetables from the street fair, begs and keeps on living. The poor woman! Who knows how long she had been thinking of killing herself, because mothers worry a good deal for their children. But what a shame against a nation.[8]

Carolina's definition of a nation's wealth is disarmingly simple: "The basic necessities must be within reach of everyone."[9]

b) *Gandhi* judged that there are enough goods in the poorest Indian village to meet the needs of all, but not enough goods in all of India to satisfy the greed of each one. Gandhi championed production by the masses, which brings dignity and livelihood to all, over mass production, which is production by a few that reduces the masses to mere consumers of others' profit-making activities.[10]

c) The student of Native American societies *Barry Lopez* considers that

> some native ideas could serve us well in this historical moment: that a concept of wealth should be founded in physical health and spiritual well-being, not material possessions; that to be "poor" is to be without family, without a tribe—without people who care deeply for you.[11]

d) *Early Fathers of the Christian Church*—John Chrysostom, Gregory of Nyssa, and Basil the Great—often preached sermons on the difference between material and spiritual riches.[12] Material goods are by nature limited and cannot be shared without diminishing the advantages each one derives from them. In contrast, spiritual goods grow in intensity and in their capacity to satisfy as they are shared. Genuine wealth, the fathers contend, resides in the internal freedom that makes one use material goods instrumentally to meet needs, and as a springboard for cultivating those higher spiritual goods that alone bring deeper satisfactions: virtue, friendship, truth, and beauty.

e) Writing in 1934 on *Technics and Civilization, Lewis Mumford* concluded that

> real values do not derive from either rarity or crude manpower. It is not rarity that gives the air its power to sustain life, nor is it the human work done that gives milk or bananas their nourishment. In comparison with the effects of chemical action and the sun's rays the human contribution is a small one. Genuine value lies in the power to sustain or enrich life. . . . The juice of a lemon may be more valuable on a long ocean voyage than a hundred pounds of meat without it. The value lies directly in the life-function: not in its origin, its rarity, or in the work done by human agents.[13]

f) The psychologist *Erich Fromm* observes that people always choose one of two modes of living:

> The alternative of *having* versus *being* does not appeal to common sense. *To have,* so it would seem, is a normal function of our life: in order to live we

must have things. Moreover, we must have things in order to enjoy them. In a culture in which the supreme goal is to have—and to have more and more—and in which one can speak of someone as "being worth a million dollars," how can there be an alternative between having and being? On the contrary, it would seem that the very essence of being is having; that if one *has nothing, one is nothing.*

Yet the great Masters of Living have made the alternative between having and being a central issue of their respective systems. The Buddha teaches that in order to arrive at the highest stage of human development, we must not crave possessions. Jesus teaches: "for whosoever will save his life shall lose it; but whosoever will lose his life for my sake, the same shall save it. For what is a man advantaged, if he gain the whole world, and lose himself, or be cast away?" (Luke 9:24–25). Master Eckhart taught that to have nothing and make oneself open and "empty," not to let one's ego stand in one's way, is the condition for achieving spiritual wealth and strength.

For many years I had been deeply impressed by this distinction and was seeking its empirical basis in the concrete study of individuals and groups by the psychoanalytic method. What I saw has led me to conclude that this distinction, together with that between love of life and love of the dead, represents the most crucial problem of existence; that empirical anthropological and psychoanalytic data tend to demonstrate that *having and being are two fundamental modes of experience, the respective strengths of which determine the differences between the characters of individuals and various types of social character.*[14]

g) The political theorist *Douglas Lummis* argues that individual riches are not the only form of wealth:

> Common wealth is not something achieved by economic development but by the political ordering of a community. . . . Common wealth may find its physical expression in such things as public roads, bridges, libraries, parks, schools, churches, temples, or works of art that enrich the lives of all. It may take the form of "commons," shared agricultural land, forests or fisheries. It may take the form of ceremonies, feast days, festivals, dances, and other public entertainments celebrated in common. . . .
>
> The *problem* of the problem of inequality lies not in poverty, but in excess. "The problem of the world's poor," defined more accurately, turns out to be "the problem of the world's rich." This means that the solution to that problem is not a massive change in the culture of poverty so as to place it on the path of development, but a massive change in the culture of superfluity in order to place it on the path of counterdevelopment. It does not call for a new value system forcing the world's majority to feel shame at their traditionally moderate consumption habits, but for a new value system forcing the world's rich to see the shame and vulgarity of their overconsumption habits, and the double vulgarity of standing on other people's shoulders to achieve those consumption habits.[15]

From these texts emerges a conception of genuine wealth whose components are:

- the societal provision of essential goods to all
- a mode of production that creates "right livelihoods" for all
- the use of material goods as a springboard to qualitatively enriching human spiritual nature
- the pursuit of material goods in function of their capacities to nurture life and enhance *being* rather than *having*
- a primacy given to public wealth, which fosters, more than do personal riches, the common good

Any evaluative ethical judgments we make about wealth and the institutions devoted to creating it need to be rooted in philosophical conceptions as to the broader purposes of human existence.

Defining Development

No less diverse than definitions of wealth are the multiple notions of development in circulation. No consensus exists as to how development should be defined, what its goals are, and what strategies should be adopted to pursue it. The economist Keith Griffin evaluates six development strategies: monetarism, open economy, industrialization, green revolution, redistribution, and socialism. He assesses empirical results yielded by each strategy in different countries on six registers: (1) resource utilization and income level; (2) savings, investment, and growth; (3) human capital formation; (4) poverty and inequality; (5) role of the state; and (6) participation, democracy, and freedom. The inconclusive results lead Griffin to conclude that "There is no best path to development."[16]

There undoubtedly exists no single best path to development, applicable everywhere and at all times. Moreover, each development paradigm and strategy admits of countless variations. Although ultimately each society must create its own model of development, it nonetheless seems possible to subsume all known strategies and paradigms under four distinct general orientations.[17] These orientations guide the choice of particular strategies, as catalogued by Griffin.

Growth

Growth strategists aim at maximizing aggregate production so as to "create a bigger economic pie." The way to create wealth quickly is to marshal domestic savings to the maximum or, if these are insufficient, to obtain foreign capital in some form (investment, loans, grants) and apply it to productive investment. Rapid growth comes not only from widening the base of productive assets, but from greater productivity in utilizing factors of production. Therefore, great importance is placed on incorporating modern technology, the single greatest multiplier of productivity.

Inequalities resulting from growth are deemed unavoidable. To redistribute wealth through revolutionary or reform measures, growth theorists argue, is merely to redistribute misery. Either the benefits of growth will trickle down to poor people at a later time, or if they do not, corrective welfare measures can be adopted by political authorities to assure equity.

Redistribution

Advocates of "redistribution with growth" argue that distributive justice—the elimination of great inequities in wealth—cannot result from trickle-down processes or even from corrective welfare policies. Equity has to be planned as a direct objective of development strategy. Accordingly, they seek not to *maximize* economic growth but to *optimize* it in the light of equity objectives. Within this paradigm, investments in education, job creation, health, and nutrition are treated not as consumer goods but as productive investments. Nutritious food and good health services add productive wealth to the nation's workforce, leading to decreases in idleness caused by illness or absenteeism and to increases in economic demand among the poor classes. Champions of this approach contend that a high level of growth is compatible with equitable distribution.

Basic Human Needs

The basic-human-needs (BHN) strategy goes beyond the redistribution model by specifying the quantifiable content of equitable redistribution. The primary task thus becomes neither to maximize nor to optimize aggregate growth, but to satisfy the basic needs of those segments of a nation's population that lie under some poverty line. Basic needs include goods and services relating to nutrition, health, housing, education, and access to jobs. The BHN paradigm does not assume that equity is necessarily compatible with high rates of economic growth. If basic needs can be met with little or no growth, so be it: true development is not measured by growth.

Even under the BHN formula, however, the ultimate goals of development are accepted as being those endorsed in the first two strategies: economic welfare for large numbers of people, technological efficiency, and institutional modernity. For BHN advocates, the best means to achieve these goals is to use scarce resources primarily to provide for the poorest.

Development from Tradition

Development from tradition departs radically from the three pathways just outlined. Its central premise is that not only the means of development but its goals are not to be borrowed from countries already "developed": any such mimetic development is spurious and distorted. In "development from tradition," the goal of development suited to a particular society should be sought within the latent dynamism of that society's value system: its traditional beliefs, meaning systems, local institutions, and popular practices. Given that culture's understanding of the meaning of life and death, of time and eternity, and of how human beings should relate to the forces of the cosmos, certain ideal images of the good life and the good society emerge. Although modern ideas, behavior, and technology are not repudiated on principle, they are critically judged to determine whether or not they contribute to the sound development of individuals and communities as defined by the traditional value system.

Traditional values are not immune to criticism, however. Gandhi himself, when evaluating the caste system or the spiritual authority of Brahmins of India, recognized that such modern values as rational inquiry and the democratic equality of persons before the law lay bare the inhuman characteristics of certain ancient beliefs. Consequently, traditional images of the good life and the good society should be critically confronted with modern alternatives to see which are more truly developed.

Both the BHN and development-from-tradition orientations assume varying forms. The BHN approach is variously labeled as "endogenous" or "self-defined" (autocentered), self-reliant, or bottom-up development. As for the tradition-rooted approach, it sometimes takes the form of an outright rejection of development. The French agronomist René Dumont considers the performance of the last forty years to be a dangerous epidemic of misdevelopment.[18] In Africa, he states, development has simply not occurred. Latin America, on the other hand, has created great wealth, ranging from sophisticated nuclear and electronic industries to cities of sparkling skyscrapers. But this growth has been won at the price of massive pollution, urban congestion, and monumental waste. Moreover, the majority of the region's population has not benefited. For Dumont, misdevelopment is the mismanagement of resources; it is the main cause of world hunger and afflicts "developed" countries as severely as it does Third World nations.[19]

Others sound the same theme: development is an irresponsible, inequitable, and destructive force that worsens the lot of poor people. The late Swiss anthropologist Roy Preiswerk judges that processes of change have led to "maldevelopment" in rich and poor countries.[20] The most absolute attack, however, comes from those who totally repudiate development, both as concept and as project. Serge Latouche, the French economist, urges us to discard development because it is a tool used by advanced Western countries to destroy the cultures and the autonomy of nations throughout Africa, Asia, and Latin America.[21] For the Mexican economist Gustavo Esteva, *development* is

> a loaded word, and one doomed to extinction. . . . From the unburied corpse of development, every kind of pest has started to spread. . . . Development has evaporated. . . . It is now time to recover a sense of reality. It is time to recover serenity. Crutches, like those offered by science, are not necessary when it is

possible to walk with one's own feet, on one's own path, in order to dream one's dreams. Not the borrowed ones of development.[22]

Ivan Illich sees development as "modernization of poverty" and the "radical disempowerment" of people to define and meet their own needs. In Illich's view, an army of expert professionals has captured a radical monopoly over diagnosis and prescriptions for society, by appropriating sole legitimacy to do so via a privileged "filtering" system of certification and "credentialization."[23] Since its creation in 1972, the Cultural Survival Movement headquartered at Harvard University has done battle to prevent development from destroying native cultures. Its founder, anthropologist David Maybury-Lewis, states that

> violence done to indigenous peoples is largely based on prejudices and discrimination that must be exposed and combated. These prejudices are backed up by widely held misconceptions, which presume that traditional societies are inherently obstacles to development or that the recognition of their rights would subvert the nation state. Our research shows that this is untrue.[24]

According to Robert Vachon of the Intercultural Institute of Montreal, development is not to be totally rejected but "radically relativized," because there exist cross-cultural "alternatives to development."[25] Accordingly, "the challenge today is not so much that of development which is global, sustainable, integral, human, democratic, etc., but rather the radical pluralism of cultures of truth, of reality."[26]

Authentic Development

The need faced by every society to make development choices thrusts three basic ethical questions to its attention:

• What is the relation between the fullness of good and the abundance of goods?
• What are the foundations of justice in and among societies?
• What criteria ought to govern the posture of societies toward the forces of nature and of technology?

Development generates multiple value conflicts over the meaning of the good life. In Ursula K. Le Guin's science fiction novel *The Dispossessed,*[27] two models of the good life vie for the loyalties of people. One model prizes collaboration, friendship, health, and a high degree of equality, achievable in an austere communitarian regime of disciplined resource use. The other prizes material comfort, individual selfishness, and competition, with its resulting inequalities, and depends on abundant resources.

A second value conflict concerns the foundations of justice in society. Should justice rest on inherited authority, on the rule of the majority, on a social contract? Are political rights and individual freedoms to be given primacy over collective social and economic rights aimed at assuring that needs are met and that society's common good is served? Do human rights have a purely instrumental value, or are they ends in themselves, worthy for their own sake?

A third set of value conflicts centers on the criteria a society adopts to frame its stance toward nature. Is nature to be viewed simply as raw material for Promethean exploitation by humans, or as the larger womb of life in which humans live, move, and have their being, and whose rhythms and laws they must respect? Should the human stance toward nature be extractive and manipulative or harmony-seeking?

Providing satisfactory conceptual and institutional answers to these three questions is what constitutes authentic development. It follows, therefore, that not every nation with a high per capita income is truly developed.[28]

One illuminating formulation of the components of authentic development is that made by L. J. Lebret, founder of the Economy and Humanism movement.[29] Lebret defines development as "the series of transitions, for a given population and all the subpopulations which comprise it, from a less human to a more human phase of existence, at the speediest rhythm possible, at the lowest possible cost, while taking into account all the bonds of solidarity which exist (or ought to exist) amongst these populations and subpopulations."[30]

The normative expressions "more human" and "less human" are to be understood in the light of Lebret's distinction between *plus avoir* ("to have more") and *plus être* ("to be more"). A society is more human or developed not when its citizens "have more," but when all are enabled "to be more."[31] Material growth and quantitative increase are doubtless needed for genuine human development, but not just any kind of growth nor increase at any price. Lebret considers that the world as a whole remains underdeveloped or falls prey to an illusory anti-development so long as a small number of nations or privileged groups remain alienated in an abundance of luxury (facility) goods at the expense of the many who are deprived thereby of essential (subsistence) goods. When such situations prevail, rich and poor societies alike suffer from an insufficient satisfaction of their "enhancement" needs.

For Galbraith the "final requirement of modern development planning is that it have a theory of consumption . . . a view of what the production is ultimately for. . . . *More important, what kind of consumption should be planned?*"[32] A sound theory of needs locates a hierarchy of importance and urgency around three categories: needs of the first order, enhancement needs, and luxury needs.[33] Authentic development does not exist when the first-order needs of the many are sacrificed in favor of the luxury needs of a few, or when enhancement needs are not widely met. For this reason Erich Fromm judges that "affluent alienation" is no less dehumanizing than "impoverished alienation."[34]

Some sixty governmental planners, project managers, and social science scholars who convened at a seminar on "Ethical Issues in Development" held 15–19 September 1986 at the MARGA Institute (Sri Lanka Institute for Development Studies) in Colombo, Sri Lanka, reached consensus that any adequate definition of development must include the following dimensions.[35]

1. An *economic component* dealing with the creation of wealth and improved conditions of material life, equitably distributed
2. A *social ingredient* measured as well-being in health, education, housing, and employment
3. A *political dimension* embracing such values as human rights, political freedom, legal enfranchisement of persons, and some form of democracy
4. A *cultural element,* in recognition of the fact that cultures confer identity and self-worth to people
5. *Ecological soundness,* understood as a mode of extracting, using, and disposing of resources that safeguards and revitalizes nature so as not to deplete it irreplaceably, poison it, or damage its life-restorative powers
6. A final dimension one may call the *full-life paradigm,* which refers to meaning systems, symbols, and beliefs concerning the ultimate meaning of life and history.

For any society, authentic development means providing optimal life-sustenance, esteem, and freedom to all its members. Therefore, the destruction of life-giving resources, the irreversible violation of nature's environments, and the indiscriminate adoption of technologies that destroy human freedoms constitute destructive development, not creative development. Like the colonial political system, however, spurious development breeds opposition, contradiction, and self-destruction: *it cannot be sustained.*

Sustainability must be assured in five domains: economic, political, social, environmental, and cultural. Long-term economic viability depends on a use of resources that does not deplete them irreversibly. Political viability rests on creating for all members of society a stake in its survival: this cannot be achieved unless all enjoy freedom and inviolable personal rights and believe that the political system within which they live pursues some common good and not mere particular interests. Environmental sustainability requires the maintenance of abundant diversity of life-forms and biosystems, a restorative mode of resource use, and disposal of wastes within nature's absorptive limits. And if development is to be socially and culturally sustainable, the foundations of community and symbolic meaning systems must be protected. Otherwise they will be steamrolled into oblivion on the pretext of the need to submit to the requirements of scientific and technological "rationality."

A sound development strategy will be oriented toward a form of economic growth whose production package centers on basic needs, job creation (largely through the adoption of appropriate technologies),[36] decentralized public infrastructure investment that produces multiple "poles" of development, an adequate social allocation ratio of public expenditures devoted to what the United Nations Development Programme calls "human priority concerns,"[37] an incentives policy to favor increased productivity in low-productivity sectors, and selective linkage and de-linkage with global markets, with the primary emphasis on domestic markets.[38]

In its report *North-South: A Programme for Survival,* the Brandt Commission declared that

> Mankind has never before had such ample technical and financial resources for coping with hunger and poverty. The immense task can be tackled once the necessary collective will is mobilized. . . . Solidarity among men must go beyond national boundaries: we cannot allow it to be reduced to a meaningless phrase. International solidarity must stem both from strong mutual interests in cooperation *and* from compassion for the hungry.[39]

In no domain is solidarity more urgently needed than in environmental affairs. The ecological imperative is clear and cruel: nature must be saved or we humans will die. The single greatest threat to nature comes from "development." This same development also perpetuates the underdevelopment of hundreds of millions of people. Therefore, the task of eliminating dehumanizing underdevelopment possesses the same urgency as the safeguard of nature. Of necessity, a comprehensive ethic of authentic development looks to the sustainable use of resources as well as to their equitable distribution. Along with this ethic we need what Ignacy Sachs, the father of "eco-development," calls an anthropological economics that simultaneously serves human needs and manages nature with wisdom.[40]

Ecology versus Development

Ecology has now become a household word. The symbolism here is illuminating, for in its Greek etymology, *ecology* designates the science of the larger household, the total environment in which living organisms exist. That total environment constitutes the "economy of nature." Nature, the support system of all life, is the larger economy (household to be managed) within which the human economy—the stewardship of "scarce" or "rare" goods—is deployed. In reinstating the ancient Greek distinction between economics and *chrematistics,* Daly and Cobb highlight two contrasting approaches to decision making regarding resource use. Chrematistics

> is the branch of political economy relating to the manipulation of property and wealth so as to maximize short-term monetary exchange value to the owner. Oikonomia, by contrast, is the management of the household so as to increase its use value to all members of the household over the long run. If we expand

the scope of household to include the larger community of the land, of shared values, resources, biomes, institutions, language, and history, then we have a good definition of "economics for community."[41]

In human economy, infrastructural and input (supply) goods need to be maintained and replenished. So too with natural support systems: biospheres and ecosystems must be constantly "recapitalized." Consequently, two procedures must be instituted in economic record keeping:

• Externalities must be internalized (natural support systems must be treated like other factors of production in cost-benefit calculations).
• Economic performance must be measured in ways that take account of nature (by introducing new, multidimensional indicators including natural depletion and replenishment).[42]

When it is faithful to its origins and inner spirit, ecology is holistic: it looks to the whole picture, the totality of relations. As a new pluridisciplinary field of study, ecology embraces four interrelated subjects: environment, demography, resource systems, and technology. Its special contribution to human knowledge is to draw a coherent portrait of how these four realms interact in patterns of vital interdependence. Ecological wisdom is the search for optimal modes and scales in which human populations are to apply technology to resource use within their environments. Both as an intellectual discipline and as a practical concern, ecology *presupposes some philosophy of nature.* Traditional human wisdoms long ago parted ways, however, in their conceptions of nature and their views as to how human beings should relate to it. All wisdoms acknowledge humans to be part of nature and subject to its laws. The common destiny of all natural beings, humans included, is generation and corruption: to be born, grow, get old, and die. But certain worldviews more than others elevate humans above their encompassing nature and assign to them a cosmic role of domination over the very nature of which they are a part. The duality of views on the relation of humans to nature is aptly expressed in the interrogatory words that serve as the title of a Sri Lankan publication, *Man in Nature, Guest or Engineer?*[43] If "man" is a guest of nature, he must obey the rules of his host. If, on the contrary, the presence of "man" in nature is as an engineer, he then has license to manipulate, handle, alter, and "engineer" nature to suit his purposes. That nature and human liberty have been seen as opposing poles in a dichotomy poses difficult questions. Are human animals *free* to treat nature as they would? Or must humans, like other animals, submit to nature's laws, or at least to its penalties? Paradoxically, human beings are free not to respect nature, but they must do so if they are to preserve the very existential ground upon which their freedom rests. Since this is so, there can be no ultimate incompatibility between the demands of nature and the exigencies of human freedom, those of environmental sanity, of wise resource stewardship, and of technology. Problems arise when ecologists and resource planners fail to look at the whole picture. Looking at the whole picture also enables theorists to transcend other apparent antinomies, chief among them the perceived contradiction between anthropocentric and cosmocentric views of the universe.

For ethicists who stress the integrity of nature, the highest values are the conservation of resources, the preservation of species, and the protection of nature from human depredations.[44] Those who stress human freedom, in contrast, take as their primary values justice—which takes the form of an active assault upon human poverty, branded as the worst form of pollution—and the need to "develop" potential into actual resources.[45] Although the two ethical orientations rank them differently, both adhere to all five values:

- The conservation of resources
- The preservation of species
- The protection of nature
- The active pursuit of justice
- The obligation to "develop" potential resources

A "nature" emphasis locates development and the elimination of human misery below biological and resource conservation in its hierarchy of values. Conversely, a "freedom" orientation places development and justice in resource allocations above environmental protection or the preservation of endangered species in its scale of values. All five values enjoy parity of moral status, however. The reason is that any long-term, sustainable, equity-enhancing combat against poverty requires wisdom in the exploitation of resources. Reciprocally, the preservation of other living species cannot be persuasively held up as a priority goal if the human species itself is threatened with degrading poverty or extinction. Nature is diminished when its human members are kept "underdeveloped." Conversely, humans cannot become truly "developed" if they violate their supportive nature.

The only authentic form of development is that which is conducted in the mode of solidarity, binding all persons and communities to each other and to the planet they inhabit. The ecological imperative is clear and cruel: nature must be saved or humans will die. The single greatest threat to nature—menacing irreversible destruction of its regenerative powers—comes from "development." This same development also perpetuates the underdevelopment of hundreds of millions of people. Therefore, the task of eliminating dehumanizing underdevelopment possesses the same urgency as the safeguard of nature.

In Conclusion: Unanswered Questions

Sustainable authentic development (SAD) is probably incompatible with the present world order, with prevailing patterns of consumption, with the regnant development paradigm, and with existing configurations of competitive global resource use. It may prove to be possible only if profound transformations occur in precisely these arenas: world order, patterns of consumption, patterns of resource use. The debate on sustainability is replete with uncertainties and difficulties. These difficult issues are here presented in the guise of four questions. How the questions are answered will determine what are the prospects for SAD.

Is sustainable authentic development compatible with a globalized economy? According to one recent commentator on global and regional trade negotiations (the GATT and NAFTA):

> The philosophy inherent in these accords is directly opposed to the idea of sustainable economic development promoted in Rio. . . . Neoliberal free trade policies are being pushed by a worldwide corporate elite bent on defining the environment as a trade barrier expressed in dollars. Governments have abetted this transformation by forging agreements that ensure a nation's powerlessness to defend itself against commercial activities that harm its citizens or the environment.[46]

Environmental sustainability may require a high degree of economic decentralization, this in recognition of the vast "diseconomies" attendant upon large-scale global production, distribution, and consumption.

Is SAD compatible with a high material standard of living, as presently defined, for all human populations? If limits must be placed on growth, there must be cutbacks in the present consumption of the "haves" and in future acquisitive aspirations of "have-nots."

Such cutbacks run counter to the momentum built up over fifty years in the "revolution of rising expectations." How, politically speaking, are they to be achieved? The example of failed central-command economies holds out the lesson that austerity cannot be imposed. And the reluctance of citizens in developed countries to accept even modest tax increases to cut deficits or to provide necessary social services suggests that sacrifices for the sake of sustainability will not be readily consented to.

Is SAD compatible with widening global economic disparities? Does not SAD presuppose, if not relative equality, at least the abolition of absolute poverty among the world's poor masses? What realistic prospects exist, however, either for abolishing absolute poverty or for diminishing global disparities? "Aid fatigue" in the rich has greatly reduced the volume of net resource transfers to the poor. Moreover, the world economy is growing too slowly for any "increased economic pie" to "trickle down" (assuming such "trickle-down" does occur) to spill its developmental benefits onto the world's impoverished populations. Leonard Silk sees a new worldwide depression as the greatest danger, for contrary to euphoric expectations at the end of the Cold War, "the peace dividend only shows up in lost jobs and falling incomes."[47] Transnational economic migrations tax national and international absorptive systems beyond present capacity. Growing disparities will but exacerbate the problem.

How can strategists promoting SAD deal with the hundreds of millions who have a vested interest in the present destructive economic dynamism prevailing in the world? What incentives, what countervailing power, and what persuasive alternative economic interests can dissuade:

• corporations from continuing to place short-term profit from natural resource extraction above long-term environmental protection;
• military establishments from their current wasteful and toxic modes of resource use and disposal;
• billions of consumers (actual and potential) from their use of certain products in the interests of avoiding remote (and uncertain) future catastrophes in the ozone or the global climate system.

Is authentic development sustainable? It may well be the only kind that can be. Authentic development, however, is monumentally difficult—difficult to desire, to implement, to sustain. Chesterton once wryly observed, "The Christian ideal has not been tried and found wanting. It has been found difficult; and left untried."[48] Here precisely lies the challenge: sustainable development must not remain untried simply because it is found difficult.

Notes

1. World Bank, "Overview," in *World Development Report 1992* (New York: Oxford University Press, 1992), 1.

2. Cf. World Bank, *World Development Report 1993* (New York: Oxford University Press, 1993), Table 30, 296–97.

3. World Commission on Environment and Development, *Our Common Future* (New York: Oxford University Press, 1987), 89.

4. Paul Streeten, "Future Generations and Socio-Economic Development: Introducing the Long-Term Perspective, " unpublished manuscript, January 1991, 3. The shorter, published version of this text does not contain the citation given; see "Des institutions pour un developpement durable," *Revue Tiers-Monde* 33; no. 130 (April/June 1992): 455–69.

5. Ibid., 1–2.

6. Paul Ekins, "Sustainability First," in *Real Life Economics,* ed. Paul Ekins and Manfred Max-Neef (London and New York: Routledge, 1992), 412.

7. Duane Elgin, *Voluntary Simplicity* (New York: William Morrow, 1981); Jeremy Rifkin, *Entropy: A New World View* (New York: Viking Press, 1980); Denis Goulet, "Voluntary Austerity: The Necessary Art," *Christian Century* 4 (8 June 1966): 748–53.

8. Carolina Maria de Jesus, *Child of the Dark* (New York: Mentor Books, 1962), 60.

9. Ibid., 39.

10. For Gandhi's views on development, see Amritananda Das, *Foundations of Gandhian Economics* (Delhi: Center for the Study of Developing Societies, 1979); and J.

P. Naik, "Gandhi and Development Theory," *Review of Politics* 45, no. 3 (July 1983): 345–65.

11. Barry Lopez, "The American Indian Mind," *Quest 78* (September/October 1978): 109.

12. Charles Avila, *Ownership: Early Christian Teaching* (New York: Orbis Books, 1983).

13. Lewis Mumford, *Technics and Civilization* (New York: Harcourt Brace, 1934), 76.

14. Erich Fromm, *To Have or To Be?* (New York: Harper & Row, 1976), 15–16.

15. C. Douglas Lummis, "Equality," in *The Development Dictionary,* ed. Wolfgang Sachs (London: Zed Books, 1992), 49–50.

16. Keith Griffin, *Alternative Strategies for Economic Development* (London: Macmillan Academic and Professional, 1989), 242.

17. On this see Denis Goulet, *Mexico: Development Strategies for the Future* (Notre Dame, IN: University of Notre Dame Press, 1983), 15–20.

18. René Dumont and M. F. Mottin, *Le Mal-developpement en Amerique Latine* (Paris: Les Editions de Seuil, 1981).

19. Bob Bergamon, "Rene Dumont on Misdevelopment in the Third World: A 42-Year Perspective," *Camel Breeders News* (Ithaca, NY: Cornell University Spring 1987).

20. Centre Europe-Tiers Monde, *Mal-Developpement Suisse-Monde* (Geneva: CETIM, 1975).

21. Serge Latouche, *Faut-il refuser le developpement?* (Paris: Presses Universitaires de France, 1986).

22. Gustavo Esteva, "Development," in Sachs, *Development Dictionary,* 6, 22–23.

23. This is the common thesis in all of Illich's writings. Cf. especially *Toward a History of Needs* (New York: Pantheon, 1977).

24. David Maybury-Lewis, "Dear Reader," *Cultural Survival Quarterly* 11, no. 1 (1987): 1.

25. Robert Vachon, ed., *Alternatives au Developpement* (Montreal: Institut Interculturel de Montreal, 1988).

26. Robert Vachon, "Dossier: Vivre avec la terre," *Horizons interculturels,* no. 29 (Spring 1993): 24.

27. Ursula K. Le Guin, *The Dispossessed* (New York: Avon Books, 1975), 20.

28. Denis Goulet, "The United States: A Case of Anti-Development?" *Motive* (January 1970): 6–13.

29. L. J. Lebret and R. Moreux, "Economie et Humanisme," *Numero Special* (February/March, 1942).

30. L. J. Lebret, editorial, *Developpement et Civilisations,* no. 1 (March 1960): 3. Cf. also Lebret, *Developpement-Revolution Solidaire* (Paris: Les Editions Ouvrieres, 1967), 82.

31. Fromm, *To Have or To Be?*

32. John Kenneth Galbraith, *Economic Development in Perspective* (Harvard University Press, 1962), 43. Italics are Galbraith's.

33. For a detailed justification of this hierarchy of needs, see Denis Goulet, *The Cruel Choice* (New York: University Press of America, 1985), 236–49.

34. Erich Fromm, ed., *Socialist Humanism: An International Symposium* (New York: Anchor Books), ix.

35. No documents have issued from the MARGA seminar; this list is based on notes taken by the author.

36. For a detailed analysis of how technologies favor or impede employment creation, see Raphael Kaplinski, *The Economies of Small, Appropriate Technology in a Changing*

World (London: Appropriate Technology International, 1990).

37. United Nations Development Programme, *Human Development Report 1991* (New York: Oxford University Press, 1991), 5–6.

38. For detailed justification and illustration see Denis Goulet and Kwan S. Kim, *Estrategias de Dessarrollo para el Futuro de Mexico* (Guadalajara: ITESO 1989).

39. Willy Brandt, *North-South: A Programme for Survival* (Cambridge: MIT Press, 1980), 16.

40. Ignacy Sachs, *Developper, les Champs de Planification* (Paris: Universite Cooperative Internationale, 1984).

41. Herman E. Daly and John B. Cobb, Jr., *For the Common Good: Redirecting the Economy toward Community, the Environment, and a Sustainable Future* (Boston: Beacon Press, 1989), 138.

42. Cf. Denis Goulet, "Development Indicators: A Research Problem, a Policy Problem," *The Journal of Socio-Economics* 21, no. 3 (Fall 1992): 245–60.

43. S. J. Samartha and Lynn DeSilva, eds., *Man in Nature, Guest or Engineer?* (Colombo, Sri Lanka: Ecumenical Institute for Study and Dialogue, 1979).

44. See, for ewxample, R. J. Berry, ed., *Environmental Dilemmas, Ethics and Decisions* (London: Chapman & Hall, 1993); J. Ronald Engel and Joan Gibb Engel, eds., *Ethics of Environment and Development: Global Challenge, International Response* (Tucson: University of Arizona Press, 1990); Tom Regan, ed., *Earthbound: Introductory Essays in Environmental Ethics* (Prospect Heights, IL: Waveland Press, 1984); H. Herbert Borman, ed., *Ecology, Economics, Ethics: The Broken Circle* (New Haven: Yale University Press, 1991); Elleen P. Flynn, *Cradled in Human Hands: A Textbook on Environmental Responsibility* (Kansas City, MO: Sheed & Ward, 1991); Henryk Skolimowski, *Eco-Philosophy: Designing New Tactics for Living* (London and New York: Marion Boyars, 1981).

45. See for example, Kenneth Aman, ed., *Ethical Principles for Development: Needs, Capacities or Rights* (Upper Montclair, NJ: Institute for Critical Thinking, 1991); Vincent Cosmao, *Un Monde en Developpement? Guide de Reflexion* (Paris: Les Editions Ouvrieres, 1984); Nigel Dower, *World Poverty: Challenge and Response* (York, England: William Sessions, 1983).

46. Douglass Stinson, "Sustainable Accords? Free Trade and the Environment," *Latinamerica Press* 25, no. 24 (1 July 1993): 1.

47. Leonard Silk, "Dangers of Slow Growth," *Foreign Affairs* 72, no. 1 (1992–93): 173.

48. *G. K. Chesterton Day by Day,* 2d ed. (London: Kegan Paul, 1912), 14. Chesterton's statement is drawn from *What's Wrong with the World?*

13

Involving Women in Sustainable Development: Livelihoods and Conservation

Rekha Mehra

Environmentalists and conservationists are becoming increasingly aware that although protected areas and wildlife preserves may be the most effective way to conserve resources and maintain biological diversity, keeping these areas truly protected is virtually impossible. In most developing countries, the establishment of parks and reserves requires either evicting people without compensation or preventing them from using the area as they have done traditionally for generations.[1] Keeping local people out often means depriving them of access to resources on which they depend for their survival and livelihood and which they may have used sustainably for the most part for a long time. It becomes difficult, therefore, to prevent "encroachment" of local people on park areas.

Over the past decade, to overcome this obstacle and gain community support for reserve areas, environmentalists have tried to combine conservation with activities designed to meet people's economic or other needs. Typically, such combined projects permit limited use of protected areas, offer support services such as schools and health care, and help communities enhance their economic opportunities in return for support of local conservation programs.[2] Development specialists, meanwhile, have become more sensitive to the need to make development efforts more sustainable and are now attempting to take better account of the relative environmental and ecological costs of alternative practices and technologies. Overall, there is a growing awareness that *sustainable development* means not only maintaining the viability of ecosystems and conserving resources and biological diversity, but also ensuring that people are able to meet their current economic needs without jeopardizing the ability of future generations to meet their own needs. This interpretation of *sustainable development* thus reconciles resource use and human needs with conservation goals.[3]

Efforts to combine conservation and resource management projects with livelihood goals have, however, had mixed results. This is mainly because their design and implementation is a complex exercise requiring attention to numerous details, as well as a fairly complex planning process that must integrate both sets of objectives, strengthen local institutions, and balance the divergent interests of local people. People's interests differ because social status, power, leverage, and participation in community life vary within communities. All these factors must be taken into account. A key differentiating factor among people, one that has often been neglected in the design and implementation of conservation and livelihood projects, is gender. There is growing evidence that this omission can be an important determinant of the success or failure of such projects. This is because women in developing countries, through their economic and household roles, have a significant impact on the use of natural resources and on sustainable development.

Women's Work and Resource Use

The majority of poor women in developing countries earn their livelihood and support their households by farming and related enterprises such as animal husbandry; thus they rely directly on the availability and quality of resources such as land, water, forests, and seeds. While patterns of participation vary, women play important and sometimes critical roles in household survival through their subsistence and income-earning activities. In many parts of Africa, for example, women are the primary food producers, contributing, on average, 70 percent of the labor for food production, 60 percent for its marketing, and virtually all the labor expended in food processing.[4] In Zaire, more women than men are involved in agriculture—94 percent of women farm, as compared with 56 percent of men.[5] In South Asia, women do almost all the work involved in transplanting rice, and they participate to varying degrees in sowing, planting, weeding, fertilizing, and harvesting.[6] South Asian women often predominate in postharvest food processing and storage.

While the exact value of women's contributions to household income is difficult to estimate because so much of their labor is unpaid, the few indirect estimates obtained by converting subsistence production to cash value show that women's shares are substantial. Among the Nso people of Northwest Cameroon, for example, women grow over 90 percent of the food consumed in the household and contribute about a fourth of all other household expenditures. If subsistence production is converted to equivalent cash value, it is estimated that on average women contribute about 41 percent of total household income while men supply the rest.[7] In Cote d'Ivoire, a time-allocation survey showed that women's own earnings provided a third of the money spent on purchased food and their own cultivation contributed three-fourths of the subsistence food consumed by households.[8]

Direct estimates of women's farm earnings in wage labor confirm the value of women's work. They show, for example, that women working as agricultural wage laborers in India are often the main or even the sole income earners in landless or near landless households.[9] In rural Bangladesh, women's earnings account for about half of household cash income.[10]

As with food production, women depend on the availability of natural resources—fodder, trees, grasses, and water—for livestock production, to which they also contribute labor and which constitutes an important source of income for them. For example, in much of the dry belt of sub-Saharan Africa, which stretches from Mauritania to Ethiopia, women own and tend small livestock such as goats, sheep, and chickens. A significant share of women's earnings in these areas are derived from livestock. In Burkina Faso, milk is a major source of income among the Fulani women.[11]

Women use trees and tree products for a wide range of items such as fuelwood, fodder, fibers for clothing and mats, roofing materials, basketry, and medicines, both to earn income and to meet household needs. In the Amazon, about a third of the work involved in rubber tapping is done by women and children.[12] In the state of Maranhão, Brazil, women comprise 86 percent of the estimated 400,000 rural workers who earn income from the vegetable oil extracted from the babassu palm kernel, which is used for the manufacture of soap and other products. The babassu palm also provides poor women with important raw materials for the production of household and market goods such as baskets, fish traps, bird cages, animal feed, and oil.[13] Baskets made by women from the leaves of palms in Botswana, Zimbabwe, and Zambia constitute an important craft export, while tubers of the grapple plant found in western Botswana are exported for use as arthritis medicine.[14]

Women also rely heavily on natural resources to meet their household obligations. The poor in developing countries meet their energy needs predominantly with biomass fuels, where these are available.[15] In many places, it is primarily women who provide for household energy needs, mainly by collecting fuelwood. In Asia and the Pacific, it is estimated that women account for two-thirds of the time spent in fuelwood collection.[16] In Africa, women provide 90 percent of the labor used in obtaining water and fuel.[17] In other parts of the world, too, women spend a great deal of time and labor collecting fuelwood, fodder, and water. The amount of time and effort required varies with the state of the environment and the availability of resources.

Women's Poverty and Constraints on Sustainable Development

Despite the important contributions women make to the economic support and nurturance of their families, the development process does not appear to have

Table 13.1

Total Number of Rural People Living Below Poverty Line[a] by Sex

	1965–70	1988	% Change
Women	383,673	564,000	47.0
Men	288,832	375,481	30.0
Total	672,505	939,481	39.7

Source: I. Jazairy, M. Alamgir, and T. Panuccio, *The State of World Rural Poverty: An Inquiry Into Its Causes and Consequences* (New York: New York University Press, 1992), 405, 422–423.

[a]Calculated on the basis of the total rural population of 114 developing countries.

benefited them. Indeed, poverty among women is widespread and growing. More women than men are poor worldwide, and the ranks of poor women are growing faster than those of poor men, especially in the rural areas of developing countries.[18] In 1988, an estimated 564 million rural women lived below the poverty line—an increase of 47 percent from 1965–70.[19] The number of men living below the poverty line increased 30 percent over the same period (Table 13.1).

An important contributing factor is the limited opportunity women have for employment—most are employed in low-paid, unprotected work or are self-employed in precarious occupations, mostly in the informal sector or in subsistence farming. In formal-sector employment, women tend to be concentrated in low-skill jobs that offer little advancement potential. They are more commonly employed, for example, in the service sectors rather than in industry. In Brazil, Chile, and Peru over 50 percent of economically active women work in the service sector.[20] Women comprise three-fourths of workers in the informal sector—where incomes tend to be lower and growth potential limited. In general, women's assets, incomes, and wages tend to be lower than those of men. The increasing number of women who work as agricultural wage laborers, for example, tend to earn less than men. In Honduras, women employed in tobacco cultivation are paid about 70 percent of the wage men earn for performing the same tasks.[21] Disparities between wage rates for men and women persist throughout the occupational spectrum.

Women, moreover, are at a particular disadvantage in attempting to overcome poverty because of a variety of additional institutional, educational, and social constraints. These constraints may also pose problems regarding women's ability to adopt certain practices that ensure environmental sustainability. Among the constraints that impede women's economic progress are lack of access to assets and productivity-enhancing resources, new technologies, training, and extension services. Few women, for example, own land, although in many places they may have the right to use land. Lack of title to land prevents women from making long-term investments and assuming the risks needed to improve their agriculture. It also prevents them from obtaining loans, because banks and other credit institutions often require land as collateral. It is estimated that just 10 percent of the agricultural credit available from formal lending sources goes to women farmers.[22] They are thus at a significant disadvantage in purchasing inputs, tools, and equipment that could enhance their productivity.

Lack of secure title to land can also prevent women from modifying current practices that harm the environment. Persuading women to grow trees and participate in social forestry projects can be difficult if they do not have land on which to grow trees, or if they are not guaranteed ownership of the fruits and timber. For instance, tree and land tenure rights are interrelated in some parts of Africa. Historically, women have not had the right to plant trees because this could give them rights over the land on which the trees were planted. In northern Cameroon, some men let their wives plant only short-lived trees such as papayas that did not confer land rights.[23]

Another factor constraining women's productivity is lack of access to education. Although some developing regions, such as Latin America, have made considerable progress over the past forty years in improving women's education, significant deficiencies persist in others. Worldwide illiteracy among women and girls actually grew from 58 percent in 1960 to 66 percent in 1985. Significant gaps also remain between girls' and boys' education, even at the primary levels, where the largest gains have been made worldwide. In 1990, just 20 percent of girls of the appropriate age were enrolled in primary school in Niger, compared with 38 percent of boys. In Senegal, primary school enrollment among girls was 49 percent, compared with 71 percent for boys.[24] Gender gaps in education are even greater at the secondary and tertiary levels.

A high rate of illiteracy and low levels of education among women have been shown to constrain productivity and may affect women's receptivity to new techniques and skills in conservation. In agriculture, an important sector for women's employment, studies show that improvements are strongly linked to education, and that educated farmers tend to be more likely to adopt modern practices. Binswanger cites evidence that literacy raises the demand for fertilizer, increases investments in draft power, and results in increased output.[25] Although no direct evidence is available regarding the links between education and the adoption of new conservation techniques and practices, it is not unreasonable to hypothesize that education may contribute to improvements in conservation practices.

Women often are not given access to the resources, technologies, and services provided by development and conservation projects and are thus unable to participate in them or benefit from them.[26] Even though women are key actors in the use of resources and in production, policy makers and project staff often assume that women do not have distinct roles and responsibilities in sustainable development. As a result, the role of women is overlooked. Project design and execution are often inappropriate with respect to women.[27] Policy makers and project designers assume that only men need to participate, and that information and technology should be targeted to men and not women. They assume either that women do not need to participate in projects or that project information will automatically reach them, or that women need the same types of information and technologies as men.[28]

There is growing evidence that these assumptions are often inaccurate. Recent studies have begun to show that women's involvement is critical in conservation and development projects. A conservation and tourism development project designed to conserve wildlife and natural resources in Western Kaokoland, Namibia, vividly demonstrated this point. It almost went awry because women were not consulted in designing a strategy to sustainably use the omurunga palm. The primary use of the palms was to make baskets for sale and local use. Project personnel noticed that since the introduction of the "sustainable use" strategy, the palm trees were actually dying at a faster rate. Closer investigation showed that the initial discussions on which the strategy was based had included only men, mostly elders. Women were, however, the primary users of the palms, from which they made baskets to hold milk, a resource that traditionally belonged to women. When project staff negotiated with men to monitor the use of palm trees, women felt their right to use and control milk had been undermined. They therefore did not feel obliged to support the conservation strategy. Once the misunderstanding was discovered, women were drawn into the discussion. They agreed to assume full responsibility for monitoring the trees, and the strategy worked.[29]

A number of other studies document the success achieved by integrating women. An example is the project that converted wastelands to income-generating silk farms in the Bankura District of West Bengal, India. Widespread deforestation and soil degradation had deprived local women of access to their traditional means of earning their livelihoods, namely, shifting agriculture and the collection and processing of forest products. As the women were poor, illiterate, and landless, alternate employment opportunities were limited. However, through the support of the West Bengal state government and the Centre for Women's Development Studies, an independent research organization, the women organized self-help groups known as *samities*. Their first project was the reclamation of 100 hectares of donated wastelands, which they planted with silk trees. Gradually, *samity* membership grew, the *samities* multiplied, and the organizations diversified from silk production to other income-generating activities.[30]

To add to the growing literature on women's role in sustainable development, in August 1992 the International Center for Research on Women (ICRW), the World Wildlife Fund (WWF), and WWF/Philippines jointly undertook a case study of a mangrove management project in Cogtong Bay on the island of Bohol in the Philippines. The main objective of the study was to determine women's involvement in the project, and if necessary, to make recommendations for enhancing their participation. An additional objective was to derive broader policy and program lessons on involving women in sustainable development.

The Cogtong Bay Mangrove Management Project: A Case Study

Found throughout the extensive coastline of the Philippines, mangroves represent a rich and valuable ecosystem. They provide nurseries and spawning grounds for fish and crustaceans and function as habitat for birds, mammals, and reptiles. By reducing erosion and controlling floods and storm surges, they protect coastal environments and maintain water quality. Mangroves also represent an important economic resource for people, providing food, shelter, and income for both traditional and commercial users—fish and shellfish for consumption and sale, fronds and timber for fuelwood, and poles for fish corrals and fences.

The widespread use of mangroves, however, has contributed to their depletion and to the decline of marine species dependent on them. About 70 percent of the 450,000 hectares of mangroves found in the Philippines early this century have been destroyed, and most of what remains is secondary growth of brush and young mangrove forests.[31] The major cause of destruction was the felling of mangrove trees for log exports during the 1960s. Other factors were a policy environment that permitted the unregulated conversion of mangrove areas for fishpond development and open access to the resource.

Over the years, the Philippine government has attempted to protect mangrove areas in a variety of ways. Measures included setting aside about 78,393 hectares as forest reserves in 1981; permitting environmental impact assessments to challenge proposed conversions of mangrove forests for industrial, tourism, or fishpond development; and encouraging local communities to assume greater responsibility for managing mangrove forests on a daily basis. In 1990, the government decentralized management of nonwilderness mangrove areas, making them available for community management, provided they were utilized sustainably.[32] The Cogtong Bay Mangrove Management Project evolved in part as a response to governmental efforts to give responsibility for resource management to local communities. The project was funded from January 1989 to September 1991 by the United States Agency for International Development (USAID) and implemented by the Network Foundation, a nongovernmental organization (NGO) with headquarters in Mandaue City, Cebu, and staff based at the project site.

The Project Site and Resource Depletion

Cogtong Bay is located in the central Visayas region of the Philippines in the southeast of the island of Bohol. The site for the Mangrove Management Project incorporated about 2,000 hectares of mangrove forest along the coast. Of this area, 1,300 hectares were vegetated, while the rest had been converted into fishponds—some legally, the rest illegally. About 52,000 people lived in the project area, in small communities scattered along the bay. The communities were poor, and unemployment was high. Average annual household income in 1988 was about P4,800 or U.S.$228, well below the Philippines' per capita GNP of U.S.$630.[33] Eighty-five percent of the people were self-employed, 68 percent of these as farmers and 9–15 percent as fishermen, but most people, in order to augment their earnings, engaged in a number of different occupations such as carpentry, handicrafts, and retail trade. Most communities along the bay had primary schools, and secondary and college education was available locally at the Bohol School of Fisheries in Cogtong, a village of 2,158 people and the project headquarters.[34] Access to health services was limited. Only 5 percent of the population had access to piped water. Secondary roads and a portion of the national highway provided access to all shores of the bay and to the provincial capital of Tagbilaran City, about 92 kilometers away.

The mangroves and other coastal resources of Cogtong Bay were being undermined as mangrove areas were cut down for firewood or converted into fishponds. Fish yields were declining both due to habitat loss and due to illegal fishing—the use of fine mesh nets, trawling, and dynamiting, which destroys coral reefs, another important fish habitat. A significant problem contributing to natural resource depletion was the inability of local officials to ensure the fair and equitable use of these resources. As a result, the richer and more politically influential residents of Cogtong Bay, and nonresidents who exploited local resources for commercial purposes, contributed disproportionately to resource depletion. For a variety of reasons, local officials were unable or unwilling to challenge illegal use of natural resources—in fact, they were themselves sometimes involved. Historically, a major cause of mangrove deforestation has been the illegal harvesting and sale of trees by wealthy entrepreneurs. Many of the fishponds that displaced extensive mangrove areas were also developed illegally, sometimes by absentee owners. Such problems caused considerable frustration and discontent among local people.

The loss of mangroves and other coastal and marine resources was not only significant from the ecological perspective but also because it threatened to undermine the livelihood of local people. Both subsistence and income-earning activities in Cogtong Bay centered on the availability of coastal and other resources. Fishing, for example, was an important secondary activity that both supplemented local incomes and augmented diets. It was done by small-scale artisanal fishermen, from small boats and with traditional gear such as handlines, cast nets, and fish corrals. Catches were relatively small, but even so, fishermen tended to sell or barter some of their catch. The best fish were sold to middlemen (or women) for resale in big provincial cities and lower-quality fish were sold in local markets or consumed at home. Oysters, clams, shells, and other marine products were also consumed and sold.

Project Objectives and Implementation

The main objective of the Cogtong Bay Mangrove Management Project was to help local communities protect and better manage coastal resources, rehabilitate mangrove areas, and promote the sustainable use of mangroves and other coastal resources.[35] A related goal was to enable participants to improve their economic situation. Specific project-related tasks were (1) to organize the residents of eight coastal communities into associations; (2) to rehabilitate 400 hectares of mangrove forest and establish individual tenure over the rehabilitated areas; (3) to install eighty artificial reefs to replace destroyed corral reefs; (4) to initiate commercial oyster and mussel culture to support local incomes; and (5) to control the use of illegal and destructive fishing methods in the project area. A key conservation strategy employed by the project was to strengthen tenure security among individuals by awarding them twenty-five-year leases over mangrove plots. Leaseholders entered into stewardship agreements with the government to keep the plots under permanent mangrove cover. For this they were awarded renewable conditional leases known as mangrove stewardship certificates (MSCs).

By June 1991 a final evaluation of the project showed that it had been moderately successful. Fishermen's and farmer's associations had been organized in eleven communities (three more than were targeted); mangrove saplings had been planted on 150 hectares; stewardship certificates had been issued to 250 individuals; participants had been trained in oyster and mussel cultivation; and just over half the targets for artificial reef construction had been met (Table 13.2). Participants had also succeeded, to some degree, in preventing illegal fishing, illegal fishpond construction, and commercial mangrove harvesting.[36] Through a program sponsored by the Department of Trade and Industries, five of the eleven associations had also established credit programs for their members.

Other project documents showed, however, that a major impediment to success was the project's inability to get access to coastal lands suitable for mangrove rehabilitation. This factor greatly slowed implementation and eventually forced staff to attempt to afforest new areas rather than rehabilitate older ones—a more difficult task, because the most favorable areas for mangrove growth are the ones originally forested.[37] In the end, only 27 hectares of mangroves were rehabilitated, instead of the 400 hectares originally planned. The rest, 150 hectares, represented new plantings.

Despite its mixed success, the project attracted attention for several reasons. First, it succeeded in securing government recognition of the principle of awarding tenure guarantees. Although the Department of Environment and Natural Resources (DENR) through its Social Forestry Program had been granting individuals tenure rights over forestlands since 1981, this practice had not been instituted for mangrove areas until the implementation of the Cogtong Bay Mangrove Management Project. Second, the project was regarded as the prototype for a larger, nationwide Mangrove Development Project (MDP) designed to place 153,000 hectares of mangroves throughout the Philippines under community management. Funding was to be provided by the Asian Development Bank (ADB). The project at Cogtong Bay was slated for expansion under the MDP and was designated the training site for NGO and DENR staff involved in the nationwide project.

Table 13.2

A Summary of Project Targets and Accomplishments, January 1989–June 1991

Activity	3-year target	2.5-year accomp.	% of target
Fishermen's associations formed	8	13	163
Mangrove			
Reforestation (hectares)[a]	75	150	200
Stewardship agreements issued	265	250	94
Artificial reef clusters constructed and placed	60	44	55
Mariculture			
Oyster plots established	18	17	94
Green mussel plots established	22	20	91
Credit obtained by Fishermen's Associations	0	5	

Source: ACIPHIL, *Terminal Report: Rainfed Resources Development Project Mangrove and Coastal Management,* unpublished, Mandaue City, Cebu, Philippines, 1992.
[a]Although reported in the evaluation as reforestation, these were new plantings.

In August 1992, when the research for this case study was done, USAID funding for the project had ended. The ADB project had not yet started. Some project activities were continuing with a small amount of bridge funding from the WWF/Philippines. The community associations appeared to be fairly well established, were continuing to hold meetings, and were continuing some activities. Project staff were unable to offer much support to the associations because just two of the eight members of the original staff were being retained to continue the work, and they were greatly overextended. In addition, they had not been paid in several months.

Women's Participation in the Project

Until August 1992, no deliberate attempt had been made by designers, donors, or implementors to integrate women into the Mangrove Management Project. A review of available project documents, including proposals to various donors made from 1988 to 1992, project correspondence from the same period, and an evaluation report did not mention women.[38] Preliminary conversations with Network Foundation office staff at the project site provided conflicting evidence about whether or not women had participated in the project and to what extent.

Initial conversations with the local community did not help clarify the situation because both women and men characterized women as "just housewives" who were involved primarily in household activities and had very little to do with economic or market activities or community work such as the conservation efforts being undertaken by the Mangrove Management Project. Closer examination showed, however, that contrary to popular belief and expression, women were actually important contributors to the local economy, active in community life, and interested in conservation. Women had also participated in the Mangrove Management Project to varying degrees.

Women, Work, and Resource Use in Cogtong Bay

The research for this study showed that, as in coastal communities throughout the Philippines, women in Cogtong Bay actually engage in a variety of economic activities and are quite active in community life. They undertake both subsistence and income-generating work in the formal and informal sectors to contribute to the support of their households. Although women in fishing communities like Cogtong Bay generally do not go fishing, they are deeply involved in processing and marketing fish and shellfish.[39] In Panacan, Palawan, for example, the United Nations Economic and Social Commission for Asia and the Pacific (UNESCAP) found equal numbers of women and men involved in fish marketing.[40]

In addition, women engage in a number of other part-time and seasonal income-earning activities, including farming for themselves or as wage laborers, retail trade, nipa weaving or mat making, raising poultry and livestock, and domestic wage work.[41] This is similar to the patterns of women's work in other fishing communities.[42] As a result, many women end up engaging in a number of different occupations simultaneously and over their lifetimes. One forty-eight-year-old woman, for example, reported having more than eight different occupations during her life including fishing, nipa weaving, snakeskin trade, fish and oyster marketing, mariculture, and firewood collection.

Contrary to what might be expected, women with many children were most actively involved in market or subsistence work. Thus, for example, one woman with six children below the age of twelve and pregnant with a seventh child reported selling fish five times a week (depending on the size of her husband's catch); farming a cassava plot (planting, weeding, and harvesting even while pregnant); raising pigs; collecting shells and traveling to Cebu (an overnight journey) once a month to sell them; tending fruit trees; and growing vegetables. Interestingly, she had started in the shell trade before marrying and after marriage continued the business with her husband's help.

Having many children appeared not to be a major constraint on women's economic participation because there was generally a grandmother or other relatives, often including older children, who cared for the younger children when the mother's work took her away from home. Studies in other fishing communities in the Philippines corroborate this finding. For example, De Castro found that in a fishing community in Panay, marital status and number of children did not affect the number and type of economic activities that involved women.[43]

In Cogtong Bay, women employed other innovative techniques to reconcile economic and household responsibilities, for example, employing their mothers-in-law or other older relatives having fewer household responsibilities to sell their fish for a small commission.

Finally, women in Cogtong Bay were also financial managers of their households. They kept the purse and made the disbursements, often making decisions independently of their husbands, except when purchasing expensive items. Women were deeply involved with ensuring that there was adequate income to feed and educate their children. This was consistent with other studies that showed that women in fishing communities throughout the Philippines were the primary financial managers of the household, responsible for budgeting money for food, household goods, school fees, clothing, and other household needs.[44] Women were also responsible for managing savings. When families experienced cash shortages, seasonal or otherwise, women were expected to obtain supplementary income through additional employment or by borrowing.[45] Small loans were generally taken by women, though men often shared in the decision to borrow larger sums.[46]

Women's livelihood in Cogtong Bay, as in other coastal areas of the Philippines, was heavily dependent on access to natural resources.[47] Fish and shellfish processing and marketing, for example, depended on the availability and quality of marine resources. Farming, kitchen gardening, and livestock rearing—other important sources of subsistence and income for the women of Cogtong Bay—required access to land and water. Changes in patterns of economic activity over the years, therefore, were frequently influenced by shifts in the availability of and access to natural resources. Some women reported, for example, that nipa weaving had been an important income-generating activity in their childhood, but because local supplies had dwindled, families did not pursue this activity any longer. Due to recent declines in fish catches, women reported wanting alternate employment and income-generating opportunities.

Not surprisingly, women appeared to be well aware of the important link between the availability of natural resources and their livelihoods, and hence, indirectly, of the importance of conservation and sustainable resource use. Notably, when asked to rank resources in order of importance, women put fish and shellfish, the two resources of greatest economic value, first. One group of women actually specified that their ranking reflected the price of the resource. When asked about resource depletion, women expressed greater concern about the decline of economic activity represented by depletion than the loss of the resource per se. However, they later went on to make the connection between habitat loss and decline of economic activity. They knew, for example, that the destruction of habitats due to dynamite fishing was partially responsible for reduced fish catches, and that shellfish were harder to collect because fishpond construction destroyed mangrove habitats.

Women's Involvement in Project Activities

Consistent with the information obtained from project documents and preliminary interviews, examination of association membership records showed that there were virtually no female members of the community associations organized by the Mangrove Management Project. However, interviews with the women themselves, later confirmed by project staff, revealed that some women did participate in project activities. A few women who were either widowed or single reported being members in their own right. However, only one married woman had membership separate from her husband, and this was because he had not wanted to join an association and she did.

Although women were thus rarely association members in a formal sense, they often attended meetings, frequently as proxies for their husbands when the men were unable to attend. Women were permitted to proxy if their husbands were ordinary members and officials of the association, but no proxy was allowed for the president. Project staff reported that in some cases, more women than men attended meetings. There were times, for example, when two-thirds of the attendees at the Cogtong association's meetings were women. Women's participation in association meetings could not be verified, however, by looking at attendance records, because they were required to sign their husbands' names if they were attending as proxies. Interestingly, even when the majority of attendees were women, meetings were conducted as if the actual members had been present, and the decisions made at such meetings were later upheld. Both male and female respondents seemed to think that male membership implied family membership in the association. Lack of official membership was not perceived as an impediment to participation in most project activities.

Among the variety of project activities, women reported being most actively involved in mangrove planting. They provided voluntary labor, harvesting mangrove propagules and planting them; in the two communities of Cogtong and Cawayanan, for example, women claimed that it was primarily they who planted and tended mangrove plantations. Women also attended meetings held to inform them about the MSCs and how they worked, and training sessions where they were taught how to plant and manage mangrove plots. On some occasions women represented more than two-thirds of the participants in mangrove planting exercises. Once again, this could not be verified by the records, which showed just a few women engaged in these activities (Tables 13.3 and 13.4).

Some women also participated in the mariculture training provided at three of the four sites visited. The training, which was done on-site over three days, involved the introduction of a simple technology—the stringing together of discarded oysters or coconut shells to make "collectors." The collectors were then installed on stakes planted in mudflats in brackish water or saltwater. Oyster spats attached themselves to the collectors and could be harvested in about eight months. Installing the stakes on which the collectors were hung required diving

Table 13.3

Percent of Women Involved in Mangrove Rehabilitation, Cogtong Bay

Site	Men	Women	% Women
Bonbon	23	3	11.5
Cawayanan[a]	30	0	0.0
Cogtong[a]	26	4	13.3
Lunsodaen	27	2	9.5
Marcelo	19	0	0.0
Minol[a]	17	2	11.0
Panas	16	0	0.0
Pangpang	20	4	16.6
Poblacion I	26	3	11.0
Poblacion II[a]	22	1	4.3
Sagumay Daku	20	2	9.1
Tombo	24	6	20.0

Source: ACIPHIL, *Terminal Report: Rainfed Resources Development Project Mangrove and Coastal Management,* unpublished, Mandaue City, Cebu, Philippines, 1992.
[a]Sites visited.

Table 13.4

Percent of Women Involved in Mariculture, Cogtong Bay

Site	Men	Women	% Women
Cawayanan (mussels)[a]	28	0	0.0
Cogtong (mussels and oysters)[a]	11	2	15.0
Minol (mussels)[a]	19	2	9.5
Poblacion II (no mariculture)[a]			

Source: ACIPHIL, *Terminal Report: Rainfed Resources Development Project Mangrove and Coastal Management,* unpublished, Mandaue City, Cebu, Philippines, 1992.
[a]Sites visited

into shallow water to make sure the stakes were secure in the marsh bottom. Care of the collectors during the breeding period included guarding them against theft. The hanging and harvesting of collectors was usually done at low tide and so did not require diving, but it did involve wading in shallow muddy waters, which was difficult and potentially dangerous because of sinkholes in the bay floor. Official records once again showed that few women participated in this activity, but project staff reported about 60 percent of mariculture trainees in Cogtong were women.

Women in Cogtong reported that mariculture was a joint enterprise, involving both women and men. The men were assigned the more difficult work of installing the stakes and hanging collectors, while the women strung the collectors together, assisted with installing stakes, helped police the waters, and did much of the harvesting. They also processed and sold the oysters produced.

Women were least directly involved in installing artificial reefs. The artificial reefs introduced through the project were L-shaped concrete structures that represented an advance over the less permanent, more commonly used bamboo structures. However, being much heavier, they were more difficult to install. The work, done communally, entailed loading the reefs onto boats and then dropping them into the bay at the designated site. This was regarded as men's work. Women provided support and felt they were involved because they cooked community meals on the days men installed the reefs.

Women's understanding of the project and its goal seemed to be best in Cogtong, where the project was headquartered. The women of Cogtong were better able, for example, to explain the problems and causes of resource depletion. This was in sharp contrast to Poblacion II, where the community appeared to be much less involved in the project. Women especially appeared to be less conscious of the project, its goals, and the need for better resource management. However, the lack of involvement may have been due to the fact that the community had been one of the last to be contacted by project staff and had only been organized for a short while.

Conclusions and Lessons Learned

Despite their active participation in a variety of project activities, the women of Cogtong Bay were effectively excluded from the main benefits of the project— they were not given leases over mangrove plots, nor were they officially permitted to become members of the community associations. Leases were awarded almost exclusively to men. In Minol, for example, just three of eighteen tenure recipients were women, two of whom were widows. In Cawayanan, the tenure was given exclusively to men; the lone female member of the Cawayanan association did not have a tenure certificate. Since a key strategy for improving mangrove management was to guarantee tenure security, this was an important omission. However, the impact of this particular factor could not be properly determined because the project faced so many other difficulties, including technical and financial problems, that it was difficult to separate out the various impacts. It was, moreover, too early to evaluate the impact of tenure security on overall management of mangrove areas. Still, in theory, a key project strategy was clearly undermined by denying women tenure.

Women's inability to gain formal membership in the community associations was not only discriminatory, it also prevented them from having access to more tangible benefits. For example, lack of membership prevented them from obtaining loans offered by the Department of Trade and Industries through some of the community associations. In fact, women were not particularly concerned about obtaining formal membership except to have access to credit. Similarly, they were eager to have tenure certificates in their own names because these could then be used as collateral for loans. This was an issue for the women, because many of them felt that lack of access to capital was the main constraint impeding their economic advancement. As wage employment opportunities in the area were limited, many women felt that the only way to improve their economic situation was to set up small businesses or expand their current enterprises, for which they needed access to capital.

In short, the failure to recognize women's roles and integrate them into the design and implementation of the project represented the loss of a significant chance to enhance women's economic opportunities. It may have undermined the mangrove conservation effort as well, although it was too early to tell yet when this study was done.

The case study, nevertheless, provided valuable insights about how to improve the effectiveness of rural community-based conservation projects. First, and most important, conservation projects should include both women and men in accordance with their respective roles and responsibilities in the use and management of resources. Differences and complementarities between women's and men's roles should be determined in the local area and at the conservation site prior to project design. Second, the views and interests of all stakeholders, including women, should be taken into account in project design and implementation. Third, conservation projects should be linked to income-enhancing activities, because this enables people to meet their short-term economic survival needs while working on the longer-term conservation goals. Within such projects, it is also crucial to ensure that equal consideration is given to meeting women's economic needs along with those of men, because as was shown in this chapter, women contribute substantially to the support of poor rural households. Fourth, women, like men, should not only be given direct access to and control over natural resources such as land, but to credit, technical assistance, and training, which are often needed to improve resource management and promote conservation. In fact, women often need these services more than men, because their access is more limited to begin with. In short, the success of conservation projects depends not only on integrating women but also in providing them full and equal access to the resources and services offered.

This chapter has highlighted the importance of integrating women into a critical aspect of sustainable development, namely, the conservation of natural resources through community-based conservation projects. It is equally important, to consider women and involve them when thinking about many other aspects of sustainable development as well. This is because, through the numerous and diverse roles women play as producers, consumers, leaders, activists, and educators in the home, marketplace, and community, they will have a significant impact upon sustainable development.

Notes

1. John C. Ryan, "Conserving Biological Diversity," in Lester Brown, et al., *State of the World* (New York and London: W. W. Norton for Worldwatch, 1992).

2. Michael Brown and Barbara Wyckoff-Baird, *Designing Integrated Conservation and Development Projects* (Baltimore: Biodiversity Support Program, 1992); John C. Ryan, "Conserving Biological Diversity," in Brown, et al., *State of the World;* Michael Wells and Katrina Brandon, *People and Parks: Linking Protected Area Management with Local Communities* (Washington, DC: International Bank for Reconstruction and Development, 1992).

3. Marcus Colchester, "Forest People and Sustainability," in *The Struggle for Land and the Fate of the Forest,* ed. Marcus Colchester and Larry Lohmann (London: Zed Books, 1993).

4. Kathleen Cloud, "Sex Roles in Food Production and Distribution System in the Sahel," in *Women Farmers in Africa: Rural Development in Mali and the Sahel,* ed. Lucy E. Creevey (Syracuse, NY: Syracuse University Press, 1986).

5. Richard H. Sines, et al. *Impact of Zaire's Economic Liberalization Program on the Agricultural Sector,* report prepared by the Bureau for Africa, Office of Development Planning, USAID (Washington, DC: Robert R. Nathan Associates, 1987).

6. Iftikhar Ahmed, "Technology, Production Linkages and Women's Employment in South Asia," *International Labor Review* 126, no. 1 (1987): 21–40.

7. Miriam Goheen, "Land and the Household Economy: Women Farmers of the Grassfields Today," in *Agriculture, Women, and Land: The African Experience,* ed. Jean Davison (Boulder: Westview Press, 1988).

8. Jennie Dey, *Women in Food Production and Food Security in Africa* (Rome: Food and Agriculture Organization of the United Nations, 1982).

9. Bina Agarwal, "Who Sows? Who Reaps? Women and Land Rights in India," *Journal of Peasant Studies* 15, no. 4 (1988): 531–81.

10. Simeen Mahmud and Wahiduddin Mahmud, *Structural Adjustment and Women: The Case of Bangladesh* (Dhaka, Bangladesh: Bangladesh Institute of Development Studies, 1989).

11. Helen Henderson, "The Grassroots Women's Committee as a Development Strategy in an Upper Volta Village," in Creevey, *Women Farmers in Africa.*

12. Janet M. Abromovitz and Roberta Nichols, "Women and Biodiversity: Ancient Reality, Modern Imperative," *Development* 2 (1992): 85–90.

13. S. B. Hecht, A. B. Anderson, and P. May, "The Subsidy from Nature: Shifting Cultivation, Successional Palm Forests, and Rural Development," *Human Organization* 41, no. 1 (1988): 25–35.

14. Malcolm L. Hunter, Jr., Robert K. Hitchcock, and Barbara Wyckoff-Baird, "Women and Wildlife in Southern Africa," *Conservation Biology* 4, no. 4 (1990): 448–51.

15. Norman Myers, "The World's Forests and Human Populations: The Environmental Interconnections," in *Resources, Environment, and Population: Present Knowledge, Future Options,* ed. Kingsley Davis and Mikhail S. Berstam (London: Oxford University Press, 1991).

16. L. Fortmann and Diane Rocheleau, "Why Agroforestry Needs Women: Four Myths and a Case Study," in Food and Agriculture Organization, *Women's Role in Forest Resource Management: A Reader* (Bangkok: FAO, 1989).

17. Food and Agriculture Organization and Swedish International Development Authority, *Restoring the Balance: Women and Forest Resources* (Rome and Stockholm: n.d.).

18. Idriss Jazairy, Mohiuddin Alamgir, and Theresa Panuccio, *State of World Poverty: An Inquiry Into Its Causes and Consequences* (New York: New York University Press for

the International Fund for Agricultural Development, 1992).

19. Ibid.

20. Mayra Buvinić and Margaret A. Lycette, "Women, Poverty, and Development in the Third World," in John P. Lewis, et al., *Strengthening the Poor: What Have We Learned?* (Washington, DC: Overseas Development Council, 1988).

21. Ibid.

22. Kathleen A. Staudt, "Women Farmers and Inequities in Agricultural Services," in *Women and Work in Africa,* ed. Edna Bay (Boulder: Westview Press, 1982).

23. Paula J. Williams, "Women, Children, and Forest Resources in Africa: Case Studies and Issues" (report presented at a symposium, "The Impact of Environmental Degradation and Poverty on Women and Children," United Nations Conference on Women and Development, Geneva, 27–30 May 1991).

24. World Bank, *World Development Report 1990* (New York: Oxford University Press, 1990).

25. Hans Binswanger, "How Agricultural Producers Respond to Prices and Government Investments" (paper presented at first Annual World Bank Conference on Development Economics, Washington, DC, 27–28 April 1989).

26. Rekha Mehra, *Gender in Community Development and Resource Management: An Overview* (Washington, DC: International Center for Research on Women, 1993).

27. Iftikhar Ahmed, ed., *Technology and Rural Women: Conceptual and Empirical Issues* (London: George Allen and Unwin, 1985).

28. Augusta Molnar, "Forest Conservation in Nepal: Encouraging Women's Participation," in *Seeds: Supporting Women's Work in the Third World,* ed. Ann Leonard (New York: Feminist Press, 1989).

29. Margaret Jacobson, "Conservation and a Himba Community in Western Kaokoland, Namibia," unpublished, 1991.

30. International Labour Office, *The Bankura Story: Rural Women Organize for Change* (New Delhi: ILO, 1988).

31. World Bank, *Philippines: Environment and Natural Resource Management Study* (Washington, DC: 1989).

32. Frederick J. Vande Vusse, *Mangrove Forests,* prepared as a staff paper for the Asian Development Bank, 1992.

33. World Bank, *World Development Report 1990.*

34. Most of the research for this case study was done in Cogtong and in three other communities, Mabini, Cawayanan, and Poblacion II.

35. The Network Foundation, "Mangrove Rehabilitation and Coastal Resource Management Project: Candijay and Mabini, Bohol," unpublished, Mandaue City, Cebu, Philippines, n.d.

36. ACIPHIL, "Terminal Report: Rainfed Resources Development Project Mangrove and Coastal Management," unpublished, Mandaue City, Cebu, Philippines, 1992.

37. Rehabilitation of mangroves involves planting mangroves in areas where they originally existed. Afforestation involves new plantings along coastal areas where mangroves did not originally grow.

38. Network Foundation, "A Proposal to the Foundation for the Philippine Environment," unpublished, Mandaue City, Cebu, Philippines, 1992. Network Foundation, "Mangrove Rehabilitation."

39. Josefa S. Francisco and Lorna Israel, *A Draft Report On Gender Needs Assessments with Fisherwomen* (Quezon City, Philippines: Women's Resources and Research Center at Miriam College, 1991). Jeanne Frances, I. Illo, and Jaime B. Polo, *Fishers, Traders, Farmers, Wives: The Life Stories of Ten Women in a Fishing Village* (Manila, Philippines: Institute of Philippines Culture, Ateneo de Manila University, 1990).

40. United Nations Economic and Social Commission for Asia and the Pacific, *Women in Fisheries* (Bangkok: 1985).

41. Nipa is a natural fiber widely used throughout the Philippines to thatch houses.

42. Francisco and Israel, *A Draft Report On Gender Needs;* Illo and Polo, *Fishers, Traders, Farmers, Wives;* Robert S. Pomeroy, "The Role of Women and Children in Small-Scale Fishing Households: A Case Study in Matalom, Leyte, Philippines," *Philippine Quarterly of Culture and Society* 15 (1985): 353–60.

43. Lourdes V. De Castro, *Role of Rural Women in the Development of Fisheries in Panay: Focus on the Socio-Cultural and Economic Variables* (Iloilo City, Philippines: University of the Philippines in the Visaya, 1986).

44. Pomeroy, "Role of Women in Fishing Households," 353–60; Theresa V. Tungpalan, Maria Mangahas, and Ma. Paz Palis, "Women in Fishing Villages: Roles and Potential" (paper presented to Coastal Resource Management, Philippines, n.d.).

45. Francisco and Israel, *Draft Report On Gender Needs.*

46. Pomeroy, "Role of Women in Fishing Households," 353–60.

47. UNESCAP, *Women in Fisheries;* Francisco and Israel, *Draft Report On Gender Needs;* Illo and Polo, *Fishers, Traders, Farmers, Wives;* Pomeroy, "Role of Women in Fishing Households," 353–60.

14

North–South Cooperation
for Sustainability

Janet Welsh Brown

Any discussion of sustainability requires a definition. In this chapter, I will use the following working definition:

> Sustainable development is a new model of development that is different from the predominant model followed by the United States and much of the non-Communist world over the last fifty years. Achieving sustainability requires (1) long-range efforts in both developing and highly industrialized countries to improve the quality of life of all people—but especially the most disadvantaged—in ways that are, over time, environmentally and economically sustainable; (2) broad public participation in decision making at all levels; and (3) access to information without which good decisions cannot be made. The emphasis and style of these efforts will necessarily vary from one society to another, and within societies.

This definition holds that sustainable development should be the goal of both the developing and the highly industrialized countries. It recognizes that sustainable development is a long process. The problems of uneven/failed development and pervasive and continuing deterioration of the environment evolved over two generations, and they cannot be corrected overnight—it will require decades. As here defined, sustainable development will be measured by improvements in quality of life, not in terms of gross national product (GNP), the standard measure of economic growth, which tells one nothing about the environmental costs of the growth, nor who benefits. A better measure is what the United Nations Development Programme calls "sustainable human development."[1] Sustainability will require a special emphasis on efforts to defeat poverty and achieve equity—within nations, between nations, and between generations. The gap between rich and poor, which widened appreciably in many industrialized and developing countries in the 1980s, exacerbates the destructive pressures that both the very rich and the very poor put on the resource base. Sustainable development, as development experts know from experience, must have the participation and "ownership" of affected groups—of forest dwellers, municipal fishermen, subsistence farmers, and urban workers. All-important among affected groups are women; leaving them out of decision making and ignoring their roles in development and resource management has led to mistakes in many countries. Lastly, this definition of sustainable development warns us against the adoption of uniform prescriptions: one-model-fits-all is not the way to sustainability.

The foregoing definition also assumes peace to be an essential condition of sustainable development, for difficult social transitions will not be undertaken when a nation's resources are all diverted to war.

Sustainability cannot be achieved without new levels of international cooperation, especially North–South cooperation, primarily because the economic and ecological problems that sustainable development seeks to overcome are themselves transnational. Air pollution, river basins, depleted fisheries, desertification, poverty, migration, and conflict respect no international boundaries. But equally important in a practical sense is the fact that no government will move in a new direction—even in a beneficial direction—if important groups of its citizenry perceive themselves to be disadvantaged by the move. We have seen a concern about presumed international advantage played out in many arenas, as in the 1991–92 negotiations for the climate treaty, when the European Community, which favored tough measures to reduce CO_2 emissions, agreed to the necessity for higher taxes on fossil fuels but made such a move contingent on similar action by the United States, which not only produces the largest share of world emissions (over 20 percent), but also has the lowest oil and gasoline taxes of any of the highly industrialized countries.[2]

New levels of international cooperation will also be required between the nations of the South and the North. Countries in the South have been enthusiastically imitating the development patterns and lifestyles of the North for at least two generations, encouraged to do so and partly financed by bilateral and multilateral assistance agencies and banks controlled by the North. They cannot now be expected to take the advice, "Do as I say, not as I do."

North–South cooperation is necessary for still another very practical reason. Just as no single country feels it can go it alone when it comes to sustainable development, neither can the North and South do without each other. The countries of the North, for instance, cannot control greenhouse gas emissions and slow climate change, nor protect the ozone layer and biodiversity, without the cooperation of the countries of the South. The highly industrialized countries of the North may use the most energy and emit the most warming gases, but energy consumption is growing much faster in the developing countries. In giants like China and India, the demand for energy is growing rapidly, while energy is used on the whole very inefficiently.[3] Similarly, the gains made by phasing out the use of chlorofluorocarbons (CFCs) under the Montreal Protocol, to protect the ozone layer, would be gravely reduced if China were to proceed with its plans to provide all households with small refrigerators—which use CFCs in the coolant. And the richest biomass in the world just happens to be in the tropical forests of the developing countries; wise management by the nations that own these treasures is essential to the worldwide goals of protecting biodiversity.

On the other hand, the Southern countries cannot accomplish all the difficult tasks necessary for sustainable development without the cooperation of the North. They will need more help, not less, in order to curb rapid population growth and educate and create jobs for the inevitable billions of people being born. They will need financial and technical assistance, debt relief, and the lowering of trade barriers that discriminate against their exports.

It became apparent in the two years of negotiations leading up to the 1992 United Nations Conference on Environment and Development (UNCED) in Rio de Janeiro, that the perspectives and priorities of the industrialized and developing countries differ when it comes to global and international environmental problems. Although the leaders of many developing countries recognize the serious economic consequences both of local and global environmental degradation, they tend to be preoccupied with their needs for economic growth. Their environmental priorities tend therefore to be those that are tangible and close to home—urban air and water pollution, erosion and salinization of agricultural land, toxic chemical contamination—rather than global warming or biodiversity loss. They tend also to be fearful that environmental protection will be too costly, and some are suspicious that they will face environmental "conditionality" from international donor countries and agencies that will further retard their progress and growth.

Furthermore, as was articulated clearly at the Earth Summit, the developing countries see the bad habits, high consumption, and excessive waste of the highly industrialized countries as the true cause of today's global environmental problems. They conclude, therefore, that the industrialized countries should themselves take the first steps toward sustainable development. This was translated into their demands at Rio for "environmental space" into which they could grow, and for the financial and technological assistance required to help them make the difficult transition to sustainable paths of development.[4]

The arguments at UNCED and since underline how much change sustainability will require in the development strategies of all countries. The search for sustainability is no mere reformist effort; it calls for fundamental, even revolutionary, change, or, to use a concept current in academic analysis, paradigm change.

As a result of intense discussion and cooperation in the months leading up to

UNCED, there is widespread agreement on the definition of sustainable development in the United States among the environmental, development, religious, and human rights groups advocating it in Washington, and widespread appreciation among them of how fundamental and difficult are the changes required.

In the developing countries as well, there is broad recognition that past and continuing notions of development based largely on the resource-intensive, high-consumption, high-waste model of the United States are *un*sustainable. Two reports put together by the Asia Development Bank and the Inter-American Development Bank/UNDP Regional Office lay out where the traditional approaches to development went wrong—that is, in discounting both environmental damage and equity.[5] The latter report, *Our Own Agenda,* says in effect that Latin American and Caribbean development has been on the wrong track for fifty years and offers prescriptions for changing course to the governments of the region. This is a startling admission in a report sponsored by agencies responsible for promoting and financing that failed model for those fifty years.

Furthermore, advocates of sustainable development share a vision of what a sustainable society might look like and ideas on how to develop and use energy, agriculture, and other resources in new ways. They draw on widely scattered cases in which governments, often in cooperation with or prodded by nongovernmental organizations (NGOs), have succeeded in making progress toward sustainability. Invariably, these projects have been developed with the full participation of the affected communities, including the participation of women.[6] In each, the creation of sustainable livelihoods is a paramount goal.

Despite real differences in official North–South perspectives, a shift toward sustainability seems to be taking place. The Earth Summit held in Rio in June 1992 addressed the whole panoply of environmental and development issues, and—except for debt, financing, and trade—reached a quite remarkable level of agreement on sustainable development. The Declaration of Principles, the 300-page *Agenda 21,* and the parallel climate and biodiversity treaties reflect the compromises made every step of the way;[7] nevertheless, in the course of the intensive two-year multilateral negotiations, the most comprehensive and most inclusive international negotiations in history, some very important concepts were ratified, concepts that are now international norms. All require reciprocity among nations and tough action at home:

• The permanent linking of environmental and economic development goals—and an understanding that no country can enjoy lasting economic progress without protecting its environment, and vice versa
• The notion of shared but differentiated responsibility for global environmental damage
• The notion that equity and justice are conditions required for sustainable development (documents issuing from the conference all require special efforts to improve conditions for the poor)

• The polluter-pays principle
• Recognition of a significant role for a wide array of nongovernmental organizations—corporations, religious groups, and environmental, population, and development organizations—many of whom have international links, which were reinforced by the UNCED experience
• A commitment from every government to pursue sustainable paths of development, made in person by 120 heads of state

Nevertheless, there remains skepticism and discouragement in the wake of the Earth Summit. Everywhere, including among the contributors to this volume, there is frustration with the lack of determined, energetic fulfillment of national commitments. Existing institutions do not seem to be providing adequate leadership. The new United Nations Council on Sustainable Development, created after UNCED by the 1992 General Assembly, was slow getting organized—holding its first "substantive" meeting in June 1993, displaying no sense of urgency, and making, until now, only the most modest advances.

How does one do sustainable development? Where does one start? Where is the necessary international assistance? How can nation-states, which bear so much of the responsibility for implementation, break through the institutional barriers and political obstacles that are in fact embedded in their own institutions and politics? For the barriers to sustainable development lie not just in misguided policy or inappropriate technology, in this writer's opinion, but in the national and international institutions and national politics that continue to reward the beneficiaries of the unsustainable model of development with wealth and political clout. How can we change the power equation within nations and between nations?

Resistance to change is completely human and understandable. On a personal level, we all resist change—in our diets or teaching methods, even when we know the changes will benefit our health or our students. On a political level, the affected interests resist—with vigor. The interests with the most economic and political power are likely to be the ones who benefit from the unsustainable status quo. They are the big wealthy commercial (and even corporate) farmers, in India and in California, who benefit from underpriced water for irrigation and government programs that promote the green revolution, and the industries or transportation sectors that benefit from subsidized fuels.

In the United States, for instance, one industry after another achieved exemption in 1993 from President Clinton's proposed BTU tax, just as in the previous administration the energy industry's persistence undergirded U.S. opposition to specific targets and timetables for lowering greenhouse gas emissions and helped weaken the climate treaty. In 1992 the pharmaceutical corporations successfully fought U.S. participation in the biodiversity treaty. Even in cases when the proposed change promises economic benefits such as the lower fuel costs that result from greater efficiency, or long-term access to rich biomasses, such powerful special interests will resist the changes, and expend significant resources in doing so.[8]

Institutional resistance may inhibit a global move toward sustainability. For instance, getting the United Nations Statistical Office to alter its standards for national accounts and include simple measures for natural resource accounting is a formidable task. Even if the will were there and powerful nations were advocating the change, the transition to new accounting methods would be slow and burdensome.

Another example of institutional resistance is offered by the World Bank, which, because of its importance in setting worldwide patterns and styles of development, plays a crucial role. The bank has had good environmental policies on the books since bank president Robert McNamara's day. Five years ago, it reviewed and strengthened those policies, instituted regular environmental reviews of all its projects, and staffed up more adequately for the task. In 1992, it adopted new policies on energy, calling for greater investments in fuel efficiency and less-polluting alternatives, and pricing that reflects realistic environmental and social costs. In 1993, the bank similarly overhauled its policies for selecting and funding water projects. But today the lending patterns of the institution have not perceptibly changed. The World Bank continues to fund mostly large-scale, capital-intensive projects in energy, agriculture, and industrial development— projects that fly in the face of the concept of sustainability —because loan officers have not internalized the concept of sustainable development, and because they continue to be rewarded for moving large sums of money rather than for helping governments plan for sustainable development.[9] What national governments and international institutions are experiencing, and finding so difficult to break out of, is *institutionalized unsustainability*.

Students of international environmental politics will often encounter the lament that institutions are inadequate to deal with the complex, multinational, and global nature of the environment-development problem, especially in national governments, on whose initiatives the follow-up for UNCED so heavily depends. This institutional inadequacy, now much discussed among academics, has in fact been the object of nongovernmental organizations' criticism for a generation. With all due respect to my academic colleagues, they did not discover this inadequacy. For twenty-five years citizen groups around the world, finding their governments inadequate to the task, have organized opposition and worked on alternatives: at the local level, around issues such as lead poisoning in Galveston, or water shortages in Gugerat; at the national level, in the United States, to create NEPA, the Clean Air Act, and drinking water legislation; and in Germany to develop national recycling regulations. In Malaysia and the Philippines, national environmental organizations like Friends of the Earth and local affected communities focused on the failure of government agencies to enforce the law. In the Philippines they took action themselves and effectively stopped illegal logging in some areas. In Malaysia, they went to jail. On the international level, NGOs around the world launched multiyear campaigns to secure and strengthen the climate and biodiversity regimes.

Preparation for UNCED gave great impetus to NGOs and greatly expanded the international links among environmental and development NGOs, North and South. Electronic mail and fax machines allow easy access to information and have facilitated and lessened the cost of international cooperation among NGOs. UNCED also stimulated the organization of corporate leaders for sustainable development, most notably the international Business Council for Sustainable Development, while other business coalitions organized to resist the climate and biodiversity agreements. Indeed, international politics—especially where environmental issues are concerned—are no longer just for state players.[10] Some environmentalists would even say environmental issues are too important to be left to governments alone. There are many examples.[11]

The New World Dialogue for Environment and Development in the Western Hemisphere, organized in early 1991, is an NGO effort. Thirty citizen leaders from South and North America organized to pressure their governments to deal with the rapidly growing environmental degradation and persistent poverty in the Americas.[12] It was admittedly an elitist venture, carried out by self-selected men and women who were not part of their national political administrations but had influence in national politics and connections with national environmental and development constituencies.

The group set out to negotiate the kind of North–South agreement that they thought hemispheric governments ought to. Though participants were all South and North Americans, the group meant its pronouncements to have a more general application and to serve as a model for UNCED commitments. A *Compact for a New World* was the result.[13] The twenty-six-page document was published in the form of an open letter to the heads of state and legislators of the American nations. It made recommendations for North–South bargains on eight interrelated issues: forests and biological diversity, energy, pollution control and prevention, poverty, population, science and technology, trade and investment, and financing. The recommendations were not easily arrived at; there were struggles among the members of the New World Dialogue over the content and language of every paragraph, starting with an argument over whether or not to include population on the agenda at all, an argument in which the Latin American men were pitted against the women and a few North American men.

The *Compact for a New World* has some characteristics worth noting:

• It recognizes that all eight initiatives are organically connected and must be dealt with together. New sustainable development models cannot be created without attention to trade, debt, and equity issues, as well as the usual roster of development and environmental problems.

• It calls for reciprocity. The compact is not a set of prescriptions just for the South. It says, for instance, that the management of temperate forests in the

United States and Canada—and in Chile and Argentina—must also meet tough new standards for sustainability, even as the management of tropical forests must.

• In so far as possible, members of the New World Dialogue tried to formulate their recommendations in terms of specific goals, progress toward which would be visible and measurable: cut military budgets by 20 percent in five years; stabilize population by midcentury (earlier, in the high-consumption countries); create regional mechanisms for sustainable development trade.[14]

• The compact proposals assume that neither North or South can achieve sustainable development without cooperation from the governments of both the North and South. New, unprecedented levels of international cooperation—a grand North–South bargain—will be required.

The *Compact* was published in four languages in October 1991 and given wide distribution throughout the hemisphere and to a lesser degree in Europe and the Commonwealth of Nations. It was launched at simultaneous news conferences in five countries. In Costa Rica, its recommendations were discussed on a nationwide prime-time television marathon by presidential hopefuls. It was praised as a model for UNCED at a world conference of environmental gurus at the Hague. It may even have had some effect on UNCED, primarily through the Preparatory Committee meetings in Geneva in 1991 and New York in 1992, and through a series of New York preparatory meetings between New World Dialogue members and government delegations from the Americas. Influence is hard to document, however. Two of the New World Dialogue members ended up members of their official national delegations, one as head of his delegation.[15] Only in the United States was the impact imperceptible, despite high-level meetings of New World Dialogue members with State Department, Treasury, and Environmental Protection Agency officials of the Bush administration.

In the post-UNCED period, New World Dialogue members continued trying to move their governments, and in 1994 we can see that important steps have been taken. The Dialogue members agreed that the United States must take the initiative in calling for government-to-government talks. Even though the Clinton administration elevated key New World Dialogue members to power, the goal of an ongoing North–South dialogue among governments remained illusive during the Democrat's term.[16] The immediate obstacles to a high-level intergovernmental dialogue in the hemisphere were largely within in the U.S. administration, whose top foreign policy team was preoccupied as much as its predecessors with the OECD countries, the former Soviet Union and Yugoslavia, and the Middle East. For the early years, President Clinton's policy goals in inter-American affairs were the liberalizing of trade and the strengthening of democracy, goals epitomized by U.S. efforts on NAFTA and with regard to Haiti. Only in early 1994 after Vice President Gore, on behalf of the president, invited all democratically elected heads of state for a Hemispheric Summit, did there appear to be more comprehensive efforts to formulate Latin American policy, and the beginning of an attempt within the State Department to coordinate traditional economic and political concerns with environmental ones. At the Summit of the Americas, held in Miami in December 1994, sustainable development was as much a part of the agenda as trade and governance issues.

Although many governments in the hemisphere have taken formal steps within their own countries to fulfill UNCED commitments, and several are represented on the United Nations Commission on Sustainable Development, there are only a few low-key international efforts under way. The Organization of American States is considering a revival and updating of the Western Hemisphere Convention of 1941 to encourage international cooperation for the protection of parks and reserves, and the State Department has several modest bilateral efforts under way.

The most active part of the region is Central America; all seven countries acted together for once when their presidents formed the Central American Alliance for Sustainable Development in late 1993. Each president has assumed responsibility for putting his or her own house in order and has promised to cooperate within the region. This new spirit of cooperation has already spawned a regional forest treaty which some U.S. NGOs and advisers hail as a possible model for a hemispheric treaty.[17]

What does it take to achieve international cooperation, especially North–South cooperation? The Central American Alliance and two other post-UNCED examples demonstrate that it takes a combination of factors: perseverance among the developing countries, specific goals, leadership from international organizations and Northern countries, and some modest promise of funding. These qualities have all been present when the Central American Forestry Treaty, the Small Island Developing States (SIDS), and the 1994 Desertification Convention were negotiated.

Central Americans have been in the habit of working together since 1989, when Costa Rica's president Oscar Arias Sanchez and others, with the blessing of and modest assistance from USAID, formed the Central American Commission for Sustainable Development. As their first major undertaking, they organized around the goal of sustainable forestry management. The unusually participatory negotiations included representatives of many interest groups: regional networks of campesinos, the forest industry, women's organizations, and indigenous peoples. The treaty created a regional council, on which these nongovernmental groups are also represented. The council is developing regional guidelines for both forest concession management and social forestry programs. And it is aggressively fund-raising among European donors and the Inter-American Development Bank (IDB).[18]

The Small Island Developing States, which successfully concluded a Plan of Action under UN auspices in April 1994, were organized first around the 1991–92 climate treaty negotiations, where, because of their concern about global warming and sea level rise, they coalesced behind demands for a strong agreement. In the process they discovered the uniqueness of their development dilemmas and acted on their shared needs. The sympathy of Australia, which has supported the Pacific island states for some years now (out of concern about possible refugees if development fails) and Canada, which has been a particular patron of the English-speaking Caribbean countries, and a promise from UNDP of special attention and modest funding led to rapid and relatively easy international agreement.[19]

The Desertification Convention of 1994, the first international treaty to emerge from UNCED, was negotiated in a record fifteen months, despite the opposition of prestigious and powerful donor states. There were the usual arguments over regional priorities and the issue of financing, but a persistent group of African states under the banner of the Organization of African Unity, with support from European former colonial powers, a determinedly positive Dutch conference chair, and a secretariat that drafted the working documents and facilitated the work of supportive NGOs, succeeded in arriving at a consensus. Though the Africans did not get all they wanted—additional specific funds as well as debt and trade concessions—they did reach consensus on the essential elements necessary to consummate the treaty, which called for employing indigenous knowledge and experience and for the involvement of local people, especially women, in development efforts to combat desertification. It was the first such agreement to do so.[20]

There are many other possible points of entry for initiating stronger North–South cooperation. The world is entering a new era, everything is in flux, and the future—and the present—is uncertain, but certain to change. And there is, in fact, opportunity in this changing uncertainty. One law of physics is that when a body is in motion it is much easier to change its direction. Proponents of sustainable development, therefore, should find it easier to identify points of impact for change in the current fluid international situation.

Indeed, things are already happening at many levels. Local communities, provinces, and states are taking initiative, not just in the United States but throughout the world. Through the International League of Mayors, cities like Toronto, Curitiba in Brazil, and Amsterdam have made their own urban plans for achieving sustainability. The heads of the UNDP and the Inter-American Development Bank have indicated their support for a sustainable development agenda at the Western Hemisphere Summit.[21] The climate and biodiversity treaty negotiations are proceeding on schedule, and these proceedings have been boosted by early declarations from the Clinton administration that the United States would reduce its emissions of greenhouse gasses to 1990 levels by the end of the decade and would sign the biodiversity treaty. In the wake of NAFTA, there are plans among environmental organizations to pursue a "greening" of the General Agreement on Tariffs and Trade—which would assure that trade will continue to be the single most contentious international environmental issue throughout the decade.

None of these things is happening fast enough to keep pace with escalating trends in resource degradation, but in countries all over the world the people are ahead of politicians and are pushing them forward. The process is admittedly disorderly. It does not nicely illustrate theories of paradigm shift and regime formation, except perhaps to provide an example of chaos theory at work. To move events more briskly toward sustainable development, there are three things contributors to this volume and other policy analysts and activists can do:

• We can, through our academic and policy work, sharpen the public's and policy makers' visions of sustainable development in this country and others and illustrate it with images that will capture the popular imagination and supersede the myths that have dominated public perception of environmental problems and governments' potential role in solving them.
• We can listen to those development practitioners who have been trying alternative, more sustainable ways of pursuing development around the world. Their accounts of what works will dispel some of the global doomsaying popular in some circles.
• We can improve the social scientific analysis of sustainable development and the factors required for its implementation. Our colleagues in the natural sciences and some in economics have become quite proficient in their technical and policy analysis and in formulating prescriptions for global environmental problems. But most social scientists do a poor job of dissecting the political and institutional barriers that prevent nations from moving toward more sustainable development. Much better analysis will help clear away even the greatest of these barriers.

Notes

1. James Gustave Speth, administrator-designate, United Nations Development Program, at a United Nations press briefing, New York, 15 June 1993; United Nations Development Programme, *The Human Development Report, 1994* (New York: Oxford University Press, 1994).

2. World Resources Institute, *World Resources 1992–93* (New York: Oxford University Press, 1992), 204–11, 346. Simon Hall, "Adoption of EC Energy Tax Unlikely, Diplomats Say," *Journal of Commerce,* 4 June 1993; Alexander MacLeod, "Remember Rio? Britain to Tax Polluters," *Christian Science Monitor,* 2 February 1994; *Daily Environment News,* 12 July 1994, A–2.

3. World Bank, *World Development Report 1992* (New York: Oxford University Press, 1992), chap. 6.

4. *Consumption Patterns: The Driving Force of Environmental Stress* (report prepared for the United Nations Conference on Environment and Development, Indira Ghandi Institute of Development Research, Bombay, October 1991).

5. Asian Development Bank, *Economic Policies for Sustainable Development* (Manila: Asian Development Bank, October 1990); Latin American and Caribbean Commission on Development and Environment, *Our Own Agenda* (Washington, DC, and New York: Inter-American Development Bank and United Nations Development Programme, September 1990).

6. Waafas Ofusu-Amaah, et al., *Success Stories of Women and the Environment: "Partners for Life"* (official document of the Global Assembly of Women and the Environment, Miami, October 1991); Michael Paolisso and Sally W. Yudelman, *Women, Poverty and the Environment in Latin America* (Washington, DC: International Center for Research on Women, 1991); and Julie Fisher, *The Road from Rio: Sustainable Development and the Nongovernmental Movement in the Third World* (Westport, CT, and London: Praeger, 1993).

7. *Agenda 21, Rio Declaration on Environment and Development,* and *Statement of Forest Principles,* final text of agreements negotiated by governments at the United Nations Conference on Environment and Development, 3–14 June 1992, Rio de Janeiro, Brazil (New York: United Nations, 1993).

8. In the 1970s and early 1980s, major U.S. electric utilities in California and New York spent millions fighting environmentalists' demands for efficiency, and least-cost pricing demanded in the regulatory system by the Environmental Defense Fund; see David Roe, *Dynamos and Virgins* (New York: Random House, 1984). Today, those same companies boast of their leadership in efficient, environmentally conscious production, and sell their know-how to other states and developing countries.

9. World Bank, *The World Bank Annual Report 1993* (Washington, DC: World Bank, 1993); Hillary F. French, "Rebuilding the World Bank," in *State of the World 1994,* ed. Lester R. Brown, et al. (New York and London: W. W. Norton, 1994); *A Statement of Friends of the Earth before the Senate Appropriations Sub-Committee on Foreign Operations Concerning Foreign Aid Appropriations for the World Bank, IMF, Asian Development Bank, Inter-American Development Bank, Export-Import Bank, UNEP and Other UN Agencies, BERD and AID, June 15, 1993* (Washington, DC: Friends of the Earth, 1993).

10. Gareth Porter and Janet Welsh Brown, *Global Environmental Politics* (Boulder: Westview Press, 1991), 56–66; Paul Kennedy, *Preparing for the Twenty-First Century* (New York: Random House, 1993), especially chaps. 3, 4, 5, and 7; Michael Clough, "Grassroots Policy Making," *Foreign Affairs* 73, no. 1 (January/February 1994): 2–7.

11. Fisher, *Road from Rio;* Harsh Sethi, "Survival and Democracy: Ecological Struggles in India," in *New Social Movements in the South: Empowering the People,* ed. Ponna Wignaraja (London: Zed Books, 1993), 122–48.

12. For a description of those problems see World Resources Institute, *World Resources, 1990–91* (New York: Oxford University Press, 1990), chap. 3.

13. World Resources Institute, *Compact for a New World* (Washington: World Resources Institute, October 1991).

14. Janet Welsh Brown and Lee Kimball, "Needed: New Rules and Mechanisms for Dealing with Trade and Environment Issues in the Western Hemisphere," in *Difficult Liaison: Trade and the Environment in the Americas,* ed. Heraldo Muñoz and Robin Rosenberg (New Brunswick and London: Transaction Publishers, 1993), 205–23.

15. José Arnoldo Gabaldón, former Venezuelan minister for the environment (the first to hold such an office in the hemisphere), was head of his delegation. He played a significant role in getting a last-minute agreement on several controversial issues. Alvaro Umana Quesada was a member of the Costa Rican delegation.

16. Albert Gore, Bruce Babbitt, and Alice Rivlin became respectively vice president, secretary of the interior, and director of the Office of Management and Budget in the Clinton administration. Fernando Henrique Cardozo became foreign minister, then finance minister, and finally president of Brazil. Arthur Eggleton is Canada's president of the Treasury and minister of national infrastructure. And James Gustave Speth was named head of the United Nations Development Programme in 1993.

17. Bill Mankin, *Initial Thoughts on Using the Central American Forest Treaty as the*

Foundation for a Western Hemisphere Agreement beginning at the 1994 Summit of the Americas (Washington, DC: Global Forest Project [Sierra Club and NAS], March 1994).

18. Interviews with Bruce Cabarle, World Resources Institute, 20 April 1994, October 1994.

19. "Bold New Initiatives for Small Island Developing States," *Update* 7, no. 9 (May 1994); "UNDP Commits to Follow-Up Activities to Assist Small Island Developing States," *United Nations Development Program, Update* 7, no. 10 (May 1994): 2; "Summary of the UN Global Conference on the Sustainable Development of Small Island Development States, 25 April–6 May 1994," *Earth Negotiations Bulletin* 8, no. 28 (9 May 1994).

20. "Summary of the Second Session of the INC for the Elaboration of an International Convention to Combat Desertification, 13–24 September, 1993," *Earth Negotiations Bulletin*, no. 2 (30 September 1993): 11; UN Government Liaison Service, "Second Session of the Desertification Negotiations, Geneva, 13–24 September 1993," *E and D File, Briefings on UNCED Follow-up* 2, no. 13 (October 1993).

21. Letter from Enrique V. Iglesias, president, Inter-American Development Bank and James Gustave Speth, administrator, United Nations Development Programme, to Vice President Albert Gore, 21 December 1993.

Part Four

Challenges of Transition

Introduction

The need to begin a transition to a more sustainable world is well established. Other sections of this book have focused on the nature of sustainable societies and sustainable development, the philosophical basis for designing such societies, and institutional and value changes that may be required. Since it is unlikely that much progress in this direction can be made simply by "muddling through," a long-term strategy for this transition must be devised.

This section begins with two chapters that are rather optimistic about such a transformation. Alan Miller examines the changing role of existing large multinational corporations in environmental preservation and comes to some hopeful conclusions. His account of many of the initiatives taken by environmentally aware corporations suggests the possibility of a transformation from within. As human environmental values change, so will demand for "green" products. Astute multinationals will be able to respond to these demands and capture world markets. Whether there will be enough corporate incentives to create a "zero-pollution economy," however, remains to be seen.

Kenneth Dahlberg is concerned with a transition to a food system capable of feeding a larger future world population in a more ecologically sound manner. He examines prospects for the transition from an environmentally disruptive industrial mode of agricultural production to a regenerative system. It is not only an exploding human population that treads heavily on the Earth; an explosion of livestock has also had negative environmental impacts. The existing fossil fuel–based agricultural system—it can require up to ten calories of fossil fuel energy to put one calorie of food on the table—cannot be sustained into a post–fossil fuel era. Dahlberg concludes by suggesting various ways that a regenerative food and fiber system can be created to replace industrial agriculture.

A transformation of human values is clearly a critical aspect of the transition to a more sustainable world. In his chapter, Lester Milbrath identifies the important elements of the "industrial value paradigm" and contrasts them with the types of values required by a new environmental paradigm (NEP). He argues that a "paradigm shift" is a required part of the transition. The second part of his chapter deals with potential strategies for and sources of change. He points out that the difficulties of capturing public attention in a complex world filled with competing messages.

Michael Marien picks up on this theme in his chapter. He stresses information overload—"infoglut"—and competing priorities as factors that deflect attention from sustainability issues. The total amount of information is growing exponentially, and this glut can be a paralyzing force and a formidable barrier to change. Similarly, the contemporary world is experiencing many types of simultaneous transformations, and sustainability issues are often the ones most remote from individual experience. Marien's sobering conclusion is that it is doubtful that there is any shared image of what "winning a war for sustainability" means, nor are there many clear indications of progress in this direction.

This section concludes with two chapters that take a close look at current attempts to build more sustainable societies. Oluf Langhelle writes about the Norwegian experience. Keeping in mind that Prime Minister Gro Harlem Brundtland was one of the major forces behind the Brundtland Commission report on sustainable development, Norway's progress—or lack thereof—is of more than passing interest. Langhelle is clearly disappointed by the Norwegian experience and finds that even though Norway has the highest carbon-dioxide-emissions taxes in the world, emissions in the year 2000 are likely to be 13 percent higher than in 1989. He acknowledges a worldwide wave of mistrust in government but maintains that strong government leadership will be required to give impetus to sustainability efforts.

Walter Corson concludes this section with an overview of attempts to measure progress toward sustainability. He identifies several different dimensions of the concept through a review of studies done on the local, state, and national levels. He also compares such data for ten industrial countries in an attempt to identify factors associated with the development of both environmental and socioeconomic sustainability.

15

Corporations as Agents for a Sustainable Society

Allan S. Miller

The modern corporation needs to expand and widen its vocabulary to become more environmentally accurate and culturally enduring. Without this new vocabulary, capitalism will become the commercial equivalent of the Holy Roman Empire: an amorphous global-corporate state taking what it needs and forcing smaller governments into financial subjugation, since no governing body can retain political legitimacy without money, credits, investment, and the sanction of the international business community. Biologically speaking, such unbalanced dominance will precipitate the demise of global capitalism, just as it brought down Rome.

Paul Hawken, *The Ecology of Commerce*[1]

The best way to predict the future is to invent it.

Alan Kay, Apple Computer Company

For much of the modern (post-1960) environmental movement, corporations have been widely viewed as being largely responsible for environmental degradation. The profit motive, it was argued, inherently conflicts with pollution control. Unless forced to do otherwise—and some limits have evolved through civil-law remedies such as nuisance suits—industry would take advantage of the air and rivers.[2] The power of the "corporate villain" perspective is evident in the structure of U.S. environmental laws, which tightly regulate corporate discharges but are much less stringent about pollution from the public sector, agriculture, and individual behavior.[3]

While some corporations have always made a point of staying ahead of environmental regulations, some business leaders have begun to posit in recent years that industry can become a positive force for environmental change. Examples include *Changing Course,* prepared by the Business Council for Sustainable Development, an organization of international business leaders;[4] *Beyond Compliance: A New Industry View of the Environment,* a World Resources Institute book;[5] *The E-factor: The Bottom-Line Approach to Environmentally Responsible Business,* by Joel Makower;[6] and *The Environmental Economic Revolution,* by Michael Silverstein.[7]

The most influential of these works to date is undoubtedly *Changing Course,* prepared under the leadership of a Swiss industrialist, Stephen Schmidheiny, to provide a business perspective on sustainable development for the 1992 United Nations Conference on Environment and Development. The authors envision a world in which corporations play a leading role in achieving sustainable development, both to benefit the planet and in the interests of their own bottom lines. The need to merge corporate pursuit of profits with the constraints imposed by global environmental imperatives is a central theme. In the words of Ben Woodhouse, a Dow Chemical official, corporations are coming to realize that "the degree to which a company is viewed as being a positive or negative participant in solving sustainability issues will determine . . . their long-term business viability."[8] The book advances several arguments supporting the proposition that environmental leadership is synonymous with business leadership.

Why Should Corporations Be Environmental Leaders?

Various reasons have been proposed as to why corporations should move "beyond compliance" to integrate environmental quality with more traditional economic objectives.

First, numerous examples are cited to support the notion that "pollution prevention pays"—the 3P program popularized by the 3M Company. *Changing Course* includes thirty-eight case studies to demonstrate that "companies can achieve commercial success while reducing their burden on the environment."[9] The 3P program of 3M is one of the oldest, begun in 1975. The company claims that more than 3,000 employee-initiated projects have prevented more than 1 billion pounds of polluting emissions and saved more than $500 million. Makower describes how the Gillette Company cut the amount of water it uses to make razor blades by over 80 percent with a recirculation system, saving $1.5 million a year.

The 3P idea is not unique to the industrialized countries. A company producing rayon in India, for example, found itself forced to become more efficient because of increases in the price of wood pulp caused by deforestation. Over a six-year period, a series of internally generated ideas for improving efficiency and reducing costs allowed a 20-percent increase in production, together with significant reductions in energy, chemical consumption, and emissions. The economics were so favorable that a senior corporate executive referred to the need for pollution control measures as "a blessing in disguise."[10]

It is noteworthy that a relatively small number of companies and executives dominate the literature on the "greening" of business; in particular, large chemical and electronics companies are well represented, while producers of basic commodities and small firms are rarely active players. It may be that the chemical and electronics industries share characteristics that facilitate an environmentally proactive strategy that may be less common in or absent from other sectors. For example, these industries are relatively research-intensive and accustomed to rapid technological obsolescence, factors consistent with the flexibility and adaptiveness needed to test new ways of manufacturing. In contrast, mature industries with low profit margins and research budgets may find it more difficult to accept new goals.[11]

An interesting contrasting thesis has been proposed on the basis of research in the United Kingdom.[12] This work suggests that large multinational companies are more likely to adopt a strategy of environmental leadership because their higher profile, relative to that of smaller firms, makes them more susceptible to a wide range of pressures from government and consumers. The same authors posit that these larger firms are more responsive to social and community responsibility issues. The authors therefore argue that size and public exposure is more determinative than sector.

These case histories raise as many questions as they answer, particularly with respect to the economic costs and benefits of the practices described.[13] If benefits typically exceed costs, these examples would suggest enormous and wide-ranging investment opportunities. Yet if this is the case, why should environmental goals be necessary? The profit motive alone should be a sufficient incentive for firms to take advantage of opportunities to save money while enhancing environmental performance. Some unexplained market failures seem to be at work, but their extent and boundaries are undefined. Surely not every environmental requirement or pollution-prevention project is profitable, a point emphasized in *Changing Course*.[14] Is there also no evidence of diminishing returns? That is, is it just as profitable to eliminate the last one percent of pollution as to eliminate the first fifty? And if the case is so compelling, why aren't all companies rushing to get on the pollution-prevention bandwagon?

There are, so far, arguably no complete answers to these questions. However, the effort to provide answers has prompted an important debate on opportunities to integrate environmental and economic goals. Ashford and Porter argue that stringent environmental controls may require the reengineering of technology in ways that yield cleaner and more productive manufacturing processes.[15] Ironically, halfhearted policies, although politically expedient, may have worse effects than anticipated because they result in inefficient, end-of-the-pipe solutions that cost more, decrease efficiency, and contribute to reduced competitiveness.

A corollary of this thesis is that some event or mechanism is necessary to trigger the sort of wholesale rethinking that can lead to major improvements. The success stories described in *Changing Course* were not random events; in most cases, they were forced by regulation. It may be possible to create incentives, partnerships, and other nonregulatory measures that have similar effects, but the clear message of the last decade appears to be that there is no substitute for tough regulations.

The example of chlorofluorocarbons (CFCs) and ozone depletion illustrates this. Studies of available technologies in the early 1980s indicated that there were no chemical substitutes for CFCs. However, the dramatic evidence of on-going ozone depletion over Antarctica led to international scientific and governmental consensus that something must be done. The result was astonishing technological innovation in just a few years. Affordable substitutes have been found for virtually all CFCs, even as scientists have identified additional chemicals that must be eliminated. It is now accepted that the ozone layer will benefit from a nearly complete global phase-out of CFCs in less than a decade with no detectable macroeconomic impact. This is a monumental achievement, especially considering the widespread use of these chemicals in critical high-technology sectors of the economy, including electronics, defense, and aerospace.[16]

William Cline's argument is more direct: countries that correctly anticipate the future direction of global market demand will gain competitive advantage.[17] One likely trend in current markets is increased environmental protection, with the possible inclusion of significant reductions in greenhouse gases, principally carbon dioxide (CO_2) and methane (CH_4). Japan and Europe already have each taken steps in anticipation of this demand, with a bevy of policies and domestic requirements. Authorities in these countries take ultimate responsibility for the disposal of these products at the end of their useful life cycles. One end result is an unfolding revolution in German manufacturing, to promote disassembly and recycling.[18] Those firms that design and implement these processes first will realize competitive advantage, despite short-term costs. In particularly large markets, the automotive market being the prime example, the race is quickly becoming global. Large manufacturers know the importance of selling worldwide. Thus, General Motors already has announced plans for car redesign that will meet German requirements.

The German example provides another insight into the perception that environmental regulation can be pro-competitive—the growth in world trade. The rising proportion of the world economy attributable to traded goods and services is a striking post–World War II development. World trade has increased from a little over $300 billion in 1950 to $3.58 trillion in 1990 and now represents almost 20 percent of the gross world product.[19] One implication of this trend is that a growing proportion of manufactured goods must satisfy the standards of all major markets, not simply those of the home country. In the past, for example, automobile producers could cater to purely national tastes. As the take-back policy indicates, this is no longer true in many cases.

The influence of trade also may explain the quicker response of some multinationals to global environmental concerns. The 350 largest multinational corporations account for almost 40 percent of total trade.[20] However, a cautionary note is required: the environmental consequences of free-trade regimes is not necessarily benign. Environmental groups and others warn that free-trade agreements may be used to challenge strong national environmental regulations. In some cases, they have led pollution-intensive manufacturers to relocate in countries with lax environmental laws and enforcement.[21]

Developing countries generate a relatively small percentage of world trade, but their economic development is often greatly influenced by standards set in major markets. For example, China and India may not attach a high priority to protecting the ozone layer, but they do hope to export appliances and consumer electronics to industrialized countries that do. Under the Montreal Protocol, their products, if made with ozone-depleting chemicals, could be banned from import. Even if not banned, they may be incompatible with standards and components adapted to meet protocol requirements in the largest markets, the industrialized countries. The United States is so far the only nation with minimum energy efficiency standards for appliances, but adoption of similar standards in other large markets in Europe and Asia would undoubtedly greatly influence the design and manufacture of those products in developing countries.

Another common theme of environmental business literature is an emphasis on the importance of management leadership. A successful pollution-prevention program, *Changing Course* asserts, "ultimately comes down to desire." The goal of "eco-efficiency" is not solely or even primarily a matter of technology, but requires "profound changes in the goals and assumptions that drive corporate activities, and change in the daily practices and tools used to reach them . . . a break with business-as-usual mentalities and conventional wisdom that sidelines environmental and human concerns."[22]

The kind of leadership described may be more consistent with the culture of some industries than others, which may also help explain the seemingly greater interest in environmental quality of the chemical and electronics industries. The research and technology emphasis in these sectors may make them more likely to promote managers comfortable with meeting new challenges.

There are other factors driving interest in the environmentally responsible corporation, particularly the demands of shareholders. The total investment in socially screened portfolios has ballooned from $40 billion less than a decade ago to more than $700 billion today. The number of mutual funds based on social responsibility criteria jumped from 12 to 25 in the last three years.[23] A related factor is the influence of a growing number of shareholder resolutions seeking the adoption of stricter environmental standards, such as those developed by the Coalition for Environmentally Responsible Companies (the CERES principles). In February 1993, the Sun Company became the first Fortune 500 company to adopt the CERES principles, albeit in a modified form.[24]

Public Policy and the Environmentally Responsible Corporation

The role of government in promoting the greening of business is a critical issue. Silverstein is among a minority who perceive this trend as inevitable and government intervention therefore largely irrelevant. As noted above, Porter's hypothesis depends on strong environmental regulations to energize and focus corporate efforts. Porter and many others also emphasize the adverse effects of many existing environmental regulations, which can discourage the use of experimental new technologies and production practices.[25]

This phenomenon is well documented in a collection of case studies prepared by the California Environmental Business Opportunities Project, a private effort started in 1992 to provide California businesses with products and services that advance both environmental and economic goals. The case studies showed that existing environmental regulations can be a significant barrier to the adoption of new environmental technologies, due to the cost and uncertainty associated with the approval of new processes, even when they are significantly superior to existing ones.[26] In a recent study of a refinery managed by the Amoco Oil Company, conducted jointly by the U.S. Environmental Protection Agency and Amoco, the authors concluded that the company could reduce pollution and save millions of dollars if standards were imposed for emissions from the entire refinery, rather than on selected components within the plant boundaries.[27]

The most widely cited example of a regulatory program that allows the flexibility needed to foster innovation is the acid rain program. Under a law adopted in 1990, utilities in the Midwest and Northeast are required to reduce their emissions of sulfur dioxide by roughly half, or 10 million tons a year. However, all power plants will not have to meet the same standard. Instead, each utility will be able to comply by whatever means it finds most economical, including the implementation of nontraditional measures such as reducing electricity needs by promoting conservation by its customers. Still more flexibility is afforded by a provision that allows emission trading; a utility may exceed its requirements and obtain credits for sale to other companies unable to comply as cheaply. The resultant market in emissions is expected to save utilities $1 billion a year. Ironically, however, the program has been hampered by state utility regulators reluctant to permit their utilities to profit from the trades.

The benefits of public-private cooperation in Japan are sometimes cited as evidence that significant environmental progress can be achieved without regulation.[28] For example, Japanese industry has been gradually eroding U.S. dominance in the development of fuel cells. A technology originally developed for use in the space program, the hope is that fuel cells will produce low-cost electricity on a small scale with little pollution and can be used in buildings, possibly in trucks and buses, and eventually in cars.

Despite their promise, the commercial development of fuel cells has been slow and expensive, and government support in the United States has been modest and inconsistent. In contrast, Japan's Ministry of International Trade and Industry has worked with utilities and technology companies to subsidize the commercial development and deployment of fuel cells, spreading the cost among large firms who are in a position to benefit from the long-term success of the venture. The government's role has been primarily to coordinate activities and promote constructive competition among suppliers, rather than to guarantee a market or provide large subsidies, as is sometimes demanded by firms engaged in long-term research in the United States.[29]

Recently, there have been some encouraging results with more collaborative models of technology cooperation in the United States. Beginning in January 1991, the EPA launched a program of voluntary greenhouse-gas-reductions.[30] The evolution of these programs was largely dictated by the Bush administration's cautious attitude toward the greenhouse issue. Because of skepticism about the state of science and concern about the economic consequences of policies to reduce fossil-fuel consumption, the Bush administration adopted a policy of "no regrets"—that is, it would take only those measures that would yield other benefits, so that there would be no regrets if the climate problem did not prove to be as serious as many predicted.[31] Although this constraint left little room for new initiatives other than tree planting and voluntary programs, these programs are proving to be very successful. In expanded form, they are central to the Climate Change Action Plan President Clinton announced on 20 October, 1993.[32] This plan identifies fifty actions that collectively are expected to fulfill the President's promise to meet the initial goal established by the climate convention: a reduction of emissions of greenhouse gases to 1990 levels by the year 2000.

The flagship of the EPA's voluntary programs is the "Green Lights" program. In this program, corporations and state and federal agencies agree in writing to survey and upgrade the lighting in their buildings with the most energy-efficient, cost-effective systems. State-of-the-art lighting technology can reduce the use of electricity by over 50 percent. Since lighting accounts for over 20 percent of U.S. electricity consumption, or about 120 million metric tons of carbon emissions, the potential for reducing pollution is enormous. In return, the EPA provides technical assistance on lighting technology and financing options. The EPA also offers something less tangible but perhaps far more valuable—the public relations benefits of being a Green Lights Partner.

Traditional economic theory suggests that such a program should not accomplish much; the Green Lights contract is, after all, a promise to do only what is in a company's economic self-interest. Assuming a reasonably effective market for lighting technology, companies should already be adopting equipment that performs reliably and saves money. Yet in less than three years, the EPA has signed up more than 1,100 participants. These include many of America's largest enterprises, which own more than 3 billion square feet of building space—5 percent of all commercial space in the country. Participants average 65-percent savings on their lighting costs and a 20–40 percent internal rate of return on their investments. The Climate Change Action Plan will expand the program to achieve efficient lighting in 16 billion square feet of commercial and industrial space, reducing CO_2 emissions by 2.5 million metric tons from the projected levels in 2000.

Why is Green Lights so successful? The EPA's experience demonstrates that there are many subtle barriers to pollution prevention and improved energy efficiency, including difficulties evaluating new technologies and procurement systems that remove most of the incentives for investing in energy conservation (e.g., the plant manager pays the higher cost for the equipment but cannot keep the savings from reduced energy costs). The Green Lights program also changes the decision-making process—no longer is the issue simply a question of cost; now it is an opportunity to demonstrate environmental leadership.[33]

The EPA also cosponsored another voluntary program to help advance technology, the Super-Efficient Refrigerator Program, which has been dubbed the "Golden Carrot" program because of its unique incentive features. A minimum energy-efficiency standard for refrigerators is already set by the Department of Energy. However, the standard is, in practice, limited to technologies already used commercially. Much better refrigerators could be produced, but manufacturers are reluctant to invest in retooling without assurances that consumers will be willing to pay the modest extra cost. Meanwhile, many utility companies offer rebates and other financial incentives to their consumers who purchase highly efficient appliances, because the reduced demand for electricity reduces the need for more costly investments in new power plants.

The most innovative feature of the Golden Carrot program is its investment pool. The pool was created by contributions from utility companies, who coordinated their financial incentives to offer almost $30 million in rebates to the refrigerator manufacturer able to demonstrate the ability to produce and sell units 50 percent more efficient than 1990 models, and 25 percent more efficient than federal standards call for. The refrigerators must also eliminate the use of ozone-depleting chemicals found in current models. The winning bidder, picked in June 1992, was Whirlpool; the product they proposed will be the most energy-efficient, ozone-friendly mass market refrigerator in the world.[34] Consumers win through reduced pollution and lower electricity bills, with savings of over $250 million in annual electricity payments, or 10 to 35 percent for the average household.

The Climate Action Plan identifies a series of similar programs for other sectors of the economy. The Climate Challenge seeks to obtain commitments from electric utilities to reduce their greenhouse gas emissions. Eight have agreed to stay at or below 1990 levels, while 50 more have expressed a willingness to achieve less ambitious targets. Other programs cover a wide array of activities, including improvements in the energy efficiency of buildings, improvements in natural gas transmission to reduce methane emissions, cooperation with beef and swine producers to reduce methane from agricultural wastes, and a partnership with aluminum producers to reduce emissions of carbon tetrafluoride. One of the few regulatory proposals is that landfills be required to capture methane gases released by decaying waste. Medium to large landfills are expected to sell these gases at a profit, so even in this instance the regulatory burden is modest.

The Climate Action Plan is largely devoid of strategies for improving the efficiency of automobiles. This problem is addressed in President Clinton's "green car" initiative announced on 29 September 1993.[35] Its goal is to develop "a practical, affordable automobile up to three times more fuel efficient than comparable vehicles today [one that gets about 80 miles per gallon] and to do so in about ten years."[36] The agreement, announced by the President together with the heads of GM, Ford, and Chrysler, is intended to achieve commercial production of a "green car" by 2010.[37]

Another major EPA effort to obtain voluntary cooperation from industry is the "33/50" program. This strategy was developed by the Pollution Prevention Office of the EPA as part of an effort to establish standard methods for measuring source reduction and provide measurable goals by which progress can by judged. The agency targeted 15 to 20 high-risk chemicals and established a voluntary goal of reducing releases of these chemicals by 33 percent by 1992 and 50 percent by the end of 1995.[38] More than 700 companies have committed themselves to meeting these goals.

The Importance of Monitors and Measures of Environmental Performance

Other than regulation, the most important motivator for the greening of business may by consumer demand. This theme runs through the books by Makower and Silverstein, who report many signs of consumer responsiveness to environmental labeling and marketing. This trend is reinforced by surveys indicating that consumers are increasingly concerned about the environmental and social reputations of the companies from whom they buy goods and services.

And corporate concern about environmental reputation is evident from the response to the Toxic Release Inventory (TRI), a report on hazardous materials production and storage required annually by the 1986 Community Right to Know Act. The TRI inventory was first released in 1989. It revealed far greater quantities of toxic emissions than had been expected—more than 7 billion pounds in 1987, from more than 18,000 reporting companies. Information is reported by company and location, so the TRI facilitates localized reporting and media coverage, producing headlines like "Ten Largest Toxic Emitters Statewide," and "Local Firm Heads List of Toxic Emitters."

Many corporations appear to have made significant reductions in their emissions since the TRI was first released. The 1993 report for 1991 shows discharges of 3.4 billion pounds, despite an increase in the number of reporting firms. To what extent this is due to changes in reporting practices rather than changes in industry practice is difficult to determine, but the impact of this nonregulatory reporting requirement appears to be significant on the basis of anecdotal evidence.[39]

These kinds of pressures, however, depend highly on mechanisms for measuring and reporting corporate environmental performance. A benefit of the TRI is that it lists about 300 specific chemicals that must be reported. The EPA is proposing to expand its coverage significantly so that companies cannot avoid being reported by shifting to substances that are not on the list but are almost as bad as those that are.

Defining environmental quality is far more difficult in the realm of consumer products. This is made evident by a visit to any large grocery store, where a growing number of products seek to distinguish themselves by claiming environmental superiority. If the consumer is unable to reliably compare these claims, some incentive for environmental progress will be lost.[40]

The technical issues associated with setting environmental standards for consumer products are challenging. For example, should a product be rated environmentally superior because it is made from recycled materials, even if it is otherwise inefficient and ill-suited for its intended purpose? Are disposable diapers environmentally inferior to cloth diapers, or should incentives be given to encourage their manufacture in the most environmentally superior form, since they are widely preferred?

The technical complexities may be even greater when comparing company-wide performance and reputation, as was done in a recent article in *Fortune* magazine recognizing the best and worst of American industry. Is it most relevant to look at each firm's recent efforts to improve, or should companies with serious problems never be rewarded? Sheer size may condemn companies such as Du Pont to appear forever on the list of the country's largest polluters.

Standards and self-reporting also must be verified, which presumes some credible means of audits and enforcement. An increasing number of companies now undertake voluntary environmental audits and make special annual reports, but the vast majority do not. This has led to concerns about the reliability and consistency of corporate environmental claims.

The Limits of Social Responsibility

How far can an environmentally responsible corporations go toward promoting the goals of sustainable development? Makower writes, "In the pursuit of quality, the goal is to continually decrease waste and pollution; it follows that the ultimate goal of environmental quality is to achieve zero waste and pollution." Silverstein asserts that environmental progress appears to be moving "at a fast enough pace so that at least theoretically . . . we could 'have it all,' in the sense of widespread material prosperity and natural preservation."[41] His argument, too, would appear to be predicated on the technological potential for a zero-pollution economy.

However, it is far from evident that all our environmental problems can be solved by means of a purely corporate focus. Gladwin warns that corporate environmental reform may be a

> necessary but not sufficient condition for sustainable development. . . . Unless we learn how to drastically shift economic opportunity, technology, capital, and primary social service provision toward the poor of this planet, then it is possible the greening in rich nations merely amounts to a rearranging of the deck chairs on a "Global Titanic."[42]

Until we more clearly establish the conditions for a sustainable society, the extent to which corporations can help achieve this goal will remain debatable. In the meantime, there should be no doubt that given proper incentives, corporations can make a major contribution to reducing the negative impact of manufactured goods on the environment.

Notes

1. Paul Hawken, *The Ecology of Commerce: A Declaration of Sustainability* (New York: Harper, 1993), 11.

2. The profit-maximizing purpose of corporations is enshrined in laws that allow the shareholder to sue for the failure to pursue profitable opportunities. This principle is arguably a radical change from early American views of the role of the corporation, which many colonists viewed as an agent of the Crown in need of close regulation. See Richard Grossman and Frank Adams, *Taking Care of Business* (Cambridge, MA: Charter, 1993).

3. A relatively small group of writers such as Commoner, Bookchin, and Ophuls, have taken this view to its logical conclusion and argued that sustainable development can be accomplished only with fundamental changes in capitalist economies.

4. Stephen Schmidheiny, *Changing Course: A Global Business Perspective on Development and the Environment* (Cambridge: MIT Press, 1992).

5. Bruce Smart, ed., *Beyond Compliance: A New Industry View of the Environment* (Washington, DC: World Resources Institute, 1992).

6. Joel Makower, *The E-factor: The Bottom-Line Approach to Environmentally Responsible Business* (New York: Plume, 1994).

7. Michael Silverstein, *The Environmental Economic Revolution: How Business Will Thrive and the Earth Survive* (New York: St. Martin's Press, 1993).

8. Schmidheiny, *Changing Course,* 11.

9. Ibid., 184.

10. Ibid.

11. As discussed below, there may be significant opportunities for innovation and improved efficiency, even in the case of mature industries such as lighting and refrigerators. External incentives, however, were necessary to capture these opportunities.

12. Hugh Williams, James Medhurst, and Kirstine Drew, "Corporate Strategies for a Sustainable Future," in *Environmental Strategies for Industry,* ed. K. Fischer and J. Schot (Washington, DC: Island Press, 1993).

13. "A Special Report: Environment and the Economy," *Science* 260 (25 June 1993): 1883–96.

14. See also Office of Technology Assessment, *Industry, Technology, and the Environment* (Washington, DC: U.S. Government Printing Office, 1994); and Rene Kemp, "An Economic Analysis of Cleaner Technology: Theory and Evidence," in Fischer and Schot, *Environmental Strategies for Industry.*

15. Nicholas Ashford, "Understanding Technological Responses of Industrial Firms to Environmental Problems: Implications for Government Policy," in Fischer and Schot, *Environmental Strategies for Industry;* Michael Porter, *The Competitive Advantage of Nations* (New York: Free Press, 1990).

16. Richard Benedick, *Ozone Diplomacy* (Cambridge, MA: Harvard University Press, 1991).

17. William Cline, *The Economics of Global Warming* (Washington, DC: Institute for International Economics, 1992).

18. Frank Den Hond and Peter Groenewegen, "Solving the Automobile Shredder Waste Problem: Cooperation Among Firms in the Automotive Industry," in Fischer and Schot, *Environmental Strategies for Industry.*

19. Lester Brown, Hal Kane, and Ed Ayres, *Vital Signs* (New York: W. W. Norton, 1993). See also Ronald Ehrenberg, *Labor Markets and Integrating National Economies* (Washington, DC: Brookings Institution, 1994).

20. Brown, Kane, and Ayres, *Vital Signs.*

21. Herman Daly, "The Perils of Free Trade," *Scientific American* 269 (November 1993): 50–57; see also Daniel Esty, *Greening the GATT* (Washington, DC: Institute for International Economics, 1994).

22. Schmidheiny, *Changing Course,* 10.

23. *Kiplinger's Personal Finance Magazine* (October 1993): 37.

24. Kuszewski, "Sun Company Joins CERES," *On Principle* 3, no. 1 (Spring/Summer 1993): 1, 5.

25. Bad regulation may help to explain why the United States spends more on environmental protection than any other country yet lags behind its competitors in several key areas of environmental technology. For example, a high proportion of expenditures associated with the Superfund program have gone so far to administration and litigation rather than cleanup of sites contaminated by hazardous wastes.

26. California Environmental Business Opportunities Project, *Breaking Down Barriers: Creating Environmental Business Opportunities for California,* first-year report, August 1993.

27. Some environmentalists argue that, properly understood, the Amoco study illustrates deficiencies in the existing regulatory system that allow opportunities for companies to ignore significant emission reductions. Eliminating loopholes, they argue, would greatly reduce the extent of these opportunities and therefore the benefits of more flexible regulations. More research is required to determine which view is more accurate.

28. Curtis Moore and Alan Miller, *Green Gold: Japan, Germany, the United States, and the Race for Environmental Technology* (Boston: Beacon Press, 1994).

29. Linda Cohen and Roger Noll, "Privatizing Public Research," *Scientific American* 271 (September 1994): 72–77.

30. U.S. Environmental Protection Agency, *The Climate is Right for Action: Voluntary Programs to Reduce Greenhouse Gas Emissions,* ANR–43, October 1992.

31. See Bromley, "The Making of a Greenhouse Policy," *Issues in Science and Technology* 7, no. 1 (Fall 1990): 55–61; Gray and Rivkin, "A 'No Regrets' Environmental Policy," *Foreign Policy* 83 (1991).

32. The White House, "Climate Change Action Plan," 20 October 1993. The Presi-

dent first proposed to expand the green programs in a package of measures promoted as an "economic stimulus." This proposal was rejected by Congress due to concerns about the federal deficit.

33. Stephen DeCanio, "Agency and Control Problems in U.S. Corporations: The Case of Energy-Efficient Investment Projects," *Journal of the Economics of Business,* 1994.

34. The criteria used in the bidding process assured that manufacturers would use only proven technology; much better designs are therefore possible. The environmental group Greenpeace has also criticized all the large refrigerator companies for replacing ozone-depleting compounds (CFCs) with HFC 134$_a$, a greenhouse gas.

35. See generally, "Reinventing the Automobile—and Government R&D," *Science* 8 (October 1993): 172.

36. The White House, "A New Partnership for Cars of the Future," (29 September 1993).

37. Developments subsequent to the announcement of the green car initiative illustrate some of the difficulties inherent in even such seemingly nonthreatening collaborative efforts. The auto industry is seeking federal support to stop California and a growing number of northeastern states from adopting requirements for the introduction of "zero-emission vehicles" beginning in 1998. Federal clean air standards for automobiles are uniform and preemptive, except for the state of California and other states choosing to adopt California standards. The auto industry argues that it should not be required to meet the California standards when it is attempting to produce entirely new technologies to meet much more ambitious goals.

38. U.S. EPA, "Pollution Prevention Strategy" (January 1991). There is some dispute about progress toward meeting these goals; an environmental group report in October 1992 found that only 13 percent of firms releasing these chemicals had agreed to participate, while a March 1993 EPA report asserts that the 50-percent goal will be met. See R. Percival, et al., *Environmental Regulation: Law, Science, and Policy, 1993 Supplement,* (1993): 44–45.

39. Patricia Dillon and Michael Baram, "Corporate Management of Chemical Accident Risks," in Fischer and Schot, *Environmental Strategies for Industry* .

40. Presumably this will not apply to internal incentives for the adoption of measures that save money and reduce pollution. It is relevant with regard to the growing evidence of consumer preference for products from companies with good reputations on social matters.

41. Silverstein, *Environmental Economic Revolution,* 193.

42. Thomas Gladwin, *The Meaning of Greening: A Plea for Organizational Theory in Environmental Strategies for Industry* (Washington, DC: Island Press, 1993), 56.

World Food Problems: Making the Transition from Agriculture to Regenerative Food Systems

Kenneth A. Dahlberg

Introduction

The transition from current industrial modes of agricultural production to more sustainable and regenerative food and fiber systems is one of the key elements in the much larger transition of all societies to sustainability in a post–fossil fuel era. The magnitude of this latter transition ranks with the other great transitions: from hunting and gathering to agricultural to urban civilizations to modern industrial societies.[1] Each of these transitions has involved a basic restructuring of the interactions and relationships between natural systems, social systems, and technological systems, something that dramatically affects both energy and resource use. Also, as in each previous transition, a basic reconceptualization and restructuring of all aspects of society, including food systems, is involved.

What the current transition means for food and agriculture is threefold. First, there is a need to reconceptualize food and agriculture in systemic terms that will better connote the interlinkages between agriculture, food, environments, resources, and technologies. Such a reconceptualization clearly needs to be placed in the general framework of sustainability. However, current concepts of sustainability neglect food and agriculture and will need to be broadened to include regenerative food and agricultural systems. Second, we need to re-assess our current understandings of world food, agricultural, and hunger problems using these broadened concepts. Third, we need to start restructuring current obsolescent industrial food and agricultural systems and to start building more sustainable systems at all levels. In this chapter, each of these challenges will be discussed in detail.

The Conceptual Challenges of Sustainability

The debate about sustainability has started the process of reconceptualization that is required if we are to identify the *real* problems facing industrial societies, and the sources of these problems. Only when we can do so will we be able to come up with genuine and workable alternatives. Yet there are real weaknesses in current concepts of sustainability.

The debates about "sustainable agriculture" illustrate a number of these. The term *regenerative food and fiber systems* is used here in preference to the more commonly accepted one, *sustainable agriculture,* for several important reasons. First, it emphasizes the need to regenerate both natural and social systems over time. For example, the regeneration of farms and farm families involves everything from sustainable cultivation practices that are environmentally benign to farm and rural economics, to good local education and health care, to general rural viability, and to inheritance laws. Second, a focus on regenerative systems requires not only multidecade analysis, but the inclusion of issues of social justice, intergenerational equity, and interspecies equity. Third, it suggests the need for systems thinking and approaches rather than linear and specialized approaches—which will require a shift from a narrow focus on production systems to an examination of complete food and fiber systems. Finally, the term is less easily co-opted than *sustainable agriculture* or *sustainable development.*[2] In general then, regenerative food and fiber systems are best understood in terms of process and context, wherein their capacity to coadapt in specific natural and cultural environments enables them to provide human and other populations with their basic food and fiber needs over multiple generations.

The above points apply to much more than agriculture. Indeed, it can be argued that current concepts of sustainability need to be broadened and redefined in terms of regenerative systems. This requires moving much more toward a *contextual analysis model* that can describe at each relevant level of analysis the real-world distribution of phenomena in space and time. This is in contrast to universal/generalization models, which do not conceptually sort out phenomena by levels and time frames and generally aggregate and average data. Such aggregation and averaging typically masks crucial contextual variables and patterns.

Contextual analysis involves several important dimensions: sensitivity to the time frame employed; use of systems approaches; use of different levels of analysis; and inclusion of externalities and the informal sectors of society. Let us examine these.

The natural sciences have had the greatest clarity regarding the *time frames* they employ and the corresponding scope, levels of analysis, and types of data required, as well as the degree of detail that can be captured for a given time frame.[3] Such clarity is not found in the work on global change. For example, current global change models are dependent upon national data sets that are organized by economic sector—agriculture, forestry, fisheries, etc.—which do not recognize the systemic overlappings between renewable resource systems. There is also little recognition that broader concepts and data sets are needed at the regional and global scales.[4]

Systems approaches tend to challenge linear and reductionist approaches and their functional specialization. This suggests the need for interdisciplinary and interfield work. Typically such interdisciplinary work as is done takes place within a given field (i.e. the natural sciences or the social sciences or the applied sciences). What is needed is interdisciplinary work that crosses both disciplines and fields.

Also crucial is the use of different *levels of analysis* to determine the relevant systems and subsystems. Hierarchy theory—which has only recently been used in ecology—offers a useful model. However, the term carries connotations that "higher" systems are superior, which they are not. Different concepts and data sets are required for each level of analysis. Also, care must be taken to map out the major influences from the systems immediately lower and higher.[5] And the natural, social, and technological subsystems at any given level need to be integrated.

The *inclusion of externalities and the informal sectors of society* involves a number of dimensions, which also vary according to the time frame and level of analysis chosen. To illustrate the range of challenges here, let us point out additional dimensions that need to be included at the global/longer-term level by elaborating upon the useful work done by John Holdren and his associates in trying to analyze and integrate environmental, population, resource, and technological issues. They developed the $I = P \times A \times T$ equation to illustrate the interrelationships. In the equation, I stands for environmental impact, P for population, A for affluence (generally measured by energy use/capita) and T for the damage done by the technologies employed.[6]

While the $I = PAT$ equation has been a very useful heuristic device to demonstrate and clarify the global population/environment/resources problematique, it needs to be expanded conceptually in several important ways to overcome the biases of different disciplines and fields as well as to include informal and political factors. First, in dealing with populations, we need to go beyond the anthropocentrism of demographers. At a minimum, livestock populations need to be included, since livestock currently consume 38 percent of all grain production and are a major source of pressure upon land and water resources (see below). In addition, the interactions and population dynamics of other species and organisms, especially exotics and diseases, need to be included to gain some sense of global trends and dynamics.[7]

Other major dimensions of population that are missing or not integrated in most current analyses are cultural and political factors. United Nations population data, as well as many national data sets, are organized jurisdictionally and do not provide information on the spatial distribution of different ethnic, religious, or economic groups. This is because of the highly political nature of population data at a national level, where the relative size and rates of change of different ethnic and/or religious groups can become a major factor in self-determination movements, regional conflicts, family planning efforts, and so on. Other population-related issues are also highly political, especially those dealing with such issues as women's roles and rights, abortion, and sex education.

In regard to affluence, care must be taken to go beyond the narrow assumptions of economists. Most analyses of affluence and consumption accept existing economic concepts of free markets and free trade—which clearly are being challenged by new concepts of sustainability.[8] Work also needs to be done to identify and internalize the social, health, and environmental consequences of production processes that economists largely ignore by defining as externalities. Work along these lines in food and agriculture soon leads to a recognition that basic reform with regard to land tenure, corporate chartering, and the operation of financial systems may be needed if we are to move in more sustainable directions.

Two crucial dimensions are missed in most analyses of the technology factor of the equation. One relates to the structural dimensions of technological systems; infrastructural patterns (centralized or decentralized) generally will shape the institutions that are built upon and around them, and correspondingly, the organizations that derive from them.[9] The other involves two central myths of industrial society: that science and technology lead us to social progress; and that individual technologies are neutral. These myths are a great source of power for those promoting new technologies, such as the military and multinational corporations. They are also a major source of influence for local developers. These social myths are being challenged by the increasing development of assessment systems, social, environmental, and technological, and of new social and health indicators that identify the real-world costs and benefits of specific technologies and/or projects. By showing that with every technology or project there are winners and losers, these social myths are both demystified and politicized. This is as it should be, since, as E. F. Schumacher pointed out, these technological choices are ultimately political choices. Therefore, they should be made in the political realm and not left to experts.[10]

Thus, as we move from "sustainable agriculture" to "regenerative food systems," major theoretical and conceptual changes are required. Equally, there is a comparable need to broaden general concepts of sustainability in order to understand and address the issues and needs of regenerative systems. Contextual analysis offers a valuable approach for pursuing these broader needs. However, as we broaden our conceptual awareness and develop new tools, we also need to apply them to world food and agricultural problems so that we can get a more complete and realistic view of the challenges facing us there.

Reassessing World Food Problems

As many studies have shown, modern industrial societies are now encountering various global constraints or limits. These "collisions" threaten the life-supporting capabilities of the biosphere, which in turn threatens industrial societies. The same vicious circle is found in industrial agriculture. The ways in which the unsustainability of industrial agriculture increases the unsustainability of industrial societies can be seen in four major classes of global constraints and/or threats.[11] Only by understanding these larger sources of the unsustainability of industrial agriculture will we be able to develop viable alternatives.

The Explosion of Livestock and Human Populations

Since the time of Malthus, there has been an awareness of the linkages between population growth rates and hunger. The easy technological approach has been to focus on increasing production rather than addressing the deeper and more difficult source of most hunger: poverty. On the population side, the easy availability of fossil fuels has been a major factor in facilitating the population explosion of humans. The intensive use of fossil fuels in modern agriculture and agribusiness has also facilitated a population explosion of livestock. If we include livestock populations in our demographics, we come up with rather different rankings of the most populous countries.[12] Also, as argued above, it is clear that we must include livestock in the $I = PAT$ equation in order to gain a fuller picture of general population pressures upon the environment. This also means that, as with humans, the resource use per animal, the type of feed (whether edible by humans or not), and the production technologies employed (and their energy- and resource-intensity) need to be included.

On a global scale, this explosion of livestock populations is a significant source of environmental destruction and degradation. Since 1950 there has been almost a doubling of the population of large livestock (cattle, pigs, sheep, and goats), from 2.3 to 4 billion. In the same period, poultry populations have increased from 3 to 11 billion. In 1992, livestock consumed 38 percent of the world's grain.[13] The intense energy and water consumption of industrial livestock production leads to high levels of water pollution, the erosion of soil (needed for grazing and for the cultivation of feed grains), and deforestation.[14] These negative trends feed back into agriculture, reducing production through the same loss or degradation of soils and water. In addition, losses of biodiversity and of crop and animal germplasm increase the risks of production losses from pests and diseases.

What all of this suggests is that three basic changes are essential if we are to avoid major population collapses over the longer term. First, "national security" must be reconceived; meeting the immediate needs of hungry people around the world, and the simultaneous promotion of the more fundamental political and social reforms that will reduce poverty and empower women so that population growth rates will decrease, must become national security priorities. Second, and in a very parallel manner, the focus of "food security," which is presently on immediate "curative" measures for the hungry, must be expanded to include and stress the development of healthy and sustainable food systems that provide for most people most of the time. Third, given the impacts described above, measures to reduce the livestock population explosion need to be included in both. This really involves developing new approaches that encourage more equitable and healthy diet patterns between and within countries.

Linkages between Fossil Fuel Use, Agriculture, and Global Climate Change

The ways in which the global use of fossil fuels leads to such problems as acid rain, ozone depletion, and global warming. have been widely reported. There has been much less discussion of the linkages of fossil-fuel use to food and agriculture. The few specialized studies done on agriculture typically do not include fiber crops, nor production in the informal sector from household and community gardens. The value of such garden production, rural and urban, in the United States is estimated to be $18 billion—which is roughly equivalent to the value of the corn crop![15] More important, these studies do not include data on the complete *food system*—production, processing, distribution, storage, use, and disposal. Thus, in addition to all of their energy facets, food systems include social, health, and symbolic facets, among many others.

Departments of agriculture and forestry are ubiquitous. Yet I am not aware of any country, state, or city that has a ministry or department of food, which is reflected by—and perhaps helps to explain—the fact that we have neither organizations nor data sets on food systems.[16]

Some energy studies done in the 1970s did look at industrial food systems and highlighted their great energy inefficiency—some 10 calories of energy are required to deliver 1 calorie of food on our dinner plates.[17] Also, while the number of farmers in the industrial countries has declined dramatically since the turn of the century, the numbers employed in the total food system have remained fairly constant, as food processors, distributors, retailers, and restaurant workers have been added. However, these studies also ignored much of the informal economy, giving us only a partial indication of the true size and importance of food and fiber systems. Thus, since much more fossil fuel is used in industrial food and fiber systems than most people are aware, improving their energy efficiency ought to be a major element in addressing global climate-change issues.

Without this, the spread of modern industrial food and fiber production systems through green revolution–type technologies will generate increasing amounts of greenhouse gasses. In turn, this will have negative effects on industrial food and fiber production. Again, the few specialized studies that have been done tend to provide a misleading picture. Specific crops are studied and estimates given as to how average changes in temperature, moisture, and/or carbon dioxide concentrations will affect production. Some studies suggest which regions and countries might be winners or losers.[18]

The larger picture is much more complex and disturbing. Crops are adapted to specific regional weather patterns. Changes in the *variability* of the weather (something projected for the temperate zones) will be much more disruptive than the projected changes in the *averages*.[19] But what about the "new" favorable climate zones that may emerge? Climate modelers have tended to ignore the tremendous amount of capital and human investment made in agriculture. For example, if the temperate zones "move north," the United States will face several dilemmas. One is that the Colorado River basin may dry up—leaving its dams as some sort of latter-day pyramids. Another is that it is unlikely that urban majorities will support the massive capital investment required to construct new dams and irrigation networks and to retrain farmers and extension personnel at a time when they will want to protect their coastal cities from rising sea levels—which will require huge amounts of capital for dikes and/or relocation programs.

At a more global level, there is little awareness that from the perspective of human ecology, the real energy problem is not a scarcity of energy but too much energy forcibly being channeled through both natural and social systems—a process that in general simplifies their structures, reduces their diversity, and makes them more vulnerable to collapse. A final point here relates not to fossil fuels but to the increasing appropriation by humans—and livestock—of the natural energy produced by all plants through photosynthesis. Of the net global primary production of photosynthetic energy (the energy fixed by plants beyond their own life-process requirements), approximately 25 percent is now consumed or lost through human activities.[20]

The Loss of Cultural Diversity and Biodiversity

In industrial agriculture, the main food crops are provided by species and habitats that are highly managed to keep them at a pioneer stage of ecological succession. Wheat, maize, and rice are regularly planted, cultivated, and harvested in monocultures that are heavily fertilized, treated with pesticides, and often irrigated in order to maximize the production of what are primarily pioneer species.[21] In addition to the very high energy and environmental costs of this, the vulnerability of these vast tracts of monocultures to massive disease and/or outbreaks of pests means that we could face the equivalent of a modern-day potato famine with any of our major grain crops. Indigenous systems—which have demonstrated their sustainability over the centuries—are typically complex and mimic the later stages of succession. The process of "development" in agriculture has typically meant replacing these more complex indigenous systems with the genetically *and* culturally more simple systems of industrial agriculture.[22] Agriculture as a field and plant breeders and crop germplasm collectors in particular have neglected the economic, structural, and cultural factors that are integral to agriculture and food. In terms of crop germplasm, only a few anthropologists have explored the close linkages between cultural diversity and biodiversity. For example, in the Peruvian highlands different tribes cultivate different species of potatoes at different altitudes.[23]

This lack of awareness of how industrial "development" has simplified cultures and social systems also permeates much of the futures literature. Visions of a "global village," whether electronic or otherwise, neglect the fundamental importance of cultural diversity, much less its links to biodiversity. A more appropriate image would be a diverse world with many different types of cities and regions, all founded upon a "globe of villages." The modern industrial vision and its blindness to diversity is in sharp contrast with that of indigenous peoples, for whom areas of biodiversity crucial to the regeneration of species are sacred— something that reflects their realization that these habitats and species are the *sources* of life.[24]

Thus, both the loss of biodiversity and the difficulty of portraying the real risk involved in such losses can be seen as a profound commentary on the inherent weaknesses of industrial paradigms and of several Western cultural beliefs. In terms of successfully navigating the larger transition to a post–fossil fuel era, such losses point to a key dilemma of industrial societies: that they are undermining, weakening, and/or destroying the multitude of renewable resource systems, natural and culturally constructed, upon which they will become more dependent in the future. The unsustainability of current patterns of agriculture, forestry, and fisheries illustrates this. Particularly striking are monocultural practices, clear-cutting in forestry, and the use of drift nets.

The Growth of Economic Inequality

The expansion of industrial societies and the economic inequalities that have grown with them have been facilitated by two important myths. One is the belief in the beneficence of "the market" and its "hidden hand"; the other the belief that technology is beneficent yet neutral.[25] Couched in larger visions of social progress achieved through reason and science, these two myths, combined with the development of fossil fuels, made possible the development of technological systems and organizations that have exploited both natural and social environments. They have made socially and politically acceptable the uncounted "externalities" of economics and the "side effects" or "the price of progress" of technologies. The result has been increasingly unequal economic systems—with the rich becoming more powerful, whether at the local, national, or international level.[26]

Inequalities in agriculture historically grew out of the dispossession of native lands and the subjugation of peasants. Today, the green revolution, together with an ever increasing emphasis on cash crops for export, have marginalized peasants and subsistence agriculture. Past inequalities have led to native uprisings, peasant revolts, and other forms of resistance. In regions where inequalities are great today, such as Central America, peasants and rural people continue to respond by revolting or causing major disruptions. Thus, existing indigenous or modern modes of sustainable agriculture are fragile and threatened in areas where social justice is lacking. Also, the historic separation and inequalities that have developed between urban and rural peoples have been compounded by the increasing power of corporate and commodity groups to make national and international agricultural policy. All of these trends have been rationalized in terms of "progress," and the use of science and technology to expand productivity and markets.

These social myths are now being used to defend the status quo and have thus taken on ideological dimensions. Sadly, they have also weakened efforts at reform. While there has been some demystification of conventional economics and its theories of "trickle-down," there has been much less demystification of the non-neutrality of technologies and technological systems. Indeed, this may be one of the key cultural mental blocks in the way of reform. The continuing power of these myths can be seen in debates over biotechnology. While its promoters emphasize its "great potential," few are aware that this can be realized only if there are major institutional restructurings and reforms that will ensure it is used for public purposes and benefit.[27]

Clearly, these four classes of global constraints and/or threats present formidable challenges to the building of regenerative food and fiber systems.

Building Regenerative Food and Fiber Systems

To build new, regenerative systems, several things are needed. It will be essential to maintain and enhance those remaining indigenous and traditional food and fiber systems that have demonstrated their regenerative capacities over the centuries. Seeking to do this, we learn from these systems and cultures as we attempt to build new ones.[28] However, if we are to succeed, there will have to be a restructuring and decolonization of current world agricultural, forestry, and fishery systems and their supporting research establishments.[29] In addition, as discussed above, all of this needs to take place within the larger requirements of a transition to a post–fossil fuel era.

To begin, there is the much discussed need for fundamental changes in worldview. A crucial part of this is a shift from the historic utopian vision of rational industrial societies built any- and everywhere to a new *eu*-topian vision of different good communities rooted in a variety of good places.[30] This is something that ultimately will require us to move from universal/generalization thinking, models, and concepts to some type of contextual analysis that is grounded in specific periods, places, and processes.[31] From there, shifts will be required in the evaluative criteria we employ—whether for society at large or for particular subsystems like food. Basically this involves a shift from economic growth and productivity criteria to health criteria—where the health of interacting natural, social, and technological systems at different levels is evaluated over multiple generations.[32] We will also have to re-embed both economics and technology into their surrounding natural systems and social institutions.[33] And for this to happen, the myth that technologies are neutral must be dismantled both conceptually and politically. Let us consider how this applies to the transition to regenerative food and fiber systems.

Restructuring and Decolonizing Industrial Agriculture, Forestry, and Fisheries

For many, part of the vision of a "global village" is a "global supermarket" run by multinational corporations and facilitated by free trade both in inputs (germplasm, equipment, fertilizers, pesticides) and in outputs (commodities and processed foods). Processing that adds value will continue to be done in the industrial countries or by Third World subsidiaries of the multinationals. At the same time, Western diets and nutritional approaches—diffused by food multinationals and global advertising—will gradually come to predominate, perhaps with a few local specialties admixed for "spice."[34] While this global supermarket can be expected to offer a wide variety of standardized products to those who can afford them, energy inefficiencies will be very high and the social and environmental costs great. Thus there will be continued talk of the need for more foreign aid and better international systems to provide "food security" for the poor countries.

To restructure and decolonize these emerging multinational regimes, a number of things will be needed. One involves efforts to "internalize" the social and environmental costs of industrial agriculture, both conceptually and practically.[35] Such internalization would help reduce the price differentials between "conventional" food and organic food domestically. Yet to reduce similar international price differentials, a rethinking of the nature of trade, a restructuring of trade regimes, and a broadening, the types of negotiators involved in trade policy will be required.[36] Other crucial changes include a strengthening of the ability of states and other political units to regulate the increasing power of multinational corporations (MNCs). Ultimately, this will require a redefinition of the legal concepts that have given corporations so much power and free reign. Key here are the "limited-liability" corporation and the legal fiction that corporations are "persons" entitled to the same constitutional rights as individuals.[37] Many other measures to re-embed these corporate and bureaucratic embodiments of the currently dominant economic paradigm into a larger democratic and social framework are also needed, from land reform to political and tax reforms.

In terms of agriculture and agricultural research, a number of basic conceptual and structural changes will be needed, including the development of new conceptual models that are systems-based and contextual. The shift in evaluative criteria from production/productivity to the health of systems will require significant institutional changes in thinking and incentives. Among these are the development of research and educational programs that focus on farming and food systems at different levels, rather than upon specific crops and commodities. Besides the changes this will require in agricultural colleges, a corresponding shift in agricultural support policies will be required—a move away from supporting specific commodities to supporting farm families and rural redevelopment.

Maintaining and Enhancing Indigenous and Traditional Food Systems

As indicated above, these food systems are reservoirs both of cultural diversity and biodiversity. Their maintenance as such ultimately depends upon Western societies developing a greater and deeper appreciation of their value. It also depends upon finding ways to institutionalize systems approaches to research and policy making. Conceptual and bureaucratic fragmentation—a basic component of industrial "divisions of labor"—has meant that few have understood the full dimensions of diversity. It is no accident that a greater appreciation for biodiversity has emerged along with the growth of ecology.

As indicated above, anthropologists have tended to do the best research on indigenous food systems and their dependence upon cultural diversity and biodiversity. Good work on traditional peasant agricultures is more scattered.[38] Sadly, those who collect and study crop germplasm have traditionally been interested only in the seeds they collect. The resulting "passport" document listing all the "vital characteristics" includes only information on the plant itself, plus some data on general climate and soil conditions. Thus, the great seed banks of the world are reduced to genetic "libraries" that contain little or no information on the cultural, economic, cultivation, preparation, taste, or other human dimensions of the food crops and the food that the seeds produce.[39]

Historically, agricultural policy making at the national level has been flawed not only by a similar fragmentation, but by its isolation from and resistance to urban issues. Agricultural policy is typically dominated by large landowners, rural elites, powerful commodity groups, and increasingly, the food industry. At the international level, trade negotiations, especially the GATT negotiations, are strengthening the corporate element of this coalition at the expense of the rural and farmer element.[40] What this means in terms of diversity is that now even national diversity in industrial agriculture is threatened with homogenization. It would therefore seem clear that the preservation of indigenous and traditional agriculture depends upon the simultaneous building of new regenerative food and fiber systems, and the restructuring and decolonization of industrial agriculture.

New and Integrative Approaches to Food and Fiber Systems

Much of the rhetoric of sustainable agriculture calls for localizing food systems. Yet most proponents deal only with the role of farming in this. Regenerative food and fiber systems must include cities and towns and must be built at many levels, from the household on up (again, a significant degree of restructuring and decolonization from the top down will have to accompany this). Also, these systems have to be designed to create greater self-reliance at each level.[41] At each level the following needs and opportunities can be seen.

The household offers great potential for families, however defined, to reduce their dependence upon the larger formal economy. A wide variety of services and production for home use can be carried out in the household. The multiple linkages and loops between food, energy, water, composted wastes, gardens, and self-reliance have been nicely illustrated in *The Integral Urban House,* which argues that redoing existing housing and ways of life should be re-created to make them less resource and job dependent.[42]

There is also an increasing interest in re-creating neighborhoods to make them more self-reliant.[43] Besides promoting community gardens, neighborhood centers, and local grocers, the basic landscapes of cities need to be rethought in terms of the natural systems that interweave them. Rather different approaches may be required for smaller towns as compared to large urban centers.[44]

At the city level there is increasing interest in food policy councils, which seek to understand and coordinate the various food system policies and activities of a city.[45] Few people are aware of the high economic and employment value and potential of local and regional food and horticultural systems in the formal economy, much less in the informal economy. For example, in the Delaware Valley in Pennsylvania, between 20 and 25 percent of the labor force is employed in food, horticulture, and agriculture, and food ranks third in venture capital expenditures.[46] Fewer still are aware of the larger food and energy flows and cycles of cities. A useful image of the needed shift toward systems thinking and new evaluative criteria is evoked by the name of the "Healthy Cities and Communities" program of the World Health Organization. While currently focused on public health matters, this concept could easily be expanded to include the long-term health of all of the natural, social, and technological systems of a city. As noted above, the shift from economic and production criteria to health criteria is one of the key elements in building more regenerative and sustainable systems.

Cities and metropolitan areas exist within regions. Calls to make cities and their regions more self-reliant have clustered around concepts of bioregionalism, landscape ecology, and urban agriculture.[47] Another metaphor might be "foodsheds"—at least for the food-related aspects of regions. There are a number of traditional and new approaches for increasing self-reliance with regard to food. Farmers' regional markets can be expanded and their produce made available to the poor through innovative food stamp programs. New risk-sharing arrangements between farmers and consumers, community supported agricultures (CSAs), are increasing in number.[48] Some states are promoting food grown within the state through labeling and promotional campaigns.

The variety of terms and concepts for the food systems found at these lower levels reflect the general conceptual vacuum that exists there. At higher levels, we start relying on more traditional conceptual language typical in economics, law, and politics. However, this is inadequate to capture the systemic dimensions; broad-gauge critiques are needed to do this and to reveal real alternatives. One useful example is the critique of "hard energy paths" made by Amory Lovins. By critiquing these centralized, capital- and energy-intensive, highly complicated systems, he is able to show us genuine alternatives.[49] What I have termed industrial agriculture might also be termed the "hard agricultural path." Analogous concepts in other sectors are needed to help us recognize alternatives.

Economic sectors, especially energy and agriculture, are important elements of national and international policy. At both levels, "sustainable agriculture" is primarily understood by most agricultural researchers and policy makers to mean reducing the environmental impacts of industrial agriculture.[50] Linkages to the larger search for "sustainable development" are mentioned only rhetorically. And ironically, the industrial countries do not see their own need to pursue the rural (re)development they recommend to the Third World.

At the international and global levels, there have been extensive discussions of sustainable development and global change. Neither has examined the crucial role of renewable resource systems at the regional level, where contiguous states are interwoven with complex land tenure and land use patterns, climatic regimes, trade patterns, dietary preferences, and so on. These must be understood to pursue regenerative—or sustainable—strategies effectively.[51]

Globally, the Gaia hypothesis has attracted a wide range of people seeking alternatives, in contrast to the more common image of the "global village." The Gaia hypothesis suggests that the surprising constancy over the millennia of the life-supporting proportions of the earth's atmospheric composition can only be explained by the fact that the biosphere is a self-regulating system. It is postulated that, within limits, the atmosphere remains life-supporting through the adaptation of both life-forms and physical processes, such as cloud cover, to major changes—climatic, volcanic, or other—which would otherwise produce dramatic changes in atmospheric composition.[52] With its blend of an integrated earth science and goddess imagery, the Gaia hypothesis clearly is both ecologically based and holistic and appeals to a wide range of people seeking reforms and alternatives to Western industrial and cultural models. In contrast, the "global village" image is linked to high-tech electronics and information superhighways and can be seen as the latest elaboration of industrial society.

In summary, whatever the alternative images at each level, any actual movement toward regenerative systems will still have to be based upon a shift to health criteria and upon a fundamental respect for biodiversity and cultural diversity as the sources of life and social viability. We need new institutions and technological systems that embody and express this respect and are not crippled by myths of technological neutrality. Since food and fiber systems are one interface between natural and social systems at all levels, if not the major one, the construction of regenerative food systems will be one of the central components of the transition to a post–fossil fuel era.

Notes

1. John W. Bennett and Kenneth A. Dahlberg, "Institutions, Social Organization, and Cultural Values," in *The Earth as Transformed by Human Action*, ed. B.L. Turner II (Cambridge: Cambridge University Press, 1990), 69–86.

2. For a discussion, see Kenneth A. Dahlberg, "Sustainable Agriculture—Fad or Harbinger?" *BioScience* 41, no. 5 (May 1991): 337–40.

3. Examples include not only geological time frames and theories covering millions of years, but evolutionary theory (a multicentury time frame), where the scope is broad but the detail captured is minimal (i.e., one can talk about the fitness or adaptation of *species*, but not of groups or individuals). Successional theory or landscape ecology (approximately a century) offers less scope but more detail (i.e., one cannot talk about the broad evolutionary processes but can identify changing patterns involving particular populations as well as species). With classical ecosystem theory there is even less scope, but much greater detail. One cannot talk about successional changes but can describe complex interactions of populations with changing energy and resource flows.

A similar trade-off can be seen in maps, where a global map provides great scope but little detail, while national maps provide less scope but more detail, and city maps provide great detail but very little scope. If one tries to project the course of a river or railroad outside a city map, the risks of error are great. Analogously, one can argue that the social sciences (with certain exceptions) have tended to focus on detailed analysis, using time frames and concepts limited in scope, and that they are poorly equipped to deal with the much broader scope, longer-time-frame issues that are involved in the sustainability debate.

4. For a discussion, see Kenneth A. Dahlberg, "Renewable Resource Systems and Regimes: Key Missing Links in Global Change Studies," *Global Environmental Change* 2, no. 2 (June 1992): 128–52.

5. For example, it is the health of "lower" units-whether cells in organs, microorganisms in the soil, or individuals in social units-that determines the health of the "higher" systems, although the latter can also have a major influence on the health of the former. There is, of course, no one "natural" way the different levels are or should be organized.

6. See Paul R. Ehrlich and Anne H. Ehrlich, *Healing the Planet* (Reading, MA: Addison-Wesley, 1991), 41–46; John P. Holdren, "Population and the Energy Problem," *Population and Environment* 12: 231–55; and Robert Goodland, Herman Daly, and John Kellenberg, "Burden Sharing in Transition to Environmental Sustainability," *Futures* 26, no. 2 (March 1994): 146–55.

7. For analyses of the historic importance of such factors, see Alfred Crosby, *Ecological Imperialism: The Biological Expansion of Europe, 900–1900*, (New York: Cambridge University Press, 1986); and Cecil Woodham Smith, *The Great Hunger* (New York: Harper & Row, 1962).

8. Herman E. Daly, "The Perils of Free Trade," *Scientific American* 269, no. 5 (November 1993): 50–57.

9. See, for example, Julian Steward, et al., *Irrigation Civilizations* (Washington, DC: Pan American Union, 1955). In modern times, the funnel-shaped infrastructural patterns laid down in colonial Africa and Asia—where all trade was funneled through one or two major ports—still hamper efforts at rural and regional development.

10. As Schumacher expressed it, "Today the main content of politics is economics, and the main content of economics is technology. If politics cannot be left to the experts, neither can economics and technology." E. F. Schumacher, *Small is Beautiful* (New York: Harper Torchbooks, 1973), 149. While there has been some effort to reintegrate the academic disciplines of political science and economics with the recent work on political economy, neither discipline has sought any systematic inclusion of technology and technological systems in their work.

11. A fifth major threat—that of the proliferation of nuclear weapons and other weapons of mass destruction—will not be addressed here. In many ways, however, the fundamental shifts in worldviews and priorities that are required for military conversion will greatly facilitate efforts to address the other major threats.

12. Using various conversion ratios, Georg Borgstrom came up with the following "biological ranking of nations": Argentina 6th rather than 23rd; Ethiopia 11th rather than 25th; and Japan 21st rather than 5th. See Georg Borgstrom, *The Hungry Planet* (New York: Macmillan, 1965).

13. See World Resources Institute, *World Resources: 1992–93* (New York: Oxford University Press, 1992), Table 18.3, 276–77. The application of industrial production techniques to livestock—where both genetic-engineering techniques and industrial-style "confinement facilities" are used—raises a host of additional ethical, economic, environmental, and health questions.

14. The latter has been seen in the so-called "hamburger connection," where tropical rain forests in Central and South America have been cut down to provide grazing land for cattle destined for use in fast-food hamburgers. For a strong and detailed discussion from an animal-rights perspective, see Jeremy Rifkin, *Beyond Beef: The Rise and Fall of the Cattle Culture* (New York: Dutton, 1992).

15. See "National Gardening Fact Sheet" (Burlington, VT: National Gardening Association, 1989). The size of the informal sector and of urban agriculture in the Third World is even larger. For a discussion, see Jac Smit and Annu Ratta, "Urban Agriculture: A Tool to Reduce Urban Hunger and Poverty," *Hunger Notes* 18, no. 2 (Fall 1992): 7–12.

16. The concept itself is now attracting increasing attention among a small handful of scholars and activists. Of course, a number of people have done extensive work on the various components of food systems, but it is quite uneven and often fragmented. Also, its name notwithstanding, the main focus of the Food and Agriculture Organization of the United Nations with regard to food has been the development of hunger relief programs, such as its World Food Program.

17. John Steinhart and Carol Steinhart, "Energy Use in the United States Food System," *Science* 184 (1974): 307–16. Roughly one-third of the energy use occurs in production, one-third in processing and transportation, and one-third in local marketing and household refrigeration and cooking. These energy studies need to be updated and expanded to include the energy costs of handling the waste stream.

18. See Martin L. Parry, *Climate Change and World Agriculture* (London: Earthscan in association with IIASA and United Nations Environment Program, 1990).

19. As all farmers know, it is not the average rainfall that counts, but how much rain falls where during which part of the growing season. The same applies to droughts and early or late frosts. See Michael Glantz, ed., *Societal Responses to Climate Change: Forecasting by Analogy* (Boulder: Westview Press, 1988); and David E. Sahn, ed., *Sea-*

sonal Variability in Third World Agriculture: The Consequences for Food Security (Baltimore: Johns Hopkins University Press, 1989).

20. Paul Ehrlich and Anne Ehrlich, *Healing the Planet,* 33–34. Humankind's terrestrial activities consume approximately 40 percent of net global primary photosynthetic production.

21. Pioneer species are those that appear and grow quickly in a habitat affected by a major disruption (e.g., a fire or flood). They are gradually replaced by slower-growing species as succession proceeds. Modern agriculture is designed to prevent natural succession from occurring. Wes Jackson at the Land Institute in Salina, Kansas, is researching how various prairie grasses found in the "perennial polycultures" of prairies might be upgraded and harvested, thus creating a sustainable production system that would remove the need for annual plowing and planting.

22. Ecologists define complexity in terms of the number and distribution of distinct species in an ecosystem. In these terms industrial societies and industrial agriculture are not complex but are rather "complicated" systems with little redundancy. They are like a mechanical clock, which has many interlocking parts but only a few "species" (gears, springs, bearings, etc.). Like a clock, these complicated systems are subject to collapse when any one of their basic components fails.

23. Stephen B. Brush, "The Environment and Native Andean Agriculture," *American Indigena* 40 (1981): 161–72. In this case, cultural simplification through "development" clearly threatens the loss of crop biodiversity.

24. Similarly, modern defenders of biodiversity need to go beyond utilitarian and economic arguments about the value of biodiversity as a resource to stress that it is the ultimate *source* of living systems and their regeneration and thus worthy of a more fundamental kind of protection than *re*-sources.

25. A common example of the myth of technological neutrality is expressed in the bumper sticker "Guns don't kill, people do." This in spite of the fact that the design principle of guns is to deliver a high-speed projectile with deadly accuracy. Other sources of nonneutrality include the scale of technologies (where larger technological systems require particular organizational patterns) and the physical and social environment in which they develop. The midwestern plow is a particularly good example of the latter; its design reflects the deep and moist soils and a social environment where land plots were large, and there was a relative scarcity of labor. "Transfer" of a midwestern plow to countries like India or Pakistan—which have thin soils and monsoon climates and where labor is widely available—thus results in major physical and social disruptions.

26. At the international level, free-trade ideologies are being expanded in such agreements as the GATT and NAFTA to cover many new areas of economic activity—something that will likely increase these disparities. For a discussion of the limitations of free-trade concepts, see Daly, *Perils of Free Trade.*

27. See Kenneth A. Dahlberg, "The Value Content of Agricultural Technologies," *Agricultural Ethics* 2, no. 2 (1990). For a valuable analysis of how the logic of genetic engineering in seed production is antithetical to the adaptiveness and diversity of using open-pollinated varieties, see Brewster Kneen, *The Rape of Canada* (Toronto: NC Press, 1992). Kneen's detailed case study of rape seed also shows how biotechnology has been used to turn grains that have been part of the "commons" into a privately controlled commodity.

28. Miguel A. Altieri, *Agroecology: The Scientific Basis of Alternative Agriculture* (Boulder: Westview Press, 1987).

29. For a discussion of the concept of "decolonization," see James Robertson, *The Sane Alternative* (St. Paul, MN: River Basin Press, 1979).

30. Maynard Kaufman, "The New Homesteading Movement: From Utopia to Euto-

pia," in *The Family, Communes, and Utopian Societies*, ed. S. Te Selle (New York: Harper Torchbooks, 1972), 63–82. For new urban approaches see Herbert Girardet, ed., *The Gaia Atlas of Cities: New Directions for Sustainable Urban Living* (New York: Gaia Books, 1992); and Richard E. Stren, et al., *Sustainable Cities: Urbanization and the Environment in International Perspective* (Boulder: Westview Press, 1992).

31. See above and Kenneth A. Dahlberg, "Regenerative Food Systems: Broadening the Scope and Agenda of Sustainability," in *Food for the Future*, ed. Patricia Allen (New York: John Wiley, 1993), 75–102.

32. This also nests such evaluations in a larger evolutionary/adaptive framework.

33. For a classic statement on this, see Karl Polanyi, *The Great Transformation* (Boston: Beacon Press, 1957).

34. For example, Japan now has the second largest number of McDonalds outlets in the world. For a general discussion, see Joan D. Gussow, *Chicken Little, Tomato Sauce and Agriculture: Who Will Produce Tomorrow's Food?* (New York: Bootstrap Press, 1991).

35. For a discussion of the different aspects involved, see Kenneth A. Dahlberg, ed., *New Directions for Agriculture and Agricultural Research* (Totowa, NJ: Rowman & Allenheld, 1986); Michael J. Dover and Lee M. Talbot, *To Feed the Earth* (Washington, DC: World Resources Institute, 1987); and Patricia Allen, ed., *Food for the Future* (New York: John Wiley, 1993).

36. Doctrines of "free" trade have historically been promoted by the dominant trading countries. Today, these doctrines have also become an ideological defense for the operations of the MNCs. "Fair" trade addresses some of the labor and environmental "externalities" of trade. "Sustainable" trade involves the more fundamental rethinking called for here.

37. These two legal concepts—really social innovations—greatly facilitated industrialism. The inability of classical regulatory restraints like antitrust laws to control the expanding market and political power of oligopolies and MNCs suggests the need for this type of basic rethinking. A prime example in agriculture is the power of the five U.S. grain-trading companies, which control some 80 percent of the market.

38. See Margery L. Oldfield and Janis B. Alcorn, eds., *Biodiversity: Culture, Conservation, and Ecodevelopment* (Boulder: Westview, 1991).

39. Equally, research in small and/or exotic animals and livestock has been neglected. See Noel Vietmeier, *Microlivestock: Little-Known Animals with a Promising Economic Future*, Board on Science and Technology for International Development (Washington, DC: National Academy Press, 1991). I remember the frustrations expressed by an Israeli researcher who convincingly argued the virtues of promoting camel's milk over cow's milk in North Africa, but who could get no funding.

40. For example, French farmers and rural France will suffer if current GATT proposals are implemented. Equally, the Japanese and Koreans are expected to sacrifice a major cultural symbol—rice and its local but higher-cost production—upon the altar of "free" trade. Clearly, even under rethought policies of "sustainable" trade, there would be questions about how to distinguish between legitimate and nonlegitimate forms of protectionism. For a detailed discussion of the consequences of trade liberalization for agriculture, see Mark Ritchie, "Agricultural Trade Liberalization: Implications for Sustainable Agriculture," in Daly, *The Case Against Free Trade*, 163–94.

41. Approaches to self-reliance do not seek the autarchy of self-sufficiency. Rather, they seek a type of bottom-up economic federalism based upon each lower system's providing for itself as much as possible before joining with higher-level systems to provide for unmet needs. Besides the increased energy efficiencies they offer, such approaches can also maintain and/or increase diversity. Clearly, changes in this direction will take time, and a transition strategy will be needed.

42. Helga Olkowski, et al., *The Integral Urban House* (San Francisco: Sierra Club Books, 1979). Like many other out-of-print books from the 1970s, this valuable work should be updated and reissued.

43. For an imaginative high-tech vision of this for a New York City neighborhood, see Richard L. Meier, "Sustainable Cities Will Feed Themselves: Design of a Working Model of an Urban Ecosystem for New York" (paper presented at the World Futures Society meeting, Washington, DC, 29 June 1993).

44. One visually imaginative example for a smaller city is contained in Richard Britz, ed., *The Edible City Resource Manual* (Los Altos, CA: William Kaufman, 1981), which shows a series of stages by which city land-use patterns in Eugene, Oregon, could be rearranged to promote neighborhood food systems.

45. See *Municipal Food Policies* (Washington, DC: U.S. Conference of Mayors, October 1985); and Kenneth A. Dahlberg, "Food Policy Councils: The Experience of Five Cities and One County" (paper presented at the joint meeting of the Agriculture, Food, and Human Values Society and the Association for the Study of Food and Society, Tucson, 11 June 1994).

46. Ross Koppel, *Agenda for Growth* (Philadelphia: Food and Agriculture Task Force, 1988).

47. On the latter, see Christopher R. Bryant and Thomas R. R. Johnston, *Agriculture in the City's Countryside* (Toronto: University of Toronto Press, 1992); and Smit and Ratta, "Urban Agriculture."

48. Each member of the community supported agriculture buys a "share" at the beginning of the growing season and offers ideas on the vegetables and fruits to be grown; each share is generally calculated to provide for a family of four. At least weekly over the growing season, members receive their share of that week's produce. The farmer thus receives capital at the beginning of the growing season and the members share in the production risks, receiving more or less, depending upon the weather and outbreaks of pests and crop disease. Most CSAs are organic.

49. These are "soft energy paths," which are decentralized, energy diffuse, labor intensive, and locally manageable and repairable. See Amory B. Lovins, *Soft Energy Paths* (San Francisco: Friends of the Earth, 1977).

50. See National Research Council, *Alternative Agriculture* (Washington, DC: National Academy Press, 1989); and Food and Agriculture Organization, *Sustainable Agricultural Production: Implications for International Agricultural Research* (Rome: FAO, 1988).

51. Dahlberg, "Renewable Resource Systems and Regimes."

52. James Lovelock, *Gaia: A New Look at Life on Earth* (New York: Oxford, 1979). Gaia is the name of the Greek goddess of the earth. Lovelock sees his hypothesis as extending Darwin's theory of evolution to include the physical environment. He argues that geophysics and biogeochemistry are not adequate to analyze the interactions involved and has called for an integrated earth science which he terms "geophysiology." See James Lovelock, "Rethinking Life on Earth," *Earthwatch* (September/October 1992): 21–24.

17

Becoming Sustainable: Changing the Way We Think

Lester W. Milbrath

A Curious and Tragic Irony

In primitive cultures, tribal structures and life patterns were tuned to the exigencies and routines of nature. The first tutelage of most children was in the ways of nature. Persons with deep environmental concerns would not have stood out as distinctive in primitive society.

In contrast, the dominant thinking in modern society is highly anthropocentric. The leaders of our institutions assert that humans can dominate and manage nature and that it will continue to serve our purposes into the indefinite future; in effect, that our current way of thinking and living is sustainable. It is becoming increasingly apparent to many people, however, even to many who adhere to the dominant modern belief structure, that we will have to change some of the ways we have been thinking and behaving. What kinds of changes must be made, how transforming must they be, and how can we induce the requisite change?

In our modern context, persons who have learned to think environmentally are challenging the societal belief structure. The media in North America today portray environmental ideas as new, challenging, even radical. The term environmentalism has come to stand for a distinctive set of beliefs, values, and concerns that are not characteristic of mainstream society.

The author gratefully acknowledges the many contributions of Yvonne Downes and Kathleen Miller, who worked with him on an earlier paper that covers most of the material discussed in the first part of this chapter.

In this chapter I will identify and discuss key premises about which there is considerable disagreement between the conventional way of thinking—the dominant social paradigm (DSP)—and new, environmental thinking—the new environmental paradigm (NEP). A social paradigm incorporates beliefs about how the world works physically, socially, economically, and politically. A dominant social paradigm may be defined as a society's belief structure, which organizes the way most people perceive and interpret the functioning of the world around them.

My thesis in this chapter is that achieving a sustainable society will require us to supplant the DSP with a belief structure much like the NEP. This will be exceedingly difficult to accomplish; as we will discover, the DSP has most of the advantages in the competition for the allegiance of ordinary people. I also will critically examine the likely success of an array of strategies frequently employed to win the allegiance of people to the NEP.

Unlearning and Relearning

Every person functions daily by means of an unspoken set of premises about how the world works; they are essential just for getting through the day. Most people simply accept the premises that are handed to them by their culture, the DSP; they do not question them, and they do not observe others questioning them. For that reason, the premises behind the DSP are usually hidden and are assumed rather than articulated in discourse. Therefore, unlearning a belief paradigm that has become accepted in a society and relearning a new, more adequate one is much more difficult than learning most other kinds of beliefs. Deeply held paradigm premises are constantly reinforced by a society's dominant institutions, especially by the media. Those who challenge their validity have great difficulty finding an audience, and equally great difficulty being understood by those who have unquestioningly accepted the dominant premises.

The DSP was generated in European culture and has become so manifestly "successful" in overpowering other cultures that the premises underlying the DSP currently shape public discourse all around the planet.

Recent scientific understanding as to how natural systems work, however, challenges many of the premises underlying modern industrial society. Environmental thinking, the NEP, has accepted this new perspective on natural systems, while most of the rest of society, especially the leaders of its dominant institutions, still follow the conventional premises underlying the DSP.

Human beliefs and values shape much that humans do; but we humans cannot repeal or alter the laws of physical systems. If we wish to live, our only viable choice is to act in accordance with the imperatives of Earth's natural systems. The key imperatives concerning natural systems that govern human behavior, and that underlie the NEP, are listed in Table 17.1.

The first two points in Table 17.1 deny the premises of the DSP that natural systems are stable, they recover quickly from injuries and perturbations caused

Table 17.1

Imperatives of Nature's Systems

1. Biogeochemical patterns do change. Humans inadvertently can, and are, changing them.
2. These systems constitute a web of life that is interlocked and highly complex. Human-induced perturbations can produce chaotic behavior in earth systems.
3. Species diversity is essential for ecosystem stability.
4. Earth is a semiclosed system in which space and resources are finite.
5. All creatures, plant and animal, seek organic (maturational) growth and development.
6. Growth in populations of reproducing species is exponential when unchecked. Since persistent doubling is impossible, given finite limits, population growth must be limited.
7. Most animal species survive by finding a niche, utilizing support from one or more other species. Cooperation, not competition, is the key to survival.

by humans, and that their continual good functioning can be relied on indefinitely. In contradiction, modern environmental science recognizes that the cumulative effects of human actions—just our doing better and better those things we have always thought were good and right—can drastically alter the functioning of biogeochemical systems. It is perilous for us to perturb those systems, for we do not fully understand and therefore cannot anticipate all the consequences of those perturbations, some of which may be powerful and irreversible.[1] Furthermore, environmentalism challenges the traditional premise that the future can be predicted by extrapolating past trends.

The third imperative in Table 17.1 makes the crucial point that biodiversity is essential to ecosystem stability. Humans increasingly violate that imperative. Ecosystems with many interrelated species recover better from external changes and shocks that in more simplified systems might destroy a vital link. Recent research also shows that fields with diverse plant communities are more biologically productive and consume more CO_2 than fields devoted to a single species.[2] Yet all over the planet, growing numbers of humans, seeking sustenance and prosperity, are slashing down forests, cultivating more and more land, destroying the habitats of other creatures, and emphasizing monocultural agriculture. Human actions that reduce diversity and resilience will not only injure the targeted systems but will also, in the long run, injure the humans that depend on them.[3]

The fourth imperative in Table 17.1 asserts that space and resources are finite. We humans can, and currently do, live beyond our means.[4] Furthermore, livable space is finite. Our dissatisfaction with crowding very likely will limit our growth in numbers before the absolute physical limit is reached.

The fifth and sixth imperatives deal with growth, which is an honorific concept in today's world; nearly all societies and all institutions adhere to the premise that we can keep growing both numerically and economically. We would not hold that belief if we fully understood doubling times. We can roughly estimate doubling times by dividing the rate of growth per year into 70. For example, something growing at the rate of 2 percent per year would double in 35 years. When numbers are already high, doubling will add an enormous increase. We should expect that, at present growth rates, the current world population of 5.5 billion will double in about 40 years. The *net growth* in human population *every two days* would fill a city the size of San Francisco.

As nature's pattern discloses, a population of any creature that has plenty of life-supporting resources can grow so swiftly that it uses up its resource base, goes into overshoot, and necessarily must die back to a sustainable level. By its excess it may have reduced the carrying capacity of its ecosystem, thus injuring other creatures as well.[5] Nonhuman creatures cannot foresee overshoot and dieback and cannot learn how to avoid them. The learning capacity of humans enables us to foresee overshoot and dieback; that capability places a moral obligation on us to limit the growth both of our population and of our economic activity; otherwise, we shall be culpable for the death by overshoot of many millions of humans and other creatures.

Modern industrial society glorifies competition, heaping wealth and fame on winners and dominators. Some modern biologists say that a belief in the survival of the fittest in fierce competitive struggle is a misreading of fossil evidence.[6] Ecosystems do have predators, but in most cases, surviving species find a niche and utilize support from other species. Cooperation is more survival-positive in nature than competition. Strength and power are not necessarily keys to survival.

Not only do the adherents of the DSP fail to understand and accept the imperatives of natural systems, their beliefs differ in many other key respects from those of proponents of the NEP. The ways in which a new society that orders itself according to the NEP would differ from contemporary society, which orders itself according to the DSP, are highlighted in Table 17.2.

Readers should bear in mind that while the ensuing discussion centers on the contrasts between the DSP and the NEP, not everyone's belief structure would fall neatly into one camp or the other. A survey conducted in the early 1980s in England, Germany, and the United States disclosed that only about 20 percent of adults adhered closely to the full panoply of beliefs characterizing either the DSP or the NEP. The remaining 80 percent either took beliefs from both camps or had poorly developed beliefs that were difficult to characterize.[7]

The discarding of an old social paradigm and the adoption of a new one is a complex and difficult process of social learning; we should expect to find some who lead, others who cling to the familiar paradigm, and many groping to make sense of the conflict in ideas. Many DSP beliefs have served society well in the past, but we are now moving into a very different world, and we need a set of beliefs that accurately represent how that world works if we hope to continue to live in a sustainable relationship with our planet's life systems.

The paradigms discussed here are not political agendas, although they cer-

Table 17.2

Fundamental Value and Belief Differences Between the DSP and the NEP

Dominant Social Paradigm (DSP)	New Environmental Paradigm (NEP)
priority on economic growth and development, focus on short-term or immediate prosperity	priority on ecosystem viability, focus on long-term sustainability
continuation of economic growth justifies dangers of perturbing biogeochemical systems	perturbing biogeochemical systems is rarely if ever justifiable
perpetual economic growth; unrestricted population growth	growth beyond replacement must be halted for sustainability
accept risks to ecosystems to maximize wealth	avoid risks to the ecosystem and overall societal well-being
reliance on markets to spur growth and ensure a bright future	reliance on foresight and planning to ensure a bright future
emphasis on immediate materially oriented gratification	emphasis on simplicity and personal enrichment
emphasis on hierarchy and authority	emphasis on horizontal structures that maximize interaction and learning
centralized decision making and responsibility	greater personal and local responsibility
emphasis on private over public goods	ensure protection and supply of public goods
excessive faith in science and technology	skepticism and critical evaluation of science and technology
reliance on mechanistic simple cause/ effect thinking and narrow expertise	recognition of need for holistic/integrative thinking
emphasis on competition, domination, patriarchy	emphasis on cooperation, partnership egalitarianism
violence needed to maintain society	aversion to violence—seek order without it
dominance and social order	based on learning and consensus
subordinate nature to human interests	place humans in ecosystemic context
emphasize freedom so long as it serves economic priorities	emphasize freedom so long as it serves ecological and social imperatives

(continued)

Table 17.2 *(continued)*

Contrasting Policies/Strategies/Approaches

maximize growth even at the cost of polluting	reduce waste and avoid pollution even at economic cost
encourage conspicuous consumption	discourage conspicuous consumption
emphasize work to fill economic needs	emphasize fulfillment in work
utilize whatever resources needed to maximize current economic activity to benefit current generation	conserve and maintain resource stocks for future generations
emphasize profitable use of nonrenewable resources; rely on market to resolve resource shortages	emphasize renewable resources; plan for resource shortages
encourage development and virtually unrestricted deployment of science and technology	critically evaluate and, as needed, restrict deployment of science and technology
use hard/large-scale technology	use soft/ "appropriate" technology
emphasize development of nuclear energy	phase out nuclear energy
sacrifice other species for economic gain	protect other species, even at economic cost
encourage monocultures to maximize output and wealth for humans so as to allow unlimited population growth	restore/preserve ecosystem diversity and resilience requiring limits to population size
emphasize high-yield (intrusive) agriculture	emphasize regenerative/appropriate agriculture
rely on markets; minimal use of planning	utilize both planning and markets

tainly have political and policy ramifications. Many of the beliefs in the NEP column could not be translated directly into a successful political program. For example, a candidate for public office in the United States in the last decades of the twentieth century may personally believe that economic growth must be curbed if our society is to become sustainable; yet, he could not openly espouse limiting economic growth and hope to be elected. Democratic elections virtually ensure that candidates must espouse society's dominant social paradigm.

The current dominant paradigm promotes economic growth as an irreproachable social good that is also the preferred means to reduce poverty and inequality. Faith in growth extends to population growth, which is believed not only to be possible but also useful in spurring economic development. Believers in the

DSP assume that markets are the best mechanism for maximizing economic growth and human welfare; they reject most planning, especially by government. High consumption is encouraged to spur further growth and jobs. The long-term future is given little thought, and classical economic theorizing assumes that future generations will find new ways to produce and consume at great rates.

The environmentalists advocating the NEP see the world very differently. They argue that the presumption that economic growth, high consumption, and unrestrained population growth can continue indefinitely are dangerously fallacious. The lifestyles spawned by such beliefs will swiftly deplete resources; more important, they are likely to interfere with the integrity of biogeochemical systems, leading them to behave unpredictably and thus injure living creatures. Unpredictably turbulent earth systems, such as a chaotic climate, would have devastating consequences for society and the global economy. Turbulence in earth systems could not only spoil the dreams of the growth advocates but could also destroy much of our civilizational infrastructure, causing poverty and death around the globe.[8] NEP advocates argue further that unfettered markets do not protect ecosystems, and that we must use foresight and planning to ensure the future we want. Environmentalists believe we must abandon highly consumptive ways of life, and they point out that lifestyles with less material consumption can be equal in quality if not actually superior to lifestyles seeking to consume more and more.

Many of the remaining contrasts derive from the basic one just discussed. Hierarchy and centralization are advocated by the DSP to maximize efficiency and growth. Command-and-control hierarchical structures are valued because they facilitate the efficient manipulation of personnel and material elements, but they inhibit learning and flexibility. Many institutions have discovered in recent years how hierarchical structures stifle the capability of staff to quickly learn and adapt. Competitive pressures have induced many of them to restructure using horizontal communications and semi-autonomous work teams, so as to encourage faster learning. These teams are encouraged to communicate with each other rather than wait for permission from superiors. Similarly, governments and private firms are discovering that regular and frequent interactions with the public help them to learn and to avoid problems they might not otherwise have anticipated.

To advocate the use of structures designed to maximize learning and personal responsibility is not to suggest we should seek a world of millions of autonomous entities each going its own way. Our world is now so crowded, and human power so great, that such a global society would almost certainly cause life systems to be severely injured, perhaps even to collapse. This criticism applies even to democratically controlled local governments; people can democratically choose to destroy their own ecosystem. Much as we value democracy and autonomy, they do not outweigh the value of life and the ecosystems that support it. For example, in most of today's world we allow each family to decide how many children to have; the cumulative consequence of that freedom is an epidemic of humans that is crowding other species from their niches, depleting scarce resources, creating wastes that nature cannot absorb, and threatening the continued good functioning of life systems.

The DSP emphasizes the use of market mechanisms to maximize private goods and gives little weight to public goods—which always raise hated taxes—while environmentalists perceive environmental public goods—e.g., clean air, water, and soil—to be absolutely essential. In general, they perceive public goods to be just as important for quality of life as private goods. They recognize that public action (planning) as well as taxes must be used to ensure that public goods are well provided.

Adherents of the two paradigms also have different perspectives on science and technology. DSP adherents have great faith that science and technology can provide the solution to almost any problem that arises. They believe science and technology can be relied on not only to solve practical physical problems but also to cure social ills. They emphasize the use of science and technology for continuous economic growth, which they believe will itself resolve many other social problems. They assert that science and technology have been so wondrously helpful that they should be strongly promoted; they will develop much more effectively if they are left unsupervised.

On the other hand, NEP adherents point out that science and technology easily become the servants of those who provide money for "sci-tech" development and control its deployment (the establishment). Some technologies, such as nuclear power, are now so powerful that they can change the way the world works; they even have the potential to destroy everything we have built. Furthermore, despite built-in safeguards, huge dangerous technologies do fail—as in the case of Chernobyl, Bhopal, the *Exxon Valdez*—and wreak great havoc on humans and the ecosystem.

The environmentalist's critique of blind faith in science and technology should not be seen as an antiscience stance. Environmentalists value and support scientific inquiry, because new knowledge is needed to enhance our understanding of how the world works and to help us solve many urgent problems. However, they urge careful evaluation of possible future consequences before a technology is developed and deployed. Environmentalists are more likely to view the world as a system made up of subsystems, requiring the estimation of the systemically generated second, third, and fourth order of consequences of a proposed action.

If economic efficiency, growth, and power play a lesser role in life, a society can more easily reject patriarchy and domination. NEP adherents urge partnership—equitable, mutually advantageous relationships—in marriage and in the workplace. They even urge that this perspective should become the accepted norm in relationships among nations. Environmentalists strive to avoid violence and seek policies that alleviate the sources of violence.

This new ecological way of thinking makes clear that humans are part of the large ecosystem, and that all humans—in fact, all creatures—are closely linked in the earth's living systems. They reject the anthropocentric belief that it is appropriate for humans to dominate nature.

The DSP emphasizes freedom in the market and the unfettered development and deployment of whatever people can dream up. Freedom for the strong generally results in exploitation of the weak, as well as injury to life systems. NEP advocates love and nurture freedom, but they recognize the necessity for society to restrict actions that would injure communities, ecosystems, and earth systems. They believe economic freedom should not be allowed to override society's top priority, ecosystem viability. In the world they envision economics will not become unimportant, but limitless economic growth can no longer serve as the predominant value by which we measure our rights, our successes, and our options.

The last part of Table 17.2 illustrates some of the more specific policies that the two paradigms would promote, which are consistent with the differing fundamental values and beliefs of the two paradigms. One could say in summary that DSP defenders highly value economic wealth, power, and control of their environment—including control of other people; they would expand throughput of all materials and would willingly risk ecosystem degradation and the disruption of global biogeochemical systems to maximize those values. They see the world and how it works very differently from advocates of the NEP, whose top priority is protecting the good functioning of planetary life systems, and who would limit human population, economic activity, and waste to achieve it. The NEP advocates would live more lightly on the earth, conserve and husband resources, cherish other species and other humans, use regenerative methods to nourish uncultivated ecosystems (such as forests) and to restore the productivity of soils and cultivated ecosystems.[9]

The Challenge of Environmental Thinking to the Dominant Beliefs of Modern Society

NEP thinking challenges the traditional story about reality that is dominant in contemporary society. The challenge is deeper and broader than the challenge of Marxism to capitalism. Adherents of the two paradigms talk past each other; there is mutual incomprehension as each side struggles politically to dominate public policy making. This mutual incomprehension is a major cause of the much decried gridlock of contemporary politics. Even when policy is made, it is often unsuccessful because the implementers do not all follow the same script, or because the world does not work as presumed by the policy makers. The average person has difficulty comprehending the conflicting stories about reality, the conflicting premises lying behind the stories, the gridlock, the botched implementation of policy, and finds it impossible to know what to expect from leaders. How is it possible for people to learn a new environmental paradigm in such a sea of incoherence?

Despite the incoherence, we cannot choose not to learn. Change will come whether we want it or not, and with it learning, because by its very design, thrust, and values, modern industrial society is incompatible with the imperatives of natural systems; therefore, it cannot be sustained.

The particular belief structure dominating thought in a society is typically made up of images that in part reflect reality and are part myth. Intellectual history suggests that a paradigm shift occurs when the dominating story becomes more and more out of synchrony with reality, the gap between reality and image creates tension, leading some people to change their beliefs while others stubbornly hold on to the old story.

The emerging paradigm may be hidden from public consciousness for a time. Casual observation will not readily disclose the extent to which people are moving toward a new paradigm, because nearly everyone continues to use the old rhetoric that is embedded in the DSP, even though their inner thoughts already are moving on to a new interpretation of reality. They use the old rhetoric because when the DSP is the "only game in town," it is the only way to be understood.

The shift from the DSP to the NEP has not progressed far enough at this time to allow the key concepts of the NEP to regularly enter our public discourse. The problem of being understood is made especially difficult by the fact that the NEP is such a fundamental and profound challenge to the central premises of the DSP. A society operating on NEP values and beliefs would be strikingly different from modern society.

At least 50 million people worldwide have adopted key elements of the NEP.[10] Millions more sense that society's ideas about reality are changing. Most also can sense from political struggles and gridlock that emerging new ideas will be vigorously opposed. Simultaneously, many are aware that we have no choice but to change, even if they personally are unwilling to change right now. Either we change thoughtfully with foresight or we will become victims of change that we did not prepare ourselves to meet. If we persist on our present trajectory we will bring about the collapse of some of nature's life-support systems—as always, death will be nature's most powerful teaching device.

The Strategic Dilemma of Change Agents Working for a Sustainable Society

In the realm of social change as well we must change our way of thinking. Many feel there is an urgent need to help others learn about the NEP and have decided to become agents of social change. It is not clear, however, what strategies are most likely to successfully stimulate the new learning. One cannot choose strategies without a theory as to how social change comes about. Ironically, many people are not conscious that they have a theory of social change; they are especially unlikely to be aware of the key premises lying behind it, and thus do not know how it influences their decisions about which strategies are likely to work and which to fail. We will develop better theories, and thus better strategies, if we become consciously aware of their hidden premises and subject them to critical analysis.

In the sections that follow I will outline my reasons for taking certain positions. I begin by reviewing what we know about social change, and especially about how to bring it about.

Sources of Social Change

Forces External to Society

Planetary Physical Changes. These include volcanic eruptions, climate change, earthquakes, and violent weather. Civilizations have died, cities have been abandoned, and mass migrations undertaken because both natural and human-induced physical changes made their societies unsustainable.[11]

Conquest. The religious map of Europe was in fact determined primarily by force of arms. Even though colonialism's most brutal practices are no longer tolerated internationally, colonial impact on societies around the globe has been profound and long-lasting. The North America of today is vastly different than it would have been had the European invaders never arrived.

Powerful New Technology. Such technology can overwhelm a society; this phenomenon is most typical of new armament. Fear of falling behind developmentally is the driving force behind most arms races. The race creates an accelerating positive feedback loop, because countries competing for dominance must each produce more powerful technology than their rivals. History is replete with instances in which a powerful new technology—the stirrup, gunpowder, nuclear energy—has permanently changed society.

Attractive New Technology. Advocates of economic growth like to call such seductive technologies "locomotive technologies." In our lifetime we have witnessed the transformation wrought by such attractive technologies as television, the automobile, and computers. Regretfully, we haven't yet learned to evaluate such "saviors" and their unintended consequences, and to figure out ways we might control them.

Dynamic Forces within a Society

The sources of these are much less apparent.

Technological Discovery and Enrichment of Resources. Not only businesses but entire societies have prospered or languished as new technologies have produced new resources and relegated others to obsolescence. The price and scarcity of copper has been profoundly affected by being replaced in many uses by fiber optics and PVC piping. Petroleum discovery transformed Saudi Arabians from poor desert nomads to the richest per capita population in the world—and also profoundly changed their country's Islamic culture.

Decline of the Oral Mythic and Ascendance of the Theoretic. The culture of our forebears was strongly influenced by oral mythic traditions that bonded people with each other and to the Earth. The ascendance of theoretic culture and especially the expansion of society's external memory has accelerated change and subverted oral mythic wisdom. Society's external memory is global and grips all nations in global economic and security structures: it forces globalization upon us. Yet by subverting the mythic, it simultaneously makes it more difficult to achieve mythic bonding with global institutions. Thus we paradoxically find simultaneous thrusts for greater globalization and greater localization in today's world. How can we bond sufficiently with each other and with the Earth to deal effectively with global environmental threats when we are losing the affective bonding that unites our efforts? Is it possible to reinstate mythic bonding in a world society that accentuates theoretic aspects of life and is developing a huge external memory?

Growth and the Increasing Dominance of Society's External Memory. Our external memory, enhanced by swift and copious computer technology, facilitates change by allowing nearly infinite searching. People can express their autonomy and increase their learning without depending on authority. Ironically, these external memory structures subtly exert greater and greater control over our lives—preventing changes and forcing others upon us. Persons wishing to be players in today's policy decision making must use computers, faxes, E-mail, and databases. As we rely increasingly on external memory, we may be unaware of how it changes the way we conceive of problems, interpret the world and especially the future, relate to other people, find our place in the community. The autonomy we thought it would give us may be stolen back without our being aware of it. What metaphor can we use to describe this burgeoning factor in our lives?

Changes in the Business Cycle. Such changes are a complex composite of billions of transactions made for individual gain with little if any consideration of their impact on the workings of the whole system. Despite the huge institutional apparatus of modern economics and its statistics, we do not come close to understanding the dynamics at work in business cycles, and we are not sure whether they can be guided or controlled.

Adjustments to Newly Perceived Realities. Society is constantly creating new realities that individuals and institutions must react to; they may be economic (e.g., gain or loss of a job), diminished or enhanced health, increasing violence, birth or death, pollution, increased crowding/congestion, new laws, new programs, new institutions, new scarcities, etc. These new realities prompt new family patterns, physical mobility, status mobility, belief changes, value changes, and new lifestyles.

Intentional Efforts to Induce Change. Most change agents typically use political social-economic methods to induce change. They try individually and in concert with others to make new laws, new regulations, new programs, new incentives, changes in prices, improved social relations, corrections to social ills, even new social paradigms. Much time, effort, and money is currently wasted on attempts to induce change that have no chance of success. People will become better change agents if they critically evaluate the probable impact their proposed efforts will have on the total set of forces determining the future. Much more careful and systematic monitoring of the implementation and success of past programs would enhance social learning.

Forces Operating within Individuals

Individuals are constantly in transition, even though we recognize enduring qualities in everyone that we usually identify as personality. People change as they mature, learn, and adjust to reality. They learn and change as they dip here and there into the external memory. They may deliberately try to change their personal reality by finding new economic resources, and by means of new intimate relationships, new or transformed institutional settings, new laws, new court decisions; by migrating, traveling, and so on. People change, regardless of whether they want to, as they move through their lives, struggle with disease, cope with misfortune. Any effort to induce or guide social change must take place within this dynamic kaleidoscope of continual change in myriad individual human lives.

Barriers to Social Change

Once persons have learned the beliefs, values, and norms of a society and have worked out a lifestyle that works in that society, they are reluctant to change what seems to be working reasonably well. Many people have a deep psychological investment in the institutional structure of the society. Their personal identities are tied into the continued success of those institutions. It requires more effort to change than not to, and instability is disconcerting. The greater the change contemplated, the greater the reluctance to undertake it. Those who would change a dominant social paradigm face a daunting barrier in the comfortable inertia of those whose thoughts are embedded in the DSP.

But many are not comfortable with things as they are and deeply desire that one or another aspect of life could be changed. Everywhere in the world, there is a rising clamor for change. However, it is highly doubtful that people would agree on what kind of change is needed, or on the appropriate strategies for achieving it.

Nearly all thrusts for social change are opposed, by those who either do not want the proposed change or want a different kind of change. The capability of the establishment, the DSP, to resist thrusts for change is so multifaceted and so powerful that a fulsome discussion is not possible here. Listing the DSP's major devices for resistance may be helpful, however.

1. The DSP's major defense is its control of most forms of the support that change agents require to launch their campaigns. If a change agent is seen as a threat, she or he can be denied grants, jobs, promotions, contracts, access to the media, loans, publication, etc.
2. Messages from change agents are routinely marginalized by the media, by public officials, by establishment institutions such as churches and schools.
3. As noted, most people perceive their fortunes to be tied to the continued dominance and success of the establishment—messages for change are seen as a threat.
4. If a threat to the established order persists despite the above defenses, the establishment can resort to tougher measures such as diffusing disinformation, theft, subversion, kidnapping, even execution—and make it all look legal.

Another barrier, whether strategic or not, is that no matter what message is put forward, hardly anybody is listening. Because television is so ubiquitous, it would seem possible to reach every home at one time, but viewers in developed societies have so many choices, including shutting off the set, that no one can call a televised town meeting—not even the president of the United States. Infoglut is an enormous barrier to coherent thinking about a society's future.

In the United States, the plethora of messages available to thrust at people has reached the point of absurdity, and it's growing worse. There are thirty, forty, fifty cable channels coming into most urban homes twenty-four hours a day, and soon there will be more. In the average American home the TV is being viewed forty-seven hours a week. People can also choose from among many thousands of videos. Persons with computers and modems can search thousands of data bases, bulletin boards, and interactive networks. In 1989, $125 billion was spent on advertising in America, while only $140 billion was spent on all public and private higher education. From June 1989 to May 1990 approximately 10,000 articles on the environment appeared in America's newspapers and magazines (the twentieth anniversary of Earth Day was observed in April 1990).[12] With this huge information overload, it's little wonder that most of the time we can only preach to the converted.

I do not feel that I understand the full implications of our communication environment in North America, but some things seem clear. While this huge external memory and glut of messages may make it difficult for anyone to manipulate the American people, it also makes it nearly impossible for us to think together as a nation, or even locally, as a community. Many people are able to disconnect from societal discourse and suffer no serious consequences. Most of the time we don't know what other people are thinking, nor how many of them think like us. We are told that we have lots of autonomy, but we are deficient in the social bonding that could help to make us feel more like a community. Most people have no clear personal basis for deciding which messages are important. When people are asked in opinion polls what the important issues for the nation are, they tend to select those the media recently told them were important.

In this morass of messages, change agents should be extremely skeptical of their ability to reach and change people with conventional theoretic messages delivered in books, speeches, newspaper and magazine articles, and letters to the editor.

Where Should Our Change Efforts Be Focused?

Change agents frequently disagree about where their efforts should be focused and on the extent of the reforms they should recommend. Is it more effective to focus on changing the thinking and behavior of individuals, or should change messages be directed to larger aggregates such as institutions, communities, and nations? Should we be working for piecemeal reform, which usually can be achieved in the short run, or is it more effective in the long run to seek wholesale societal transformation?

Individual/Personal Change

In some respects personal change cannot be separated from societal change. Societal transformation will not be successful without change at the personal level; such change is a necessary but not sufficient step on the route to sustainability. People hoping to live sustainably must adopt new beliefs, new values, new lifestyles, and new worldview. But lasting personal change is unlikely without simultaneous transformation of the socioeconomic/political system in which people function. Persons may solemnly resolve to change, but that resolve is likely to weaken as they perform day-to-day within a system reinforcing different beliefs and values. Change agents typically are met with denial and great resistance. Reluctance to challenge mainstream society is the major reason most efforts emphasizing education to bring about change are ineffective. If societal transformation must be speedy, and most of us believe it must, pleading with individuals to change is not likely to be effective.

Piecemeal Change

Can we transform an unsustainable system by working for piecemeal change (reforms) within the system. Will new laws, new regulations, better enforcement, new programs, new institutions, new technologies bring about a sustainable society?

Modest changes, which are more readily achievable, are unlikely to transform the system sufficiently to make it sustainable. Changes that have the potential to strongly influence behavior—a $3.00-per-gallon tax on gasoline in North America—would be so bitterly resisted by stakeholders as to totally marginalize messages proposing them. We may know what needs to be changed to make a society sustainable but messages urging the appropriate changes cannot be heard by the people who would have to adopt the changes.

We need not and should not abandon efforts for piecemeal change but we must simultaneously realize that at best, they buy us time to attempt a paradigm shift. They cannot, by themselves, bring about the transformation to sustainability.

Fundamental Change—Paradigm Shift

For most contemporary societies to become sustainable, paradigm shift is essential, but it is the most difficult form of social change to achieve. Without paradigm shift, most personal value and lifestyle changes by individuals are unfulfillable, marginalized, and overwhelmed. Individual changes are more likely to become permanent when the majority in society begin "reading from a new text" and are "on the same page." Without that social support, most piecemeal efforts with real transformative potential are easily misunderstood, hard to implement, and easily circumvented.

Conventional wisdom tells us that big societal changes take a long time. Yet, if we critically examine that belief in the light of history, we discover that sometimes change comes astonishingly swiftly, even a change as great as the dissolution of the Soviet Union. We also can discern that the pace of paradigm shift is speeding up. Elgin makes the point that while it took humans about fifty thousand years to evolve out of the hunter-gatherer era into the agricultural era and five thousand years to evolve out of the agricultural era into the industrial era, we are already evolving out of the industrial era after only three hundred years.[13]

But can a paradigm shift be planned for? Can we work toward it strategically and systematically? We may be the first generation ever to set ourselves such a task. We will not know if it can be done until it is tried. I believe we will most effectively work for transformative social change if we keep our focus on bringing about paradigm shift while simultaneously making piecemeal changes wherever possible and working on individual change as well.

Why Not a Gradual Unplanned Transition to a New Paradigm?

As noted, most previous paradigm shifts were gradual, almost invisible; they just seemed to happen over a long period of time. Why not let that process, whatever its dynamics, just happen in the future? Why not be optimistic that the appropriate changes will be made as we go along and proceed as best we can with the life we have now?

The main difficulty with that line of reasoning is that maintenance of our present trajectory is likely to cause a severe breakdown of Earth's life systems long before a century has passed. Breakdown will cause excruciating anguish, massive death, and drastic loss of the carrying capacity of the planet.

By planning ahead and taking appropriate action to try to forestall collapse, or at least to mitigate its most devastating consequences, we may avoid much anguish and death. When the possibility of imminent collapse becomes plausible to billions of people—we humans are the only creatures able to foresee such a possibility—there is likely to be a small window of opportunity that can be used to avert breakdown—if we are prepared to take advantage of it.

Brief Critique of Most Common Methods and Strategies for Change

Education. Almost every list proposed for achieving sustainability includes an admonition for more and better education. Despite all the admonitions, the day-to-day practice of education changes very little. If we reflect more deeply on that strategy, we recognize that most education is designed to reinforce the dominant social paradigm, and those who control funds and make educational policy are determined to make sure it continues to do that. Educational initiatives and programs that question or challenge the dominant social paradigm are rebuffed, contained, easily subverted, and generally unimplementable. Hence, attempting to use education to change society is a weak, time-consuming strategy at best.

Once a new paradigm begins to assume credibility, education might be reformed to be more ecological, holistic, and integrative, and more oriented to the long term. It might then become very useful for imprinting the new paradigm and helping to implement it in everyday life.

Better Science and Technology. The proven power of science and technology makes some people confident, even complacent; they assume that sci-tech will come to the rescue with the invention of new ways to make society sustainable. Persons holding this belief misunderstand both science and politics. Science has so far failed to combine its power with any foresight about society's trajectory, or with the ability to make wise value and moral judgments. Science and technology are indissolubly linked to the establishment and thrive or die with it; witness the writhing throes of disorder and death in Soviet science upon the dissolution of the Soviet state.

Is our crises of sustainability a technical problem resolvable by technical means? The belief is usually that technological deliverance will take the form of some new technology that will constantly expand carrying capacity so that there will be no limits to growth. But even if it were possible to keep more and more people alive, the social and quality-of-life problems that would flow from a burgeoning human population would be dreadful. At best, new technology might buy us some time but it cannot bring about the multitude of socioeconomic/ political transformations that must occur to make a society sustainable.

Books, Op-Ed Pieces, Professional Papers, Conferences. Thoughtful analyses are very useful in clarifying our ideas about where we want to go, but they are very ineffective means of getting there. Few people read books containing such analyses; such messages are likely to reach only the converted. A book that was read by a million people would be considered a runaway best-seller but it would reach only one half of one percent of the adult American population. Books that demonstrate the ability to reach and convert even a small minority of people—say 15 or 20 percent—to new paradigm thinking would come under attack and could be marginalized, maligned, and otherwise subverted by the defenders of the DSP—and their media lackeys.

Documentaries and TV Specials. Televised messages can reach a larger audience, but seldom one large enough to make a noticeable difference. A superb documentary like *Race to Save the Planet* was given wide publicity when it was shown on public television in the early 1990s. Yet, it probably reached no more than five million people, and it's very likely that a large share of those were already interested and sympathetic. Persons with little interest, those it would be most important to reach, would simply tune to something else. If this means of communication started to have an effect, the DSP defenders would probably try to subvert it.

Documentaries are very useful for educating the converted and in schools and other educational settings—they can make points more effectively than is possible with words alone. They can also be used to mobilize concerted action among the converted.

Social Movements, New Political Parties, Networking. North Americans tend to believe that people organized into groups have an impact that individuals cannot achieve. Even though messages seeking support for such groups are literally thrust at people, the average person hardly ever recognizes their existence. Such messages are routinely marginalized, rebuffed, and subverted by the dominant media. In this ongoing contest, the defenders of the dominant social paradigm hold nearly all the cards. Ideas that challenge the DSP have almost no chance of reaching the masses unless conditions are so bad that people everywhere are desperately tuning in to new messages that promise some kind of salvation. Most groups seeking societal transformation spend a great proportion of their effort just nourishing the membership; this may lend meaning to their lives but should not be confused with effective action to bring about social change.

Intentional Communities, Local Experiments, Bioregionalism. Some people believe that if we can develop sustainable local communities, the lessons learned there will readily spread to the larger society and eventually the world. There is no doubt that we can learn valuable lessons from such experiments, but they do not constitute a viable model for bringing about paradigm shift. Mainstream North American society is already so crowded, urbanized, and resource-consumptive that models working in small communities cannot be applied to the larger society. Most North Americans are so caught up in modern society and have such a strong interest in maintaining its present trajectory that they can't imagine adopting the kind of sustainable lifestyle found effective in small local communities; messages urging them to do so will easily be marginalized by the DSP-oriented society. There might have been a chance a hundred years ago for people to adopt such models—plenty of utopian models were offered then, but few were implemented—now it is a hundred years too late.

Messages Directed to Political Leaders. Citizens typically communicate with their leaders by means of letters, phone calls, E-mail, and lobbying. If the message concerns a change that falls within the general parameters of the present system—that does not try to change the paradigm—it has some chance of being meaningful; these kinds of messages are especially useful for addressing local problems. When there is a call for a major transformation, however, the message is unlikely even to be understood and is easily countered by opposition.

Activism in a Traditional Political Party. Wanting mainly to win in the present system, a traditional party cannot hear a message for basic change. Trying to change fundamentally the policy thrust of an existing political party is a waste of time. Groups with differing ideas are constantly vying with each other to capture party leadership. Even if a group wins, it is likely soon to be overturned. Because electoral choices ultimately determine the long-run policy thrust of parties, working to change the electorate is more likely to bring about change than becoming active in a party.

Messages Embedded in Entertainment. People will attend to, even seek out, communications that entertain them. Entertainment that incorporates messages urging basic changes are frequently offered to people, but do they have any significant effect? Messages embedded in entertainment must be very subtle or else the entire show will be dismissed as "preachy." The effects of the messages, if any, are therefore also very subtle and very difficult to trace unambiguously to their source. At best, this strategy to bring about social change is likely to be very slow, but a succession of such efforts could accumulate to create a potential for fast social learning should the right conditions facilitate that in the future.

Vicariously Carry People Through Their Future History in Feature Films or a TV Series. Conceivably, a drama that portrays the future that awaits us if we continue on our present trajectory could be sufficiently gripping to attract the attention of those who aren't listening. If such a gripping drama could be filmed and shown to fifty or a hundred million people, it might get the attention of those who are not now listening. It would have to be a blockbuster and would constitute *only an opening* that must be followed up by more solid information. If done right, it could stimulate millions of discussions that explore the deeper meanings in the story. Many existing organizations for social change could provide opportunities for that discourse. Political channels must be kept open to allow people to express their displeasure with the dynamics inherent in the present potentially disastrous system, and to provide people the opportunity to demand a change of course.

Of course, defenders of the DSP would quickly grasp the danger in such a powerful message and would seek to halt, contain, or subvert it. The proponents of transformation must anticipate that and try to deflect the attack, but the contest is unequal, and the greater power of the DSP may abort or subvert the project. Is it worth a try?

Necessary and Facilitating Conditions for Paradigm Shift

The Necessary Condition—Great Dissatisfaction with the Present System

Dissatisfaction must be focused on the system, not simply on individuals or parties that are perceived to be doing a bad job within a fundamentally good system (the situation we have now in the United States). So long as people see their continued happiness as being tied to the success of the present system, they are unlikely to hear messages urging change. Theoretical or hypothetical arguments about impending doom are easily avoided, denied, and marginalized. Claims to be able to fix the system (a la Clinton) will always win out over pleas to dump the system. Many people will see abandonment of the present system as the threat of death.

People will begin to accept messages urging transformation to a new paradigm and a better life when they see continuation of the system as more threatening than change.

Facilitating Conditions

None of these conditions are sufficient for a paradigm shift, even if all are present.

Natural Control of Excess. Grim as it sounds, without death there could be no new life. The world is overpopulated with humans and swiftly becoming more so. The planet's life systems cannot support twelve to twenty billion humans, and there must also be viable habitat for other creatures or human life cannot be good. Morally we cannot reduce our population by murdering people or deliberately allowing them to starve, so attrition must and will occur by disease, famine, or system collapse. Such calamities open the way for rejection of the outdated beliefs and values, inappropriate institutions, and foolish life-styles that now block progress toward sustainability.

Open, Easy, Fast, Accurate Communication. There must be no limit to learning. Even if other aspects of the old system collapse, every effort must be made to insure that the communication system stays intact; it is essential if we are to carry on the learning required for a successful transformation to a sustainable society.

Visions of a Better System. When the present system will no longer support a decent life, people will seek visions of alternative ways of living. Such visions could be presented in books, dramas, feature movies, community visioning sessions, and so on.

An Enlightened Dedicated Leadership Cadre. They should stand ready to provide rationale and leadership for the institution of a new sustainable paradigm when conditions are ripe for its acceptance. This crucial leadership cadre was missing in the Soviet Union when its system collapsed.

A Solid Science and Knowledge Structure. The proposed new paradigm and the system for implementing it should not be vulnerable to scientific charges of invalidity. Scientists should be enlisted to help design the changes and to support them as valid and necessary for sustainability. Scientists can also contribute many practical solutions.

Social Movements to Implement a New Paradigm. When conditions are right for paradigm shift, the minds of many people will open to new ideas. In that context, social movements can be effective in mobilizing people for the transition and in constructing the necessary new institutions.

Educational Programs. Educational reform that was not possible under the old system will become feasible when people's minds are open to new ideas. We should prepare in advance the plans to institute the needed new educational system.

Weighing the Prospects for Success

The immediate prospects for effective action to bring about a sustainable society in advanced industrial countries are very poor; at the moment, little can be done. Yet it is difficult to believe that humans will be able to continue their gluttonous exploitation of the earth for very long. Rapid global population growth, combined with resource depletion, loss of the ozone layer, desertification, deforestation, and climate change will disrupt socioeconomic/political systems. People who chose to ignore the environmental problems looming on the horizon may suddenly be confronted with the grim consequences of their apathy. Facing disruption, injury, and possibly death, people are likely to once more seek to bond with each other and with the earth. In order to do that, they will need a new mythic story about their proper place in the cosmos. They will also be more likely to seek theoretic learning. We should be visioning this transition and planning our strategy to help lead society through the transformation.

Notes

1. Union of Concerned Scientists, "Warning to Humanity" (Washington, DC: Union of Concerned Scientists, 1992); Donella H. Meadows, Dennis L. Meadows, and Jorgen Randers, *Beyond the Limits: Confronting Global Collapse and Envisioning a Sustainable Future* (Post Mills, VT: Chelsea Green, 1992); Cheryl Simon Silver and Ruth S. DeFries, *One Earth, One Future: Our Changing Global Climate* (Washington, DC: National Academy of Sciences Press, 1990).

2. Yvonne Baskin, "Ecologists Dare to Ask: How Much Does Diversity Matter?" *Science* 264 (8 April 1994): 202-3.

3. Edward O. Wilson, "Threats to Biodiversity," in *Managing Planet Earth: Readings from Scientific American* (New York: W. H. Freeman, 1990), 49-59.

4. Donella H. Meadows, Dennis L. Meadows, and Jorgen Randers, *Beyond the Limits*.

5. William R. Catton, Jr., *Overshoot: The Ecological Basis of Revolutionary Change* (Urbana, IL: University of Illinois Press, 1980).

6. Lynn Margulis and Dorian Sagan, *Microcosmos: Four Billion Years of Evolution from our Microbial Ancestors* (New York: Summit Books, 1986), 14-15; Mary Clark, "Looking for Unity: On Getting the Assumptions Right" (paper presented at the Conference on Unity of Knowledge, Capri, Italy, 9–14 June 1992).

7. Lester W. Milbrath, *Environmentalists: Vanguard for a New Society* (Albany: State University of New York Press, 1984).

8. Joel J. Kassiola, *The Death of Industrial Civilization: The Limits to Economic Growth and the Repoliticization of Advanced Industrial Society* (Albany: State University of New York Press, 1990); and Lester W. Milbrath, "The Societal Impacts of Chaos in the Climate System," in *Coherence and Chaos in Our Uncommon Futures—Visions, Means, Action: Selections from the 13th World Conference of the World Futures Studies Federation,* ed. Mika Mannerma, Sohail Inayalullah, and Rick Slaughter (Turku, Finland: Finland Futures Research Centre, 1994), 297-301.

9. Readers dissatisfied with this sketchy comparison of the two belief systems should consult Lester W. Milbrath, *Envisioning a Sustainable Society: Learning Our Way Out* (Albany: State University of New York Press, 1989) for more extensive evidence and argument.

10. Riley E. Dunlap, George H. Gallup Jr., and Alec M. Gallup, *Health of the Planet: A George H. Gallup Memorial Survey* (Princeton, NJ: Gallup International Institute, 1993); Milbrath, *Environmentalists.*

11. Albert Gore, *Earth in the Balance: Ecology and the Human Spirit* (New York: Houghton Mifflin, 1992), chap. 3; Clive Ponting, *A Green History of the World: The Environment and the Collapse of Great Civilizations* (New York: St. Martin's Press, 1992); Brian M. Fagan, *The Journey from Eden: Peopling Our World* (New York:

Thames & Hudson, 1990); Emmanual LeRoy Ladurie, *Times of Feast, Times of Famine: A History of Climate Since the Year 1000* (Garden City, NY: Doubleday, 1971); Joseph A. Tainter, *The Collapse of Complex Societies* (Cambridge: Cambridge University Press, 1988); Kevin D. Pang, "The Legacies of Eruption," *The Sciences* 31, no. 1 (January 1991): 30-35.

12. Robert Rehac, *Greener Marketing and Advertising: Charting a Responsible Course* (Emmaus, PA: Rodale Press, 1993).

13. Duane Elgin, *Awakening Earth: Exploring the Evolution of Human Culture and Consciousness* (New York: William Morrow, 1993), 226.

18

Infoglut and Competing Problems: Key Barriers Suggesting a New Strategy for Sustainability

Michael Marien

If we are to have a future at all, it must be sustainable in many respects. But is this probable?

In the next few decades, it does not seem likely that most societies, especially so-called "developing" societies, will have evolved in any substantial way toward any reasonable degree of sustainability. The major reason for this near-term pessimism becomes apparent when we consider the barriers to such evolution. Two important barriers are considered here: infoglut and competing problems.[1] To my knowledge, these barriers have not been identified or discussed by any advocate of a sustainable society. However fundamental these are thought to be, it would seem some thought and action might be invested in their direction. This, of course, is the perennial hope of every author, that people are listening, comprehending, and believing. In an age of infoglut, as suggested here, the chances are small.

More likely than not, I fear, the unpleasant problems of infoglut and competing issues will continue to be ignored. This will lead to more wasted effort, and the transition to sustainability will be further delayed—perhaps beyond the point where an adequate number of sensible measures can be undertaken to create a lasting relationship between nature and humankind.

Information Society versus Sustainable Society

Hundreds of terms have been proposed over the last three decades to define what our society is, what it is becoming, and what it ought to be.[2] At present, there are three major competing survivors: *information society, sustainable society,* and *postmodern society.* Remarkably, none of these three survivors was mentioned before the mid 1970s.

Even more remarkable is that these three concepts are seldom, if ever, considered together. Those who write about an information society, which is very achievable and possibly desirable, do not consider sustainability or postmodernism. Those who write about sustainability, which is desirable and possibly achievable, do not consider the information society or postmodernism. And those who write about postmodernism, which according to many observers is the emerging cultural *zeitgeist,* do not consider the information society or the need for a sustainable society.[3] Postmodernism will not be considered here, however, so as to keep the argument relatively simple and to focus on the relationship between information society and sustainability.[4]

The term *sustainable society* was first used as the title of a 1977 book by Dennis Pirages.[5] In the next few years, several other books and reports mentioned sustainability, notably those from the Worldwatch Institute and the 1979 Woodlands Conference.[6] The concept received a great boost by the World Commission on Environment and Development in its 1987 report, *Our Common Future.*[7] From that point, use of *sustainability* spread rapidly up to and past the landmark 1992 UNCED meeting in Rio.[8] The widespread use of this term, at least among those concerned with environmental issues, is remarkable. Equally remarkable is the absence of any controversy over "sustainability." People are either fervently for sustainability, or they ignore it. In contrast, the Club of Rome's 1972 *Limits to Growth* report sparked a decade of heated intellectual controversy about growth and scarcity. In hindsight, it might well be argued that this debate impeded action and was needlessly divisive. In contrast, sustainability is a broad umbrella, albeit with several definitions, under which many can unite. More important, it suggests action of some sort.

The notion of an information society is equally noncontroversial and action-evoking. It apparently first surfaced in Japan in the late 1960s[9] as the focus of *The Plan for an Information Society,* which was submitted to the Japanese government in 1971. The project manager for this ambitious national plan, Yoneji Masuda, described the information society for Western readers in his highly idealized book, published in 1980.[10] A U.S.-based journal, *The Information Society,* began publication in 1982. Predecessors include such terms as "the age of cybernation," widely used in various forms during the 1960s, "the electronic age" and "the age of information," both proposed by Marshall McLuhan in 1964, "the knowledge society," described by Peter Drucker in 1969, and the ungainly "technetronic society," suggested by Zbigniew Brzezinski in 1970. In late 1993 and early 1994, the image in vogue was the immensely evocative metaphor of "the information superhighway."

Why should advocates of a sustainable society be concerned with the emergence of an ever expanding cornucopia of information and information technology (IT), together constituting "information society"? Several years ago, I listed sixty actual or potential impacts of computers and other forms of IT, assessing them as positive, negative, or mixed.[11] The positive impacts, such as mass storage of information, mind extension through expert systems, computers as tutors, and automatic language translation, slightly outnumbered the negative ones. But if one looks at the quality of the impacts, the negatives—unemployment, invasion of privacy, an accelerated sense of time, the destruction of sense of place, aggravated rich-poor differences—outweigh the positives. Tom Forester of Griffith University ably summarizes the many negative arguments, suggesting that the information society is a multifaceted megamistake.[12] This early warning may well be followed by many more, but very few people are disposed to listen now. The information society is proceeding at a rapid pace, with little to stop it—we will be computerized, networked, and flooded with ever more information once the new "superhighways" are in place.

One of the greatest negative impacts of the emerging information society is the pervasive problem of information overload, or "infoglut," which arises from more people sending more communications in more variegated ways than ever before. China has a serious problem of human population explosion, which it tries to address; we in the West have a serious problem of information explosion, which we generally ignore. But examine your own life and ask anyone around you, and the response is unanimous: we are more and more busy trying to keep up, yet fall further and further behind as we initiate, digest, and respond to E-mail, fax messages, letters, phone calls, printouts, journals, magazines, newsletters, newspapers, books, audiotapes, CD-ROMs, memos, fliers, advertisements, catalogues, Post-it notes, signs, cable television, and videocassettes.

The $I = P \times A \times T$ formula considered elsewhere in this volume can readily be adapted to $I = P \times O \times T$ so as to allow us to better understand infoglut. $P =$ population and $T =$ technology remain the same; $A =$ affluence becomes $O =$ occupation. Thus the $I = P \times O \times T$ formula explains the growing infoglut impact (I) resulting from more people (P) in more service occupations producing and distributing information (O), using ever more information technology (T).

Does this ever growing info-abundance make us happier and wiser? Or are we besieged and confused? If the latter, is it simply a matter of cultural lag, we need time to adapt to this evolutionary jump? Or are we creating a monster—making a megamistake? The advocates are blissfully acritical. And the critics—such as Donald N. Michael and Theodore Roszak, who assert that information leads to increasing complexity and decreased productivity;[13] Orrin Klapp, who charges that more information leads to boredom and noise;[14] and Neil Postman, who fears that we are amusing ourselves to death and succumbing to "technopoly"[15]—have yet to be answered.

Regardless of whether we think of IT as boon or bane—or both—the IT revolution is not only unfolding but accelerating. Two recent commentators make a persuasive argument that despite the many impacts of infotech over the past two or three decades, the major impacts will come in the next decade or so.[16]

The impact of IT on the quest for sustainability, similar to its impact on society in general, must be viewed as a complex mix of positives and negatives. On the plus side, data on various environmental problems, satellite photos from outer space, and a burgeoning literature on environmental issues and sustainable futures can illuminate many facets of a complex realm. On the minus side, there is already a glut of information on saving the planet and remedying a wide variety of environmental problems. My brief overview of this literature in the October 1992 issue of *Futures* cites 312 items in 255 notes, with an appendix listing 68 futures-relevant environmental periodicals, both scholarly and popular. A recent bibliography of environmental literature briefly describes 3,084 items, including dozens of periodicals not on my preliminary list.[17] And the *World Directory of Environmental Organizations,* now in its fourth edition, describes the activities of some 2,200 selected environmental groups worldwide.[18]

All of these books, journals, and organizations may be necessary and useful. But there is also much duplication and competition. The haunting verse of Edna St. Vincent Millay, written over fifty years ago, seems more timely than ever:

> Upon this gifted age, in its dark hour,
> Falls from the sky a meteoric shower
> Of facts . . . they lie unquestioned, uncombined.
>
> Wisdom enough to leech us of our ill
> Is daily spun; but there exists no loom
> To weave it into fabric . . . [19]

The shower of facts continues unabated, but there are now many looms that bring environmental information together in reports, annuals, yearbooks, almanacs, and agendas. Still, most of them are not widely known, some are superficial, and none stands out;[20] neither does any of the hundred or so environmental journals. There is no single person or organization to speak for sustainability. The number of people and organizations involved in the pursuit of sustainability defies comprehension. Efforts at coordination are weak and scattered.[21] With hundreds of generals each going their own way, can "the battle to save the planet" ever be won? Lester R. Brown, who supplied this military metaphor,[22] does not elaborate on how the battle should be fought. The metaphor might be rejected by some as overly militaristic and hierarchical. But even in a large scientific endeavor, such as the "sociocultural genome-project" proposed by Dennis Pirages,[23] some degree of coordination and overall strategy is necessary. The need for a new rationality of integrated thinking and theory is greater than ever, at a time when specialization and irrationality appear to be growing.

The "environmental movement" is large and variegated, so much so that few if any can grasp its dimensions. A further problem is understanding those outside "the movement," or ironically, the environment of environmentalism. The broad category of nonenvironmentalists includes a small but active and growing anti-environmentalist opposition,[24] and a larger mass of uninvolved people who may be sympathetic, neutral, or simply uninformed.

Although the antienvironmentalists are small in number, many are politically sophisticated and well funded by corporations and conservative foundations. Should environmentalists engage them in the mass media? To date, the hostiles have been ignored.[25] Yet they were empowered in the United States during the Reagan and Bush administrations, and their influence now dominates Congress and could well return to the White House if the Clinton administration stumbles in its first term.

Perhaps of more immediate concern is the large group of people who ignore or undervalue environmental issues. One can only speculate as to why; the answer is likely to be complex. Many are probably distracted by the vast feast of information, much of it entertaining escapism. Many are citizens who are not involved in politics in any way, and those who give a vast range of social and economic issues higher or exclusive priority. Many professionals who should be incorporating "green" perspectives into their thinking seem to have "environmental blind spots."[26] Ideology seems to produce these blind spots—or low intellectual standards. Perhaps the blindered professionals are sympathetic but don't know how to adopt a greener and more truthful perspective. Perhaps they don't know enough about the issues to bring them into their work. Quite possibly a green perspective is beyond the presently accepted boundaries of their specialty. Research on this question promises to be useful for advancing sustainability.[27]

If the multifaceted transition to sustainability is to succeed in the next few decades, it will probably be necessary to cope with infoglut in society and within the environmental movement, while recruiting more citizens to the environmentalist perspective and greening the worldviews of many more professionals. In this latter regard, there has been a recent greening to some degree among professionals in the social sciences, notably in economics, religion, architecture, education, health, psychology, criminal justice, urban affairs, engineering, and business. With appropriate pressures, these intellectual beachheads could very well be expanded.

Infoglut means there is greater competition to be heard. Those in the advertising industry understand this emerging situation very well and are motivated to get their commercial messages out, thus adding to infoglut. Some possibilities for improved social marketing of sustainability:

• Aim crisp messages at broad audiences, e.g., publish letters in the op-ed pages of major newspapers.[28] The conservatives understand this strategy very well;[29] environmentalists seem to be more comfortable—as most of us are—in addressing like-minded colleagues in relatively obscure journals.

- Engage the antienvironmentalists. It is doubtful that they will be converted, but many neutral bystanders might be—or at least be kept from being converted to the opposition. Debate can be educational; as a result, environmentalists might learn to tailor their messages to make them more immune from intellectual attack.[30]
- Promote a nationally syndicated green columnist. Indicative of how far the environmentalists have to go is the fact that in the United States there is still no nationally syndicated columnist—a green George Will who is read by millions daily. (In Canada, however, David Suzuki is widely known for his weekly syndicated column and his weekly TV show, *The Nature of Things*). Donella Meadows, who writes a weekly column for a local newspaper in New Hampshire,[31] has tried to get national syndication in the United States, but without success.
- Promote an annual "Green Top Ten"—books selected by an authoritative group or individual for consideration by schools, colleges, and libraries. This could be contrasted with the escapism and triviality so prevalent on the widely circulated fiction and nonfiction best-seller lists.
- Promote green Nobel prizes. The Nobel prizes, established early in this century, are irrelevant in an emerging age of sustainability. They munificently reward thinking that contributes to traditional disciplines—and in many instances to the global problematique—rather than thinking aimed at the multidisciplinary problems of promoting sustainability. In recognition of this, the Right Livelihood Awards were established in 1980 as an alternative Nobel Prize,[32] but they are not well known, and should be much more widely publicized.
- Support widespread, general civic education for all ages, with an emphasis on sustainability-related thinking. Educators should be arguing for better "intellectual nutrition" in our information-glutted society, in the same way that nutritionists urge us to eat more vegetables and whole grains, rather than fat, sugar, and empty calories.
- Develop and promote a new vocabulary to replace such obsolete and misleading Cold War terms as *First World* and *Third World* and such economic labels as *developed* and *developing*. Five possibilities: Strongly Progressing Nations, Somewhat Progressing Nations, Nonprogressing Nations, Somewhat Regressing Nations, and Strongly Regressing Nations (such as Haiti and Ethiopia). This new vocabulary would focus attention on sustainability and encourage periodic global assessment of the transition to sustainability.[33]
- Publicize the dysfunctions of the Knowledge Industry. Too many people are trained and rewarded for triviality; too many people accept without question the industrial-era structure of higher education institutions, and too few are urging new multidisciplinary programs in sustainability, world futures, and/or general culture.

Sustainability versus Competing Issues

Despite extensive efforts to cope with infoglut, other issues, whether worthy or not, compete for the attention of policy makers and the public. Some are specific to certain countries and times: much political energy in the United States is invested in the abortion issue, and in legislating a new health care system. In Canada, there is perennial concern over the question of Quebec's secession. Many other issues having to do with government deficits, jobs and the economy, education, health, crime, illegal drugs, corruption, violence, infrastructure, transportation, homelessness, poverty, immigration, human rights, and—increasingly—issues of race, gender, and ethnicity seem to be more or less present in all countries.

Perhaps the best current illustration of competition from other problems is the preoccupation of Al Gore, author of the remarkably thoughtful and farsighted *Earth in the Balance,* with the national economy. In his years as vice president of the United States, he has not visibly pursued any of the elements of his proposed Global Marshall Plan which would make "the rescue of the environment the central organizing principle for civilization."[34] Rather he has been spearheading a major effort to "reinvent government" and reduce unnecessary spending.

The move toward sustainability is arguably the key long-term transition today, but it is not the only one taking place. We live in what I call an "era of multiple transformations," with many momentous changes occurring simultaneously. As noted by Donald N. Michael, this leads to increasing incoherence. "Because of the incoherences, the sought-after products and processes are unlikely to be either fruitful or enduring. The pressures for short-term responses to critical issues will also increase and, given the incoherences, dominate social action."[35] Or, as memorably stated by David Rejeski of the United States Environmental Protection Agency, "the immediate always drives out the important."[36]

Yet another way to articulate this problem of sustainability not receiving its due is to consider the widespread tendency to discount the future. This is a long-standing concern of Harold T. Linstone, who observes that events appearing to be far removed from one's immediate neighborhood in space and time are greatly discounted.[37] Alternatively, Linstone describes how the individual looks at the future as if through the wrong end of a telescope,[38] which affects many decisions.

In the absence of a global ecocatastrophe or a widely touted "Earth Summit" such as the UNCED in Rio, the long-term cause of sustainability suffers when considered along with other issues of greater immediacy and palpability. The general remedy is for environmentalists to become active on other issues and to link them to sustainability.[39] If this strategy is adopted, as argued by Robert C. Paehlke, environmentalism can gain a mass following, evolve into the new wave of progressivism, and become fully developed into a coherent ideology for our times—the first to be deeply rooted in the natural sciences.[40] Stated alternatively by Martin W. Lewis, a "Promethean environmentalism" would strive for a broader coalition—and by doing so reject the romantic views of "ecoextremists."[41] But this will not be easy. Many environmentalists are not disposed to expand their horizons, to work for the greening of cities, business, education, agriculture, and foreign policy. And many embrace a utopian idealism that inhibits effective action in the real world.

Three Scenarios for Nonsustainable Future

As of the mid 1990s, there are no societies that can be called "sustainable" by any definition. All are still heavily under the influence of obsolete industrial-era thinking, reinforced by outdated industrial-era institutions of higher learning and their restricting academic disciplines. Yet many individuals, corporations, NGOs, and nations are breaking loose and initiating promising action in the direction of a sustainable future.[42] Over the next few decades a few countries—probably Japan and nations in Northern Europe; possibly the United States, Canada, and other members of the OECD—may approach what today is thought to be "sustainability," although our definition of the desired end is likely to change.[43] In contrast, most countries, especially poor ones and new ones hastily born of ethnic splintering, will probably fall far short of any reasonable ideal.

All of this adds up to three scenarios that suggest how sustainability will *not* be realized. The first and especially the second best describe the present moment; all three scenarios are equally probable in the next few decades.

1. False Success

Compelling arguments for sustainability are widely heard, and it appears that the transition to sustainability is well under way, due to improved environmental protection and some degree of technological and/or social transformation. Progress is apparent in international environmental agreements, in programs to promote birth control and recycling and to reduce pollution and toxic waste in full costing of motor vehicle usage, and in new energy technologies such as fusion or hydrogen and cost-effective improvements in renewable energy sources and energy efficiency. The 169 national reports on environment and development, prepared for the 1992 UNCED, have led to regular reporting by most nations on progress toward sustainable development.[44] The feeling of widespread activity and progress is enhanced by ignoring or downplaying negative indicators such as declining per capita fish catch, rising Third World debt, and increasingly common shortages of fresh water.[45] Politicians proclaim a premature victory, and other goals take on a higher priority. Environmentalists are better organized than in the past, but their protests that more is needed are ignored.

2. Minimal Success/Regression (More of the Same)

Intellectuals, a variety of UN agencies, and NGOs continue to advocate sustainability of some sort, but with little if any coordination. National governments pay lip service to the notion of sustainability, or ignore it, due to the press of other issues such as deficits, crime, health care, education, inadequate infrastructure, and international crises. Environmental progress is made on a few fronts but offset by worsening conditions in other areas, a mixed picture reflected by forty-two global indicators reported in the early editions of the Worldwatch Institute's annual *Vital Signs*.[46] There is no widespread sense either of marked success or regression.

3. Evident Regression

Consciousness of environmental problems and the idea of sustainability lose their prominence for economic, political, and/or cultural reasons: a widespread and prolonged economic depression, a major war or sustained terrorist activity, success of conservative regimes that downplay the extent of environmental problems and exaggerate the extent of environmental progress, a widespread plague that dwarfs the already considerable impact of AIDS, new information and bio-medical technologies that give the illusion of general progress, ever more quantities of trivial and escapist information drowning out essential messages, a public increasingly weary of doom and gloom from environmentalists and futurists, ever more intense cultural conflict over issues of race, gender, ethnicity, birth, and death.[47] In addition to these distracting and displacing forces, the fragmentation and incoherence of those who advocate sustainability and desirable futures continues to worsen.

The common themes of these scenarios have to do with political priorities and the strength and incidence of other competing concerns. Political priorities are established by the quantity and quality of argument for and against the various issues, and by the perceptions and dispositions of the public and their elected leaders (what is commonly referred to as "political will"). In the emerging information-rich societies, it is by no means clear that political priorities are more rationally determined. Conversely, there may be reason to suspect that the information society is the enemy of sustainable society.

In Sober Conclusion

Despite increased understanding of environmental problems and recent actions taken in the direction of a sustainable society, it is doubtful that progress is being made. Nor is there any consensus about what "winning the war" entails. Any of the three scenarios sketched above seems more likely than genuine success.

Two of the many barriers to attaining sustainability have been explored here. Infoglut, the product of the burgeoning information society, creates a plethora of entertaining and commercial distractions from our many problems, and often makes these problems more difficult to comprehend, for those few who are willing and attempt to fully understand them. Other major problems, more immediate or more readily grasped, serve to displace interest in pursuing sustainability. To substantially reduce these barriers there must be much greater outreach to counter infoglut, and a much greater effort to integrate sustainability concerns into other issues.

But who will do this? Although the scale required of the sustainability effort is that of a world war, the existing organization is quite unlike that of the military, which has centralized planning and can rapidly deploy its ample resources to areas where they are needed. The environmental movement is vast, nonhierarchical, and fragmented. It is good at tackling specific grassroots issues, at holding conferences, at writing high-minded books, reports, papers, almanacs, guidelines, and lists of 101 ways to save the earth. The movement is not good at conceiving and implementing top-level strategy to reposition itself for greater success.

It is possible, but unlikely, that some major eco-catastrophe, such as critical global warming, will soon occur, and that it will supply a galvanizing force for good works; far more likely than this secular Armageddon is more of the same, or dynamic stagnation.[48] I encourage any argument as to why this is not our very probable future.

Notes

1. Other barriers are listed by Walter Corson in "Changing Course: An Outline of Strategies for a Sustainable Future," *Futures* 26 (March 1994): 2.
2. Michael Marien, *Societal Directions and Alternatives: A Critical Guide to the Literature* (LaFayette, NY: Information for Policy Design, 1976).
3. A rare exception to this generalization is David Ray Griffin and Richard Falk, eds., *Postmodern Politics for a Planet in Crisis* (Albany: State University of New York Press, 1993).
4. There are scores of books on postmodernism, mostly by writers in the humanities. For a social science point of view, see Pauline Marie Rosenau, *Postmodernism and the Social Sciences: Insights, Inroads, and Intrusions* (Princeton: Princeton University Press, 1992).
5. Dennis Pirages, ed., *The Sustainable Society* (New York: Praeger, 1977). The main focus of this book was on the growth debate, which permeated the 1970s. Today's focus on "sustainability" sidesteps the issue.
6. Denis Hayes, *Repairs, Reuse, Recycling:First Steps Toward a Sustainable Society,* Worldwatch Paper 23 (Washington, DC: Worldwatch Institute, September 1978); Lester R. Brown, *Building a Sustainable Society* (New York: W. W. Norton, 1981); James C. Coomer, ed., *Quest for a Sustainable Society* (Elmsford, NY: Pergamon, 1981); Harlan Cleveland, ed., *The Management of Sustainable Growth* (Elmsford, NY: Pergamon, 1981).
7. World Commission on Environment and Development, *Our Common Future* (New York: Oxford University Press, 1987).
8. Michael Marien, "Environmental Problems and Sustainable Futures: Major Literature from UCED to UNCED," *Futures* 24, no. 8 (October 1992): 731–57.
9. Kenichi Kohyama, "Introduction to Information Society Theory," *Chuo Koron,* Winter 1968. Cited by Yoneji Masuda in *Changing Value Patterns and Their Impact on*

Economic Structure, ed. Yoshihiro Kogame (Tokyo: University of Tokyo Press, 1982; distributed in the United States by Columbia University Press), 174.

10. Yoneji Masuda, *The Information Society as Post-Industrial Society* (Bethesda, MD: World Future Society, 1981), 3. As a historical note, it is illuminating to recognize that *information society* and *sustainable society* are the contemporary counterparts of the two diametrically opposed uses of *post-industrial society*. See Michael Marien, "The Two Visions of Post-Industrial Society," *Futures* 9, no. 3 (October 1977): 415–31. The essay concluded that "there is no evidence that any writer holding either of the two visions of post-industrial society has any appreciable understanding of the opposing vision."

11. Michael Marien, "IT: You Ain't Seen Nothing Yet," in *Computers in the Human Context: Information Technology, Productivity, and People*, ed. Tom Forester (Cambridge: MIT Press, 1989), 41–47.

12. Tom Forester, "Megatrends or Megamistakes? What Ever Happened to the Information Society?" *The Information Society* 8, no. 3 (July/September 1992): 133–46.

13. Donald N. Michael, "Governing by Learning: Boundaries, Myths, and Metaphors," *Futures* 25, no. 1 (January/February 1993): 81–89; Theodore Roszak, *The Cult of Information*, rev. ed. (Berkeley: University of California Press, 1994).

14. Orrin E. Klapp, *Overload and Boredom: Essays on the Quality of Life in the Information Society* (Westport, CT: Greenwood Press, 1986): Orrin E. Klapp, *Opening and Closing: Strategies of Information Adaptation in Society* (New York: Cambridge University Press, 1978).

15. Neil Postman, *Technopoly: The Surrender of Culture to Technology* (New York: Alfred A. Knopf, 1992); Neil Postman, *Amusing Ourselves to Death: Public Discourse in the Age of Show Business* (New York: Viking, 1985).

16. William E. Halal, "The Information Technology Revolution: Computer Hardware, Software, and Services into the 21st Century," *Technological Forecasting and Social Change* 44, no. 1 (August 1993): 69–86; David Ronfeldt, "Cyberocracy Is Coming," *The Information Society* 8, no. 4 (October/December 1992): 243–96.

17. Yale School of Forestry and Environmental Studies, *The Island Press Bibliography of Environmental Literature* (Washington, DC: Island Press, 1993).

18. Thaddeus C. Trzyna and Roberta Childers, eds., *World Directory of Environmental Organizations* (Sacramento: California Institute of Public Affairs, 1992).

19. Edna St. Vincent Millay, *Huntsman, What Quarry?* (New York: Harper and Brothers, 1939), 92.

20. For example, *Choosing a Sustainable Future: The Report of the National Commission on the Environment* (Washington, DC: Island Press, January 1993).

21. The Global Tomorrow Coalition in Washington, DC, made a modest attempt to coordinate major U.S. environmental groups.

22. Lester R. Brown, et al., *State of the World 1991* (New York: W. W. Norton, 1991), 3.

23. See Dennis Pirages' introduction to this volume, in which he proposes a "sociocultural genome project."

24. See six items in *Future Survey* 15, no. 7 (July 1993): 14–15; especially Carl Deal, *The Greenpeace Guide to Anti-Environmental Organizations* (Berkeley: Odonian Press, March 1993).

25. For many years I have pondered a phrase from John Steinbeck's *Sea of Cortez* (New York: Viking Press, 1941, 31), wherein he muses that "men really need sea-monsters in their personal oceans." Is this characteristic of men, or of women? In any event, there seems to be a very strong correlation between ideology and sea-monster need: the right wing has an obsessive need for monsters (first communism; now environmentalists, Muslims, and Zhirinovsky), while the left wing, which, loosely, includes many environ-

mentalists, seems to have little need to create a larger-than-life enemy. Thus, while conservatives actively attack environmentalists, especially those on the radical fringe, who make easy targets, the environmentalists seem inclined to ignore any opposition.

26. As an illustration of the "environmental blind spot," consider Samuel P. Huntington, "The Clash of Civilizations," *Foreign Affairs* 73, no. 3 (Summer 1993): 22–49, in which it is stated that world politics is entering a new phase in which the fundamental source of conflict will be cultural. Alternative possibilities, such as conflict over scarce resources and environment-related policies, are not considered.

27. Some clues are provided by Lester W. Milbrath, *Envisioning a Sustainable Society: Learning Our Way Out* (Albany: State University of New York Press, 1989).

28. Doug McKenzie-Mohr and others are investigating this matter for Canada's National Round Table on the Environment and the Economy, created in 1988 to reach across institutional lines to identify paths to sustainable development. Contact National Round Table Secretariat, 1 Nicolas Street, Ottawa, Canada KIN 7B7.

29. David Shenk, "Why Liberals Still Can't Compete with Conservatives in the TV Talk Show War," *Washington Post*, 8 August 1993, C1, describes how well conservatives do on TV with their absolute, aggressive, and confrontational style. The conservatives are also very skilled at commanding their share of op-ed essays in major newspapers.

30. One of the rare public confrontations between an environmentalist and an anti-environmentalist involved a bet between Paul Ehrlich and Julian Simon on the prices of five metals over the course of the 1980s. Simon bet that they would fall; Ehrlich, assuming scarcity, thought they would rise. The prices of all five metals declined—an embarrassment for the environmentalist forces. See John Tierney, "Betting the Planet," *New York Times Magazine*, 2 December 1990, 52ff.

31. Donella H. Meadows, *The Global Citizen* (Washington, DC: Island Press, 1991).

32. Paul Ekins, *A New World Order: Grassroots Movements for Global Change* (London and New York: Routledge, 1992), describes the recipients of the Right Livelihood Award and their projects.

33. See Hazel Henderson, "The Role of Social Indicators and Sustainable Development," *Futures* 26: 2, on the importance of indicators and reporting.

34. Al Gore, *Earth in the Balance* (Boston: Houghton Mifflin, 1992), 273.

35. Donald N. Michael, "Forecasting and Planning in an Incoherent Context," *Technological Forecasting and Social Change* 36 (August 1989): 79.

36. Comment by David Rejeski at World Future Society Seventh General Assembly in Washington, DC, Wednesday, 30 June 1993.

37. Harold A. Linstone, "Communications in Futures Research," in *The Study of the Future: An Agenda for Research*, ed. Wayne I. Boucher (Washington, DC: National Science Foundation, 1977), 203.

38. Harold A. Linstone, *Multiple Perspectives for Decision Making* (New York: North-Holland, 1984), 21.

39. Sally Lerner, "The Future of Work in North America," *Futures* 26: 2.

40. Robert C. Paehlke, *Environmentalism and the Future of Progressive Politics* (New Haven CT: Yale University Press, 1989).

41. Martin W. Lewis, *Green Delusions: An Environmentalist Critique of Radical Environmentalism* (Durham, NC: Duke University Press, 1992).

42. Corson, "Changing Course," fn 1, and *Future Survey* 15 (November 1993): 11.

43. See Dennis Pirages' introduction to this volume.

44. United Nations Conference on Environment and Development, *Nations of the Earth Report* (Geneva: UNCED, 1992, 1993), three volumes.

45. Lester R. Brown, Hal Kane, and Ed Ayres, *Vital Signs 1993: The Trends That Are Shaping Our Future* (New York: W. W. Norton, June 1993).

46. Ibid. In *State of the World 1993* (New York, W. W. Norton, 1993), 4, Brown, et al. state that despite many local gains, "the broad indicators showed a continuing wholesale deterioration in the earth's physical condition."

47. Michael Marien, "Cultural Trends, Troubles, and Transformations: A Guide to Recent Literature," *Futures* 25 (May 1993): 414–30.

48. Such a scenario is suggested by Duane Elgin in *Awakening Earth: Exploring the Evolution of Human Culture and Consciousness* (New York: William Morrow, 1993).

19

Norway: Progress
Toward Sustainability?

Oluf Langhelle

According to Norway's minister of environment, Torbjorn Berntsen, "No country has this far managed to transform the positive formulations about sustainable development into practical policy." Making this transformation would require a strategy; a strategy, to be fruitful, requires an understanding of the problems to be solved and the goals to be reached. To discuss Norway's progress toward sustainability, thus, implies a notion of what sustainability is.

I shall first give a brief description of the goal of sustainable development, and then a description of how this goal is conceived by the Norwegian government, notably by our prime minister, Gro Harlem Brundtland, and Torbjorn Berntsen, minister of environment. Even though they have more or less the same understanding of what sustainable development is, the question of how to achieve it and what the implications are seems to be causing a growing tension between the two. This tension can thus be interpreted as a conflict over what strategy to use; the tension is also evident in the actual environmental policy of Norway. My claim, therefore, is not only that a governmental rift is imminent in Norway, but also that we have a "schizophrenic policy" on sustainable development.

Sustainable Development

There are several definitions and conceptions of sustainable development. In the case of Norway and Prime Minister Gro Harlem Brundtland, the natural starting point is, of course, the World Commission on Environment and Development. *Our Common Future* defined sustainable development as "development that meets the needs of the present without compromising the ability of future generations to meet their own needs."[1] Fundamental to this definition, according to the report, are two concepts:

• The concept of *needs,* in particular the essential needs of the world's poor, to which overriding priority should be given
• The idea of limitations imposed by the state of technology and social organization on the environment's ability to meet present and future needs

In John A. Dixon and Louise A. Fallon's classification, the concept of sustainable development found in the Brundtland report is labeled a "social-physical-economic-concept,"[2] where the goal of development is not a sustained level of a physical stock or physical production, but some increase in societal and individual welfare. This is also very explicit in *Our Common Future*: "The satisfaction of human needs and aspirations is the major objective of development."[3]

As Raino Malnes points out, this goal of development is constrained by what he calls the "proviso of sustainability." The prerequisites of development derive, in Malnes's words, "in large measure from the natural environment, and these prerequisites are particularly vulnerable to destruction through development itself."[4] In *Our Common Future* this implies that to be sustainable, development "must not endanger the natural systems that support life on Earth: the atmosphere, the waters, the soils, and the living beings."[5] This is the minimum requirement for sustainable development.

But even the narrow notion of physical sustainability implies, according to the report, "a concern for social equity between generations, a concern that must logically be extended to equity within each generation."[6] Thus one can identify two different dimensions of justice connected to the concept of sustainable development:

Figure 19.1 **Dimensions of Justice**

| | | **Geographical Scope** | |
		The Nation-State	**Globally**
Temporal Scope	Within generations	I. Equity within a current national generation	II. Equity within a current global generation
	Across generations	III. Equity across national generations	IV. Equity across global generations

These different dimensions of social justice, together with the physical or ecological limits, are the paramounts of sustainable development. Development has to fulfill *both* to be sustainable. This is also how sustainable development is conceived in *Caring for the Earth*. Sustainable development here means "improving the quality of human life while living within the carrying capacity of supporting ecosystems."[7]

There seems to be, as Dixon and Fallon also note, "little debate that some version of sustainable development is a desirable goal. The debate is mainly how to pursue the goal and how to measure progress toward it."[8] The vagueness of the goal itself, however, also creates problems. It is, for instance, unclear what is required by social justice. Is it the satisfaction of vital needs, vital aspirations, or both? Is it global equality in living standards and patterns of consumption, or is it a minimum satisfaction of vital needs?

What national goals regarding sustainable development should be is thus not only dependent upon the question of how to pursue and measure progress but also on a further clarification of sustainability itself. A narrow notion of physical sustainability does not rescue one from this; it begs the same questions. Physical sustainability has the same global and temporal scope. These dimensions, therefore, have implications for what should be seen as national goals in both perspectives, physical or equitable.

There is, however, a tension between these inherent goals of sustainable development. This is very clearly put by Gro Harlem Brundtland: "Our dilemma is that all countries—at the very best—are pursuing two potentially conflicting goals: to improve environmental quality and to ensure a high level of economic activity so that tomorrow's societies will hold more promise for the majority of people."[9] The question, therefore, is how to reconcile these two inherent goals of sustainable development in practice.

Sustainable Development and Norway's National Goals

On 19 and 20 January 1994, Norway's minister of environment, Torbjorn Berntsen, hosted a Symposium on Sustainable Consumption in Oslo. The meeting was an attempt by Berntsen to put sustainable consumption on the international agenda. "Our first and most pressing challenge," Berntsen states in the report from the symposium, "is to mobilize public support and political will for sustainable production and consumption patterns."[10] Berntsen gives the following reason:

> If all developing countries follow our example of unsustainable practices, the result would be ecological collapse. But it is morally impossible to deny these countries the basic welfare we take for granted. Our task is to explore and act on measures now, by developing new models of consumption, and by sharing our wealth more justly. . . . We must ensure that the patterns of consumption

build on solidarity across borders and generations. We must search for models that can be applied worldwide. Producers of cars, refrigerators or computers work in global markets. They have to think globally.[11]

The same position is taken by Brundtland:

> An average person in North America consumes almost 20 times as much as a person in India or China, and 60 to 70 times more than a person in Bangladesh. It is simply impossible for the world as a whole to sustain a Western level of consumption for all. In fact, if 7 billion people were to consume as much energy and resources as we do in the West today, we would need 10 worlds, not one, to satisfy all our needs.[12]

These statements are very much to the point. Taken together, they are an acknowledgment of the geographical and temporal scope of sustainable development. They also seem to be in accordance with *Our Common Future,* which states that "sustainable development requires the promotion of values that encourage consumption—standards that are within the bounds of the ecological possible and to which all can aspire."[13] From this perspective, a sustainable Norway is dependent upon adjustments to equity considerations within and across global generations and ecological limits.

The question, however, still remains: What is needed to make these adjustments and to reconcile the ecological and the human imperative? Gro Harlem Brundtland suggests "five possible elements, or challenges, of an Agenda for Change, to meet the challenges of the twenty-first century. These challenges can be summarized as follows:

• We must choose to leave enough "Environmental Space" for future generations, recognizing that our planet has limited capacity to absorb the byproducts of industry.[14]
• Renewable energy must gradually replace nonrenewable energy.[15]
• We must reconcile economic policy with the laws and limitations of nature.[16]
• A new generation of instruments for transport must be developed.[17]
• The total amount of waste, which is a result of production and consumer patterns, must be reduced to a minimum.[18]

These challenges are examples of what is needed, according to Brundtland, to achieve sustainable consumption patterns. They are no doubt challenges of utmost importance. They need, however, closer examination. The rest of this essay, therefore, will focus upon three central questions: What would it take to realize these challenges? What has Norway actually done in regard to these challenges? And how do you bring about the necessary changes?

The Costs of Sustainability

Prior to the Oslo conference on sustainable consumption, the following headline appeared in the largest newspaper in Norway over an interview with Torbjorn Berntsen: INCREASED GROWTH MEANS INCREASED SUFFERING. This was a reference to Berntsen's statement that

> the growth in prosperity we are striving for in Norway will imply increased suffering in the rest of the world. This means further environmental deterioration, the opposite of sustainable development. . . . The problem is that now no matter how environmentally sound our industry gets, or how environmentally correct our products get, any growth in the North will contribute negatively to the global distribution policy. . . . We Norwegians must realize that there is no more space for further growth in prosperity.[19]

Even though Berntsen later denied having used the term "any growth in the North," these statements, in Jon Hille's view, represent some of the most radical ever spoken by a responsible politician in the Western world.[20] They are in sharp contrast to Gro Harlem Brundtland's main conclusion on how to achieve the challenges of the Agenda for Change. Her message is the same as that in *Our Common Future:*

> Some view decline in the standard of living for industrialized countries as necessary steps in bringing total global consumption to a sustainable level. The Commission [World Commission on Environment and Development] did not, however, conclude that such measures were needed, nor that they were desirable. Global change requires thriving economies, large-scale investment, and technological change. Neither change nor full employment will come about as a result of reduced economic activity.[21]

The basic conclusion, is, then, that it is the content of economic growth that has to change.

"Environmental space" for future generations and developing countries can, in Brundtland's view, be achieved in two ways: (1) By sharing resources in a more equitable manner. This would still "leave enough for all peoples to attain an acceptable standard of living."[22] (2) By the development of new technology. New technology, however, also seems to make redistribution superfluous: "Through the development of new technology and more efficient use of energy and raw materials most people in industrialized countries can also maintain their material standard of living, and at the same time gain a better quality of life."[23] Since Brundtland earlier concluded that we would need ten worlds, not one, for the world as a whole to sustain a Western level of consumption for all, simple arithmetic, as Jon Hille points out, [24] would imply that the resources-use per unit of consumption can be reduced by a factor of more than ten.

Another implication of Brundtland's strategy, however, is that in this perspective, sustainable development has no real costs. There are no trade-offs whatsoever for anyone or anything. And not only does new technology and growth with a different content secure the "environmental space" for future and present generations, it is also supposed to create new jobs for the 34 million people out of work in member nations of the Organization for Economic Co-operation (OECD). This has to be a joint operation: "We are compelled to address both unemployment and the necessary transition towards sustainable development as one combined operation."[25] Technology and growth will thus reconcile the environmental and human imperatives.

In the minister of environment's yearly account for the parliament, Berntsen adopted a position more in line with the prime minister's. His formulations, though, seemed a bit reluctantly made and are none too convincing, in view of what he had said earlier:

> As we all know, it is a considerable economic activity that is necessary to uphold the welfare and standard of living in our own country. Reduced growth will, among other things, mean that we must be willing to reduce the growth on our total consumption and welfare goods. Reduced growth could also delay the alteration to more environmentally sound means of production. In the debate on these issues, I have argued that it is possible that the inherent dynamic in our economic system can and will result in economic growth. OECD thinks we will have a growth between 2.5 percent and 3 percent in GDP in the years to come. This should make us more capable of accelerating adjustments in a sustainable direction.[26]

It is hard to see how these statements could be reconciled with Berntsen's earlier position. But not only are the conclusions vague, it is also difficult to determine what Berntsen actually prescribes here. One can still argue that there are signs of a rift in the Norwegian government between the prime minister and the minister of environment.

In addition, the statements made by Gro Harlem Brundtland and Torbjorn Berntsen leave one a bit confused with regard to two very important questions: Is it possible or impossible for the world as a whole to sustain a Western level of consumption for all? Does social justice imply the satisfaction of vital needs, vital aspirations, or both? From their own arguments it seems it is impossible to achieve a universal level of consumption that is also ecologically sustainable—without major changes in the total level of consumption. If this is not possible, then the question becomes, what trade-off has to be made? Sooner or later, I think, this question has to be raised again at the governmental level.

The confusion over what sustainable development actually requires of Norway, however, is evident not only in official statements but also in Norway's actual policy.

Norway's Policy

What has Norway actually done to meet the challenges of sustainable development? If one looks at the environmental issues first, there seems to be progress in some areas, but little or no progress in others. Norway has managed to reduce emissions of CO_2 by 73 percent from 1980 to 1992. The number of cancer-causing chemicals has been reduced by 66 percent from 1988 to 1992.[27]

In regard to climate changes, the Norwegian parliament has decided on a preliminary goal of stabilizing CO_2 emissions at 1989 levels by the year 2000. In light of international recommendations to reduce global emissions by 60 percent immediately,[28] this must be said to be a very modest goal.

From 1989 to 1991 Norway reduced its CO_2 emissions by 4 percent. According to the Norwegian Pollution Control Authority, this was due to reduced consumption of gasoline and fuel oil. After 1991, however, emissions again increased, even though 1991 was the year Norway introduced its tax on CO_2 emissions. In 1993 emissions were at the same level as in 1989, about 35.5 million tons, or 0.2 percent of global emissions.[29] Even though Norway has one of the highest CO_2 taxes in the world, this doesn't seem to have any major impact on emissions.

According to the Norwegian Pollution Control Authority, the increase from 1991 to 1993 can be explained by higher production of oil and gas and increased freight traffic. The greater concern, however, is that estimates show that without further action, emissions will increase by 13 percent from 1989 to the year 2000, about 70 percent of which will be due to increased emissions from the oil industry.[30]

The CO_2 estimates are also part of the government's *Long-term Planning Document*.[31] In this document the government lays out its intentions for the next four to thirty years. This document raises several interesting questions with regard to sustainable development. As Stein Hansen[32] points out, the budget presupposes that income and spending will double by the year 2030; furthermore, this supposition is not questioned in the budget. How we are to combine the stated policy goals of economic growth and stabilizing CO_2 emissions is thus a very open question, so open as to strain credibility. As a contribution to sustainable consumption patterns, Torbjorn Berntsen's own comment tells it all: "The goal of a doubling of Norwegian consumption by the year 2030 is completely wild. Should India strive for the same thing as us, the world would collapse."[33]

But there are other environmental goals that will probably not be met in time, including several of the goals set by the Norwegian parliament and the North Sea Declaration on the reduction of emissions of environmentally damaging chemicals. Target goals for emissions of six of the ten chemicals given the highest priority by the Norwegian Pollution Control Authority, which include cadmium, fluorine, copper, and zinc, will not be met.[34]

Redistribution from North to South has been one of the major issues in the sustainable development debate. At the Rio "Earth Summit" in 1992, Gro Harlem Brundtland urged the OECD countries to increase their aid efforts.[35] This has also been a declared goal of Norway's government, but even so, the 1993 Norwegian budget resulted in the most dramatic cut ever. According to OECD the drop was as large as 11 percent, reducing aid to 1.01 percent of Norway's gross national product (GNP). Denmark, with development assistance at 1.02 percent of GNP, has become the country that gives the largest share.[36]

In its budget proposal for 1994, the Norwegian government did not seem very interested in taking the lead back. The proposal reduced development aid by a total of 100 million Norwegian kroner, with aid to Africa cut by 5 percent, and to Asia by 3 percent. At the same time, aid conditional upon the purchase of Norwegian products was to increase by 26 percent.[37] The budget proposal, however, was turned down by the parliament, who managed to restore the aid. Even so, according to Bjorn H. Amland, aid now plays "an important role in promoting the Norwegian export industry, especially within the telecommunication and hydropower sectors."[38]

Strategy

These examples, in my opinion, show the "schizophrenic" character of the Norwegian policy on sustainable development. Both Berntsen and Brundtland, however, acknowledge that further steps have to be taken. The key question, as they see it, is how far Norway can go on its own. Our CO_2 taxes were, in Brundtland's words, "so much higher than in other countries that we were forced to take one small step backwards." And she further observed, "At present countries are watching each other, waiting to move in order to guard what they see as their competitive edge."[39] This is, of course, not particularly promising. But it cannot be the only reason for the lack of progress. It remains difficult to explain the fact that Norway is unable to fulfill its own self-imposed obligations.

There must thus be other constraints. According to Brundtland, our economic systems "so far do not yet take sufficient account of harm done to people's welfare or the environment." Her conclusion is straightforward: "Where the market is insufficient, we will have to act politically."[40] In this regard the job of the political system is to correct market failures. The more interesting question, however, is where is the market seen as insufficient, and politics as necessary?

Since the ideological wave of neoliberalism or libertarianism, the mistrust of political governance has been widespread, and the market has been viewed as more and more "sufficient" for sustainable development. The influence of this ideology is important with regard to sustainable development for two reasons: because this ideology alters the relationship between the democratic process and the market process, and because the ideology questions the very possibility of reaching collective goals through the democratic process, and thus the goal of sustainable development.

It was, according, to Arthur Seldon, Friedrich Hayek's thinking "which largely inspired the 'Thatcherite Revolution' in economic policy." In Seldon's words, Hayek believed in two essential principles: "That government, essentially incompetent, should be minimal; and liberty should come before equality."[41] Chanddran Kukathas describes Hayek's project as an attempt to show that "the nature of mind and the limited powers of human reason make institutions aimed at organizing society to achieve some desired end, or reconstructing it in accordance with some preferred pattern of distribution, largely unworkable."[42]

This skepticism toward planned change is also expressed by Jon Elster: "If one considers planned change as a process where one seeks the best available means to realize a given goal, the probability of failure is high."[43] The market, being conceived as a spontaneous order by Hayek is superior to the political system by being far more rational: "We have no ground for crediting majority decisions with that higher, superindividual wisdom which, in a certain sense, the products of spontaneous social growth may possess. . . . Those spontaneous processes which free communities have learned to regard as the source of much that is better than individual wisdom can contrive."[44] The substitution of politics with the market for realizing collective goals, is called "Utopian nonengineering" by Vernon.[45]

This "nonengineering" seems to be reducing the scope of the politically feasible; the measures that are seen as useful are limited more or less to incentives and disincentives. From this perspective, political action consists in trying "to ensure that incentives and disincentives act in harmony with the needs of our society today and in the future."[46] Berntsen's new measures to combat a polluting industry consist of "a further development of the cooperation with the industry. There will be taken initiatives to voluntary agreements concerning among other things deliberations and declarations of intentions connected to reduction of emissions which are not covered by the CO_2 tax." The plans for these agreements are supposed to be ready sometime in 1994. Within the transport sector, the government "will assess the need for more information and increased use of traffic controls to make people fully aware of how to drive more energy and fuel efficient."[47]

It would be an exaggeration to assert that these are hard measures, and sufficient for a transition to a sustainable society in Norway. More hard-hitting and efficient means, though, are just what Harald Rensvik, director general of the Pollution Control Authority, wants in the form of binding legal regulations: "An important aspect of legal regulations is to have reasonably sure possibilities of sanctions. This demands thorough supervision by the authorities, and possibilities for legal action. Today, these kinds of instruments tend to be referred to rather patronizingly as 'command and control instruments,' and not of the type to be developed. This is a complete misunderstanding, and underestimation of these instruments' importance."[48]

The findings of Martin Janicke and Helmut Weidner seem to support Rensvik's view. After summarizing twenty-four different cases of successful environmental policy, they conclude, among other things, that "our examples show that governmental command and control remains a strong implement in environmental policy." And further, that "public administrations have . . . played the most important role in improving environmental quality." New types and modes of governmental intervention are, according to Janicke and Weidner, still "needed and possible."[49] Even though Jon Elster (1984) views the likelihood of failure through planned change as high, there are, according to Elster, circumstances where such attempts have better prospects for success: "Such change can have better prospects if the process is supported by a conception of what a just arrangement of society is. Not instrumental rationality, but normative conceptions should guide the process of change."[50] The concept of sustainable development in itself can thus be a major driving force for its own attainment. We have in Norway at least a tradition of constraining and subordinating the market to the collective goals of the community. A transition to a sustainable society requires a revival of this tradition and the skills of political engineering. This will, however, take a lot more courage than the Norwegian government is currently demonstrating.

Notes

1. World Commission on Environment and Development, *Our Common Future* (New York: Oxford University Press, 1987), 43.
2. John A. Dixon and Louise A. Fallon, *The Concept of Sustainability: Origins, Extensions, and Usefulness for Policy,* Division Working Paper no. 1989–1, The World Bank, Environment Department, 2.
3. WCED, *Our Common Future,* 43.
4. Raino Malnes, *The Environment and Duties to Future Generations: An Elaboration of Sustainable Development,* Report 1990/2, Fritjof Nansen Institute, 5.
5. WCED, *Our Common Future,* 44–45.
6. WCED. *Our Common Future,* 43. For discussion on the logic of this see William M. Lafferty, Oluf Langhelle, and Nils Christian Stenseth, *Sustainable Development: The Goal of Development and the Conditions of Sustainability* (1995).
7. IUCN/NEP/WWF, *Caring for the Earth: A Strategy for Sustainable Living* (Gland, Switzerland: 1991), 10.
8. Dixon and Fallon, *Concept of Sustainability,* 7.
9. Gro Harlem Brundtland. "The Challenge of Sustainable Production and Consumption Patterns," in *Symposium: Sustainable Consumption,* Ministry of Environment (Oslo: 1994), 26.
10. Torbjorn Berntsen, foreword to *Symposium: Sustainable Consumption, Ministry of Environment,* Ministry of Environment, 4.
11. Torbjorn Berntsen, "Opening Address," Norway, *Symposium: Sustainable Consumption,* Ministry of Environment, 24.
12. Brundtland. "Challenge of Sustainable Production," 26.
13. WCED, *Our Common Future,* 44.
14. Brundtland, "Challenge of Sustainable Production," 30.
15. Ibid., 31.
16. Ibid.

17. Ibid., 32.
18. Ibid.
19. *Aftenposten,* 19.01.94 (my translation).
20. Jon Hille, "Forbruk og miljo," in *Miljoarboka 1994* .
21. Brundtland, "Challenge of Sustainable Production," 28.
22. Ibid., 30.
23. Ibid.
24. Hille, "Forbruk og miljo."
25. Brundtland, "Challenge of Sustainable Production," 28.
26. Torbjorn Berntsen, *Miljovernpolitisk Redegjorrelse,* 1994 (my translation).
27. SFT, *Forurensning i Norge* (1994): 5–6.
28. Miljoverndepartementet, *Drivhuseffekten, virkninger og tiltak,* Raport fra Den Interdepartementale Klimagruppen, 1991, 33.
29. Emission of other gases contributing to climate change were estimated at 12.4 million metric tons CO_2 equivalents in 1993; see SFT, *Forurensning i Norge,* 1994, 8–11.
30. Ibid.
31. Finans og tolldepartementet, *Langtidsprogrammet 1994–1997,* St. meld, no. 4 (1992/93).
32. Stein Hansen, "Hvor er baerekraften?" in *Tidskrifiet Alternativ Frantid* (February 1993): 49–63.
33. *Aftenposten,* 19.01.94. (my translation).
34. Norges Naturvernforbund, "Nar ikke seks av ti mal for miljogifter," in *Natur & miljo,* no. 15 (1994): 3.
35. Miljoverndepartementet, *FN-konferansen om miljo og utvikling,* report, 1992, 49.
36. *Development Today* 4, no. 10 (1994): 2.
37. *Redd Barna-avisa* (September/October 1993): 5.
38. *Development Today,* 2.
39. Brundtland, "Challenge of Sustainable Production," 31.
40. Ibid., 30.
41. Arthur Seldon, "Professor F. A. Hayek," *The Independent,* 25 March 1992.
42. Chandran Kukathas, *Hayek and Modern Liberalism* (Oxford: Clarendon Press, 1989), 4.
43. Jon Elster, "Skeptiske tanker om samfunnsplanlegging," *Forskning og Framtid* 1 (1994): 27.
44. Friedrich A. Hayek, *The Constitution of Liberty* (Chicago: University of Chicago Press, 1960), 110.
45. Cited in Kukathas, *Hayek and Modern Liberalism,* 215.
46. Brundtland, "Challenge of Sustainable Production," 30.
47. Berntsen, *Miljovernpolitisk Redegjorelse,* 12.
48. Harald Rensvik, "The Role of the Authorities: From Pollution Watchdog to Catalyst for Sustainable Development," in *Symposium: Sustainable Consumption,* Ministry of Environment, 95.
49. Martin Janicke and Helmut Weidner, eds., *Successful Environmental Policy: A Critical Evaluation of 24 Cases* (Berlin: Edition Sigma, 1994), 13.
50. Elster, "Skeptiske tanker om samfunnsplanlegging," 27.

20

Measuring Sustainability: Indicators, Trends, and Performance

Walter H. Corson

Introduction

Current rates of population growth and resource consumption may not be ecologically sustainable for more than a few decades; they are resulting in harm to our air, water, land, and other natural resources and are jeopardizing our future well-being. Recently the rate of environmental decline has greatly accelerated. On average, resource use nearly tripled between 1950 and 1990. This growth, combined with widespread use of harmful technology and a doubling of human population, resulted in roughly a sixfold increase in human impact on the global environment during the four decades. This estimate is based on the formula stating that environmental impact (I) is the product of the number of people (P), resource use per person (R), and environmental degradation from technologies employed in resource use (T): $I = PRT$.[1] These factors are also central to the concept of global carrying capacity, defined as "the maximum human population that the Earth can support indefinitely on a specific resource base and at a specific level of technology."[2] Human activity is now altering the Earth's basic life-support systems and cycles, including the atmospheric system and carbon, nitrogen, sulfur, hydrologic, and biologic cycles.[3] Biologists have estimated that humans are appropriating, directly or indirectly, nearly 40 percent of the Earth's terrestrial food resources.[4]

Evidence of increasing human impact on the environment includes rising levels of greenhouse gases in the atmosphere, increased acid damage to forests and lakes, depletion of the protective ozone layer, increasing shortages of fresh water, accumulation of toxic wastes, pollution of groundwater and surface waters, soil erosion and degradation, desertification, loss of forests and other habitats, depletion of marine fisheries, and extinction of plant and animal species.[5] Many of these changes are occurring rapidly, and some are largely irreversible. An entire country can be deforested in a few decades; a region can lose most of its topsoil in a generation; the ozone layer can be significantly depleted in a decade.[6]

In addition to these ecological threats, the widening gap between rich and poor nations, the persistence of poverty and malnutrition, and the growing incidence of crime, wars, and war-related death all pose serious questions regarding the economic, social, and political viability of communities and societies around the world. In many regions, rapidly growing populations, scarce resources, and environmental degradation are exacerbating ethnic, cultural, and religious differences and increasing the potential for instability and conflict.[7] The accelerating degradation of natural resources and the extent of unmet basic needs in some areas may prove to be unsustainable in the foreseeable future. While the issues of ecological and societal sustainability are not yet high priorities on most political agendas, they could soon become central foci of decision making at all levels of government. Societies need to recognize the full environmental, economic, and social costs of human activities and to develop strategies and methods for moving to ecologically and socially sustainable paths.

This chapter defines sustainability as a multidimensional concept and reviews a variety of programs and studies that use environmental and social indicators to assess quality of life, performance, and sustainability for communities, states, business firms, nations, and the world as a whole.

Dimensions of Sustainability

The long-term aspect of sustainability is central to the widely cited definition of sustainable development from the 1987 report of the World Commission on Environment and Development, *Our Common Future*: "Development that meets present needs without compromising the ability of future generations to meet their own needs." A survey of works on the topic suggests that sustainability is a multidimensional concept with a number of interrelated aspects, including ecological, environmental, economic, technological, social, cultural, ethical, and political factors.8 To define and develop measures for monitoring progress toward a sustainable future, the author reviewed a wide range of data and identified more than a hundred indicators divided among twelve dimensions of sustainability; examples are given in Table 20.1.[9]

Ecological and Societal Sustainability

The concept of sustainable development may involve inherent conflicts between shorter-term economic and social goals and longer-term ecological sustainabil-

Table 20.1

Aspects of Sustainability	Dimensions of Sustainability	Examples of Indicators
Ecological/ Environmental	Natural resources and environment	Energy use Air quality
Economic	Transportation Economy	Mass transit use Unemployment rate
Ethical	Socioeconomic equity	Percent of population in poverty
Social-Cultural	Social environment Population Health Education Culture Recreation	Crime rate Population change Infant mortality rate High school graduation rate Circulation of printed materials Area devoted to public parks
Political/ Governmental	Political participation Government effectiveness	Voting rate Efficiency of government

ity. Conditions and practices considered socially desirable, such as high incomes and living standards, may result in environmental degradation and be ecologically and biophysically unsustainable. And practices that appear sustainable in a local context may not be sustainable if they excessively deplete resources from surrounding areas or other regions.[10]

Different socioeconomic factors may have different effects on ecological sustainability; for example, a high level of education could contribute to ecological sustainability, while a high income level may have a negative ecological impact. Examination of the links between socioeconomic and ecological indicators could help clarify to what extent different aspects of development are ecologically sustainable.

Indicators and Indexes of Sustainability

Indicators are generally designed to make complex phenomena or conditions quantifiable, perceptible, and understandable. Environmental and social indicators can provide measures of the health and viability of ecological and social systems. Among environmental indicators, three types can be distinguished: *pressure* or stress indicators that measure the causes of environmental problems (such as pollutant emissions); *state* or impact indicators that gauge environmental quality (such as pollutant concentration); and *response* indicators that reflect efforts to improve the environment (such as regulations to reduce pollution). A *policy performance* indicator is a normative measure that compares an existing condition with an explicit standard or target (such as an allowable or desired level of pollution). To be useful in public policy making, indicators should be aggregative (capable of being combined into composite indicators), time sensitive (able to show a trend), related to cause and effect, policy-relevant, verifiable, and reproducible.[11]

Information is available for the development of indicators to estimate the degree of ecological and socioeconomic sustainability for communities and nations, and to assess progress toward sustainability at the local, regional, national, and global level. Data exist for all important dimensions and sectors, including natural resources and the economic, social, and political sectors. Taken together, data for the various sectors of a community or nation can comprise a "sustainability profile." Numerical data (such as a country's population growth rate) and nonnumerical information (such as the extent of a country's family planning program) can both be converted to indicators. Numerical indicators can be direct measures of a variable (such as the concentration of a pollutant), or indexed or scaled values (such as a pollutant's concentration relative to highest and lowest observed levels). Following practices widely used in index construction, direct measures can be used to calculate or estimate scale values, with data judged "least sustainable" given a value of 0, and those deemed "most sustainable" a value of 1, 10, or 100. Data falling between these limits can be expressed as index numbers proportional to the data's position in relation to the lower and upper limits. Index numbers for several indicators in a given sector (e.g., environmental or economic) or for a given issue (e.g., air quality) can be combined or averaged to create sectoral or issue indexes; these can be further aggregated into overall sustainability indexes for individual communities, regions, or nations. Although combining several indicator values into a composite index (such as the index of leading economic indicators) can give an overall assessment of conditions (such as the general state of the economy), the composite index lacks the detail reflected by the individual indicators. A composite index should be interpreted in conjunction with its individual components.[12] The construction of composite indexes of sustainability is illustrated later in this chapter.

When employed together with numerical targets, indicators can be used to compare current environmental, economic, and social conditions with desired performance levels, to show trends over time, and to allow comparisons between different regions. Performance levels can be defined and calculated as the extent to which current data for the indicators approach or exceed target levels (by expressing the data as a percentage of the target figure). Performance indicators and targets can help define and publicize new standards and measures for assessing progress, and can help us judge the effectiveness of policies and programs.

Community Programs

A number of urban areas are using numerical indicators and targets to assess their quality of life and progress toward sustainability.[13] The Sustainable Seattle project defines sustainability as the area's "long-term cultural, economic, and environmental health and vitality." Their latest report lists 40 proposed indicators selected for data development, grouped into four broad areas: environment (including biodiversity, air quality, topsoil loss, wetlands); population and resources (including population growth, water use, solid waste, energy, transportation, land use, food); economy (including employment, income, poverty, housing affordability, health care spending); and culture and society (including infant health, crime, community service, voting, literacy, library use, participation in the arts). The report gives trend data for 20 of the indicators between 1980 and 1992, and characterizes the trends as "moving toward sustainability" (4 indicators), "moving away from sustainability" (11 indicators), or "neither toward nor away" (5 indicators). Of the 6 indicators reflecting resource and environmental trends, 2 showed movement toward sustainability and 4 showed movement away. Future targets for the indicators are being considered.[14]

The Greenville County project includes 63 indicators in nine categories: population, economics, education, family, health, public safety, mobility, voter participation, and environment. The report gives trend data for 59 indicators between 1987 and 1992: 21 indicators showed improvement, 23 worsened, and 15 exhibited no clear trend. Of the four environmental indicators, 3 showed improvement and one worsened.[15]

Pasadena's Quality of Life Index is designed to periodically assess the community's overall health. The program includes 112 indicators covering ten areas: environment, health, drugs, education, the economy, housing, arts and culture, recreation and open space, transportation, and community safety. The environmental indicators include air quality, water conservation, energy efficiency, solid waste and recycling, trees, and environmental education. Many of the indicators are compared with other local, state, and national data. Quantitative targets have been established for more than a third of the indicators.[16]

The Pasadena report gives trend data for a number of the indicators: of 21 showing clear trends, 13 were positive and 8 negative. Of the 6 environmental indicators, 3 improved and 3 showed no clear trend. The extent to which current data for 18 of the indicators approached or exceeded the designated target level (a measure of performance expressing the data as a percentage of the target figure) varied from a high of 138 percent (for vehicular deaths) down to a low of −210 percent (for cases of syphilis); the average performance rating for the 18 indicators was 57 percent. Of the 18 indicators, half had values that were at least 80 percent of the target figure.

Jacksonville's program has used 74 indicators to monitor the quality of life on an annual basis since 1983. The indicators reflect trends in nine areas: the economy, public safety, health, education, the natural environment, travel mobility, government and politics, the social environment, and culture and recreation. Between 1983 and 1992, 35 of the indicators showed improvement, 23 worsened, and 16 exhibited no clear trend. Of the 7 indicators measuring environmental trends, 3 improved, 2 worsened, and 2 showed no definite trend.

Of the 72 indicators for which Jacksonville has established targets for the year 2000, the extent to which current data for the indicators approached or exceeded the target level (a measure of performance) varied from a high of 123 percent (for septic tank permits) down to a low of −86 percent (for net job growth); the average performance rating for all 72 indicators was 64 percent. Of the nine areas, the natural environment had the highest average rating (96 percent); the social environment had the lowest average rating (29 percent). Of the 72 indicators, 42 percent had values that were at least 80 percent of the target figure.[17]

Urban Indicator Surveys

A number of recent surveys have analyzed environmental, economic, and social factors that influence the quality of life in urban areas, and that affect whether they can maintain acceptable living standards and remain ecologically and socioeconomically sustainable over the long run. Two of these surveys are summarized here.

Cities: Life in the World's 100 Largest Metropolitan Areas

The Population Crisis Committee used ten criteria to rate each metropolitan area's standard of living: public safety, food costs, living space, housing standards, communications, education, public health, peace and quiet, traffic flow, and clean air. For each indicator, a rating between 1 and 10 was assigned, with 10 being the highest rating; for each city the ten ratings were totaled to give an overall urban-living-standards score with a possible maximum of 100. City scores ranged from a high of 86 for Melbourne, Montreal, and Seattle-Tacoma to a low of 19 for Lagos, Nigeria.[18] The results show a negative correlation between living standards and urban growth rate: the fifty cities with the highest living standards had an average population growth rate less than half that of the fifty lowest-ranked cities.

Urban Stress Test

Zero Population Growth used a five-point scale to rate 192 U.S. cities on eleven categories using 30 indicators to assess social, economic, and environmental conditions. The categories were population change, crowding in housing, educational attainment, violent crime, community economics, individual economics, birthrate and infant mortality rate, air pollution, hazardous waste sites, water quality and availability, and quality of sewage treatment. In each category, a score of 5 represents a "most stressful" condition; a rating of 1 denotes "least stressful." Each city's scores were averaged to give a combined overall urban stress score. These scores ranged from a high of 4.2 for Gary, Indiana, to a low of 1.6 for Cedar Rapids, Iowa. The study shows a positive correlation between the stress scores and population size: the average score for cities with fewer than 100,000 people was 2.5; the average for cities of a million or more was 3.8.[19]

State Programs

At the state level, Minnesota and Oregon are using indicators and setting numerical targets. Minnesota's Milestones program includes twenty general descriptive goals and 79 indicators with quantitative targets for the years 1995, 2000, 2010, and 2020. The indicators are designed to measure progress in a number of areas, including economic viability, health, education, community safety, community services, housing, environmental quality, recreation, participation in government, and government effectiveness. For 25 of the 79 indicators, the data show changes from 1980 to 1990; 13 of these demonstrated progress toward the targets, 6 exhibited movement away from the targets, and 6 displayed no clear trend. Of the 12 environmental indicators, 5 improved, one worsened, and 6 showed no clear trend.[20]

The extent to which current data for 49 of the indicators approached or exceeded the designated target level (a measure of performance) varied from a high of 110 percent (for hazardous waste generation) to a low of 0 percent (for highway litter); the average performance rating for all 49 indicators was 75 percent. The average rating for 13 environmental indicators was 69 percent. Of the 49 indicators, 61 percent had values that were at least 80 percent of the target figure.

Oregon's Benchmarks program includes 272 indicators pertaining to people, quality of life, and the economy, with data for some indicators from 1970 to 1992, and numerical targets for 1995, 2000, and 2010. Areas covered include health, education and worker training, housing, crime, transportation, cultural activities, environmental quality, civic and political participation, government effectiveness, economic viability and diversity, income, employment, and energy use. A number of the 272 indicators are designated as critical measures of Oregon's human, environmental, and economic well-being. Of the 37 critical indicators for which trend data is given, 17 showed progress toward the targets, 13 reflected movement away from the targets, and 7 displayed no clear trend. Of the 5 critical environmental indicators, 2 improved, 2 worsened, and one showed no trend.[21]

Of the 51 critical indicators that included both current data and a target value for the year 2000, the extent to which the data approached or exceeded the designated target level varied from a high of 101 percent (the percentage of forestland and of agricultural land preserved) to a low of 41 percent (teenage pregnancy rate); the average performance rating for all 51 indicators was 69 percent. The average rating for 6 environmental indicators was 78 percent. Of the 51 indicators, 53 percent had values that were at least 80 percent of the target figure.[22]

In Colorado, a nongovernmental organization has identified 41 socioeconomic and environmental measures of sustainability and compiled trend data for 33 indicators of three types: social (crime, health, education and literacy); economic (employment); and environmental (air and water quality, energy and resource use, toxins and hazardous waste, solid waste, agriculture, forests and habitats, population). Of the 16 socioeconomic indicators evaluated, 11 showed movement away from sustainability and 4 suggested movement toward sustainability. Of the 17 environmental indicators evaluated, 13 reflected movement away from sustainability and 4 suggested progress toward sustainability.[23]

State-Level Environmental Indicator Surveys

The Institute for Southern Studies has developed an index to measure environmental conditions at the state level. For each of the fifty U.S. states, the index contains 256 indicators that emphasize the links between natural ecosystems, the built environment, and human health. The indicators include data in thirteen categories: air pollution, water pollution, energy use and production, transportation efficiency, hazardous and solid waste, community health, workplace health, agricultural pollution, forestry and fish, recreation and quality of life, state policy initiatives, and leadership in Congress. The study gives a total "green" index score and overall rank for each state. The total score is the sum of the state's ranks for all 256 indicators, with each indicator carrying equal weight; the state with the smallest combined score has the highest overall rank. The state ranked first is Oregon with a score of 4,583; the state ranked last is Alabama with a score of 8,658.[24]

Based on the 179 indicators in the study that measure environmental conditions, there is a negative correlation between environmental quality and population size. The 25 states ranked lowest on environmental quality have a combined population of 151 million, 55 percent greater than the combined population of the highest-ranked 25 states, which have a combined population of 97 million.

In a more recent study, the institute used 40 indicators to evaluate each U.S. state's economic performance and the degree of environmental stress statewide. The 20 economic indicators include annual pay, job opportunities, and business start-ups; the 20 environmental indicators measure factors ranging from toxic emissions and pesticide use to energy consumption and spending for natural resource protection. The study shows that states with the best environmental records offer the best job opportunities and the best climate for economic development.[25]

In its 1994 *Information Please Environmental Almanac,* the World Resources Institute compared U.S. states and Canadian provinces on per capita energy use, toxic chemical releases, per capita water use, and greenhouse gas emissions. The almanac provides current data for more than 60 indicators covering population, income, energy, transportation, water, solid and hazardous waste, pollutants, biodiversity, and environmental and natural resource expenditures.[26]

Environmental Ratings for Business Firms

The Council on Economic Priorities' 1991 report, *The Better World Investment Guide,* rated 100 U.S. companies on twelve social, economic, and environmental criteria. Environmental performance for 52 of the companies was rated as positive, mixed, or poor. Of this group, 28 larger companies had assets of over $5 billion, and 24 smaller firms had assets worth less than $5 billion.[27] The survey results showed that the smaller companies had much better environmental ratings.

In a second analysis of environmental performance, the council assigned environmental ratings to 142 U.S. companies; 69 were classified as large, 32 were considered small, 12 were gas and oil companies, and 29 were supermarket chains.[28] Four rating categories were used: good, fair, neutral (neither positive nor negative), and poor. The small companies had by far the best environmental ratings, followed by the supermarket chains. Three-fourths of the large businesses had fair, neutral, or poor ratings, and all but two of the gas and oil companies were rated as poor.

National Environmental Programs

Government agencies and nongovernmental organizations in various countries are developing indicators to measure ecological, environmental, and socioeconomic aspects of sustainability. A number of nations are establishing goals and using indicators to monitor environmental trends. Canada, France, the Netherlands, Norway, and the United Kingdom have all developed national environmental plans that include targets for reducing solid waste generation and emissions of carbon dioxide (CO_2), sulfur dioxide (SO_2), nitrogen oxides (NO_x), and ozone-depleting chemicals.

Carbon Dioxide Emissions

All five nations have established targets to stabilize CO_2 emissions by 2005 or earlier. The Dutch plan calls for stabilization by 1994–95. Of the five nations, Canada has by far the highest per capita CO_2 emissions (16.5 tons per year) and showed the greatest increase in emissions (27 percent) since 1971. The Netherlands, with the most rigorous goal for reducing emissions, has the second-highest per capita CO_2 emissions (12.8 tons) and the second-highest increase in emissions since 1971 (19 percent). France, which along with the United Kingdom has the least rigorous target for reducing emissions, also has, along with Norway, the lowest per capita emissions (7.1 tons) and the greatest decrease in emissions since 1971 (12 percent).

Sulfur Dioxide Emissions

Canada and Norway have set the most rigorous targets for SO_2 emissions; both plan reductions of 50 percent by 1994. Of the five nations, Canada has by far the highest per capita SO_2 emissions (123 tons), while Norway has the lowest (10.7 tons); both countries are incurring significant acid damage from emissions in neighboring countries. The Netherlands, with the second-lowest per capita emissions, has the least rigorous target, a cap on emissions by 2000, rather than a reduction. Among the five nations, the Netherlands and Norway have achieved the largest reductions in SO_2 emissions since 1971 (75 percent and 73 percent, respectively), compared with reductions of between 44 percent and 56 percent for the other three nations.

Nitrogen Oxide Emissions

The national plans for Canada and France omit targets for NO_x reduction; the Dutch plan calls for a cap on emissions, and both Norway and the UK plan reductions of 30 percent. Of the five nations, Canada showed the greatest emissions increase between 1970 and 1991 (41 percent) and has by far the highest per capita emissions (72.3 tons). With its large nuclear power program, France exhibited the smallest emissions increase (14 percent) and has the lowest per capita emissions (26.6 tons). Norway's target of a 30-percent cut may reflect its relatively high per capita emissions (50.7 tons) and relatively large emissions increase since 1970 (37 percent).

Municipal Waste and Recycling

All five national plans include a goal of reducing waste and/or increasing recycling of materials. Only the Canadian plan contains a specific waste reduction target of 50 percent; France and the UK set recycling targets of 50 percent, and the Dutch plan calls for increasing the overall recycling rate from 20 to 33 percent. In terms of indicators, Canada has the highest per capita municipal waste generation (601 kilograms per year), the second-highest increase in waste generation between 1980 and 1990 (27 percent), and the lowest recycling rates for paper (20 percent) and glass (12 percent). France has the lowest per capita waste generation rate (328 kilograms) and the second-highest recycling rates for paper (46 percent) and glass (29 percent). While the Netherlands is relatively high on per capita waste generation (497 kilograms), it showed the smallest increase in generation between 1980 and 1990 (5 percent) and has the highest recycling rates for paper (50 percent) and glass (67 percent).[29]

In addition to the issues of climate change, ozone depletion, acidification, and waste, goals in the five national plans reviewed show concern about toxic and radioactive substances, urban air pollutants, water quality, natural areas, and noise. The targets in these five national plans reflect the varying importance each country attaches to the different issues; they also represent different degrees of commitment to their achievement. Although the Canadian plan contains national initiatives, the federal government shares authority with the provincial governments. The French plan is not a document of the entire government, and its course of implementation is uncertain. The Dutch plan may have the broadest political acceptance of all the plans. The Norwegian plan lacks a concrete program for implementation, and compared with the others, the United Kingdom's plan is less detailed regarding specific measures and probable costs.[30] The Dutch plan is probably the most detailed of the national plans; it contains eight major issue themes: climate change, acidification, eutrophication, toxic substances, solid waste, disturbance of local environments, dehydration of soils, and waste of resources. Numerical goals are being identified for each issue.[31]

While the United States lacks a national environmental plan or strategy, a federal interagency working group is identifying indicators of sustainable development, and the Environmental Protection Agency is developing national environmental goals. And within the Department of Commerce, the Bureau of Economic Analysis is designing a system of national resource and environmental accounts that includes the depletion and degradation of natural assets.[32]

Environmental Trends in the Netherlands

The Netherlands has used composite indicators to monitor several aspects of environmental quality between 1980 and 1991. The indicator of the potential for climate change is the weighted summation of the Dutch annual discharge or use of CO_2, CH_4, N_2O, chlorofluorocarbons (CFCs), and halons, expressed in CO_2 equivalents; the indicator declined by 16 percent between 1980 and 1991. The indicator of the potential for stratospheric ozone depletion is the weighted total of the annual production of eight types of CFCs and halons in ozone-depletion equivalents; the indicator fell 56 percent over the period. The acidification indicator is the weighted sum of annual emissions of SO_2, NO_x, and ammonia (NH_3) in acidification equivalents; it dropped 39 percent over the period. The eutrophication indicator is the weighted total of annual releases of phosphates and nitrates; it declined by 10 percent during the period. A composite indicator of toxic emissions showed a decline of 11 percent, and a composite indicator of solid waste declined by 8 percent between 1980 and 1991. Finally, these six composite indicators were further aggregated into a composite pollution index; it dropped 16 percent over the period.[33]

Environmental, Economic, and Social Trends in the United States

The author has analyzed 65 environmental, economic, social, and political trends in the United States between 1970 and 1993. Of 37 environmental and natural resource trends, 12 were judged to be generally positive (showing improvement or movement toward sustainability), 20 were considered to be negative (moving away from sustainability), and 5 were mixed (having both sustainable and unsustainable aspects). All of the air quality trends were positive, the water quality and supply trends were more positive than negative, while the trends for wildlife, natural habitats, and waste were generally negative.

Of the 28 economic, social, and political trends, 5 were positive, 18 were negative, and 5 were mixed. The 8 economic indicators were equally divided between mixed and negative. The 14 social indicators reflected 4 positive trends (improvements in education, life expectancy, and infant mortality, and a drop in drug use); 9 of the remaining 10 trends were negative. Analysis of correlations among the socioeconomic trends showed significant Pearson coefficients between the consumer price index and the unemployment rate, with a two-year time lag ($r = +.73$), and between the unemployment rate and the poverty rate, with no time lag ($r = +.61$).[34]

Between 1950 and 1992, the U.S. gross domestic product (GDP) per capita increased by 107 percent (in constant 1982 dollars). An alternative indicator of economic progress has been developed by Clifford Cobb; his measure, the genuine progress indicator (GPI), corrects the per capita GDP for a series of social and ecological factors so as to differentiate between the costs and benefits of economic activity. The GPI accounts for factors such as unemployment, income distribution, pollution, and natural resource depletion. Whereas per capita GDP more than doubled between 1950 and 1992, Cobb's per capita GPI showed a 26-percent *decline* for the same period.[35]

Fordham University's Institute for Innovation in Social Policy has published the *1994 Index of Social Health,* a composite measure of sixteen social problems affecting children, youth, adults, the elderly, and all ages. The individual components of the index are calculated as a deviation from the best-ever performance in each category, which has a value of 100. The index has been compiled yearly since 1970, when it had a value of 74. It reached a high of 77 in 1973, declined 47 percent to a low of 39 in 1991, and rose slightly to 41 in 1992. Among the trends noted in the latest report are a worsening of child abuse nearly every year since the mid 1970s, a decline in average weekly earnings each year since 1987, and nearly a 50-percent improvement in the poverty rate among the elderly since 1970.[36] The decline in the Fordham study's composite index after 1970 is consistent with the predominance of negative social trends in this author's U.S. study summarized above.

Environmental Trends in Industrial Nations

The National Center for Economic Alternatives used a composite index to measure recent environmental trends in nine industrial nations. The index combines 21 broadly accepted indicators covering six categories: air pollutants (6 indicators), water quality and use (6 indicators), wetlands and woodlands (2 indicators), industrial and agricultural chemicals (3 indicators), municipal and nuclear waste (2 indicators), and passenger car traffic and energy consumption (2 indicators). The study calculated the percentage change in each indicator between 1970 and 1990, computed the average change within each of the six categories, and then combined the six averages into a composite average change for the period. The results show an overall decline in the composite environmental index for all nine nations. The decline ranged between 11 and 14 percent for the Netherlands, Denmark, and the United Kingdom; between 16 and 22 percent for Sweden, West Germany, Japan, and the United States; and between 38 and 41 percent for Canada and France. The drop in Canada's index stems in part from large increases in fertilizer use and industrial chemical production; the drop in the French index was partly due to increased nuclear waste generation and pesticide use.

For seven of the nine nations, negative trends outnumbered positive trends; for Canada and the United Kingdom, twice as many trends were negative (14) as positive (7). Only the Netherlands and Japan showed more positive trends (11) than negative (10). And for all nine nations together, the negative trends for the 21 indicators outnumbered the positive by 105 to 82. The trends were largely positive for air pollutants, slightly positive for water quality, mixed for wetlands and woodlands, and predominately negative for chemicals, waste, automobile traffic, and energy use. The report notes that each nation achieved some improvements, including reductions in sulfur dioxide emissions and motor vehicle emissions. The study concludes that in all nine nations, agriculture, chemical manufacture, transportation, and waste generation are the pollution sources most difficult to control; the report raises doubts about the ability of industrial nations to reverse negative environmental trends.[37]

Sustainability Indexes for Industrial Nations

To examine sustainability at the national level, the author selected ten industrial nations ranging in population size from Switzerland to the United States. Indicators were identified for most of the twelve dimensions of sustainability listed earlier. For natural resources and the environment, 25 indicators were chosen; and for the economic, social, cultural, and political dimensions, 33 indicators were selected. Of the 25 environmental indicators, 15 measure pressure or stress (such as pollutant emissions), five measure state or impact (such as pollutant concentration), and five measure response (such as recycling rates).

For each indicator, data for the most recent year available was converted to a value on a scale of 0 to 100, with 0 the least sustainable (most environmentally or socioeconomically harmful) value among all industrial nations, and 100 the most sustainable (least harmful) value.[38] The 25 scaled environmental measures were grouped in the 15 subindex categories shown in Table 20.2 below. Then a composite *environmental sustainability index* (ESI) was computed by weighting

Table 20.2

Sustainability Indexes for Ten Industrial Nations

	USA	JAP	GER	ITA	UK	FRN	CAN	NE	SW	SWZ
Population, millions	251	124	63.2	57.7	57.4	56.4	26.6	14.9	8.5	6.7
Environmental Sustainability Subindexes										
Energy (2)	29	69	41	59	44	51	26	39	78	93
Gasoline price (1)	0	54	52	100	52	71	24	70	88	52
Aluminum consumption (1)	0	0	0	42	71	50	4	42	21	37
Materials recycling (3)	45	77	76	66	37	63	27	96	66	83
Municipal solid waste (1)	0	74	86	89	80	89	38	63	86	70
Hazardous waste (1)	62	98	73	91	77	96	100	42	99	96
Greenhouse gas emissions (1)	49	81	80	96	85	97	59	89	98	100
Acidification (3)	20	67	55	73	58	63	10	69	54	86
Common air pollutants (1)	22	—	76	100	65	92	0	94	71	97
Ozone-depleting emissions (1)	53	0	70	72	70	72	75	79	89	100
Fresh water (2)	39	71	75	64	80	76	61	71	94	91
Food and agriculture (2)	77	15	50	4	36	27	100	18	60	31
Forests (2)	23	57	28	38	50	25	47	17	59	20
Habitat protection (1)	38	22	100	14	69	31	17	34	13	9
Wildlife (3)	52	45	76	72	57	60	92	77	78	66

Environmental Sustainability Index (25)	34	52	63	65	62	64	45	60	70	69
	USA	JAP	GER	ITA	UK	FRN	CAN	NE	SW	SWZ
Socioeconomic Sustainability Subindexes										
Transportation (4)	16	51	25	27	20	23	43	17	37	15
Economy (5)	72	88	73	35	52	59	67	71	71	76
Socioeconomic equity (3)	38	58	53	58	52	53	48	75	91	34
Human development (3)	91	100	60	27	77	85	99	84	93	94
Housing (1)	82	44	87	21	—	36	100	—	90	95
Telephones (1)	88	57	61	51	46	64	86	70	89	100
Newspapers and radios (2)	66	64	46	16	53	28	34	38	59	51
Security (2)	34	94	69	65	71	62	83	85	89	84
Population (4)	44	42	86	80	68	64	44	71	73	66
Health (2)	54	100	45	51	52	64	72	74	81	77
Education (1)	100	72	78	11	87	87	96	70	78	78
Political participation (3)	42	48	68	83	42	40	61	91	95	100
Government stability and effectiveness (2)	50	88	86	53	30	52	72	77	98	100
Socioeconomic Sustainability Index (33)	60	70	64	39	54	55	70	69	80	75

Table 20.3

Environmental Sustainability Index		Socioeconomic Sustainability Index	
1. Sweden	70.3	1. Sweden	80.3
2. Switzerland	68.7	2. Switzerland	74.6
3. Italy	65.3	3. Japan	69.7
4. France	64.2	4. Canada	69.6
5. West Germany	62.5	5. Netherlands	68.6
6. United Kingdom	62.2	6. West Germany	64.4
7. Netherlands	60.0	7. United States	59.8
8. Japan	52.1	8. France	55.2
9. Canada	45.3	9. United Kingdom	54.2
10. United States	33.9	10. Italy	39.5

each subindex equally and calculating the average value of the 15 subindexes.[39] Similarly, the 33 scaled socioeconomic measures were grouped in the 13 subindex categories in Table 20.2, and a composite *socioeconomic sustainability index* (SSI) was computed as the average of the 13 indicators.[40] In Table 20.2, the number in parentheses after each subindex denote the number of indicators it includes.

Values for the individual subindexes and the two composite indexes are given above for the ten nations, in order of decreasing population size: United States (USA), Japan (JAP), West Germany (GER), Italy (ITA), United Kingdom (UK), France (FRN), Canada (CAN), the Netherlands (NE), Sweden (SW), and Switzerland (SWZ). The numbers provide environmental and socioeconomic profiles for each nation.[41] For example, the U.S. environmental profile suggests that compared to other nations, U.S. gasoline prices, aluminum consumption, and solid waste generation are relatively unsustainable; while the U.S. socioeconomic profile shows that the nation is relatively sustainable in terms of education and human development.

The EDI and SSI ratings are listed in descending order in Table 20.3. Sweden and Switzerland rank first and second, respectively, on both the environmental sustainability index and the socioeconomic sustainability index. Japan, Canada, and especially the United States have relatively low ESI ratings; their scores are well below those for the West European nations.

Correlations among the Indicators

The relationships between the ESI, the SSI, and some of the subindexes in Table 20.2 were analyzed using plots and the Pearson product-moment correlation coefficient r.

ESI and population size show a strong negative correlation ($r = -.78$): the higher a nation's ESI, the smaller its population. (But Canada falls well below the curve, having both a low ESI and a relatively small population.)

ESI and the population index have a strong positive correlation ($r = +.79$): the higher the ESI, the higher the population index. (A high population index results from a low population growth rate, low birthrate, and high availability and use of birth control.) The seven West European nations are high on both indexes, while the United States, Canada, and Japan are relatively low on both.

ESI and SSI exhibit virtually no correlation for the ten nations as a group ($r = +.03$). However, Sweden and Switzerland have the highest values for both the ESI and SSI.

ESI and the economic index show very little correlation for the seven European nations, but a weak negative relation for all ten countries ($r = -.26$). Japan, with the highest economic index, has a relatively low ESI. (The economic index includes per capita gross domestic product, unemployment rate, inflation rate, budgetary balance, and trade balance.)

ESI and per capita gross domestic product exhibit a moderately strong negative correlation for all nations except Switzerland: ESI drops as per capita GDP rises. (For the ten nations together, $r = -.50$.) Switzerland has the second highest values for both, consistent with the fact that much of the country's income comes from financial and other environmentally benign activity.

ESI and voter turnout have a strong positive correlation ($r = +.92$): the higher the ESI, the greater the percentage of eligible voters that vote in national elections. (Voter turnout is one of three components of the political participation index.)

SSI and population size exhibit a moderate negative relation for the seven West European nations: SSI decreases as population size rises. (For the ten nations together, $r = -.26$.)

The energy index shows a moderate positive correlation with gasoline price ($r = +.52$), and a stronger positive correlation with the greenhouse gas emission index ($r = +.73$). (The energy index includes per capita energy use and percent of energy from renewable sources.)

In summary, for the group of ten nations examined, countries with a high environmental sustainability index tend to have small populations, low population growth rates and effective family planning programs, a relatively low gross domestic product per person, and high voter turnout. Although there may be serious methodological problems involved in comparing large, heterogeneous industrial nations with small ones,[42] the data suggest that populous industrial nations with high economic output may be less ecologically sustainable than industrial nations with smaller populations and smaller economies. The United States and Japan, with large populations and relatively low ESIs, have major impacts on the global environment;

for example, the United States accounts for 18 percent of global greenhouse gas emissions, and Japan is by far the world's largest importer of wood.[43]

Other National Surveys

A number of other studies have assessed the quality of life and the economic and social status of nations; several of these surveys are summarized below.

Trends in World Social Development: The Social Progress of Nations. The study used economic, social, and political indicators to measure the ability of 124 nations to provide for their citizens. Among the factors included in the study's index of progress were economic growth, health and welfare provisions, literacy, education, political participation and stability, women's rights, and geographic desirability. Based on 1983 data, the five nations rated best were (in order) Denmark, Italy, West Germany, Austria, and Sweden; those rated worst were Angola, Ethiopia, Chad, Guinea, and Afghanistan. Of the 124 nations included in the study, the United States ranked twenty-seventh.[44]

The International Human Suffering Index. In 1992 the Population Crisis Committee compiled an index of human suffering for 141 countries, based on ten measures of human welfare: life expectancy, daily calorie supply, clean drinking water, infant immunization, secondary school enrollment, GNP per capita, rate of inflation, communications technology, political freedom, and civil rights. Each of the ten measures was ranked from 0 (best) to 10 (most distressful); the index is the sum of the ten measures. The five countries with the best living conditions were (in descending order) Denmark, the Netherlands, Belgium, Switzerland, and Canada; those with the worst conditions were Mozambique, Somalia, Afghanistan, Haiti, and Sudan. The United States ranked eighth.[45] The data show a positive correlation between the suffering index and annual population increase: the 70 countries with the highest index values had an average growth rate more than twice that of the 71 nations with the lowest suffering index values.

World Military and Social Expenditures 1993. The study ranked 140 nations based on their relative economic and social standings on ten indicators covering income, education, and health. Based on 1990 data, the five top-rated nations were Sweden, Iceland, Denmark, Norway, and Switzerland; the lowest-rated nations were Ethiopia, Mozambique, Somalia, Afghanistan, and Chad. The United States ranked ninth.[46]

Human Development Report 1994. Produced by the United Nations Development Programme, the study computed a human development index for each of 173 countries; the index is based on the average of separate ratings for life expectancy, educational attainment, and per capita gross domestic product. The highest-ranked countries were Canada, Switzerland, Japan, Sweden, and Norway; the lowest-ranked countries were Guinea, Burkina Faso, Afghanistan, Sierra Leone, and Niger. The United States ranked eighth.[47]

In spite of the different indicators employed in these four surveys, the results for the highest- and lowest-ranked nations show similarities; all but two of the top-rated nations are West European, and all but two countries with the lowest ranks are in Africa. Sweden and Switzerland, which had the highest two scores for the author's ESI and SSI indexes, ranked among the top five nations in two of the surveys summarized above, and among the top seventeen in the other two surveys.

Global Indicators

As noted earlier, many global environmental, economic, and social trends appear not to be sustainable over the long run. The author examined 66 global environmental and socioeconomic trends since 1950. Each trend was characterized as positive (movement generally toward sustainability), negative (movement generally away from sustainability), or mixed (having both positive and negative aspects).[48]

Of the 43 natural resource and environmental trends analyzed, 25 (58 percent) appear to be negative (worsening), 12 (28 percent) are generally positive (improving), and 7 have both positive and negative elements. Of the 23 socioeconomic trends, 10 (43 percent) appear to be negative, 8 (35 percent) seem to be positive, and 5 have positive and negative aspects. The trends are predominately negative for resource use, the atmosphere, water, agriculture, forests, biological diversity, transportation, refugees, socioeconomic equity, and military conflicts. Positive trends are apparent for health, education, energy use, the population growth rate, military spending, and nuclear weapon stocks. On balance, the indicators show an overall trend away from sustainability. Many negative trends show no sign of slowing, and several have accelerated, including deforestation, soil erosion, and loss of plant and animal species.

The data summarized in this chapter raise serious questions about the long-term ecological and societal sustainability of large industrial nations, and of the planet as a whole. A more thorough analysis of environmental and societal trends might help resolve the continuing debate between the optimists who see a bright future for human civilization and the pessimists who fear serious ecological and social decline.[49]

Analysis and Discussion

Based on the studies reviewed in this chapter, there appears to be general consensus that resource use, the natural environment, and economic, social, cultural, and political factors are all significant dimensions of the quality of life and of sustainability. It seems useful to distinguish between the ecological-environmental components of sustainability and the socioeconomic elements, although there is clearly overlap and interdependence between the two areas. For example, human population has been treated here as a socioeconomic factor, but people are obviously a dominant factor in the ecological dimension, and a strong case can be made for including population in both the environmental and socioeconomic dimensions. Most of the studies described here include both environmental and socioeconomic indicators; they used several methods to rate communities, states, and nations with regard to these dimensions.

Size, Growth Rate, and Quality of Life

Results from a number of the studies suggest that large-scale or rapidly growing organizations and societies—including corporations, communities, and nations— tend to rate lower on quality of life indicators and may be less sustainable over the long run than smaller, slower growing entities.[50] The Zero Population Growth survey shows that large urban areas are more stressful than smaller communities, and the Population Crisis Committee's study of the world's one hundred largest cities reveals a positive correlation between rapid population growth and low living standards.

The Institute for Southern Studies' *Green Index* shows that U.S. states with large populations on average have lower environmental ratings than less populous states, and the studies by the Council on Economic Priorities indicate that large corporations generally have poorer environmental records than smaller firms.

At the national level, PCC's *Human Suffering Index* shows a clear relation between rapid population growth and high levels of suffering, and the author's study of ten industrial nations demonstrates a correlation between large populations and low environmental ratings.

Integrative Indicators

While each of the indicators used in these projects probably assesses some aspect of sustainability, some indicators are more relevant than others, and there may be better single measures of sustainability than any of those used in the programs reviewed. One such indicator might be a measure of the extent to which a community or nation addresses its ecological and socioeconomic problems in an integrated way, and designs measures that alleviate several problems at once.[51] For example, at the community level, the imperatives of supplying food and energy, dealing with municipal waste, and providing jobs can be addressed in an integrated manner. Thus, municipal sewage can be processed to produce biogas fuel and protein to feed fish, thus providing food and employment.[52] As another example, the city of Curitiba in Brazil seeks to meet the demands of a rapidly growing population through integrated approaches to transportation, waste management, and urban design. High-density housing developments are located along transport lines, bags of garbage are traded for food and transport vouchers, and the city is reported to be largely self-sufficient.[53] An outstanding example of an integrated industrial ecosystem is in Kalundborg, Denmark, where a number of enterprises exchange a variety of materials, including process steam, water, fertilizer, chemicals, waste products, and other materials.[54]

This important aspect of sustainability might be reflected in an indicator that assesses to what extent a community or nation practices integrated resource management, perhaps measured by estimating the degree of communication between people and offices responsible for diverse areas such as energy, transportation, waste management, and economic development; or by estimating the degree of interaction between different levels of government, or between the public and private sector.

An important related element of sustainability is the efficiency with which a jurisdiction manages resources, such as energy and water, and provides services, such as public transportation and waste management. At the local level, efficiency can be measured as the cost per person for delivery of resources and services, or as the number of government employees relative to total population. Integrated and efficient resource management and service delivery can improve environmental quality, conserve resources, and save money. At the national level, resource efficiency can be gauged by the ratio of inputs to outputs, that is, the weight or volume of raw materials used relative to gross national product.[55]

A final aspect of sustainability that could be reflected in indicators is the extent to which the prices of goods and services include estimates of the full environmental and social costs of their production, provision, use, reuse, and disposal. Subsidies for commodities such as energy, water, and agriculture encourage waste and inefficient use; whereas full-cost pricing can promote efficiency and lead to more sustainable resource use. Such an indicator could measure the difference between the price paid directly by the user and the estimated total environmental and social costs, including all indirect, external, or hidden costs.[56] Increased prices and taxes for goods and services to cover these costs could be offset by lower taxes on income, savings, and other productive activities.[57]

Indicators and Policy Making

Perhaps the ultimate tests of an indicator are whether its use increases public awareness of the condition it is designed to measure, and whether it contributes to improvement. Indicators such as rates of unemployment and crime are widely used in evaluating public policy; policy-relevant indicators and targets that measure other dimensions of sustainability could be valuable policy-making tools.[58]

Conclusion: Curbing the Impacts of Population, Resource Use, Technology, and Poverty

This chapter began with the estimate that the environmental impact of human activity increased roughly sixfold between 1950 and 1990, based on the formula that impact is the product of population, resource use, and technology ($I=PRT$). It was noted that the Earth's carrying capacity is a function of these three factors, and that human activity is already altering the Earth's basic life-support systems. Given the current global trends of increasing population, resource use, and environmental degradation summarized earlier, it seems clear that unless these trends are reversed, a serious deterioration in the quality of life may be inevitable in the foreseeable future.

To reduce environmental impacts, all three factors in the $I = PRT$ equation must be addressed. A vigorous family planning effort worldwide could curb population growth. Growth in resource use could be slowed if prices rose to include the full costs of resources. Environmental damage from resource use could be sharply reduced through technological changes, such as improved information systems that could greatly increase the efficiency of resource use.[59] Education could increase ecological and societal literacy, which could facilitate all three of these changes.[60] And finally, by alleviating poverty and providing the poor with access to education and employment, we could help slow population growth, protect natural resources presently being degraded in developing countries, and make resource-efficient technologies affordable for the poor. If combined with adequate public support, political commitment, and resources, programs employing environmental and socioeconomic indicators and targets could help reverse ecological degradation, reduce poverty, and move communities and societies toward a sustainable future.

Notes

1. For a similar formula, see Paul R. Ehrlich and Ann H. Ehrlich, *Healing the Planet: Strategies for Resolving the Environmental Crisis* (Reading, MA: Addison-Wesley, 1991), 7.

2. Cynthia P. Green, "The Environment and Population Growth: Decade for Action," *Population Reports*, series M, no. 10 (May 1992): 23.

3. B. L. Turner, et al., eds., *The Earth as Transformed by Human Action: Global and Regional Changes in the Biosphere over the Past 300 Years* (Cambridge and New York: Cambridge University Press, 1990).

4. Peter Vitousek, et al., "Human Appropriation of the Products of Photosynthesis," *Bioscience* 36, no. 6 (June 1986): 368–73.

5. See Mostafa K. Tolba, et al., *The World Environment 1972–1992* (London and New York: Chapman & Hall, 1992); Lester R. Brown, et al., *Vital Signs 1994: The Trends that Are Shaping Our Future* (New York: W. W. Norton, 1994); World Resources Institute, *World Resources 1994–95* (New York: Oxford University Press, 1994); Donella H. Meadows, et al., *Beyond the Limits: Confronting Global Collapse, Envisioning a Sustain-*

able Future (Post Mills, VT: Chelsea Green, 1992); and Lester R. Brown, et al., *State of the World 1993* (New York: Norton, 1993), 5–11.

6. Thomas F. Homer-Dixon, "On the Threshold: Environmental Changes as Causes of Acute Conflict," *International Security* 16, no. 2 (Fall 1991): 100–101. On the irreversibility of changes such as species loss, toxic contamination of soil and groundwater, and the buildup of greenhouse gases in the atmosphere, see Robert U. Ayres, "Cowboys, Cornucopians and Long-run Sustainability," *Ecological Economics* 8, no. 3 (December 1993).

7. On the increasing frequency of wars and war-related deaths, see Ruth L. Sivard, *World Military and Social Expenditures 1993* (Washington, DC: World Priorities, 1993), 20–21. On the growing potential for violent conflicts, see Thomas F. Homer-Dixon, et al., "Environmental Change and Violent Conflict," *Scientific American*, February 1993, 38–45; Robert D. Kaplan, "The Coming Anarchy," *The Atlantic Monthly* 273, no. 2 (February 1993); Matthew Connelly and Paul Kennedy, "Must It Be the Rest against the West?" *The Atlantic Monthly* 274, no. 6 (December 1994); and Samuel P. Huntington, "The Clash of Civilizations?" *Foreign Affairs* 72, no. 3 (Summer 1993).

8. See Walter H. Corson, "Changing Course: An Outline of Strategies for a Sustainable Future," *Futures* 26, no. 2 (March 1994): 207.

9. For a complete list of these indicators and data sources, see ibid, 213–15. The natural resources and environment dimension includes seventeen groups of indicators covering energy and minerals, solid and hazardous waste, atmosphere and climate, air pollution and acidification, ozone layer depletion, noise, freshwater quality and quantity, food and agriculture, land and soil, forests, other natural habitats, wildlife, and marine resources. The social environment dimension includes four groups of indicators covering housing, utilities, security, and human development.

10. On how urban settlements appropriate resources from surrounding regions and deplete their carrying capacity, see Richard Stren, et al., eds., *Sustainable Cities: Urbanization and the Environment in International Perspective* (Boulder: Westview Press, 1992), 11–12. See also Mathis Wackernagel, *How Big Is Our Ecological Footprint? Using the Concept of Appropriated Carrying Capacity for Measuring Sustainability* (Vancouver: Task Force on Planning Healthy and Sustainable Communities, University of British Columbia, 1993).

11. Albert Adriaanse, *Environmental Policy Performance Indicators* (The Hague: Dutch Ministry of Housing, Physical Planning and Environment, 1993), 7–13. On defining, classifying, and selecting indicators, see J. A. Bakkes, et al., *An Overview of Environmental Indicators: State of the Art and Perspectives* (Nairobi: United Nations Development Programme, June 1994), 1–7; Rob Swart and Jan Bakkes, eds., *Scanning the Global Environment: A Framework and Methodology for UNEP's Reporting Functions* (Nairobi: United Nations Environment Programme, August 1994), 7–13; and World Bank, *Monitoring Environmental Progress,* 35–37.

12. See John C. O'Connor, *Toward Environmentally Sustainable Development: Measuring Progress,* (Washington, DC: World Bank, draft of 16 January 1994), 13. A recent World Bank report on indicators notes a general movement toward aggregated measures for specific issues but cautions against "striving for a 'magic number' that pretends to capture the complexity of sustainable development:" World Bank, *Monitoring Environmental Progress,* 1.

13. Walter H. Corson, *Defining Progress: An Inventory of Programs Using Goals and Indicators to Define and Measure Quality of Life, Progress, and Sustainability at the Local and State Level* (Washington, DC: Global Tomorrow Coalition, 1995).

14. *The Sustainable Seattle 1993 Indicators of Sustainable Community: A Report on Long-Term Trends in Our Community* (Seattle, WA: Sustainable Seattle, November 1993).

15. *Community Indicators: A Report Card for Greenville County* (Greenville, SC: Community Planning Council of Greenville County, August 1993).

16. *The Quality of Life in Pasadena: An Index for the 90s and Beyond* (Pasadena: Pasadena Health Department, 1992).

17. *Life in Jacksonville: Quality Indicators for Progress* (Jacksonville, FL: Jacksonville Community Council, November 1993). In the performance ratings for Jacksonville and Pasadena, a negative percentage resulted from a current indicator value more than twice as high as the target value.

18. Population Crisis Committee, *Cities: Life in the World's 100 Largest Metropolitan Areas* (Washington, DC, 1990).

19. Zero Population Growth, *Urban Stress Test* (Washington, DC: Z.P.G., 1988). For additional ratings of U.S. communities using a variety of environmental and social indicators, see Zero Population Growth, "Children's Stress Index," *The ZPG Reporter*, May 1993; and the Green Cities Index and the Green Metro Index compiled by the World Resources Institute in the 1992 and 1994 editions of *The Information Please Environmental Almanac* (Boston: Houghton Mifflin). See also John Tepper Marlin, *The Livable Cities Almanac* (New York: Harper Collins, 1992); David Savageau and Richard Boyer, *Places Rated Almanac*, 2d ed. (New York: Prentice Hall, 1993); and *America's Top Rated Cities: A Statistical Handbook*, 5 vols. (Boca Raton, FL: Universal Reference Publications, 1993).

20. *Minnesota Milestones: A Report Card for the Future* (St. Paul, MN: Minnesota Planning, December 1992).

21. *Oregon Benchmarks: Standards for Measuring Statewide Progress and Government Performance*, report to the 1993 legislature (Salem, OR: Oregon Progress Board, December 1992).

22. In the performance ratings, a negative percentage resulted from a current indicator value more than twice as high as the target value.

23. Daniel D. Chiras, *Sustainable Development in Colorado: A Background Report on Indicators, Trends, Definitions, and Recommendations* (Evergreen, CO: Sustainable Futures Society, June 1994).

24. Bob Hall and Mary Lee Kerr, *1991–1992 Green Index: A State-by-State Guide to the Nation's Environmental Health* (Washington, DC: Island Press, 1991).

25. Bob Hall and Mary Lee Kerr, "Gold and Green," *Southern Exposure*, Fall 1994.

26. World Resources Institute, *The 1994 Information Please Environmental Almanac* (Boston: Houghton Mifflin, 1994).

27. Council on Economic Priorities, *The Better World Investment Guide* (New York: Prentice Hall, 1991).

28. Council on Economic Priorities, *Shopping for a Better World 1992* (New York: Council on Economic Priorities, 1991).

29. Information on national targets is from Julie Hill, *National Environmental Plans: A Comparative Survey of the National Plans of Canada, France, the Netherlands, Norway, and the UK* (London: Green Alliance, January 1992). Data on emissions, waste generation, and recycling is from *OECD Environmental Data Compendium 1993* (Paris: Organization for Economic Cooperation and Development, 1993).

30. Hill, *National Environmental Plans*.

31. Adriaanse, *Environmental Policy Performance Indicators*.

32. *Interim Report of the Interagency Working Group on Sustainable Development Indicators* (Washington, DC, 18 July 1994). See also Phillip A. Greenberg, *Toward a U.S. Green Plan: Thinking About a U.S. Strategy for Sustainable Development* (San Francisco: Resource Renewal Institute, October 1993).

33. Adriaanse, *Environmental Performance Indicators*; and Allen Hammond, et al., *Environmental Indicators: A Systematic Approach to Measuring and Reporting on Environmental Performance in the Context of Sustainable Development* (Washington, DC:

World Resources Institute, 1995). The composite pollution index was constructed by weighting each of the 6 indicators based on the difference between its current value and the long-term target for sustainability.

34. Walter H. Corson, "State of the Nation: Trends That Are Shaping America's Future," unpublished manuscript, December 1994.

35. Clifford Cobb and Ted Halstead, *The Genuine Progress Indicator* (San Francisco: Redefining Progress, August 1994). The GPI increased by 32 percent between 1950 and 1969 but then declined by 43 percent between 1969 and 1992. For an earlier version of the GPI, see Clifford W. Cobb and John B. Cobb, Jr., *The Green National Product: A Proposed Index of Sustainable Economic Welfare* (Lanham, MD: University Press of America, 1994).

36. Fordham Institute for Innovation in Social Policy, *1994 Index of Social Health: Monitoring the Social Well-Being of the Nation* (Tarrytown, NY, 1994). The 16 measures include infant mortality, child abuse, children and elderly in poverty, teen suicide, drug abuse, high school dropouts, average weekly earnings, unemployment, health insurance coverage, highway deaths due to alcoholism, homicides, food stamp coverage, housing, and the gap between rich and poor.

37. National Center for Economic Alternatives, *Index of Environmental Trends: An Assessment of 21 Key Environmental Indicators in 9 Industrialized Countries over the Past Two Decades* (Washington, DC: National Center for Economic Alternatives, April 1995).

38. An individual "subindex" for each indicator was computed by calculating its value as a percentage of the value for the most sustainable nation. In many cases, two or more subindexes were averaged to produce a composite subindex. For example, the freshwater subindex for the United States is a composite of two numbers: (1) water withdrawals in cubic meters per person, and (2) withdrawals as a percentage of available freshwater resources. For 1, the United States had the highest value (least sustainable use) among industrial nations, 2,167 cubic meters per person, so the U.S. index is 0. For 2, the highest value (least sustainable) was 88 percent (for Israel), the lowest value (most sustainable) was 0 percent (for Norway), and the U.S. value was 19 percent; the U.S. index is [100 × (88 − 19)] 88 = 78. The composite freshwater index for the United States is the average of 1 and 2: (0 + 78)—2 = 39.

39. The environmental sustainability index includes the following 25 measures, each converted to a value on a scale of 0 to 100 (see note 38) and then weighted equally: energy use (requirements per person, percent from renewable sources); gasoline price; aluminum consumption; materials recycling (aluminum, glass, paper); municipal solid waste; hazardous waste; greenhouse gas emissions per person; acidification (sulfur and nitrogen emissions per person, acidity of rainfall); common air pollutant emissions per person; ozone-depleting emissions per person; fresh water (withdrawals per person and as a percent of water resources); food and agriculture (pesticide use, cereal exports per person); forests (percent of land in forest and woodland, percent change in forest and woodland); percent of land area protected; and wildlife (percent of threatened mammal species, bird species, and plant taxa). As an alternative to combining all 25 environmental measures in a single composite index, they could be grouped in several subindexes, e.g., for energy and raw materials, air quality, water quality, agriculture and forests, and habitats and wildlife.

If valid criteria could be established, individual components of a composite index could be given different weights in proportion to their importance in the overall index. For example, environmental factors that harm the Earth's basic life-support systems (such as groundwater pollution), that are changing rapidly (such as rapid deforestation) or that are irreversible (such as species loss) could be weighted more than less harmful factors or factors undergoing slow or reversible changes. In the absence of such valid criteria, most studies (such as the United Nations Development Programme's *Human Development Report*) give equal weight to the components of a composite index.

40. The socioeconomic sustainability index includes the following 33 measures, each converted to a value on a scale of 0 to 100 and then weighted equally: transportation (passenger cars per 1,000 people, ratio of public to private vehicle travel, ratio of passenger travel by rail to travel by air, and ratio of freight moved by rail to freight moved by air); economy (gross domestic product [GDP] per person, unemployment rate, inflation rate, budget deficit or surplus as a percent of GDP, and trade deficit or surplus as a percent of GDP); equity (income inequality, parliament seats held by women, and years of schooling for females as percent of males); human development (life expectancy, education, and income per person); housing (average number of persons per room); utilities and communication (telephones per 1,000 people); culture and communication (newspaper circulation and radios per 1,000 people); security (homicides per 100,000 people and military spending as a percent of spending for education and health); population (rate of increase, birthrate, access to birth control, and percent of married couples practicing contraception); health (life expectancy and infant death rate); education (schooling index); political participation (percent voting in national elections, political freedom index, and civil rights index); and government stability and effectiveness (communal violence and government effectiveness). As an alternative to combining all 33 socioeconomic measures into one composite index, they could be grouped in several subindexes, e.g., economy and transportation; equity; human development, education, and health; population; housing; communication; and politics and government.

This compilation of composite national indexes is a preliminary first step in index construction; no effort was made to assess the quality of the original data, or to group individual indicators into the pressure, state, and response categories. For a discussion of data quality, see O'Connor, *Toward Environmentally Sustainable Development,* 12–16.

41. For examples of environmental quality profiles, see Bakkes, et al., *Overview of Environmental Indicators,* 39–40. Many studies have developed indexes to compare the performance of a nation (or other jurisdiction) on a given criterion (a) to that nation's performance at another time, or (b) to a different nation's performance at some point in time. Many studies have also combined such individual indexes into composite indexes, usually giving equal weight to the individual subindexes by adding or averaging the individual subindex values. For example, the United Nations Development Programme's Human Development Index for nations combines three indicators, each measured in different units—literacy, life expectancy, and income per person—by setting a minimum and a maximum for each indicator dimension and then calculating where each nation stands in relation to these scales, expressed as a value between 0 and 1; the scores for the three dimensions are then averaged into an overall index. For details, see the United Nations Development Programme, *Human Development Index 1994* (New York: Oxford University Press, 1994), 90–92. For lists of environmental and socioeconomic indicators, and for examples of composite indexes and problems associated with their use, see Bakkes, et al., *Overview of Environmental Indicators,* 37–44, 55–70; and O'Connor, *Towards Sustainable Development,* 7–8, 12–13.

Most of the data in Table 20.1 are for 1990 through 1992. Data sources include World Resources Institute, *World Resources 1992–93* (New York: Oxford University Press, 1992); United Nations Environment Programme, *Environmental Data Report 1991–92* (Cambridge, MA: Basil Blackwell, 1991); Organization for Economic Cooperation and Development, *Environmental Data Compendium 1993* (Paris: OECD, 1993); United Nations Development Programme, *Human Development Report 1993* (New York: Oxford University Press, 1993); Lester R. Brown, et al., *Vital Signs 1993* (New York: W. W.

Norton, 1993); Sivard, *World Military and Social Expenditures 1993;* Population Crisis Committee, *World Access to Birth Control* (Washington, DC: Population Crisis Committee, 1990); Population Crisis Committee, *Population Pressures: Threat to Democracy* (Washington, DC: Population Crisis Committee, 1990); Population Crisis Committee, *The International Human Suffering Index* (Washington, DC: Population Reference Bureau, 1992); Population Reference Bureau, *1993 World Population Data Sheet* (Washington, DC: Population Reference Bureau, 1993); and Andrew Shapiro, *We're Number One: Where America Stands and Falls in the New World Order* (New York: Vintage Books, 1992).

42. A recent World Bank report notes that "invidious comparisons are almost unavoidable when large, ecologically heterogeneous nations are reported alongside small, rather homogeneous ones": World Bank, *Monitoring Environmental Progress,* v.

43. WRI, *World Resources 1992–93,* 208, 289.

44. Richard J. Estes, *Trends in World Social Development: The Social Progress of Nations, 1970–1987* (New York: Praeger, 1988).

45. Population Crisis Committee, *International Human Suffering Index.*

46. Sivard, *World Military and Social Expenditures 1993.*

47. UNDP, *Human Development Report 1994.*

48. Details are given in the author's working paper, "Global Sustainability: World Environmental and Social Trends, 1950–1992."

49. See Norman Myers and Julian Simon, *Scarcity or Abundance? A Debate on the Environment* (New York: W. W. Norton, 1994). For pessimistic views, see Ayres, "Cowboys, Cornucopians and Long-run Sustainability;" Lindsey Grant, *The Cornucopian Fallacies* (Washington, DC: Environmental Fund, 1982); and "World's Leading Scientists Issue Urgent Warning to Humanity," Union of Concerned Scientists press release, 18 November 1992. For optimistic views, see Ronald Bailey, ed., *The True State of the Planet* (New York; Free Press, 1995); and Gregg Easterbrook, *A Moment on The Earth* (New York: Viking, 1995). Easterbrook argues that most environmental changes in the West are more positive than commonly understood, and that human degradation of the environment is of a lower order than many other stresses during the earth's long history.

50. On the relation between the size of business firms and their ecological impact, see Paul Hawken, *The Ecology of Commerce: A Declaration of Sustainability* (New York: Harper Collins, 1993), chap. 6.

51. See Brian Burrows, et al., *Into the 21st Century: A Handbook for a Sustainable Future* (Twickenham, England: Adamantine Press, 1991), chaps. 10, 11.

52. See Pliny Fisk and Gail Vittori, *Sustainable Cities as a Part of a Global Ecology* (Austin, TX: Center for Maximum Potential Building Systems, n.d.); and Richard L. Meier, "Ecological Planning and Design: Paths to Sustainable Communities," unpublished manuscript, University of California, Berkeley, March 1993.

53. Marcia D. Lowe, *Shaping Cities: The Environmental and Human Dimensions,* Worldwatch Paper 105 (Washington, DC: Worldwatch Institute, October 1991); Hawken, *The Ecology of Commerce,* 213–14.

54. Robert L. Olson, *Technology for a Sustainable Future* (Alexandria, VA: Institute for Alternative Futures, 1994), 13.

55. For the local level, see John Hart, *Saving Cities, Saving Money* (Sausalito, CA: Resource Renewal Institute, 1992). For the national level, see World Bank, *Monitoring Environmental Progress,* iv, 13–15.

56. For example, in the early 1990s, energy consumers in the United States paid between $400 billion and $500 billion a year in direct energy costs; additional "hidden" costs not paid directly by consumers, in the form of subsidies, health effects, military costs, and other external expenses have been estimated at between $100 billion and $300

billion. See Harold M. Hubbard, "The Real Cost of Energy," *Scientific American* 264, no. 4 (April 1991). David Pimentel has estimated that the total unpriced costs of the U.S. food system may be between $150 billion and $200 billion per year, compared with about $700 billion spent annually on food and fiber products: "Environmental and Social Implications of Waste in the U.S. Agriculture and Food Sectors," *Journal of Agricultural Ethics* (1990): 8.

57. Robert Repetto, et al., *Green Fees: How a Tax Shift Can Work for the Environment and the Economy* (Washington, DC: World Resources Institute, November 1992); Ernst von Weizsaecker and Jochen Jesinghaus, *Ecological Tax Reform* (London and Atlantic Highlands, NJ: Zed Books, 1992).

58. On how publicizing environmental and social trends could help change public policy and individual behavior, see Walter H. Corson, "Priorities for a Sustainable Future: Education, the Media, and Tax Reform," *Journal of Social Issues* (forthcoming); and Corson, "State of the Nation."

59. Olson, *Technology for a Sustainable Future*, 51–54.

60. David W. Orr, *Ecological Literacy: Education and the Transition to a Postmodern World* (Albany: State University of New York Press, 1992); Corson, "Priorities for a Sustainable Future"; Corson, "Changing Course," 211.

About the Editor

Dennis Pirages is professor of government and politics and director of the Harrison Program on the Future Global Agenda at the University of Maryland. Elected as a lifetime fellow of the American Association for the Advancement of Science, he has been working on sustainability questions since the publication of his *The Sustainable Society* in 1977. He is the author or editor of nine other books, including most recently *Global Technopolitics: The International Politics of Technology and Resources* and *Transformations in the Global Political Economy.*

Contributors

Michael A. Alberty is a Ph.D. student in the Department of Government and Politics at the University of Maryland at College Park. He is currently a visiting research fellow at the Center for Advanced Study at the University of Illinois at Urbana–Champaign. His main research interests involve environmental justice issues and natural resource policy. He is coeditor of *Green Planet Blues: Environmental Politics from Stockholm to Rio.*

Gar Alperovitz, political economist and historian, is president of the National Center for Economic Alternatives. He is also senior research scientist at the University of Maryland at College Park's Department of Government and Politics and a fellow of the Institute for Policy Studies. His books include *Rebuilding America* (with Jeff Faux); *Atomic Diplomacy: Hiroshima and Potsdam;* and *The Decision to Use the Atomic Bomb.* He is currently working on a book on theoretical models of alternative political-economic systems "beyond capitalism and socialism." He publishes regularly in academic and popular publications ranging from *The New York Times* and *The Washington Post* to *Technology Review, Foreign Policy, International Security,* and *The Atlantic.*

Janet Welsh Brown is senior fellow at the World Resources Institute, where she does policy research in international environmental politics and U.S. policies toward developing countries. She is co-author of *Global Environmental Politics,* and editor and author of several other books and articles. She is currently a member of a joint U.S.–Chinese team studying the United Nations, and a member of the New World Dialogue on Environment and Development in the Western Hemisphere. A former executive director of the Environmental Defense Fund, she has also served as a consultant on environmental, international, and equity issues; been a professor at Howard University and the University of the District of Columbia; and been a visiting professor at the University of Washington. She is a member of the boards of directors of Higher Education Resources, Inc., and Friends of the Earth–USA.

Peter G. Brown is a professor at the School of Public Affairs at the University of Maryland at College Park. He is interested in the problems of environmental policy formation and philosophy in public policy. Among his most significant publications are *Markets and Morals; Energy and the Future;* and *Food Policy: The Responsibility of the United States in the Life and Death Choices,* both of which he edited.

Ken Conca is assistant professor of government and politics at the University of Maryland at College Park. His research and teaching interests include international environmental politics, North–South politics, the role of social movements in world politics, Latin American politics and society, and the political economy of science and technology. He is coeditor (with Ronnie D. Lipschutz) of *The State and Social Power in Global Environmental Politics* and a coauthor of *The Highest Stakes: The Economic Foundations of the Next Security System.*

Walter H. Corson is a senior associate at the Global Tomorrow Coalition in Washington, DC. He also directs the environmental politics program in the Graduate School of Political Management at George Washington University. His research interests include developing indicators of ecological and societal sustainability and identifying priorities for reversing unsustainable environmental and social trends. His publications include *The Global Ecology*

Handbook and *Changing Course: An Outline of Strategies for a Sustainable Future.* He is a board member of the International Center for Development Policy, the Rachel Carson Council, the World Population Society, and the U.S. Association for the Club of Rome, and a steering committee member of HOLIS: The Society for a Sustainable Future.

Kenneth A. Dahlberg is professor of political science and environmental studies at Western Michigan University. He has been a Fulbright Fellow and is a Fellow of the American Association for the Advancement of Science. In October 1991 he received one of Western Michigan University's Distinguished Faculty Scholar Awards. His publications include *Beyond the Green Revolution,* which won the International Studies Association's Sprout Award in 1981; *Environment and the Global Arena; Natural Resources and People;* and *New Directions for Agriculture and Agricultural Research.* In addition to his work on global change and sustainable agriculture, he has also worked on policies to maintain genetic and biological diversity. His current research is on urban food systems and food policy councils.

Herman E. Daly is senior research scholar at the University of Maryland's School of Public Affairs. From 1988 to 1994 he was senior economist in the Environment Department of the World Bank. Prior to 1988 he was Alumni Professor of Economics at Louisiana State University, where he taught for twenty years. He has served as Ford Foundation Professor at the University of Ceara in Brazil, as a research associate at Yale University, as a visiting fellow at the Australian National University, and as a Senior Fulbright Lecturer in Brazil. He has served on the boards of advisers of numerous environmental organizations and is cofounder and associate editor of the journal *Ecological Economics.* His interest in economic development, population, resources, and environment has resulted in over a hundred articles in professional journals and anthologies, as well as four books, including *Steady-State Economics* and *Economics, Ecology, Ethics.* He is coauthor with John Cobb of *For the Common Good:*

Redirecting the Economy Toward Community, the Environment, and a Sustainable Future.

Anne H. Ehrlich is senior research associate in the Department of Biological Sciences at Stanford University and associate director and policy coordinator of the Center for Conservation Biology at Stanford. Her work has focused on issues surrounding human population, environment, resources, and agriculture, as well as environmental connections to warfare and military activities. Among her most recent and important publications are *The Population Explosion* and *Healing the Planet* (both coauthored with Paul Ehrlich); and *The Stork and the Plow* (coauthored with Paul Ehrlich and Gretchen Daily).

Denis Goulet is O'Neill Professor in Education for Justice, Department of Economics; faculty fellow, Kellogg Institute for International Studies; and faculty fellow, Kroc Institute for International Peace Studies at the University of Notre Dame. He is a pioneer in the interdisciplinary study of development ethics; has conducted field studies in France, Spain, Algeria, Lebanon, Brazil, Guinea-Bissau, Sri Lanka, and Mexico; and has held visiting professorships at universities in the United States, Canada, France, Brazil, and Poland. Goulet's major books include *Development Ethics: A Guide to Theory and Practice; The Cruel Choice; A New Moral Order; The Uncertain Promise: Value Conflicts in Technology Transfer; Mexico: Development Strategies for the Future;* and *Incentives for Development: The Key to Equity.*

Michael T. Klare is professor of peace and world security studies at Hampshire College, and director of the Five College Program in Peace and World Security Studies. He has written widely on U.S. security policy and the international arms trade. His books include *American Arms Supermarket* and *Rogue States and Nuclear Outlaws.* He is also editor or coeditor of *World Security: Challenges for a New Century; Peace and World Security Studies: A Curriculum Guide;* and *Lethal Commerce: The Global Trade in Small Arms and Light Weapons.*

Oluf Langhelle is a research assistant at the Project for an Alternative Future in Oslo, Norway, and a doctoral student at the University of Oslo's Institute of Political Science. He is interested in the concept of sustainable development and the normative and empirical relationship between democracy and sustainable development. His graduate thesis analyzed the relationship between democracy and social justice, with special emphasis on the theories of Robert A. Dahl, Friedrich A. Hayek, and John Rawls. He has published several articles on related topics in Norwegian journals and is currently coediting the book *Sustainable Development: The Conditions of Sustainability and the Goal of Development.*

Michael Marien is founder and editor of *Future Survey,* a journal of abstracts published monthly since 1979 by the World Future Society in Bethesda, Maryland. He is interested in trends, forecasts, and policy proposals regarding a wide range of domestic and global issues, notably the imperative to shape a sustainable society. Among his most significant publications is *World Futures and the United Nations: An Annotated Guide to 250 Recent Books and Reports.*

Rekha Mehra is director of the Program Support and Analysis Division at the International Center for Research on Women, where she conducts research and technical assistance on issues related to women in development, agricultural and economic policy reform, credit, women and AIDS, and the environment and natural resources. Her current work includes a study of recent developments in microfinance and credit for women, and an examination of global trends in women's employment during the past twenty years. Her publications include "Women's Land Rights and Sustainable Development," "Can Structural Adjustment Work for Women Farmers?" and "Women and Agricultural Development."

Lester W. Milbrath is Professor Emeritus of Political Science and Sociology and director of the Research Program in Environment and Society at the State University of New York at Buffalo. He has been teaching and researching the environment and society for some twenty-five years. He is especially interested in the transformation of present-day society to a sustainable one. He is the founding chair of HOLIS: The Society for a Sustainable Future. He has written three books relevant to this topic, all published by the State University of New York Press: *Environmentalists: Vanguard for a New Society; Envisioning a Sustainable Society: Learning Our Way Out;* and *Learning to Think Environmentally.*

Alan S. Miller is executive director of the Center for Global Change at the University of Maryland at College Park. He is a lawyer and policy analyst who has worked on environmental and energy issues for more than twenty years at research institutions in the United States and abroad. He is author or coauthor of several books including *Green Gold: Japan, Germany, the United States and the Race for Environmental Technology* and *Environmental Regulation: Law, Science and Policy.*

William Ophuls is an independent scholar and writer. He is the author of the prize-winning *Ecology and the Politics of Scarcity.* Following a book-length treatment of the themes discussed in this article, he plans to turn his attention to the political meaning of the epistemological revolution of the twentieth century.

Vaclav Smil is professor of geography at the University of Manitoba. His main research interests are in interdisciplinary studies of the environment, energy, population, food, economics, and public policy. Among his recent books are *China's Environmental Crisis; Global Ecology;* and *Energy in World History.* He is presently at work on *Biospheric Cycles* for the Scientific American Library.

Stacy D. VanDeveer is a Ph.D. candidate in government and politics at the University of Maryland at College Park. His research interests include international environmental cooperation and institutions, Central European political and institutional development, and the role of transnational norms in state structure, bureaucratic organization, and policy.

Stephen Viederman is president of the Jesse Smith Noyes Foundation, a mid-size philanthropy that supports organizing and advocacy on the environment and reproductive rights as they intersect with issues of social justice. In addition to his writing on sustainability, he has also focused on issues of environmental justice and ecological economics.

Thomas A. Wathen is a lawyer currently employed as a program officer for the environment at the Pew Charitable Trusts, where he works on forest protection, marine conservation, and trade policy. He previously worked for the Rockefeller Family Fund and the Environmental Grantmakers Association, where he wrote *A Guide to Trade and the Environment*. The author of books and articles on auto safety, solid waste, and small-town democracy, he has worked with consumer and environmental organizations since 1974. He has served as the executive director of three statewide public interest research groups in New York, Colorado, and Indiana.